DYNAMICS OF AGRICULTURAL DEVELOPMENT

About the Author

Dr. Amandeep Kaur is currently working as an Assistant Professor in Department of Economics at Guru Gobind Singh College for Women, Chandigarh, Punjab. She completed her Masters in Economics and Master of Philosophy from Department of Economics, Panjab University, Chandigarh and also received her Ph.D. degree in Economics from Panjab University, Chandigarh, Punjab. Her research focuses on various issues related with economics. She is particularly interested in some core economic issues like agricultural economics, industrial economics and development economics. She assisted one of the world's most renowned Indian-born economists, Professor Ajit Singh and completed research papers under his guidance on issues like crisis in euro zone. She is member of various economic societies and Associations.

Dynamics of Agricultural Development

A District Level Study

Amandeep Kaur

CONCEPT PUBLISHING COMPANY PVT. LTD.
NEW DELHI-110059

ISBN-13: 978-93-5125-287-0

First Published 2018

Published and Printed by

Concept Since 1974

Concept Publishing Company Pvt. Ltd.
A/15-16, Commercial Block, Mohan Garden,
New Delhi-110059 (INDIA)
T : 25351460, 25351794
E : publishing@conceptpub.com, *W*: www.conceptpub.com

Cataloging in Publication Data--Courtesy: D.K. Agencies (P) Ltd. <docinfo@dkagencies.com>

Amandeep Kaur (*Assistant professor of economics*), **author.**
Dynamics of agricultural development : a district level study / Amandeep Kaur.
pages cm
Includes bibliographical references and index.
ISBN 9789351252870

1. Agriculture—Economic aspects—India—Uttar Pradesh. 2. Agricultural productivity—India—Uttar Pradesh. I. Title.

LCC HD2072.A43 2018 DDC 338.109542 23

Preface

Increasing agricultural productivity remains the central concern of most of the agricultural dominant states in India. This is because; it is the major factor determining the level of income of the farming sector, meeting the food requirements of ever increasing population as well as in trade earning. Agriculture is the source of livelihood to majority of population living in the rural areas in India. Not only in rural areas, agriculture is still a demographically the broadest economic sector in many states in the country. It is the main sector of livelihood in one of the most populous state, Uttar Pradesh. About two-third of the work force of the state is employed in agriculture and the sector contributes about twenty three per cent to the gross state domestic product in the state. Not only in the state itself, agriculture sector of Uttar Pradesh occupies an important position in all India scenario. In 2013-14 the state produced 50.05 million tonnes of food grains which is 18.90 per cent of country's total production. Therefore, performance and growth of agriculture sector in the state has not only significant bearing on the living conditions of people in the state, but also for the food security of the country as a whole. Available evidence indicates that the state of agriculture development in Uttar Pradesh is not much better than the average level for the country as a whole. Furthermore in spite of having best quality land in the country and abundant availability of water resources, agriculture in the state failed to match the spectacular performance of agriculture experienced by its neighbouring states of Punjab and Haryana. Available evidence also suggest that the agriculture in the state is marked by wide inter-district disparities in growth and development from 1962-65 to 1990-93 (Bhalla and Singh, 2001). It is well-known that the Indian agriculture suffered serious deceleration since the early nineties. With only exception of Gujarat and Maharashtra, the post-reform developments adversely affected agriculture performance in remaining

Indian states including Uttar Pradesh (Bhalla and Singh, 2009). It would, therefore, be interesting to examine how different regions and districts of Uttar Pradesh performed during the post-reform period. The present study is a modest attempt in this direction.

The content of this book is divided broadly into two main categories: temporal pattern of agriculture performance in Uttar Pradesh compared with all India level and spatial pattern of agriculture performance, i.e. at the district and region level in Uttar Pradesh. The book is further divided into nine chapters with each chapter focussed on specific topic to cover the diverse perspectives of agricultural performance. The first chapter is introduction of the topic that includes brief agriculture history, objectives and the data sources. Second chapter reviews the existing literature related to our topic. Third chapter is devoted to temporal dynamics of agricultural performance in Uttar Pradesh. Chapter four analysis the pattern of agricultural growth and variations therein across districts and agro-economic regions over the period 1960-61 to 2010-11. Chapter five examines the temporal and spatial variations in the level of agricultural development (land productivity) in the state. For temporal analysis, the level of agricultural development is measured for the triennium ending 1960-63, 1970-73, 1980-83, 1990-93, 2000-03 and 2008-11. For spatial analysis, the level of agricultural development is measured for all 46 district units formed after clubbing newly formed districts (among total 72 districts) in the state. Chapter six is devoted to rigorous examination of convergence/divergence of the inter-district disparities in the state. We propose to examine the dynamics of temporal and spatial patterns of labour productivity of workers employed in agricultural sector for the last five decades in chapter seven. Sources of agricultural growth and productivity differences across regions and districts in Uttar Pradesh are identified in chapter eight and the last chapter concludes the main findings of the study.

I hope this book would be a valuable reference for researchers, students and policy experts and a useful resource for educators and agriculture economists.

Amandeep Kaur

Acknowledgements

First and foremost my heartiest thanks to the God, the almighty, for his showers of blessings throughout my research work and bringing it out in a book form.

It is my proud privilege to release the feelings of gratitude to several persons who helped me directly or indirectly to conduct this research project work. I express my heart full indebtedness and owe a deep sense of gratitude to my teacher and my guide Prof. Gurmail Singh, Vice Chancellor, Akal University, Talwandi Sabo, Panjab, for his sincere guidance and inspiration in completing this project.

Special thanks to Dr. Sawarn Singh, Assistant Director, Population Research Centre, Panjab University, whose suggestions are always valuable for me.

I have taken efforts in this project. However, it would not have been possible without the kind support and help of many individuals and organizations. I would like to extend my sincere thanks to all of them.

I also thank all my friends who have more or less contributed to the preparation of this research project. I will be always thankful to them.

Finally, I would like to acknowledge with great gratitude, the support and love of my family. They all kept me going, and this book would not have been possible without them.

The study has indeed helped me to explore more knowledgeable avenues related to my topic and I am sure it will help me in my future.

Contents

List of Figures, Maps and Tables

LIST OF FIGURES

LIST OF MAPS

TABLES

Acronyms

ADB	Asian Development Bank
ARDC	Agriculture and Rural Development Cooperation
CAGR	Compound Average Growth Rate
CSO	Central Statistical Organization
CV	Coefficient of Variation
DES	Directorate of Economics and Statistics
DMC	Developing Member Countries
FAI	Fertilizer Association of India
FGLS	Feasible Generalized Least Square
GATT	General Agreement on Tariffs and Trade
GCA	Gross Cropped Area
GDP	Gross Domestic Product
GoI	Government of India
GoUP	Government of Uttar Pradesh
HYV	High Yielding Variety
IADP	Intensive Agricultural District Programme
ICAR	Indian Council of Agricultural Research
IMD	Indian Metrological Department
Km	Kilometer
MLE	Maximum Likelihood Estimates
mm	Millimeter
NABARD	National Bank for Agriculture and Rural Development
NAFSCOB	National Federation of State Cooperative Banks Ltd.
No.	Number
NPK	Nitrogen, Phosphorous, Potassium
NSA	Net Sown Area
NSDP	Net State Domestic Product
OLS	Ordinary Least Squares
PNSDP	Per-capita Net State Domestic Product
RBI	Reserve Bank of India

R&D	Research and Development
SAP	Structural Adjustment Programme
SP	Sankhyikiya Patrika
TE	Triennium Ending
WTO	World Trade Organization
%	Percentage
R^2	Coefficient of Determination

1
Introduction

1.1. INTRODUCTION

Agriculture continues to be an important sector of Uttar Pradesh economy. About two-third of the workforce in the state is employed in agriculture and the sector contributes more than one-fourth to the gross domestic product of the state. Not only for the state of Uttar Pradesh, agriculture sector of the state occupies an important position for the country as it contributes one-third of wheat production, one-seventh of rice, about 40 per cent of sugarcane, 40 per cent of potato and about one-fifth of the foodgrain production to the country as a whole (GoI, 2014). Therefore, the performance of agriculture in the state has not only significant bearing for the people in the state, but also have significant implication for food security of the country as a whole. Available evidence indicates that the status of agriculture development in Uttar Pradesh is not much better than the average performance of the country as a whole. Furthermore, in spite of having best quality land in the country and abundant availability of water resources, agriculture in the state failed to match the spectacular performance of agriculture experienced by its neighbouring states of Punjab and Haryana (Bhalla and Singh, 2012). Available evidence suggests that the agriculture in the state is marked by wide inter-district disparities in growth and development (Bhalla and Singh, 2012). Available evidence also suggests that performance of Indian agriculture suffered deceleration during the post-reform period. Even this evidence is not uniform across spatial units. While the state of Gujarat, Bihar, Maharashtra performed exceptionally well during this period, agriculture performance suffered reverses in most of the remaining Indian states including Uttar Pradesh (Bhalla and Singh, 2012).

Many researchers examined agricultural performance in Uttar Pradesh, but we have not come across any comprehensive analysis of temporal and spatial dimensions of agricultural performance at the district-level for the state. Evidence suggests that the available district-wise studies are either focussed at the country as a whole or examined limited issues at the district-level or are focussed at micro-level analysis for a limited number of districts or are limited in coverage of crops or confined to a limited time period (Brown, 1971; Bhalla and Alagh, 1979; Bhalla and Tyagi, 1989; Bhalla and Singh, 2001, 2009, 2010, 2012; Kumar and Jain, 2013; Shaffi, 1984; Jain, 1990; Prabha, Goswami and Chatterjee, 2010; Raman and Kumari, 2012; Shafiqullah, 2013). The present study is a modest attempt of in-depth analysis of the temporal and spatial dynamics of agricultural performance of Uttar Pradesh at the district-level during the last five decades.

1.2. MOTIVATION FOR THE STUDY

The region and district-level analysis of agricultural development in a big state like Uttar Pradesh is of crucial importance on the following accounts:

1. First and foremost requirement in designing and implementing any strategy for development and modernization of agriculture is the information regarding what constraint the development of some regions/districts and what enables some others to grow rapidly and forge ahead of others. Planners and policy-makers must focus their attention on the left behind districts by drawing fruitful lessons from the districts that successfully reached a higher level of development. Only comprehensive and most updated information can be very useful to address these issues.
2. Most of the studies target state as unit for measuring disparity and neglect variations within states. Such efforts lead to limited success in achieving the objectives of balanced development. This is mainly because in a country like India, where some of the states are larger than even many nations, it is very important to analyze the factors responsible for disparities at the disaggregate level and design policies accordingly.

3. The wide inter-regional disparities can disturb the peace and harmony in a state or in any of its region. The sense of being left out and poor living conditions fuel the feelings of being ignored and deprived among the population in backward regions. Many times people in the backward regions demand for separate state as has happened in the recent past when Uttarakhand, Jharkhand and Chhattisgarh were demanded and created as separate states on similar grounds. Sometimes, sense of being ignored and deprived also leads to violence and domestic disturbances, as the country is currently facing in some regions and states. The Naxalite movement, Gorkha land issues and demand for separate Telangana owe their origin in underdevelopment and sense of deprivation. Such disturbances lead to wastage of precious human and economic resources to contain domestic discontentment. The diversion of resources further aggravates the problem of underdevelopment and poverty and leads to wastage of huge amount of money to maintain peace and harmony in such disturbed regions. To pass on aspiration of the people and for containment of such serious problems, extent and causes of underdevelopment must be known and addressed by appropriate policies and programmes.
4. Any growth process cannot be inclusive if it continues to bypass some regions and certain segments of the society. Therefore, to address our policies and programmes for attainment of (i) an inclusive growth as a main aim of the Twelfth Five Year plan with; (ii) the objective of balanced regional development adopted by the planners since long time back; and (iii) for alleviation of poverty and to provide decent level of living to people depending on agriculture, policies and programmes must be focussed on the development of the agriculturally backward regions. Identification of such policies and programmes again lies in the district-level information on crops grown, their actual and realized potential, use of modern inputs and availability of social and economic infrastructure are of crucial importance. This again requires the latest available information on the performance of agriculture at the district-level.

Besides these crucial issues any district-level information on agricultural development is also important on two other grounds:

1. With increased emphasis on district-level planning, extent, pattern and sources of agriculture development at the district-level is an essential prerequisite in designing appropriate policy initiatives for agriculture development.
2. The slowdown of agriculture growth in general and developed regions in particular and rising prices of many agricultural commodities like pulses and edible oils is threatening livelihood of poor and food security of the country. However, available evidence suggests prevalence of unexploited potentials of agricultural development in many parts of the country including Uttar Pradesh. Many initiatives under National Food Security Mission have already been implemented in identified districts and many others are required to be initiated in remaining ones. District level information is prerequisite in identifying such programmes not only for agricultural development , but also for inclusive and sustainable growth.

Before we directly identify the key objectives and hypotheses for our present study, it would be fruitful to have synoptic view of different perspectives for agricultural development, to have a peep into different phases of agriculture development and a brief review of empirical evidence on agriculture development at the sub-state (regional/district) level. This has been undertaken in the subsequent paragraphs.

1.3. AGRICULTURAL DEVELOPMENT: SOME MODELS

A rich literature, both theoretical and empirical, on processes of structural transformation of economies from low level of development and predominant agrarian in structures to modern agriculture and predominant services sector is available. This literature has articulated agriculture's role as the precursor to the acceleration of industrial growth from England in the mid eighteenth century to Japan in the late nineteenth century, and much of Asia in the late twentieth century (Bairoch, 1973; Timmer, 1988; Diao *et al.*, 2005). The discussion on the role of agriculture in structural transformation has evolved from the time of classical theorists, such as Lewis (1954), who viewed economic development as a process of transfer of resources or factors of production from the low productive agricultural sector to a modern industrial sector with higher productivity. However, many others, including Schultz (1964), Mellor (1966) and Ruttan and Hayami (1984), argued that agriculture play a central role in transition of agrarian economies through various forward, backward and consumption linkages. They argued that ignoring agriculture development can prove counterproductive to industrialization as happened in India and many other developing countries during early 1960s.

Numerous models/approaches have been proposed by scholars for agriculture development. Some of the well-known models in this context are: the Frontier or Resource Exploitation Model, the Conservation Model, the Urban-Industrial Impact Model, the Diffusion Model, Schultz Model and the Induced Innovation Model. The Frontier or Area Expansion Model is relevant in land abundant countries where public investments in transportation and rural infrastructure, rather than yield increasing innovations, have been major sources of agricultural growth. The pursuit of the Frontier Model has led to the destruction of tropical rainforests and the possible consequence of global warming that raise the questions whether continuous area expansion represents a cheap way of expanding agricultural output. The growing environmental concern therefore led to the development of Conservation Model. The model emphasized the evolution of a sequence of increasingly complex land and labour intensive cropping systems, the production and use of organic manures and labour intensive capital formation in the form of drainage, irrigation and other physical facilities to more effectively utilize land and water resources. The model is relevant in many countries such as Somalia, Botswana, Chad and Mali where extensive pastoral grazing is practiced with few external inputs. However, the historical records reveal that these low-input models are capable of producing agricultural growth of only around one per cent per year. The major challenge faced by this model is the need to develop technologies that can generate higher rates of agricultural growth in order to meet the increasing demands for agricultural products resulting from population and income growth.

The Urban-Industrial Impact Model was first of all given by Thunen (1826). The rationale of Urban-Industrial Impact Model was to develop more effective input and product markets in areas of rapid urban-industrial development. Industrial development stimulate agricultural development by expanding the demand for farm products, supplying the industrial inputs needed to improve agricultural productivity and drawing away surplus labour from agriculture. The policy implications of the Urban-Industrial Impact Model appeared to be most relevant for less developed regions of highly industrialized countries or lagging regions of the more rapidly growing less developed countries. The Diffusion Model rests on the empirical observation of substantial differences in land and labour productivity among farmers and regions. The route to agricultural development in the model was through more effective dissemination of technical knowledge and a narrowing of the productivity differences among farmers and among regions. The Diffusion Model provided the major intellectual foundation of much of the research and extension effort in farm management and production economics. During 1960s, the limitations of the Diffusion Model as a foundation for the design of agricultural development policies became increasingly apparent as technical assistance and rural development programmes, based explicitly or implicitly on this model, failed to generate either rapid modernization of traditional farms and communities or rapid growth in agricultural output.

The most influential thesis on transformation was put forth by Schultz (1964). He referred backward agriculture as traditional agriculture. The traditional agriculture was further referred as efficient, but poor due to limited technical and economic opportunities. According to him, modernization of a traditional agriculture requires that the farmers must be provided with opportunities to invest in factors which incorporate the potentialities of science and technology along with public investment in human capital. He was probably the first to put emphasis on provision incentives to the farmers through subsidies, access to new and more productive factors of production and human resource development. The central idea of the Schultz thesis was that the profitability in the use of factors as the key to agricultural transformation for the farmers trapped in a traditional agriculture. The agricultural development policy in the Schultz formulation had two principal emphases: one concerned with the quality and availability of the non-human factors, and the other with the development of the abilities of the traditional farm people. He strongly argued for the need of the policies and programmes for the provision of the non-human factors emphasized on research, science and technology and a system of distribution of factors that would make the profitable factors accessible to farmers. For long-term sustainable technological transformation, Schultz emphasized on initiation of the programmes and policies for the improvement of human abilities centred on education, training, extension services and investment in human agents through formal and informal systems.

Schultz Model is incomplete as a theory of agricultural development. Typically, education and research are public goods not traded through the marketplace. The mechanism by which resources are allocated among education, research and other public and private sector economic activities was not fully incorporated into the model. It did not explain how economic conditions induce the development and adoption of an efficient set of technologies for a particular society. Neither, it attempted to specify the processes by which input and product price relationships induce investment in research in a direction consistent with a nation's particular resource endowments. The model also ignored the role of institutions in the development process, (Hayami and Ruttan, 1985).

The limitations of Schultz Model, led Hayami and Ruttan (1985) to develop an Induced Innovation Model of agricultural development. They emphasized that the impulses for technical and institutional changes are endogenous to the system. Their model is based on the notion that countries can pursue alternative paths of technical change and productivity growth in agriculture. The changes in relative factor prices, reflecting changes in relative factor scarcities, play a determining role in guiding the search for new agricultural technologies and institutions. Technology can be developed to facilitate the substitution of relatively abundant hence cheap factor for relatively scarce expensive factors of production. For example, the constraints imposed on agricultural development by an inelastic supply of land in economies such as Japan and Taiwan can be offset by the development of high yielding crop varieties designed to facilitate the substitution of fertilizer for land. The constraints imposed by an inelastic supply of labour in countries like United States, Canada and Australia can be offset by technical advances leading to the substitution of animal and human labour with machinery. Hayami and Ruttan (1985) argued that due to differences in relative factor prices, Japan and United States followed different technological paths, but achieved the same long-term compound rate of agricultural growth of 1.6 per cent per annum over the 1880-1980 period. The classical problem of resource allocation, which was rejected as an adequate basis for agricultural productivity and output growth in the Schultz Model, was treated as central to the agricultural development process. Under conditions of static technology, improvements in resource allocation represent a weak source of economic growth. The efficient allocation of resources to open up new sources of growth is essential to the agricultural development process. For the induced innovation mechanism to guide technological change along an efficient path, two key conditions must be met. First, the changes in factor prices must reflect changes in relative factor scarcities. Second, the researchers in both the private and the public sectors must adjust their research programmes in response to changes in factor prices. A strategic implication of the model was that different nations can pursue different technological paths in response to differences or changes in relative resource endowments and factors prices over time. But to this, the countries need well functioning product and factor markets to signal resource scarcities and a set of incentives that will induce researchers to respond to those scarcities. Hayami and Ruttan's (1985), concept of induced institutional innovation states that as relative price change, incentives are created for certain groups in society to push for institutional changes that would allow the groups to benefit from the changing factor prices. For example, growth in the labour force may lead to pressures to change the institutions governing remuneration of agricultural labour from a fixed share of the harvest to a daily wage. The theory also focussed on the factors affecting the supply of and demand for such institutional innovations.

1.4. AGRICULTURAL DEVELOPMENT IN INDIA: EXPERIENCE OF FIVE DECADES

Agricultural development in post-independent India took place in three distinct phases. These are: (i) Pre-Green Revolution phase (1947-1965), (ii) Green Revolution phase (1966-1990), and (iii) Reform phase (1991 onwards).

The first phase of agricultural development began after independence. From recording of dismal performance of less than one per cent annual growth over half a century (1901-1947), agriculture in independent India rebounded and began to grow at more than 3 per cent per annum (Bhalla and Singh, 2001). This had happened despite serious setback due to partition of the country in 1947 and transfer of fertile and irrigated land to Pakistan. Upon the serious food crisis during late 1950s, the government invited the Ford Foundation team to suggest the initiatives to resolves the crises. Ten point's programmes recommended by the team of experts laid the foundation for modernisation of Indian agriculture. Rather than thinly spreading resources in a vast country like India, the team recommended intensive efforts in limited areas. Where, besides using modern inputs, appropriate price incentives were recommended to be created for the farmers. Consequently, the recommended programme was initially started in the form of 'Intensive Agriculture District Programme' (IADP) in selected 15 districts in the country in 1960. The success of the IADP led to its expansion in the broader areas in the form of 'Intensive Agriculture Area Programme'. Besides the intensification programme, many other policy initiatives were also undertaken during this period that contributed immensely in preparing a fertile ground for subsequent (Green) revolution in Indian agriculture. These includes: (i) expansion of surface irrigation facilities through investment in multi-purpose irrigation projects (like Bhakra Dam); (ii) land reforms including abolition of intermediary absentee landlordism (Zamindari System) and providing the land to the tillers, protection of tenant farmers through tenancy reforms (fixing land rents, providing security to land tenure and ownership rights under certain conditions), redistribution of land among small and landless agriculture workers by putting ceiling on landholdings and consolidation of scattered landholdings; (iii), setting up of Agriculture and Rural Development Cooperatives (ARDC) in (RBI) for supply of institutional agricultural credit; (iv) setting up of the 'Agriculture Price Commission' for recommending government the minimum support prices; (v) establishment of Food Corporation of India for implementing the minimum price support; (vi) Community Development Programme for dissemination of scientific knowledge at the village level; and (vii) strengthening and establishment of agriculture R&D system by opening up agricultural universities in major states.

However, the adverse weather conditions during the early 1960s and two wars in 1962 and 1965 with China and Pakistan resulted in aggravating the agriculture crisis and food insecurity in the country that attained serious dimension in 1985 when country began to be labelled as 'ship to mouth' economy.

Learning a lesson from very successful experiment of agricultural transformation in Mexico, the Government of India invited Dr. Norman Borlaug, the father of new HYV technology to India and suggest the ways and means to implement the same in the country. The field trail of the Mexican variety of wheat developed by him proved highly successful in Indian conditions. Subsequently, India imported the HYV seeds from Mexico and chemical fertilizers and other plant protection material from other countries. The spectacular results of the new HYV seed-chemical fertilizer-irrigation resulted in remarkable improvement in wheat yield and wheat production in the country, which began to be popularly known as the 'Green Revolution' in Indian agriculture. Phenomenal expansion of institutional credit upon strengthening of cooperative credit, nationalisation of 14 private sector banks and earmarking 18 per cent credit for agriculture sector under purity lending scheme, contributed immensely for diffusion of new technology and its adoption by small and marginal farmers, who otherwise would not have benefitted from new developments. The breakthrough in wheat yield was followed by similar technological developments in rice production upon importing of HYV rice seed developed by International Rice Research Institute, Manila, Philippines. Besides new technology and credit, many new institutions were established for making available good quality seeds and other modern inputs to agriculture as well as for phenomenal expansion of rural infrastructure, including electrification for irrigation purposes, rural road network and other agricultural markets. In the beginning, the fruits of new technology were confined to the selected regions in Punjab, Haryana and western Uttar Pradesh in the north and some coastal districts in the southern India only (Bhalla and Singh, 2001). However, the new technology made big intrusion in the eastern and central Indian states during 1980s. The green revolution technology matured during 1980s and its benefits were widespread across length and breadth of the country. Furthermore, during 1980s, Indian agriculture witnessed diversification in agriculture that resulted in fast growth in non-foodgrains output like milk, fishery, poultry, vegetables, fruits, etc. which accelerated growth in agricultural Gross Domestic Product during 1980s (Chand, 2003). The hallmark of the green revolution was that by the late 1970s, India achieved self-reliance in the foodgrains production, overcoming the painful memories of the agrarian crisis of the 1960s (Venkateswarlu, 2008). There was considerable increase in subsidies and support to agriculture sector during this period, while public sector spending in agriculture for infrastructure development started showing decline in real term, but investment by farmers kept on moving on a rising trend (Mishra and Chand, 1995; Chand, 2001). However, it is widely known that the impact of green revolution varies widely across different regions of the country. There was increase in disparities at the regional, district and state level due to differences in natural and physical resource endowments, infrastructure development including marketing opportunities and institutional setup, within which the farming community operates.

The third phase, post-reform period, began from 1991 after the initiation of economic reform process in the Indian economy. The process of economic reforms was initiated to liberalize the economy and integrate it with the world economy. The 1991 reforms focussed mainly on the industrial sector, with dismantling of industrial licensing, removal of import licensing, tariff reductions and relaxation of rules for foreign investment. Agriculture was bypassed in the terms of direct reforms, except with trade liberalization and relaxation of some controls on export of agricultural commodities. However, policies like currency devaluation, reduction in industrial protection and a shift towards marked determined exchange rates affected agriculture indirectly (Ahluwalia, 2000). The reforms also weakened the institutional support structures in agriculture and the protection to agriculture from predatory imports. Liberalization policies led to substantial decline in public investment in agriculture and hence deceleration in public sector capital formation in agriculture. Financial sector reforms resulted in significant decline in the priority sector credit lending to the agriculture sector. The agriculture sector in India failed to derive the expected benefits from liberalization. As a matter of fact, when compared with the immediate pre-liberalization period (1980-1990) agricultural growth in India recorded a visible deceleration during the post-liberalization period (1990s) (Bhalla and Singh, 2009). More specifically, this deceleration in agriculture during 1990s was attributed to the reduction in and/or stagnation of public expenditure on agricultural infrastructure, defunct extension services and biased economic reforms (Thamarajakshi, 1999; Balakrishnan, 2000; Dev, 2000; Vyas, 2001; Rao, 2003; Kannan and Sundaram, 2011). The only positive impact of the reforms was improvement in terms of trade for agriculture and opening of some opportunities such as benefits from trade and specialization, widening choices in new technology including bio-technology, increase in private investment in irrigation and marketing infrastructure like storage and transport (Ahluwalia, 2000; Dev, 2009).

Besides, economic liberalization during this phase, signing of the Uruguay round of General Agreement on Tariffs and Trade (GATT) in 1994 and subsequent implementation of the same under World Trade Organization (WTO) were initiated. The Agreement on Agriculture (AOA) under World Trade Organization aimed at reduction in trade distorting policies on domestic and export subsidies, replacing quantitative restrictions on trade with tariff and reduction in tariffs to encourage more and free trade. It was projected that trade liberalization and implementation of Agreement on Agriculture would bring large benefits to the developing countries. It was a step towards reform in agricultural trade expecting that though most of the Indian agricultural products enjoy comparative advantage, signing of World Trade Organization would further improve its competitive edge in international market (GoI, 1994). Institutions like WTO were considered essential for providing a level playing field to developing countries in international market (Rao, 2001). Reduction of production and export subsidies and rolling back of non-tariff barriers by the developed countries in compliance to the WTO requirements would provide welcome stimulus to agricultural exports from India, specifically exports of high value labour intensive agricultural and allied sector products (GoI, 1994; Bhalla 1995). Integration of domestic markets with the international markets was expected to improve the domestic terms of trade in favour of agriculture, reduce the distortions of domestic prices and inefficiency in allocation of resources. Consequently, it was hoped to boost production and productivity of Indian agriculture (Rao, 1994; Singh, 1995). On the contrary, some scholars feared that liberalization of trade could destabilise the domestic prices (Chand and Jha, 2001). Serious doubts were also raised regarding the capabilities of the resource poor, subsistence and unorganized farmers to withstand the competitive environment of the modern markets dominated by the powerful organized groups (Rao, 1994). The post-World Trade Organization trade liberalization helped India to achieve small increase in agricultural exports, whereas it resulted in sharp increase in imports of some commodities. The main reason for this adverse effect was unprecedented decline in international prices which was caused by the attempts by almost all the countries to push exports at the international level and declining public investment in agriculture, unabated degradation of natural resources, weakened support systems resulting from feeble financial positions of state governments, unresponsive research system and near breakdown of the agricultural extension services at the national level. Once again, a major step taken towards the agricultural development did not give the expected results and now the challenge to policy-makers is how to protect Indian agriculture from the impending World Trade Organization threat, enhance the competitiveness of Indian farming and make a viable and self-sustaining enterprise to improve and ensure livelihood security of the farmers.

The slowdown in agricultural sector is a matter of serious concern as it retards the overall growth in the economy like India, where little less than half of the population in the country still depends on agriculture for their livelihood (GoI, 2014). Moreover, agriculture slowdown may seriously impede the employment generation and poverty alleviation in India as there is almost one to one correspondence in agricultural growth and reduction of rural poverty (Mellor, 2000). Under these circumstances, higher agricultural growth is vital not only for ensuring food security at macro- and micro-levels in general and in agriculturally lagging states like Uttar Pradesh in particular.

1.5. EMPIRICAL EVIDENCE: A SYNOPTIC VIEW

Though a comprehensive review of available literature on national and sub-national level of the study on the topic is to be undertaken in next chapter, yet a synoptic view of selected studies on the topic concerned at all-India level in general and on the state of Uttar Pradesh in particular is presented here to get a brief overview of the available information on the topic. This is essential to identify the gaps and to provide rationale to the present study.

There are number of studies examining the agricultural performance at district-level for the country as a whole. Brown (1971) was probably the first to undertake comprehensive district-level study for the period 1956-57 to 1965-66. Thereafter, Gordan (1974) analyzed the association between agriculture output and sources of agriculture growth for the year 1960-61. Then, Bhalla and Alagh (1979) undertook district-level study for the triennium ending 1962-65 to 1970-73, analyzing the level and growth of agriculture sector and also classified the districts into high, medium and low growth categories. Bhalla and Alagh (1979) study was further extended by a number of scholars: Dev (1985) extending to 1975-78, Bhalla and Tyagi (1989) to 1980-83, Bhalla and Singh (2001) to 1990-93, Bhalla and Singh (2010) to 2003-06 and recently Bhalla and Singh (2012) extended it to 2005-08. In addition to agriculture growth and development, sources of agriculture growth as well as district-wise labour productivity was also examined in these studies. In addition, Singh (2007) carried out district-level analysis for 581 districts for the triennium ending 1990-93 to 1999-2002. Chand, Garg and Pandey (2009) analyzed agriculture productivity and linkage of agricultural productivity with poverty for 551 districts for the period 2003-04 and 2004-05. Thereafter, Kumar and Jain (2013) analyzed the level of agricultural productivity, agriculture growth, sources of agricultural growth and instability in agriculture production at the district-level (388 districts) for the period 1990-91 to 2007-08. These studies were carried out at the district-level for the country as a whole. Moreover, most of these district-level studies are for initial and end triennium averages.

At the sub-state level in Uttar Pradesh, Shaffi (1984) and Jain (1990) undertook district-level study for Uttar Pradesh examining the growth and development of agriculture sector. But these studies covered the period till 1975-76 in Shaffi (1984) and only till 1965-66 in Jain (1990) study. Moreover, Shaffi (1984) covered only 13 crops whereas Jain (1990) analyzed the impact of HYV seeds on rice and wheat crops only. Thereafter, Kumar (2000) analyzed agriculture development at district-level for triennium ending 1980-83. Recently, Prabha, Goswami and Chaterjee (2010), Pandey and Reddy (2012), Raman and Kumari (2012), and Shafiqullah (2013) also carried out district-level study in Uttar Pradesh, but these studies analyzed the level of agriculture development only and some of them examined linkages between agriculture productivity and poverty. There is no state level study for Uttar Pradesh to examine dynamics of growth and productivity at the district-level that covered both pre- and post-reform period. The present study on five decades of agricultural performance at the district-level in Uttar Pradesh is a modest attempt in this direction. In addition to analyzing agriculture growth and level of agriculture development, we also propose to analyze growth and development of agriculture workers productivity at the district-level in Uttar Pradesh during 1960-61 to 2010-11.

1.6. OBJECTIVES

The main objectives of the present study are:

1. To analyze the temporal pattern of agricultural performance in Uttar Pradesh during different policy regimes (Pre-green revolution, initial phase of green revolution, mature phase of green revolution, initial post-reform period and new millennium phase) over the last half a century (1960-61 to 2010-11).
2. To examine the spatial (district and region) pattern of agricultural performance (level of development, output growth and disparities) in Uttar Pradesh over 1960-61 to 2010-11 period.
3. To identify the sources and constraints of agricultural development at the district-level in Uttar Pradesh.

1.7. HYPOTHESES

Given the theories and empirical evidence on the main objectives, we propose to test the following hypotheses in the subsequent chapters.

1. Temporal Pattern

(i) Changing policy regimes made significant impact on temporal variations in agricultural performance in Uttar Pradesh.

(ii) Changing technological, institutional and market environment led to diversification of cropping pattern in the state from low productivity and low value coarse cereals, pulses and oilseeds towards more remunerative wheat, rice and horticulture crops.

2. Spatial Pattern

(i) Given the wide regional disparities in natural and human resource endowments, growth and development of agriculture vary considerably across districts and regions in Uttar Pradesh.

(ii) Given the regional disparities, the temporal pattern during different policy regimes may vary considerably across regions and districts in Uttar Pradesh.

3. Regional Disparities

(i) With the spread of new technology and policy initiatives for backward regions, we hypothesise the convergence of inter-district disparities in Uttar Pradesh.

4. Sources of Agricultural Performance

(i) Differences in physical and human resource endowments (land and human resources), use of modern technology (chemical and mechanical) and physical facilities (road, irrigation) are hypothesised to be responsible for inter-regional disparities in agricultural performance.
(ii) Agro-climatic conditions, such as rainfall, soil quality and other idiosyncratic features play an important role in inter-district differentials in agriculture development.

1.8. DATA AND METHODOLOGY

1.8 (i) Data Sources

To carry out the objective and test the proposed hypotheses, the present study planned to make use of three types of data sources. First, is the state level data on agriculture output for all crops grown in the state during 1960-2010 compiled by the Central Statistical Organisation (CSO) for all states in the country. Second, is the data set on area and production of different crops at the state and district-level compiled by the Directorate of Economics and Statistics (DES), Ministry of Agriculture, Government of India. Third, is the data on various inputs, infrastructural facilities, human resources and various agro-climatic indicators obtained from different individual agencies/ministries compiling information on these accounts. These are:

(i) Fertilizer Association of India (FAI) for district-wise data on chemical fertilizers consumed from 1960-2010.
(ii) Livestock Census Survey of India for district-wise number

of tractors and pumpsets for the years 1961, 1972, 1982, 1992, 2003. The Livestock Census 2007 has not collected information from agriculture machinery, therefore data for 2007 on number of tractors and pumpsets has been obtained from Statistical Abstracts of Uttar Pradesh.

(iii) The Census of India information has been used for district-wise number of agriculture workers and level of literacy in Uttar Pradesh from 1961 to 2011.

(iv) The publication of Indian Metrological Department (IMD), Pune has been used for district-wise rainfall in Uttar Pradesh for the study period.

(v) The Agricultural Census Survey information is used to estimate the structure of landholdings in terms of district-wise proportion of small and marginal farmers in Uttar Pradesh.

(vi) Various publications of Ministry of Irrigation and Water Resources and Season and Crop Reports of Uttar Pradesh are used for compiling statistics on proportion of area under irrigation for the study period.

(vii) Data on district-wise road length has been obtained from Statistical Abstracts of Uttar Pradesh.

(viii) The district-wise poverty data has been taken from study by Chaudhuri and Gupta (2009).

Given these data sources, there was some missing information for some years and on some indicators. In that case, the gaps were filled by having data from Statistical Abstracts of Uttar Pradesh for various years, district-wise *Sankhyikiya Patrika* (SP), published by Economics and Statistics Division (ESD) of Planning Department, Government of Uttar Pradesh and Chandlok, H.L. (1990), India Database information.

1.8 (ii) Methodology

The research methodology followed to carry each of these objectives and to test the proposed hypotheses is to be explained at relevant places in subsequent chapters. However, a brief information on the same is as follows:

(i) Coverage of Districts

The study proposes to examine various issues at three broad levels namely—for the state as a whole, for regions of Uttar Pradesh and for all districts in the state. Since the study propose to cover the period of last five decades from 1960-2010, therefore, it covers districts which constitute combined state up to 2000 and bifurcated in the form of two states, Uttar Pradesh and Uttarakhand currently. For consistency of temporal data, we included all the district units in these two states. Over the study period, many new districts were created as the number of districts in the state increased from 54 to begin with (includes both plain and hill districts), in 1960 to 85 in 2010. When any new district is created, no effort has been made by the official agencies to create the past information on agriculture performance. Therefore, the only situation left was to club the newly created districts into their erstwhile parental unit. In many cases, a district was created by drawing area from two/three districts. Its area was therefore allocated in the same proportion. Following this procedure, the study propose to examine the performance of agriculture for 47 district units (including hills) from 1960-2010.

(ii) Coverage of Crops

The state level analysis is based on the information on output for all crop sectors for which consistent information was generated by Central Statistical Organisation (CSO). However, similar information for all crops is not compiled by any other designated official agency including Directorate of Economics and Statistics (DES), Ministry of Agriculture. The Directorate of Economics and Statistics, Ministry of Agriculture compiles district-wise information for 35 main crops grown in the country on regular basis. Therefore, district-wise analysis of agriculture production is based on 35 crop sectors which covers almost 90 per cent of the gross cropped area in the state. We jacked up the value output for 35 crop sectors for the whole crop sector by assuming that the yield of the left over crops was same as the average yield of 35 crop sectors. To estimate the value output of the total crop sector, we used the constant 2010-11 prices which was taken from the implicit price of the National Accounts statistics for the relevant year.

(iii) Methodology

Agricultural performance at different levels is to be compared on three main accounts: (i) the compound average growth rate has been used to measure the growth performance of agriculture for different time periods to study the magnitude and direction of agricultural performance in Uttar Pradesh; (ii) the concept of land productivity is to be employed as an indicator of agriculture development in the state. The land productivity is defined as value output per unit of net sown area in that particular year for a particular geographical unit; and (iii) for measurement of labour productivity and its growth, concept of labour productivity is defined as value output of the total crop sector per worker employed in agriculture during that particular year. The agriculture workers information includes both male and female workers as well as main and marginal workers employed in agriculture sector.

The changing temporal pattern of growth in area, production and yield is to be examined both by comparing simple average growth rates as well as by including slope dummy variables in the time trend growth equations.

The regional and inter-district disparities are to be examined following the two main approaches: first is by comparing the temporal inequalities in terms of indicator of inequality which includes—Gini coefficient, share of top to bottom quintile in production and ratio of top to bottom quintile in agriculture labour/land productivity. Besides these indicators, changes in inter-district disparities in agriculture development are also to be examined by testing for sigma convergence, beta unconditional, beta conditional and club convergence.

The role of various sources of agriculture performance is to be examined using tabular analysis, graphical analysis, bivariate analysis and multivariate regression approaches. In the later case, the Random Effect Panel Data and Fixed Effect Panel Data Models would be used on the pooled district data set for the years 1980-83, 1990-93, 2000-03 and 2008-11. The data for sixties and seventies are not to be included because of non-availability of consistent and reliable information on some variables. The Panel Data Models have been chosen specifically because of its known advantage over cross-section and time series data and its ability to control many district-level attributes that are not included in the model, but are significant determinants of the dependent event (Hsiao, 2003). The models used and their associated dimensions are to be discussed at the relevant place in the concerned chapter.

1.9. ORGANIZATION OF THE STUDY

Findings of the study are to be presented as follows:

Chapter 1: Introduction
Chapter 2: Review of Literature
Chapter 3: Agricultural Performance in Uttar Pradesh: Temporal Dynamics.
Chapter 4: Pattern of Agricultural Growth in Uttar Pradesh: Variations Across Districts and Agro-Economic Regions.
Chapter 5: Dynamics of Agricultural Development in Uttar Pradesh: Variations Across Districts and Agro-Economic Regions.
Chapter 6: Convergence of Regional Agricultural Performance in Uttar Pradesh: 1960-61 to 2010-11.
Chapter 7: Dynamics of Labour Productivity in Uttar Pradesh.
Chapter 8: Sources of Agricultural Performance in Uttar Pradesh.
Chapter 9: Summary and Conclusions.

2

Review of Literature

2.1. INTRODUCTION

Having briefly introduced the topic, visiting the theories put forth by scholars for transformation of agriculture, underlying the objectives, hypotheses and research design in the previous chapter, an attempt has been made here to review the existing studies undertaken by the researches on the theme of our thesis. These studies are expected to throw useful insights on various dimensions of agricultural development at the regional and sub-regional levels. A very large number of studies on different dimensions of agricultural development at international, national and sub-national level are available in the literature. It is neither feasible nor desirable to include all the available studies in the present chapter. Only selected studies are chosen which are directly related with various objectives of the present study.

2.2. INTERNATIONAL LEVEL STUDIES

Bhattacharjee (1955) studied the resource use and productivity in World agriculture, taking 22 selected countries for 1948-50. Cobb-Douglas production function was used by taking six independent variables; population active in agriculture, arable land, fertilizer, work stock, productive livestock and tractors. He concluded that fertilizer consumption, weighted arable land and number of people active in agriculture were significant items of input whereas productive livestock, work stock and tractors did not show any significant regression. Marginal productivity of significant factors was computed that showed Marginal Productivity of fertilizer was the highest followed by labour in agriculture and weighted arable land was lowest among three.

Hayami and Ruttan (1970) found wide disparities in agricultural productivity across 38 selected countries for 1952-1966. The underdeveloped countries like India had only one-fifth of productivity level attained by the developed countries. They further classified the sources of productivity growth into three groups: resource endowments, technology as embodied in fixed or working capital, and human capital that included education, skill, knowledge and capacity embodied in country's population. It was found that these three categories accounted for approximately 95 per cent of differences in labour productivity in agriculture between selected countries. They recommended additional allocation of resources and investment in industries producing technical inputs to achieve higher output per worker through increased output per unit of area.

Nair (1980) studied the pattern of technological progress and its impact on agriculture in the sixties and seventies in 20 countries of the world. He concluded that food production registered an impressive growth rate in most of the developing countries. In India, food production registered a growth rate of 2.27 per cent per annum during the study period. Inputs like irrigation, chemical fertilizer, mechanization, high yielding varieties and insect pest control led to higher productivity in the agricultural sector. Irrigation was not found to be the explanatory variable for yield in all the countries except for India, China and Japan. Tractor use was the factor for variation in developing countries. Chemical fertilizer was crucial for higher yields. Level of irrigation, farm profitability and tractor use led to substantial use of fertilizer in India and Japan.

Kawagoe and Hayami (1983) compared labour and land productivities among the 44 countries during 1960-1980. It was found that the differences in labour productivity between developed and less developed countries were extremely large and also widened from 1960 to 1980. However, the growth of land productivity in less developed countries kept up with developed countries. A major factor for the widening gap in labour productivity was increased land-labour ratio in developed countries and decreased in less developed countries owing to population explosion. Developed countries were able to increase the labour productivity very rapidly by exploiting the opportunity opened by reduction in labour force through development of labour saving technology. The widening gap in land productivity between developed and less developed countries resulted from widening differences in land and capital per worker and widening differences in rate of growth in production efficiency that stemmed from the difference in the scientific research and development.

Naher (1997) studied the nature and degree of instability in production and yield of foodgrains and the extent to which food self-sufficiency was reached through the introduction of green revolution in Bangladesh during 1969-70 to 1991-92 and its sub-periods—phase I (1969-70 to 1976-77), corresponding to low keyed adoption of the new technology and phase II (1977-78 to 1991-92) corresponding to increased usage of technology. The study was at the aggregate and the regional level for rice, wheat, gram and total cereal production in the country. It was found that the most important impact of green revolution in the country was increase in the cropping intensity each year due to accelerated use of fertilizers, irrigation, High Yielding Variety seeds and modern technology. The foodgrain sector achieved impressive growth rates since mid-1970s and the increase in rice production, the main staple food of the country showed stable trend that helped the country towards self-sufficiency and removing the gap between availability and demand.

Wu (1997) focussed on reforms in China's agriculture since 1978, their impact on China's internal and external economies and future reforms and their possible trade implications. He found that China's post-1978 agricultural reform brought significant positive impact on the Chinese economy in general and China's rural and agricultural sector in particular. Markets replaced central planning and helped in agricultural production and trade. Agricultural resources including land and labour were increasingly reallocated in accordance with China's comparative advantage. However, the author found that China's agricultural reform was not completed because of the Government's commitment to grain self-sufficiency, control over agricultural land, labour and other resource mobility and policy interventions through erratic price changes. He concluded that if China continued to adhere to its food self-sufficiency policy, rapid industrialization would make land-intensive agriculture more costly and if it wants to keep its domestic food prices at world market levels, it will have to import more land-intensive food and diversify its resources towards more export oriented industrial goods.

Karshenas (1999) studied the role of agriculture in economic development in Sub-Saharan Africa and Asia. It was found that in the case of Asian countries, the existence of an abundant supply of labour in agriculture allowed fast rates of industrial growth to take place at low and competitive wages, creation of an adequate infrastructure and integration of the agricultural sector in the national market. This led to the complementary and mutual growth of agricultural and non-agricultural sectors. However, in the case of sub-Saharan African economies, with limited supply of labour and relative abundance of cultivable land, the non-agricultural sectors faced relatively high and steep wage curves. The lack of basic infrastructure, lack of capital and appropriate technologies to alleviate the agricultural labour constraint in most African countries prevented the integration of a large part of the agrarian economies into the national and international market. The author suggested for the substitution aspect of sectoral growth rates and the policy lessons to take into account specific country characteristics.

Kurosaki (2001) quantified the contribution of changes in crop mix to agricultural growth for the areas currently in India and Pakistan for the period c.1900-1995. A decomposition method was applied that showed a significant part of land productivity growth was attributed to changes in crop mix in post-independent India and in areas currently in Pakistan (pre- and post-independence). It was found that land reallocation toward high value crops was the main engine of agricultural growth during the pre-green revolution period (after independence) for Pakistan. In India, in contrast, the importance of changes in crop mix to land productivity growth had been increasing throughout the post-independence period. Estimated patterns of the sources of land productivity growth were found to be consistent with the hypothesis that development of rural markets and improvement in agricultural technology were key to the realization of farmers' economic rationality. He concluded that sustained growth in agriculture can be achieved with public investment in agriculture.

Debela, Heshmati and Oygard (2004) analyzed the performance of agriculture in post-reform Ethiopia by measuring technical, allocative and economic efficiency, productivity growth, and technological progress using stochastic frontier production function. The results indicated evidence of significant technical and allocative inefficiencies among the farmers and on the other hand allocative and economic efficiency deteriorated over the period. The findings from the growth accounting suggested that technological regress contributed the largest share of output decline during the period. Increased fertilizer use by 105.9 per cent did not contribute much to output growth because of the small size of elasticity of output with respect to fertilizer. The key policy agendas suggested by the authors were to reverse the land degradation process, investments in agricultural research, training, transport and communication infrastructure, rehabilitation and conservation and human capital and the government to ensure availability of credits and tenure security.

Barrios (2007) proposed agricultural growth model to verify the agricultural convergence hypothesis among 27 Asian countries that included Developing Member Countries (DMCs) of ADB excluding Japan, other non-member Asian countries and Pacific countries for the period 1995–2005. There was significant evidence of conditional convergence among some Asian countries. The effect of spatial externalities defined by participation of a country in international trade, country-specific random endowments, and temporal accumulation were found to be significantly contributing to agricultural growth. Whereas, public expenditures for agriculture and foreign aid did not record any direct effect on agricultural growth, they however facilitated countries' movement towards the steady-state production rate leading towards convergence. The author concluded that conditioning on current trade, foreign aid and public expenditures for agriculture, Asian economies would converge in agricultural growth at the rate of approximately 15 per cent per year. He suggested that to effectively achieve the goals of regional integration, careful matching among countries engaged in bilateral or multilateral agreements should be done to facilitate convergence in agricultural growth.

Breisinger *et al.* (2008) discussed the role of agriculture in growth and development of Ghana and a tool for poverty reduction during 1990-2006. It was found that the agriculture growth was more rapid than the non-agriculture sector, expanding by an average annual rate of 5.5 per cent, compared to 5.2 per cent for the economy as a whole. Agriculture supported the rest of the economy through substantial and largely invisible monetary transfers to the non-agricultural sectors. Despite the country's sound agricultural performance over the past years, it was found to be challenging for Ghana to sustain and accelerate this growth, particularly if external conditions become less favourable in the future. The authors suggested the future growth of agriculture by closing existing yield gaps and increasing the efficiency of available land use through substantial investments in green-revolution type of investments, including rural infrastructure, marketing, extension and agricultural research and development.

Afzal and Ahmad (2009) analyzed the agricultural input-output relation in Pakistan and found that the improved seed had higher relation with fertilizer (83%) and water (72%) than electricity (4%), i.e. water and fertilizers were essential to harvest the benefits of improved seed. He suggested increasing the water and energy use efficiency in future because water is a finite resource and there is acute shortage of electricity in Pakistan. Fertilizer had the strongest relationship with water (95%), followed by seed (83%) and electricity (72%), this indicated that water was essential to harvest the benefits of fertilizer and electricity. The author suggested for improvement of input use efficiency in agriculture such as reduction in per capita water availability, rise in population, less than the optimum level availability of improved seed, imbalance use of fertilizers, rise in diesel prices and electricity tariff and lack of institutions to provide timely services to farmers.

Xin and Qin (2009) studied the regional disparity of China's agricultural productivity growth by decomposing it into technical changes, efficiency changes and input accumulation per worker. The convergence test was used to analyze the determinants of regional disparity. The authors found that during 1987 and 2005, the growth of China's agricultural labour productivity depended on the accumulation of inputs and technical changes contributed more to the regional disparities in agricultural productivity growth. The increase in inputs for Western China, and the improvement in technical change for Central and Western China were found to be significant aspects to promote the growth of agricultural productivity and narrow the gap in agriculture productivity with the Eastern China.

Piya, Kiminami and Yagi (2011) focussed on the analysis of sources of land productivity in South and South-east Asian countries during 1980 to 2007. It was found that land productivity and input intensification widely varied across South and South-east Asian countries. The use of modern inputs like chemical fertilizer and tractor was found higher in South-east Asia while the use of traditional inputs like livestock and labour were found higher in South Asia. The growth accounting suggested that the growth in fertilizer and tractor usages were the main sources of land productivity growth. Average annual production growth was higher in South-east Asia compared to South Asia. Decomposition of production growth into land productivity and land area indicated that only land productivity growth explained the growth in agricultural production in South Asia while land productivity as well as land expansion explained the production growth in South-east Asia.

Rehman, Saeed and Salam (2011) analyzed the trends in area, production and yield of wheat, rice, sugarcane and cotton crops in Pakistan agriculture using component analysis model during pre-structural adjustment period (1972 to 1988) and post-structural adjustment period (1989 to 2009). They found that growth rate of major crops, except rice, was better in pre-structural adjustment period than under the post-structural period. The results of decomposition analysis found that during the pre-adjustment period, increase in output was predominant in case of wheat, rice and cotton due to the yield effect and in sugarcane crop due to area effect. In the post-structural adjustment period, the source of output growth in wheat and cotton was due to yield effect and due to area effect in sugarcane and rice crops. For the overall study period, for wheat and cotton crops, the major growth factor was the yield effect, but for sugarcane and rice it was the area effect. The aggregate result for all crops recorded that the production growth was mainly due to yield effect during the pre-structural adjustment period and due to area effect during the post-structural adjustment period. However for the overall study period 1972-2009, the area and yield effects contributed equally towards the total change in output growth for aggregate crops. The authors thereafter suggested policies focussing on developing new high-yielding varieties to increase crop production in Pakistan, research efforts to strengthen the crop breeding programmes and to develop and establish the bio-technology programmes to develop high yielding varieties of the crops suitable to agro-climatic conditions of the regions.

Taffesse, Dorosh and Asrat (2011) discussed patterns and trends of crop production in Ethiopia for all crops during 2004-05 to 2007-08 and for cereal crops from 1961-62 to 2008-09. It was recorded that five major cereals (teff, wheat, maize, sorghum and barley) occupied almost three-quarters of total area cultivated, and represented almost 70 per cent of total value added in the country. Decomposition analysis recorded that during the 1990s, most of the increase in cereal production was due to increases in area. However, in the 2000s, area and yield increases, each accounted for about half of production growth. The authors suggested increasing cereal crop yield for its growth by adopting improved seeds, chemical and organic fertilizers and to diversify and shift to higher-value crops.

Udensi *et al.* (2012) studied the determinants of macro-economic variables that affect agricultural production in Nigeria between 1977 and 2007. They found that total government expenditure on agriculture, nominal exchange rate, interest rate and total credit accessed by farmers from commercial banks were all positively related with the index of agriculture production and were all significant at 1 per cent level of significance. Government expenditure on agriculture was found to be the most important variable required to cause growth and development in the agricultural sector in Nigeria. They suggested to design sector-specific agricultural policies to facilitate increased long-term sustainable government investment in agriculture, foreign private investment in agriculture, favourable exchange rate, availability of credit at low interest rate, reduction of annual rate of inflation and farmers to respond positively to the opportunities that emanate from soaring global food prices to increase agricultural production in Nigeria.

Alamian, Eshraghi, and Joolaie (2013) analyzed the components of agriculture growth in Golestan province in Iran using multiplicative decomposition method during 1991-92 to 2010-2011. The authors found that the price growth was the main factor of agriculture growth and there was lack of an appropriate improvement in land productivity growth as well as the cropping pattern growth. The authors therefore, stressed on revision in the development policies of agricultural crops production to increase the productivity in the agricultural sector and suggested for government investment in agricultural infrastructure and research to develop high-efficiency organizations along with change in supportive policies to change the exchange rate between the agricultural items and the products of other sectors, paying attention to the exploited potentials from the pioneer farmers and its propagation among the other producers, development and propagation of more appropriate methods for cultivations, rearing and harvesting and more appropriate organization of production to increase the role of productivity factor in the production growth of agricultural products and decrease the need of increasingly growth of prices.

2.3. NATIONAL LEVEL STUDIES

Abraham and Raheja (1967) analyzed the growth of production for rice and wheat in India during 1951-52 to 1964-65 and examined the contribution of input factors like area, irrigation and fertilizer. It was found that the unirrigated area, irrigated area and fertilizer consumption accounted for about 7.14 per cent, 15.84 per cent and 77 per cent respectively in the rice production and 30 per cent, 35 per cent and 35 per cent respectively of the growth in wheat production.

Brown (1971) was probably first to undertake the comprehensive district-wise analysis of pre-green revolution of Indian agriculture. The study was based on data for 19 major crops, 320 districts including 15 Intensive Agricultural District Programme (IADP) districts during 1956-57 to 1965-66. With only exception for Ludhiana, Surat and Mandya, change in yield level of remaining 12 IADP districts was similar to other non-Intensive Agricultural District Programme districts. The author found that the inter-district variations in yield and growth rate of output were due to combined impact of favourable soil, adequate irrigation, rainfall, cost reducing technology and fertilizers used. He concluded that Intensive Agricultural District Programme districts did not show significant different performance than other non-Intensive Agricultural District Programme districts in India.

Rao (1971) analyzed the factors responsible for inter-regional differentials in the growth of crop-output during 1952-53 to 1964-65. He found that the major cause of the disparities in growth of crop-output was the difference in growth of irrigation. The public investment played a major role in bringing the growth in irrigation, private investment was mostly confined to well irrigation. It was also argued that private investment was high where public subsidies and loans were easily forthcoming and where rainfall was scanty and fluctuating. According to the author, it was doubtful whether the ability to save was an important factor in explaining inter-regional differentials in private investments in irrigation or the growth of crop-output. Since rich farmers also happen to be concentrated in the better-off areas, they were able to induce greater public investments in irrigation in their regions.

Gordan (1974) studied the factors besides agro-climatic conditions that were associated with the variations in output per acre across the districts in 16 Indian states for 12 crops (rice, wheat, jowar, gram, bajra, maize, cotton, ragi, groundnut, jute, barley and sugarcane). Regression analysis was used to measure the degree of association between dependent variable (output per acre of various crops) and 19 explanatory variables including irrigation, multiple cropping, electrification, transportation and various measures of farm size, education, health facilities and health status. The author found that controlled water flow constituted a critical input necessary to obtain maximum yields. Education was an important contribution to human capital formation than improved health. Output per acre was large on small farms than on large farms and the factors responsible for this relationship were extensive irrigation, more intensive multiple cropping and in case of rice more labour intensity.

Easter, Martin and George (1977) examined the regional difference in agricultural productivity in 73 major wheat producing districts in states of Punjab, Haryana, Uttar Pradesh, Madhya Pradesh and Rajasthan and 69 rice producing districts in Eastern regions comprising of Eastern Uttar Pradesh, Bihar, West Bengal, Orissa and Eastern Andhra Pradesh. The information on crop area and output, irrigation, fertilizer, roads, and labour was used for 1959-60 and 1961-62 period. The author found that for wheat regions, the expansion of irrigation and improvement in quality of irrigation through tubewells led to substantial increase in productivity. However, other variables turned out to be insignificant statistically. Results for rice region, also turned out on similar line with exception that irrigation variable was insignificant, whereas surface road had significant bearing on productivity differences among districts. The findings of the study did not bring out the role of modern inputs as determinants of inter-district disparities in agricultural productivity.

Alagh, Bhalla and Bhaduri (1978) argued that the main source of agricultural growth in India during 1960s was increased yield which was associated with a higher ratio of labour to land. A more intensive pattern of land use, resulting in higher yield and higher labour input per unit of land was the main source of growth of output and employment in agriculture. It was found that the districts that showed high rates of growth of agricultural output and land yield absorbed more labour per hectare and maintained higher labour productivity and *vice versa*. Growth rates were achieved in agriculture mainly in areas where rapid extension of irrigation made possible high rates of growth of cropped area, high cropping intensity and significant expansion of area under high yielding varieties.

Bhalla and Alagh (1979) studied the comprehensive analysis of inter-district variations in growth and productivity in Indian agriculture. The study was based on crop-wise information for 19 major crops and input used for triennium 1962-65 and 1970-73 and covered 282 districts from 17 major states in the country. On the basis of value output per hectare, the districts were classified into high productivity, medium productive and low productive districts. It was found that 69 high productivity districts accounted for 24.8 per cent of area, 36.4 per cent of total irrigated output, consumed 44.2 per cent of total fertilizers and employed 50.39 per cent of tractors and 45.47 per cent of tubewells for irrigation. These districts were mainly from the Western and Southern States: Punjab (9), Tamil Nadu (9), Kerala (7), Karnataka (5), Western Uttar Pradesh (5), West Bengal (5), Andhra Pradesh (5), Coastal Maharashtra (3), Haryana (1), and Gujarat (1). On the other extreme were 83 districts having low productivity less than Rs. 700 per hectare. From 30.74 per cent of total area, these contributed 15.68 per cent of total output, consumed only 12.83 per cent of total fertilizers, 11.30 per cent of tractors, 19.0 per cent tubewells and 11.80 per cent of total irrigated area in the country. Low productivity districts were mainly distributed in the Central and Eastern parts of the country. With concentration of modern inputs in highly developed and high growth districts in the country, the authors concluded that modern inputs and irrigation were major source of growth and inter-regional variations in Indian agriculture.

Alagh and Sharma (1980) studied the growth of crop production during 1960-61 and 1978-79, dividing it into two sub-periods—1960-61 to 1969-70 (pre-green revolution) and 1969-70 to 1978-79 (post-green revolution). They found that the growth rates for food-grain production rose from 1.85 per cent during the first period to 2.74 per cent for the second period, while for the period 1960-61 to 1978-79, it was 2.77 per cent. Punjab recorded the highest growth rates of 9.54 per cent and 8.01 per cent per annum for 1960-61 to 1969-70 and 1960-61 to 1978-79 whereas, Maharashtra led the second period (1969-70 to 1978-79). At the all-India level, sugarcane output grew at the rate of 2.29 per cent, 3.42 per cent and 2.93 per cent for the first, second and the third periods respectively. With regard to cotton, the trend of growth in output was 1.62 per cent for the period 1960-61 to 1978-79. During 1960-61 to 1969-70, it was 0.31 per cent which increased to 3.38 per cent during 1969-70 to 1978-79.

Dayal (1984) identified and interpreted regional agricultural productivity patterns in India. Three indexes of agricultural productivity—land productivity, labour productivity, and aggregate productivity were employed to measure and map productivity patterns in India. Large regional inequalities in the levels of productivity were recorded. Regression analysis revealed that the spatial variation of land productivity was positively related to fertilizer use, irrigation, and urban-industrial development and negatively related to population density. Labour productivity was positively associated with agricultural wages and fertilizer use and negatively with the density of agricultural workers on net sown area. Aggregate productivity was positively associated with fertilizer and irrigation use and negatively with the densities of population and agricultural workers. The significant explanatory variables in the regressions explained 61 per cent of land productivity, 57 per cent of labour productivity, and 42 per cent of aggregate productivity.

Dev (1985) extended the Bhalla and Alagh (1978) district-wise analysis of agricultural performance up to the period 1975-78. It was found that the share of 106 low productivity districts in the aggregate output declined from about 16 per cent during 1970-73 to 11 per cent during 1975-78 and that of 48 high productivity districts increased from 36 to 45 per cent during the same period. The output per unit area for high productivity districts increased from Rs. 1730 per hectare to Rs. 1829 per hectare while that for low productivity districts declined from Rs. 550 per hectare to Rs. 481 per hectare.

Ranade (1986) studied the sources of growth of agricultural productivity during 1952-53 to 1982-83 in India. He found that the change in the rice productivity was highest in the last period (1972-73 to 1982-83) and lowest in the first period. The major contribution in agriculture production in the first period came from pure yield while during green revolution period, the cropping pattern and locational effect made a significant contribution to growth. The author also found that the technological change in rice production helped in tapering comparative advantage of some states like Punjab and Haryana. The locational effect was possible only after the technological change had taken place. As a result, the contribution of pure yield effect was more in pre-green revolution period than in the post-green revolution period.

Bhalla and Tyagi (1989) analyzed agricultural performance at the district-level in 17 major states for the periods 1962-65, 1970-73 and 1980-83, examined the association between growth rates and use of modern inputs and whether the degree of regional concentration of growth had increased or declined. The analysis was carried for 19 major crops and total crop sector for 41 crops. The authors found that introduction of new technology during 1962-65 to 1970-73 led to increase in the inter-district disparities in the productivity levels. However, the spread of new technology during 1970-73 to 1980-83 led to increase in agriculture productivity as well. There was positive correlation between the levels of productivity, agriculture growth rates and use of modern inputs like fertilizers, tractors and tubewells. The authors suggested for proper policies and increased investments in the agriculture sector to increase productivity and reduce disparities.

Rana (1990) examined inequality in land productivity at the state level in India using cross-section data for the year 1983. The author found that rainfall, per capita cropped area, short term interest rate for agriculturists and soil quality index played an insignificant role in affecting the land productivity, whereas irrigation and fertilizers were the only significant factors. He suggested for controlling the variation in the land productivity through larger allocation of funds for irrigation purposes in the states where land productivity was low and more use of fertilizers in the states where its use was lower in comparison to the progressive states, providing greater facilities of credit, higher support prices for the main crops in the low productivity states and effective plans by the government to control floods and transfer water to the states lacking irrigation facilities.

Singh and Chand (1990) examined the changes in the technological factors across states/regions and analyzed the inter-state disparities in the growth of agricultural production and productivity during 1970-71 to 1986-87. Time series data on production, technological parameters, infrastructural factors, mechanical power and total foodgrains production and productivity was used to calculate state-wise changes and growth rates. Large imbalances in the growth of agricultural production among the states/ regions were recorded due to adoption of modern crop production technology, variations in the infrastructural facilities and use of mechanical power. Punjab, Haryana and Uttar Pradesh, where the changes in the adoption of new technology, development in the infrastructural facilities and use of machinery took place, agricultural production and productivity increased tremendously. However, the backward states such as Orissa, Madhya Pradesh, Rajasthan and West Bengal, where there were no changes in the technology, showed low growth rates in agricultural output. The policy suggestions included adoption of modern crop technology in the backward states/regions, more investment in the development of infrastructure facilities for irrigation, water management, land improvement, consolidation of holdings, marketing and provision of adequate credit to purchase agricultural machinery.

Alshi and Joshi (1997) studied the inter-state and inter-decadal variations in the performance of cereals, pulses and total foodgrains and yield differences due to the use of fertilizers, irrigation and HYV in India and in different states for the periods 1971-72 to 1980-81 and 1981-82 to 1990-91. The results showed that during seventies the performance of cereals varied among the states where Punjab and Haryana had the highest and Madhya Pradesh and Maharashtra had lowest yield and the disparities further increased in the eighties. In pulses also there was divergent performance among the states in seventies which continued in the eighties also. Punjab had the highest per hectare productivity while Andhra Pradesh had the lowest productivity during seventies. Foodgrains also recorded a divergent growth during seventies that further widened in the eighties and again Punjab had the highest growth followed by Haryana and Kerala whereas Rajasthan, Maharashtra and Madhya Pradesh lagged behind. There were large variations in the adoption of key inputs like irrigation, fertilizer and HYV and the states with higher level of use of these inputs exhibited higher productivity.

Bhalla and Singh (1997) analyzed the regional patterns of levels and growth of agricultural output at state level on area and output of 43 crops from 1962-65 to 1992-95 in India. The authors recorded acceleration as well as diversification in the growth rate of agricultural output in India during 1980-83 to 1992-95 as compared with the earlier periods. The period 1980-83 to 1992-95 also recorded cropping pattern changes away from coarse cereals towards rice and wheat cultivation on the one hand and towards oilseeds on the other. There was widespread acceleration in per male agricultural worker productivity in many Indian states during 1980s. The authors concluded that if high labour productivity growth would sustain then it would not only result in higher wages, but would also trigger growth in the non-agricultural sector through input-output and consumption linkages. According to the authors, there is large potential in crop diversification and exports in Indian agriculture and small and marginal farmers play an important role in the process of diversification. Therefore, appropriate institutional strategies should be devised to involve the small and marginal farmers so that they may avail the benefits of increasing growth, agricultural diversification and exports.

Singh, Rai and Karwasra (1997) examined the temporal and spatial performance of area, production and yield of foodgrain and non-foodgrain crops and the factors responsible for determining yield and acreage of the foodgrain crops across the states and the country for the three time periods: period I (1960-61 to 1967-68), period II (1968-69 to 1980-81) and period III (1981-82 to 1992-93). It was found that for foodgrains, the yield witnessed higher growth rates as compared to the acreage in the last two decades at the national level and at the state level. In case of non-foodgrains, oilseeds and cotton maintained a steady trend in growth rates. The main determinants of agricultural performance were found to be the total cropped area, yield per hectare and irrigation water followed by regulated markets and road networks. It was also found that increased use of irrigation water, fertilizers and HYV seeds could increase the yield of foodgrain crops in most of the states.

Bhide, Kalirajan and Shand (1998) examined the patterns of agricultural growth and compared it with non-agricultural sectors at the national as well as state level in India from 1950-51 to 1993-94 and tested for convergence of agricultural growth rates across states over time. They found that unlike the non-agricultural sectors, growth in agriculture was steady for almost four decades since 1950 and the statistical tests did not show any structural break in the growth pattern of agriculture. However, when trend growth in output per hectare was considered, structural breaks occurred in the mid-1960s and in 1980s. Growth rates in agriculture exhibit marked cyclical pattern at the crop as well as state levels. The crop level cycles were attributed to movements in relative prices or other factors relating to market conditions, whereas the state level cycles were related to policies. The pattern of growth rates of agricultural output of the states over short periods of 5 years indicated that all the 15 states were converging to one rate of growth; but over a longer time period of 10 years, the states with higher proportion of crop area under irrigation were registered to be converging to higher rates of growth, whereas the states with lower proportion of crop area under irrigation converged to lower rate of growth. The policy suggestions included strengthening the investment climate in agriculture, by operating on both the supply and demand factors.

Bhalla and Singh (2001) analyzed the pattern, growth and sources of agricultural development for 17 states and 282 districts for the triennium, 1962-65, 1970-73, 1980-83 and 1990-93. The study covered 44 crops at the state level and 35 crops at the district-level. It was found that during 1962-65 to 1980-83, the impact of new technology in transforming traditional agriculture was confined to North-Western and Southern regions and a few irrigated parts of Central and Eastern India. The spread of green revolution was slow during the first twenty years, i.e. from 1962-65 to 1980-83 and gathered momentum during the 1980s. There was a change in cropping patterns from coarse cereals towards oilseeds and other commercial crops. A substantial number of districts progressed to a higher level of development and growth, both in terms of land and labour productivity. The spread of new technology to the Eastern region was the most important development during 1980s. The authors suggested for balanced regional and substantial development of Indian agriculture, there is need for diversification of agriculture from low value coarse cereals to high value fruits and vegetables, investment in rural infrastructure including irrigation, rural roads and electrification, increased allocation to agriculture research and development, animal husbandry and fishing, consolidation of landholdings and continuation of policy of minimum price supports programmes.

Joshi, Birthal and Minot (2006) examined the sources of agriculture growth during 1980s and 1990s at the national and regional level in India. The analysis concluded that at the national level, technology (yield increases) was the prime mover of growth during 1980s, while rising prices and diversification were the dominant source of growth in agriculture during 1990s. At the regional level, in Northern and Eastern regions, prices increase was the most important source of growth during 1990s, whereas in Southern and Western regions, crop income growth was led by diversification into higher value crops. The policy suggestions included investment in agricultural research and development, diversification of agriculture, infrastructure improvements, and institutional development to link small farmers with markets.

Mathur, Das and Sircar (2006) examined the trends, factors and constraints and inter-regional variations in growth of agricultural production in India during 1990-91 to 2003-04. The authors recorded decline in the growth of agriculture sector during 1990s till the recent past accompanied with decline in yields per hectare in food crops. The yield of different crops in the country was below the world average except for wheat and sugarcane. The state-wise analysis also showed wide variations in growth from 28 per cent to 19 per cent for first three years and last three years—1993-96 and 2000-03. It was found that at the state level the agricultural output at current prices was significantly and positively dependent on government expenditure on agriculture, fertilizer usage, rainfall and population.

Chand, Raju and Pandey (2007) examined the trend in agricultural growth and factors for slowdown in agriculture at the national and state level since 1980s. They found that the initial years of reforms were favourable for agricultural growth, but the post-WTO period witnessed a sharp decline in the growth rate of all sub-sectors and commodity groups in the agricultural sector. At the state level, the growth rate was negative in four out of 20 major states while six states showed growth rate between 0.10 and 0.95 per cent. However, the growth rate of agriculture in most of the low productivity states was much higher than the national average during 1984-85 to 1995-96. But after 1995-96, their growth rates declined and were much lower than the national average. To revive agricultural growth, the authors suggested to exploit irrigation potential, increase power supply, fertilizer use, credit facilities to farmers, competitive markets, and improvement in terms of trade in agriculture and mitigate risk in farming.

Mishra (2007) analyzed the trends in agriculture growth and decomposed growth using Minhas-Vaidyanathan decomposition scheme in India during 1951 to 1998. It was found that introduction of high yielding varieties in wheat, maize and rice along with improved irrigation facilities led to significant increase in their yield rates and cash crops such as cotton, sugarcane and jute recorded two-fold increase in their yield rates. Decomposition analysis recorded that the percentage contribution of change in yield rate was the most dominant component of agricultural growth. And the percentage contribution of change in the gross area under cultivation was the second most important factor of agricultural growth. However, during 1981-91 and afterwards, the interaction component between area and yield was better than area effect and change in cropping pattern was only a marginal component of agricultural growth. However, interacting with changes in gross area and yield rate significantly contributed to agricultural growth.

Singh (2007) analyzed agriculture performance and labour productivity for 45 crops across 581 districts from 33 states and Union territories in India during 1990-93 to 1999-2002. Considerable variations in agriculture were recorded where 175 most developed districts contributed about 50 per cent to total agriculture production with only 27 per cent land resources, whereas on other side 231 most underdeveloped districts contributed only 27 per cent to production with 50 per cent of cultivated land. Western-Central region recorded most of the agriculturally low developed districts whereas, most of the districts in Northern region were high developed. In case of labour productivity, Eastern and North-Eastern regions recorded maximum number of low productivity districts. Agriculture growth also recorded deceleration during 1990s in majority of the districts. For rapid, inclusive, equitable and sustainable development, he suggested for upgradation in technological base, successful adoption of biotechnology and rehabilitating the productive capacity of the soil. Strengthening of research, market infrastructure and other institutions, consolidation of landholdings, formalization of contract farming and development of agro-processing industries, and human resource development.

Sahoo and Mohapatra (2008) focussed on inter-state disparities among the 15 major states of India from 1981-82 to 2002-03. The better performing states were mostly in the Western and Southern regions of the country. On the other hand, the non-performing or poorly performing states were in the Northern and Eastern regions. There was a decrease in the disparity across the states in both Net State Domestic Product (NSDP) and Per capita Net State Domestic Product (PNSDP) over the years, but the disparity continued to be very high and relatively higher in the Net State Domestic Product compared to Per capita Net State Domestic Product. There was also strong evidence of cyclical nature of the disparity across the states, implying that agriculture was highly dependent on nature and other stochastic factors that caused fluctuations in the output across time and space. The agricultural growth decelerated in the agriculturally developed states like Punjab, Haryana and Western Uttar Pradesh in the post-reform period. Some agriculturally poor states like Bihar and West Bengal had shown a significant improvement in their agricultural growth. The regression results showed that the disparity in the agricultural output was significantly and positively affected by the variations in fertilizer use and the length of *pucca* roads.

Venkateswarlu (2008) analyzed the changing policy perspectives and the performance of Indian agriculture in the post-independence period. He discussed agricultural development during: first phase of pre-green revolution period (till mid-1960s) where implementation of land reforms was undertaken; in the second phase, i.e. during the green revolution period (1966-91) when bio-chemical and mechanical technologies were adopted; and the third phase was the post-reform period when Indian agriculture was influenced by the SAP (Structural Adjustment Programme) and India's entry into the WTO. He noted that during green revolution period, India achieved self-sufficiency in foodgrain production with high yield growth. However in the post-1991 period, there was deceleration in growth rates for all crops including food and non-food and the growth rates of agricultural GDP and rural employment also decreased. The author suggested for adoption of proper plans and policies and the government to play a vital role for the development of agriculture sector.

Bhalla and Singh (2009) analyzed the impact of economic reforms on the levels and growth of land yields and agricultural output at the state and regional levels for 17 major Indian states and 44 crops. The entire period of the study was divided into initial period of green revolution (1962-65 to 1980-83), maturing of green revolution (1980-83 to 1990-93) and post-liberalization period (1990-93 to 2003-06). It was found that the spread of new technology during 1960s remained confined to irrigated states mainly the North-Western region of India. However, the new technology matured during 1980-83 to1990-93 and spread widely to more areas and crops that resulted in growth rates of yield, output and agricultural worker productivity. There was acceleration in the growth rates from 2.24 per cent in 1962-65 to 3.40 per cent and change in cropping pattern during the period. But the post-reform period 1990-93 to 2003-06 was characterized by retrogression in the level and growth rates of yield and output and slowdown in diversification towards oilseeds. The reasons for the slowdown were decline in public investment in irrigation and water management, decline in scientific research as well as slowdown in diversification.

Singh and Singh (2009) studied the temporal and spatial pattern of agricultural growth in the pre- and post-reform period across 17 major states in India. The analysis indicated that growth rates of agricultural output and productivity registered a sharp decline since the early nineties at the all-India level as well as in most of the states. There was a downtrend in the growth of area expansion, irrigation and fertilizer consumption due to decline in public sector investment in agriculture coupled with a policy of reduction in subsidy and declining support to the public procurement system. The process of economic reforms largely bypassed the agricultural sector and the external environment also did not give the expected boost to agriculture due to declining trend in world prices, continuation of the high level of subsidies in the developed countries and resort to non-tariff barriers. It was found that price reforms alone would not be an effective instrument of agricultural growth without support in the form of rural infrastructure, technology and institutional reforms.

Tripathi and Prasad (2009) evaluated performance, progress and sources of agricultural growth in India since 1950-51 to 2007-08. It was found that agricultural workforce shifted from cultivators to agricultural labours, the number of uneconomic holdings had an increasing trend, area under food crops shifted towards non-food crops, and within food crops area under cereals shifted towards non-cereals, growth trend of aggregate agriculture as well as all sub-sector of agriculture except forestry declined during post-WTO period, production and yield instability declined for almost all crops during post-reform period while area instability increased. The decomposition analysis indicated that rising output per hectare was the predominant source of agricultural growth for most of the crops and crop groups. Disaggregating of reference period in four sub-periods showed that expansion of agricultural land was the main source of agricultural growth during the period before 1965-66 and after that the contribution of increased land area under agricultural production had declined over time and increase in productivity became the main source of growth in agricultural production. The estimation of aggregate agricultural production function with both intercept and slope dummy indicated that land significantly affected the agricultural output growth during 1950-51 to 1964-65 and after that land became less significant and now labour and capital were significantly affecting the agricultural output growth.

Birthal, Singh and Kumar (2011) investigated convergence and catch-up among 15 Indian states during 1980-81 to 2004-05 and examined the role of agricultural conditions during convergence or divergence. They found that income growth accelerated in middle income states, decelerated in most rich states and neither accelerated nor decelerated in poor states. However, there was no evidence of σ-convergence as well as absolute β-convergence in income levels across Indian states, indicating no tendency of states to converge to an identical steady state. In contrast, robust evidence of conditional β-convergence was found. It was found that investment in physical infrastructure and human resources alone was not sufficient for convergence. It should be accompanied by an improvement in agricultural conditions in particular with regard to employment pressure and technological change. According to them, for convergence it was imperative to reduce employment pressure on agriculture by improving labour market linkages of agriculture with non-agricultural sectors and technology-led intensification of agriculture to promote agricultural as well as overall economic growth and speed up process of convergence.

Kannan and Sundaram (2011) discussed the trends and patterns in agricultural growth at the national and sub-national levels in India for 44 crops in 17 major states during 1967-68 to 2007-08. They analyzed that the cropping pattern in India has undergone significant changes over time with a shift from cultivation of food-grains to commercial crops. Increase in crop yield was found to be a major factor for accelerating crop production since 1960s. The authors concluded that the enhanced capital formation, better irrigation facilities, normal rainfall and improved fertilizer consumption helped to improve crop output in the country and there is further potential for enhancing yield of major crops through better soil and water management, profitable crop rotation, innovative marketing, genetic engineering and investment in farm education and rural infrastructure.

Bhalla and Singh (2012) analyzed the regional patterns of levels and growth of agriculture output, labour productivity and their association with inputs used at the district, state and regional level during post-reform period from 1990-93 to 2005-08 and compared it with agriculture performance during pre-reform period from 1962-65 to 1980-83. The study was undertaken for 44 crops and 281 districts. It was found that adoption of seed fertilizer technology along with irrigation expansion during green revolution phase led to acceleration in output growth. During initial years of green revolution, there was inequality at the regional level, but it declined thereafter. However, post-reform period led to decline in agriculture performance and growth rates declined from 3.17 per cent to 2.77 per cent per annum during green revolution phase to post-reform period. Except Gujarat and Maharashtra, growth rates declined in all states during post-liberalization period. This decline was due to decline in public investment and lack of fresh technological breakthrough in agriculture.

Chand and Parappurathu (2012) analyzed the trends in agricultural productivity at the national and state level to identify the major factors responsible for the varied performance of agriculture during 1960-61 to 2010-11 in India. It was found that green revolution technologies introduced in the late 1960s led to significant acceleration in growth from below 1 per cent to 3 per cent as well as diversification of production towards horticultural and cash crops. However, the post-reform period witnessed a deceleration of growth in most of the crops due to diversion of resources away from agriculture and decline in public and private investment. The use of primary inputs in the sector also slowed down, which led to decline in the yield levels. The retardation of growth continued up to 2004-05, after which there was a sharp recovery. According to the authors, this was mainly due to hike in public and private investment and a substantial improvement in terms of trade in favour of the agriculture sector and this led to rapid expansion of agricultural credit, reinvigorated growth in the distribution of quality seeds and favourable prices of farm products.

Kumar and Jain (2013) examined the trends in growth and instability in Indian agriculture at the district-level for the period from 1990-91 to 2007-08. They found that proportion of districts recording very low productivity declined from 9.4 per cent in TE 1991 to 3.3 per cent in TE 2007 and low productivity districts declined from 25 per cent to 17 per cent during the same period. On the other hand, the proportion of very high productivity districts increased from 11 per cent in TE 1991 to 23 per cent in TE 2007. There was also a shift in districts across the growth categories during 1990s and 2000s. During 1990s, about 60 per cent of the districts recorded low growth of less than 2.5 per cent and 21 per cent of the districts recorded high growth rate of more than 3.5 per cent. During the 2000s, the number of high growth districts increased to 35 per cent. Modern inputs such as use of fertilizer, rainfall, irrigation, sources of irrigation, human resources and road connectivity were found to be critical determinants of enhancing agricultural productivity. The authors suggested for insurance to mitigate the consequences of persisting instability in agriculture, prudent management of rainfall water, need for regionally differentiated strategies for ensuring sustainable and inclusive agricultural growth in a state and consequently in the country due to varying performance of crop sector at the district, state and national level.

Birthal *et al.* (2014) studied the patterns and sources of agricultural growth for 20 Indian states during 1980-1981 to 2009-

2010. They recorded transformation of Indian agriculture from a cereal-based production system toward high-value crops during the 1990s but food security concerns resurfaced during the first decade of the twenty first century, and the policy environment tilted in favour of cereal-based production systems, especially rice and wheat. The authors concluded that technological change and diversification toward HYVs were the major sources of agriculture growth and to sustain this growth, investment in agricultural research must be increased, agricultural research agenda must be revisited in view of the emerging challenges and market opportunities in agriculture and the agrifood industry, irrigated facilities should be enhanced, formulation of policies, development of institutions, and infrastructure that facilitate farmers' access to remunerative markets should be initiated.

Chatterjee (2014) analyzed convergence in per capita income in agriculture and identified the drivers of agriculture growth across 17 major states in India during 1967 to 2010 sub-dividing the period into 1st sub-phase (1967-1977) the period of green revolution, 2nd sub-phase (1978-1989) period of falling public investment in agriculture and 3rd sub-phase (1990-2010) period of economic reforms. The results of sigma test found that except in phase 1 when the standard deviation declined, there was no evidence of any trend in sigma convergence in any of the other sub-periods over the entire period. And further for spatial convergence analysis, strong evidence of spatial beta convergence in the entire period as well as all the three sub-phases was found. Factors that significantly drive agriculture growth were input usage, physical infrastructure and cropping pattern. However, input usage and infrastructure were significant only in the first phase. In the second and third phases, inputs were not significant, but literacy was significant. Land, irrigation, rainfall and spatial variables recorded significant impact on growth during all the phases. Therefore, the author suggested for economic policy measures targeting improvement and expansion of infrastructural support, literacy input usage and water management to promote long run agriculture growth and convergence across Indian states.

Kumar, Lala and Chaudhry (2014) examined convergence of per hectare Net State Domestic Product agriculture and catch-up among 15 Indian states during pre-WTO, post-WTO, and overall period during 1980-81 to 2000-01. The authors found that growth in

NSDP agriculture during post-reform period favoured agriculturally underdeveloped states whereas agriculturally developed states recorded deceleration. They concluded that the economic reforms initiated by government led to convergence in per hectare NSDP across Indian states whereas there was divergence during pre-reform period. According to the authors, fertilizers, public finance, small holdings, cropping pattern, investment in agricultural research and education, physical infrastructure, mechanization and diversification were the main factors that led to convergence in agriculture growth and while framing policy and designing development programmes all these variables should be included as policy inputs for getting desired policy outcome.

2.4. STATE LEVEL STUDIES

Etienne (1968) analyzed the factors influencing agricultural production in two districts—Bulandshahr, primarily wheat producing district, and Varanasi producing both wheat and rice crops in Uttar Pradesh. The author found that the state accounts for 19 per cent of the total agricultural area in India, but it shares only 9 per cent of irrigation and allotted only 14.6 per cent of funds. The problems of corruption and lack of coordination in the administration machinery of the state were some of the causes of slow growth of agriculture. He further noted that the Intensive Area Cultivation Programme and use of new high yield Mexican wheat seeds had encouraging results on production and productivity in the state agriculture.

Singh, Sirohi and Singh (1973) fitted the Cobb-Douglas production function to the data on 40 farms of two villages of Meerut district of Western Uttar Pradesh for the year 1967-68 and examined the efficiency of farm resources among different crops grown on the farm. The variable Y (the dependant variable) showing yield per acre was regressed on human labour, bullock labour, manure and fertilizer expenditure and irrigation representing independent variables. Bullock labour turned out to be non-significant, whereas, the coefficient of manure and fertilizer and irrigation were significant in all the cases. For the optimum use, the authors suggested that resources should be diverted to irrigation which had maximum return per rupee of additional investment.

Singh (1975) fitted the Cobb-Douglas production function on the data on 150 farms in Deoria district of Eastern Uttar Pradesh for

1967-68 and worked out elasticity of output with respect to land, human factor, bullock labour, manures and fertilizer and fixed capital. The value of R^2 was 0.86 and the sum of elasticities was equal to one, establishing the constant returns to scale in agriculture of Eastern Uttar Pradesh. The ratio of marginal value product to factor cost indicated that all factors except land were being used at the optimal level.

Shaffi (1984) examined agricultural productivity and regional imbalances in the Uttar Pradesh agriculture. The analysis was based on data for 13 main crops (wheat, rice, jowar, bajra, maize, pigeon pea, gram, green gram, black gram, bengal gram, ground nut, sugarcane, and potatoes) for 48 districts during 1966-67 to 1975-76. The author compared the inter-district variations in productivity by employing seven alternative methods of productivity measurements and found that the standard nutrition value unit (SNU) output per hectare method was most suitable. By employing the factor analysis and Cobb-Douglas type of production function, irrigation by canals, irrigation by other sources, chemical (NPK) fertilizer consumed and number of agricultural workers in a district had significant relationship with inter-district differentials in productivity. The first three were positively associated with productivity, whereas the last had negative association with it.

Singh and Saxena (1985) assessed agricultural development in Uttar Pradesh from 1960-61 to 1980-81. Authors found that the food-grains production during this period recorded a significant high growth (3.61% per annum) and exceeded the population growth (2.51% per annum) in the state. The authors concluded that if this trend in agriculture growth is maintained and population is controlled, production in 1990-91 and 2000-01 was predicted to be 29.9 million tonnes (MT) and 34.9 million tonnes respectively and the state would be food surplus at the end of century. Provision of incentive support prices, declaration support before sowing season, organizational support for the purchase of commodities at support prices and a timely, easy and adequate supply of essential inputs were recommended by the authors to help and promote agricultural development in the state.

Chopra (1986) compared the agricultural development in Uttar Pradesh and Bihar with agriculturally leading states of Punjab and Haryana. He noted that the state economy was basically an agrarian in nature and marked by small sized holdings and low level of development. Value of agricultural output of food-grains and main commercial crops in 1977-78 was Rs. 573 per hectare in Uttar Pradesh compared with Rs. 1779 in Punjab and Rs. 1172 in Haryana. The author concluded that the problems responsible for low productivity of agriculture were non-implementation of land reforms, predominance of small sized holdings and underdeveloped and underutilized irrigation facilities in the state. He suggested for rural electrification, diversification from food and cash crops and development of irrigation in the state for agricultural development and the state should be split up into three-four independent units for its better administration and overall development.

Jain (1990) analyzed the correlation of wheat and rice yield with the introduction of the high yielding variety seeds across 44 districts for the pre-HYVs period (1954-55 to 1965-66) and the HYVs period (1966-67 to 1980-81) in Uttar Pradesh. The author found that number of significantly positive correlations between actual yields for wheat increased in all the cases, with highest increase in the Western region. The actual yields of rice also showed an increased number of significantly positive correlations. However, between the districts of the Eastern and Bundelkhand regions, actual yield correlations of rice became less significant during the second period. The inter-district correlations for yield variability for wheat and rice recorded that the number of significantly positive correlations between districts decreased during the second period in all the regions. The inter-district correlations between the districts of the different regions showed significantly positive correlations during the HYVs period compared to the first period. Whereas, the number of negative correlations between the districts of these regions was greater during the period of HYVs as compared to the first period, for both wheat and rice crops.

Arora, Srivastava and Bhogal (1997) analyzed the agricultural growth in area, production and productivity for wheat, paddy, sugarcane, potato, oilseeds and pulses for five economic regions—Western, Central, Eastern, Bundelkhand and Hills in Uttar Pradesh. The study covered the period from 1970-71 to 1993-94, dividing it further into two sub-periods—1970-71 to 1979-80 and 1980-81 to 1993-94. The authors found that the state performed much better (4.99 per cent) as compared to the nation (1.87%) in wheat in 1970s in area, production as well as productivity. Among the regions, the Eastern region outperformed other regions in the state. However, the second period recorded deceleration in wheat growth rates. In case of paddy, oilseeds and sugarcane, the growth rates in production and productivity in 1970s were found to be non-significant, but in the second period, the state outperformed the country as a whole in terms of growth in production as well as productivity. The performance with respect to pulses was not found to be significant in both the periods. The state did well during the first period in the case of potato, but there was deceleration in the growth in area as well as production during the second period. The authors concluded that irrigation facilities and use of chemical fertilizers contributed to the variations in crop productivity in the state.

Kumar (2000) examined the levels of input utilization and spatial behaviour in the agriculture pursuit, measured the level of agriculture development and the extent of agriculture land potentiality in the development of agriculture and suggested the ways to reduce inequalities and raise the level of agriculture development in Uttar Pradesh. The study was based on the district-level data for triennium 1980-83 excluding the hill districts because of non-availability of data. The method of principal component analysis was used to measure the levels of agriculture development and to derive the component responsible for disparities in the levels of development. A set of 11 variables was grouped into two segments: (a) input utilization, and (b) related to agricultural land potentiality. Author found out that the districts in the Western regions were highly developed whereas those in the Eastern parts had very low level of development. The inter-regional differences were mainly due to availability of irrigation facilities and use of modern agricultural inputs.

Shukla (2002) examined the constraints for slow growth rate of agriculture in Uttar Pradesh and suggested strategies and policies for higher growth rates. The author found that agriculture growth was about 2.7 per cent per annum during 2001 which was slower than the other sectors growth rates. There were widespread induced fluctuations in agricultural production and growth. These fluctuations were partly weather induced and partly institutional led. There was lack of diversification in agriculture from low value crops, inadequate and inefficient infrastructure for development, the non-economic holdings were dominated in the state that could neither face the challenging position nor get benefits from liberalization. Therefore, the author suggested for a need for a new mode of organizing agriculture and production, processing and marketing into a single system.

Srivastava (2003) analyzed the temporal changes in the cropping pattern of paddy, maize, bajra, wheat, potato and sugarcane in the Western region of Uttar Pradesh during 1950-51 to 2000-01, for pre-liberalization and post-liberalization periods. The pre-liberalization period was grouped into three sub-periods: Pre-green revolution phase (1950-51 to 1966-67), green revolution phase I: 1967-68 to 1979-80 and green revolution phase II: 1980-81 to 1994-95. The author found that the technological breakthrough brought by the green revolution led by liberalization in the early 1990s led to a sharp increase in the share of paddy, maize, wheat and potato area by the triennium 1966-68 compared to 1950-52. The introduction of high yielding variety of paddy and wheat along with other improved package of practices provided the incentives to the farmers to bring land improvement and irrigation facilities which led to increase in the cropping intensity in the Western Uttar Pradesh. The findings of the study also indicated a bias of the green revolution associated technological breakthrough and liberalization against the coarse cereals in the state.

Bajpai and Volavka (2005) identified and analyzed the issues and problems associated with the agriculture sector in Uttar Pradesh since pre-green revolution period from the early 1960s. The authors examined the growth of agricultural outputs during green revolution in Uttar Pradesh and those in relation to Punjab and Haryana and also examined intra-state variations in patterns of agriculture between Western and Eastern Uttar Pradesh. The most significant variables were fertilizers, high yielding variety seeds, rainfall, irrigation, soil fertility, size of holdings and size of markets that explained the differential agricultural performance of Uttar Pradesh relative to Punjab and Haryana. During the green revolution period, only the Western region of Uttar Pradesh made good use of high yielding variety seeds relative to other parts of the state. Over time, Eastern Uttar Pradesh made strides to narrow the gap with its Western counterpart. However, disparities between the two regions persisted. The authors suggested increased focus on irrigation, research and development, infrastructure, promotion of agro-based industries and adoption of new technology as the areas that required higher public investment and government attention for growth of agriculture in the state.

Rehman, Wahab and Asif (2008) examined variations in crop productivity in Ganga-Yamuna Doab in Uttar Pradesh. Using Yang's 'Crop Productivity Index', the authors examined the crop productivity variations of 13 major crops grown in the districts of the region and the changes in productivity during 1990-94 and 2000-04. The analysis found that during the period of 1990-94, there were only four districts with low productivity, while during the period 2000-04, the number of districts increased to nine. There were variations in productivity influenced by the physical and socio-economic factors, substantial variation in respect of soil fertility, preponderance of small and semi-medium holdings and highly fragmented fields which showed low yields in farming areas. To increase the productivity of crops per hectare, the authors suggested for application of new agricultural technology brought with high-yielding varieties, dividing the Doab into a number of micro agro-climatic zones and intensive efforts to be made to evolve new high-yielding varieties suiting to each agro-climatic zone.

Prabha, Goswami and Chatterjee (2010) estimated rural poverty across 48 districts in Uttar Pradesh to measure and analyze the regional and district-level variations in the incidence, depth and severity of rural poverty and to examine the linkage between agricultural productivity and incidence, depth and severity of rural poverty across the districts of the state. The authors estimated rural poverty for four quinquennial years based on National Sample Survey Organization data for the 43rd (1987-88), 50th (1993-94), 55th (1999-2000) and 61st (2004-2005) rounds of Household Consumption Expenditure Survey reports. The authors found significant differences in the incidence, depth and severity of rural poverty across the regions and districts of Uttar Pradesh. Rural poverty was recorded high across the districts in comparison to national average. The linkage between agricultural productivity and rural poverty was found to be significant at the district-level. The authors suggested that to alleviate poverty in the rural areas of the state, the state government should make a sincere effort to improve the agricultural productivity in the districts of the state. Neglect of agriculture will hamper the growth of industries, particularly agro-based industries and weaken the macro-economic fundamentals of the state and the country as a whole.

Pandey and Reddy (2012) analyzed the agricultural productivity levels and variations in productivity for 70 districts and four regions in Uttar Pradesh during 2005-06 to 2007-08, to identify the factors that affect land and labour productivity and in turn, rural poverty in the state. The authors found that the performance of agriculture in Uttar Pradesh varied considerably across districts and regions and has strong linkages and implications for poverty reduction. Irrigation and fertilizer-use were found to be the major determinants of the level and variations of agricultural productivity in the state. Econometric analysis indicated that an increase of 10 per cent in land productivity would reduce poverty by 4.3 per cent. The dependence of workers on agriculture recorded inverse relationship and 10 per cent reduction in labour force could result in 7.7 per cent reduction in poverty. The authors suggested the need for strengthening the non-farm employment and income opportunities along with improved farm productivity through resource diversification towards high-value crops like fruits and vegetables in low productivity districts and region-specific development strategies of generating non-farm activities along with improving land productivity for reducing rural poverty in Uttar Pradesh. They also stressed on the need for public investment in irrigation and incentives to encourage agricultural diversification and intensive-use of inputs like fertilizers in the state.

Raman and Kumari (2012) analyzed district and regional level disparities in agriculture development in Uttar Pradesh. The study was conducted for 54 districts using 13 agricultural development indicators for two cross-section years 1990-91 and 2008-09. The authors found that the development of agriculture in Uttar Pradesh was polarized in Western region followed by Central region and Bundelkhand region was the least developed. The maximum number of developed districts was also recorded in agriculturally commercialized and technologically advanced Western and Central regions of the state. Western region was found to be much influenced to green and technical revolution that led to high contribution in export and food production of the state. The authors therefore suggested that to alleviate the problem of high and alarming disparity in agriculture development there should be region specific policies, specially for low developed Bundelkhand and high density Eastern regions, availability of credit and subsidy to the neediest region and need to identify the agro-climatic zones that have problems and are most backward such as Bundelkhand and Vindhyan Zone and therefore specific efforts should be made for these regions.

Goyal and Kumar (2013) studied overall production trends of agriculture in Uttar Pradesh during 1950-51 to 2011-12 and cropping pattern in the state for the period 1982-83, 1991-92 and 1999-2000. The authors recorded an increase in agriculture productivity along with improved cropping pattern and state agricultural growth rates were found to be more satisfactory than national averages. The authors suggested that huge quantities of water could be saved by diversification of cropping pattern from rice, wheat and sugarcane crops to less water consuming crops and in addition technological improvement and change in the agricultural practices in general and irrigation practices, in particular, could also help to reduce the water consumption in these crops.

Shafiquallah (2013) analyzed the spatial pattern of regional disparities, variations in the levels of agricultural development and relationship between agricultural development and 14 agriculture indicators during 2001. The spatial distribution of agricultural development recorded that majority of North-Eastern and Southern districts in the state were backward and districts from Western and Central plain regions had higher levels of development. In the analysis of level of regional disparities, the author found that *tarai* districts were backward whereas Western, Central and Southern districts were in favourable position. The relationship between levels of regional disparities recorded an increase from West to Central and Eastern region. The author concluded that the state has tremendous scope for agricultural development and social justice and balanced development can be achieved through increased irrigation facilities and giving top priority to low developed regions and districts (see Tables 2.1 and 2.2).

2.5. CONCLUSION

From International Studies

1. There is a shift from the traditional to modern agriculture due to availability of modern inputs, technological developments, research and extension in the agriculture sector.
2. There are wide inter-country, intra-country disparities in agricultural performance due to agro-climatic, infrastructure, human capital as well as technological differences.
3. Reforms in agriculture sector have contributed to better agricultural performance in the developing countries. China however reaped the maximum benefits.
4. Signs of conditional convergence among some Asian countries. However, there is neither convergence nor divergence in regional disparities in the countries like China.
5. Need to formulate policies to focus on agriculture research

Table 2.1: Key Features and Findings of Main District Level Studies in India

Author	*Objective of the study*	*Period*	*Districts included*	*Crops covered*	*Main Conclusions*
Brown (1971)	Impact of IADP programme	1956-57 to 1965-66	320	19 crops	No significant difference in performance of IADP with non-IADP districts
Gordan (1974)	Inter-district disparities and their causes	1960-61	Districts in 16 states	12 crops	Irrigation leads to higher yield, education imp. than health for human capital formation and output/ acre was large on small farms.
Bhalla and Alagh (1979)	Inter-district variations in agricultural performance and sources of growth	1962-65 to 1970-73	282	19 crops	69 high prod., 130 mid & 83 low prod. districts 50 districts recorded gr. > 4.5 %, 105 (1.5-4.5%) & 62 (0.5 to 1.5%), districts in Eastern UP, Bihar and WB recorded low growth rates, modern inputs and irrigation led to inter-district disparities.
Dev (1985)	Inter-district variations in agricultural performance	Exten.of Bhalla and Alagh (1979) 1962-65 to 1975-78	282	19 crops	Decline in output and output share of low prod. districts during 1970-73 to 1975-78 and increase in high prod. districts.
Bhalla and Tyagi (1989)	Agricultural Performance and sources of growth	Exten.of Bhalla and Alagh (1979) 1962-65 to 1980-83	282	19 crops	Acceleration in agriculture growth during 1980s, positive association between agricultural performance and modern inputs
Bhalla and Singh (2001)	Agricultural Performance and sources of growth	Exten.of Bhalla and Alagh (1979) 1962-65 to 1990-93	282	35 crops	Decline in low productivity districts, changes in cropping pattern, increase in MAWP and decline in regional disparities
Singh (2007)	Agricultural Performance and sources of growth	1990-93 to 1999-2002	581	45 crops	175 high dev. districts contribute 50% to production & low 231 districts 27%, Western-Central region under dev. in ag. prod. and Eastern region low developed in labour productivity.
Chand, Garg and Pandey (2009)	Regional variations in agricultural productivity and its linkage with poverty	2003-04 and 2004-05	551	45 crops	191 districts recorded low and 66 districts recorded very low productivity, 1% increase in rainfall leads to 0.43% increase in prod, fertilizer (0.27%) and irrigation (0.11 %). 1% incr. in land prod. reduces poverty by 0.51%. and 1% reduction in labour force leads to 0.49% decline in poverty.

(*Contd.*)

Author	*Objective of the study*	*Period*	*Districts included*	*Crops covered*	*Main Conclusions*
Bhalla and Singh (2010)	Agricultural Performance and sources of growth	Exten.of Bhalla and Alagh (1979) 1962-65 to 2003-06	281	44 crops	Low ag. growth during 1990s, no. of high gr. districts increased during 1980s but decreased thereafter, decline in disparities in ag. prod. and increase in disparities in agriculture workers productivity
Bhalla and Singh (2012)	Economic Liberalization and Agricultural Performance	1962-65 to 2005-09	281	44 crops	Economic liberalization led to decline in agriculture performance at the state as well as district level, except Gujarat and Maharashtra, all other stats faced reverses in agriculture growth.
Kumar and Jain (2013)	Trends, instability and drivers of agriculture productivity	1990-91 to 2007-08	388	45 crops	Increase in high growth districts in 2000s. The elasticity of cropping intensity was 1.17, followed by fertilizer use (0.29), irrigation (0.20), literacy (0.19), rainfall (0.17), road density (0.11) and credit (0.0003).

Table 2.2: Key Features and Findings of Main District Level Studies in Uttar Pradesh

Author	*Objectives*	*Period*	*Districts included*	*Crops covered*	*Main Conclusions*
Shaffi (1984)	Inter-district variation in ag. Productivity and examine input-output relationship	1966-67 to 1975-76	48	13 crops	Positive association between agricultural productivity, irrigation, fertilizers and negative with labour.
Jain (1990)	Compare the yield variability of wheat and rice with HYV	1954-55 to 1965-66	44	2 crops (Rice and wheat)	Correlation between yield of rice and wheat with HYV seeds.
Kumar (2000)	Analyze pattern of agriculture development and inputs used	1980-83	48	11 variables	Districts in Western region high developed and low in Eastern region and irrigation and modern inputs lead to inter-district disparities in agriculture.
Prabha, Goswami and Chatterjee (2010)	Linkage b/w rural poverty and agriculture production	1987-88 1993-94 1999-2000 2004-05	48	Not mentioned	Agriculture development mitigate rural poverty significantly
Pandey and Reddy (2012)	Linkage b/w farm productivity and rural poverty	2005-06 to 2007-08	70	Not mentioned	1% increase/decrease in agricultural productivity leads to 0.43% increase/decrease in rural poverty
Raman and Kumari (2012)	Inter-district disparities in agriculture development	1990-91 and 2008-09	54	Only Foodgrain crops included for agriculture development and 13 indicators of development	Western and Central regions high developed, Bundelkhand low developed and all development indicators except road highest in Western region
Shafiqullah (2013)	Inter-district disparities in agriculture development	2001	70	14 indicators of agriculture development and 26 to measure inter-district disparity	Marked disparities from west to central and eastern regions, literacy, urbanization, health, education and infrastructure significant in inter-district disparities.

and development, development of HYV seeds, establish bio-technology programmes, etc.

6. Growth in area effect and yield effect are major source of output growth. However, due to limitation on area expansion there should be more emphasis to yield augmenting technological changes.

From National Level Studies

1. The Green Revolution technology introduced in mid-sixties was mainly confined to irrigated North-Western regions of Punjab, Haryana and Western Uttar Pradesh and to some pockets in Coastal regions. Initially it almost bypassed major areas in Eastern, Central and Southern regions.
2. During initial phase, Green Revolution led to widening of regional disparities in Indian agriculture.
3. Indian agriculture experienced diversification from low technology and low value coarse cereal crops and pulses towards better technology crops rice and wheat, and high value commercial crops like plantation, fruits and vegetables, condiments and spices crops.
4. With the passage of time, new technology spread to newer areas and encompassed more districts, leading to widespread gains across all regions.
5. There was deceleration in the agriculture growth rates after the reform in almost all the states except Gujarat and Maharashtra. The post-reform performance of agriculture was contrary to the expectations.
6. There is shift in the sources of agriculture growth from traditional inputs like land, labour and animal capital to modern industrial sector inputs such as machinery, chemicals, pesticides, new seeds etc.
7. Development of infrastructure and institutional changes contributed immensely to agricultural performance in India.
8. Decline in public sector investment led to slowdown in agricultural growth during the reform period.
9. There exist wide regional, district as well as state level disparities due to variations in natural, human and infrastructure facilities.
10. There are some signs of convergence in agriculture growth

during shorter time period, however during longer time periods states with higher crop area under irrigation converged to higher growth rates and states with low area under irrigation converged to lower growth rates.

11. Yield effect played an important role in output growth in Indian agriculture.

From State Level Studies for Uttar Pradesh

1. Different studies for Uttar Pradesh cover different number of crops.
2. Most of the state level studies are confined to limited period of almost two decades.
3. Most of the studies have limited objectives. Therefore, many of the issues like growth dynamics, labour productivity, convergence/divergence and other spatial dimensions are ignored by most of the researchers.
4. Most of the studies focussed on identification of sources of growth and regional differentials in agricultural performance lack sophisticated econometric analysis to arrive at more definite conclusions.

2.6. GAP IN LITERATURE

1. There is no recent comprehensive district-level analysis of agricultural performance for Uttar Pradesh.
2. Majority of the studies analyzing agricultural performance are on basis of initial and end trienniums averages. This sometimes leads to erroronous estimation of growth in case any of the trienniums contains abnormal production years. Such analysis ignores well-known year-to-year fluctuations in agricultural production.
3. The intra-state analysis of agricultural performance below state levels are few and are far between.
4. A comprehensive analysis of district-level agriculture in Uttar Pradesh in post-reform period is not available.
5. Most of the studies are confined to analysis of inter-regional variations in agricultural development in Uttar Pradesh. Much literature is not available on whether these regions or districts are coming closer or moving far away in the process of

agriculture growth and development in the state. We could not lay our hands in any study analyzing the process of convergence or divergence in performance of agriculture in Uttar Pradesh.

6. With a few exceptions, most of the studies identifying sources of agricultural growth are weak on methodological account. The problems of heteroscedasticity and multicollinearity are ignored by researchers, which lead to misleading conclusions. Furthermore, the idiosyncratic factors which play significant role in agriculture sector are ignored by the researchers.
7. We did not come across any study analyzing the district or region-wise growth and level of agriculture workers productivity in Uttar Pradesh.

3

Agricultural Performance in Uttar Pradesh: Temporal Dynamics

3.1. INTRODUCTION

Having a brief peep into the existing body of vast literature on agricultural performance at the international, national and regional levels in the previous chapter, the present chapter is focussed to examine the agricultural performance in the state of Uttar Pradesh as a whole during the last half a century from 1960-61 to 2010-11. Though the main objective of our present study is to examine the district-level performance of Uttar Pradesh agriculture during the last five decades, the idea of state level analysis is to have a broader prospective regarding the overall performance of Uttar Pradesh agriculture *vis-à-vis* the country as a whole as well as with the agriculturally selected leading states in the country during the different phases of agricultural development. Besides comparative analysis, the present chapter also proposes to identify the emerging temporal dynamics of Uttar Pradesh agriculture in terms of performance of different crops, sub-group of crops as well as performance of agricultural allied sub-sectors. The chapter also proposes to decompose the agricultural production into its main contributors namely—area, yield, cropping pattern and their interactions terms to identify their changing role as contributors to growth over the period of time.

More specifically the main objectives of this chapter are:

1. To identify the temporal dynamics of agricultural growth in Uttar Pradesh.

2. To examine the temporal dynamics of changes in area, production and yield of different crops.
3. To examine the temporal dynamics of the changing contribution of area and yield as contributors to overall production over time.

Given these objectives, we propose to test the following hypotheses in this chapter:

(i) Changing policy regimes made significant impact on temporal variations in agricultural performance in Uttar Pradesh.
(ii) Changing technological, institutional and market dynamics led to diversification of cropping pattern in the state from low productivity and low value coarse cereals, pulses and oilseeds towards more remunerative wheat, rice and horticultural crops.

The chapter is organized as follows. After introduction, objectives and hypotheses in this section, section 3.2 details methodology followed in the present chapter. Section 3.3 presents pattern of agricultural growth in Uttar Pradesh and its comparison with the country as whole and the states of Punjab and Haryana as well. The section also presents the sub-sector-wise and crop-wise growth of agriculture in the state. Pattern of agricultural development in terms of land and labour productivity is detailed in section 3.4. Section 3.5 examines the diversification of crops in the state of Uttar Pradesh and section 3.6 presents the decomposition of agricultural growth during different periods over the last five decades. The concluding section 3.7 summarizes the findings of this chapter.

3.2. METHODOLOGY

To study the dynamics of temporal variations in agricultural growth and development in Uttar Pradesh, we employed the following measures:

3.2 (i) Estimation of Growth: Growth of area, production and productivity are estimated by calculating compound average growth rate as follows:

$$\text{Annual growth rate } (G_t) = [(V_t/V_{t-1}) - 1] \times 100$$

$$\text{Compound annual growth rate (CAGR)} = \sum_{t=1}^{T} G_t/T$$

where,

V_t – Value of indicator (like area/production/inputs) in year t.

V_{t-1} Value of indicator (like area/production/inputs) in year t-1

T – Number of years for which CAGR is to be estimated.

3.2 (ii) Coefficient of variation: The growth rates provide information on the extent of development, but not about robustness of growth over time. To examine the same over time, we estimated the standard deviation and coefficient of variation in growth over time during different phases of agricultural development in Uttar Pradesh as follows:

$$\text{Standard Deviation} = \left[\sum_{t=1}^{T}\left(G_t - G^2/T\right)\right]^{1/2}$$

$$\text{Coefficient of Variation} = \frac{\text{Standard deviation}}{\text{Mean}}$$

3.3 (iii) Estimation of land and labour productivity: Level of agricultural development is generally measured in terms of partial factor productivity of the fixed factor employed in production. Land and labour productivity are two such popular measures. In the literature on partial factor productivity in agriculture, there is no hard and fast rule regarding the choice between the land and labour productivity measures. However, most of the studies undertaken in developing countries prefer land productivity whereas labour productivity is the preferable index for analysis of agricultural development in the developed countries. Basic reason behind this seems to be scarcity of land in developing and labour in developed countries. However, to have a broader view, we preferred to use both of these measures for analyzing the level of agricultural development in Uttar Pradesh.

In the empirical literature on agricultural development, land productivity is measured in two ways. First is the value output per unit of the gross cropped area (GCA) and the second is the value output per unit of the net sown area (NSA). Both of these lead to same conclusions if the cycle of different crops grown over time or across regions is uniform. However, they may lead to different conclusions if the situation is not so. In the state of Uttar Pradesh both seasonal and perennial crops are grown simultaneously. For example, sugarcane is a major crop in Uttar Pradesh and is of almost double of the lifespan of other major crops like wheat, jowar, pulses and rice. Therefore, gross cropped area based measure of land productivity can lead to wrong conclusions. Consequently, we preferred to define the level of agricultural development as value output of all the crops grown in the state per unit of the net sown area as follows:

$$\text{Land productivity} = \frac{\text{Total value of crop output in the state}}{\text{Total net sown area in the state}}$$

$$\text{Labour productivity} = \frac{\text{Total value of crop output in the state}}{\text{Total number of agricultural workers in the state}}$$

3.4 (iv) Crop diversification: To measure dynamics of diversification in Uttar Pradesh agriculture, we estimated share of output and area under each crop in total crop sector as follows:

In case of share of area, we used the following formula:

$$\text{Crop area share} = \frac{\text{Area under crop}}{\text{Gross croped area}} \times 100$$

In case of output share, the formula used is:

$$\text{Crop output share} = \frac{\text{Value output of crop}}{\text{Total value output}} \times 100$$

3.5 (v) Decomposition of total output growth: There are number of additive and multiplicative methods to estimate the contribution of different elements (area, yield, cropping pattern, etc.) to the output growth. Minhas and Vaidyanathan (1965) were probably the first to decompose output growth and compute the influence of individual components by using four factor model. Later on Minhas (1966) extended it to a seven factor decomposition model, considering the other interaction terms since the four factor model is not useful when the interaction term is relatively larger. Later on, Prabha (1971), Sagar (1977), Narain (1977) further modified and expanded the Minhas (1966) decomposition model. Whereas, Prabha (1971) modified the model by converting the absolute growth into relative growth, Sagar (1977) expanded it into seven components namely—three pure components—area, yield and prices and their four interaction terms (Area-Price, Area-Yield, Yield-Price and Area-Price-Yield). Narain (1977) modified Minhas and Vaidyanathan (1965) model by explicitly introducing a locational component to interpret the yield effect in agricultural growth. All these approaches are referred to as additive schemes since they decompose absolute growth in terms of the sum of individual growth components.

In the literature, there is an alternative multiplicative scheme also, which decomposes the relative growth of output into growth rates of components. The first multiplicative scheme was introduced by Dayal (1966). Thereafter, Parikh (1966), Shetty (1970), Sagar (1980), Jamal and Zaman (1992), etc. developed new multiplicative schemes as alternatives to the existing ones.

In our study, we preferred to use Prabha (1971) decomposition approach as the same is more comprehensive scheme of decomposition and provides better information about contribution of various sources to overall growth. We start with the following identities as provided by Minhas and Vaidyanathan (1965):

$$P_o = A_o \Sigma i W_i C_{io} Y_{io} \quad \dots (1)$$

$$P_t = A_t \Sigma i W_t C_{it} Y_{it} \quad \dots (2)$$

where,

P_o and P_t – are the total value of crop production (all crops) in the base (0) and final (t) years respectively.

A_o and A_t – are the area under crops in the base and final years respectively.

Wi – stands for the price per unit of the ith crop and is kept constant throughout the computation.

C_{io} and C_{it} – denote the area under the ith crop as a proportion of the total area in year '0' and 't' respectively.

Y_{io} and Y_{it} – represent the yield per acre of the ith crop in base and final years respectively.

All these indices, both in the base (0) and final (t) years are triennium averages to smoothen the weather induced yearly variations.

Taking difference between P_t and P_0 from (1) and (2) and on simplifying the terms, we get:

$$P_t - P_o = \underset{\text{(Area effect)}}{(A_t - A_o)\,\Sigma i W_i C_{io} Y_{io}} + \underset{\text{(Yield effect)}}{A_t \Sigma i W_i C_{io}(Y_{it} - Y_{io})} + \underset{\text{(Crop pattern effect)}}{A_t \Sigma i W_i C_{it}(C_{it} - C_{io}) Y_{io}} + \underset{\text{(Cropping pattern and yield interaction effect)}}{A_t \Sigma i\, W_i (C_{it} - C_{io})(Y_{it} - Y_{io})}$$

Thereafter, Prabha (1971) slightly modified the above scheme of decomposition by dividing each term by P_o and thus converting absolute growth into relative growth such that in the process the weights become explicit. The scheme used is the following:

(Area effect) (Yield effect) (Cropping pattern effect)
(Area and yield interaction effect) (Area and cropping pattern interaction effect)
(Yield and cropping pattern interaction effect) (Area, yield and cropping pattern interaction effect)

Where,

P_{io} – represents the value of output of the ith crop in the base year '0'

P_{io}/P_o – denotes the fraction of the total value of agricultural output contributed by the ith crop. The rest of the notations are the same as used in the previous scheme.

EMPIRICAL FINDINGS

3.3. PATTERN OF AGRICULTURAL GROWTH IN UTTAR PRADESH

3.3 (i) A Comparative Analysis

To study the pattern of agricultural growth in Uttar Pradesh, we begin with comparing the performance of Uttar Fradesh agriculture *vis-à-vis* the country as a whole as well as with Punjab and Haryàna—two

Northern-Indian leading states in adoption of green revolution technology and level of agricultural development. We estimated the growth rates for overall period from 1960-2012 as well as by subdividing it into five phases of agricultural development in the country. These are: pre-green revolution (1960-61 to 1965-66), initial green revolution (1967-68 to 1980-81), mature green revolution (1981-82 to 1990-91), initial post-reform (1991-92 to 2000-01) and new millennium phase (2001-02 to 2012-13). For estimation of growth, we have chosen the Net State Domestic Product (NSDP) generated in agriculture sector for total agricultural production. It may be mentioned that the state-wise Gross State Domestic Product (GSDP) series is not available for the period as a whole. Similarly, the state-wise value of crop output and value of other allied sectors is not available for whole of the study period.

The information on the growth of NSDP—both phase and state-wise is detailed in Table 3.1. Comparison of agricultural growth in Uttar Pradesh *vis-à-vis* the country as a whole during all five different phases reveals that Uttar Pradesh continued to be among agriculturally backward states in the country as the agricultural growth in the state during all the periods is less than the growth for the country as a whole. The green revolution technology seems to have made a significant contribution to agricultural development in the state as

Table 3.1: Growth of Agriculture NSDP: 1960-61 to 2012-13

	Period	*Compound annual growth rate (per cent per year)*				*Coefficient of variation (per cent per year)*			
		Uttar Pradesh	*Punjab*	*Haryana*	*India*	*Uttar Pradesh*	*Punjab*	*Haryana*	*India*
Pre-Green Revolution	1960-61 to 1965-66	0.04	2.36	-0.36	0.56	295.0			15.43
Initial Green Revolution	1967-68 to 1980-81	2.78	4.20	5.34	3.26	2.30	0.97	2.69	2.59
Mature Green Revolution	1981-82 to 1990-91	3.25	5.31	5.63	3.53	1.12	1.02	2.79	1.70
Initial post-Reform	1991-92 to 2000-01	2.12	2.99	1.92	2.36	2.34	1.33	3.06	2.00
New Millennium	2001-02 to 2012-13	2.36	1.16	3.63	2.96	0.66	2.10	1.60	1.93

Source: (i) Chandlok, H.L. (1990), *India Database*, *The Economy*, Volume 1, New Delhi, The Policy Group.

(ii) Online data from GoI, *Ministry of Statistics and Programme Implementation*, (www.mospi.nic.in).

the growth rate in the initial phase of green revolution jumped to 2.78 per cent per annum compared to almost nil growth (0.04 per cent per annum) during the pre-green revolution period. Growth further accelerated to 3.25 per cent during the mature phase of green revolution during 1980s compared with 2.78 per cent per annum growth during the initial phase of green revolution. Comparison of growth with Punjab and Haryana suggests that the state agriculture could not benefit as much from the green revolution technology as the neighbouring states of Haryana and Punjab succeeded in gaining.

Agricultural growth during the initial decade of the economic reforms (during 1990s) decelerated in Uttar Pradesh to 2.12 per cent from 3.25 per cent during 1980s. Interestingly, there was lesser gap in growth of agriculture in the state *via-à-vis* agriculture in Punjab and Haryana states during 1990s. During the new millennium (2001-2012), agricultural growth accelerated, but marginally to 2.36 per cent compared to 2.12 per cent during the last decade of the twentieth century. Comparatively, the pace of acceleration was much less in Uttar Pradesh as compared to upsurge in the growth in the country as a whole and its neighbouring state of Haryana. Interestingly, it was almost double than that of Punjab during this period but it was mainly because of very high level of agricultural development in Punjab and potential of increase in area under cultivation and yield of its main crops, wheat and rice are approaching saturation levels. Both these arguments seem to be not relevant for the state of Uttar Pradesh. On the whole, it seems that the state of Uttar Pradesh performed not very well during the last half a century. The state benefitted from new technology introduced in Indian agriculture during 1960s, but gains were not that substantial as attained by its neighbouring states of Haryana and Punjab.

Besides growth, Table 3.1 also presents the variation in growth of agricultural production during different phases as well as in chosen states with coefficient of variation. Interestingly, it comes out that the magnitude of coefficient of variation for the whole state of Uttar Pradesh is less than for the country as a whole and for most of the phases it is less than the corresponding magnitude of coefficient of variation for the states of Punjab and Haryana. This seems to suggest that compared to country as a whole as well as Punjab and Haryana, agricultural growth in the state of Uttar Pradesh is less amenable to yearly fluctuations. Both growth and its dispersion taken together, seems to suggest that despite the slow growth, agricultural performance in Uttar Pradesh has been comparatively more resilient to weather induced instability in production and growth. Why agriculture in Uttar Pradesh performed not so well? And why it was more stable compared to others is an interesting analysis? The same would be undertaken in subsequent analysis in this chapter as well as in the following chapters.

3.3 (ii) Performance of Uttar Pradesh Agriculture: Sub-sector-wise Analysis

Having examined the overall performance of agriculture in terms of Net State Domestic Product (NSDP), this section presents component-wise growth of different sub-sectors of agriculture in the state of Uttar Pradesh and the country as a whole. The idea is to find out on which particular account and for what particular period the state agriculture performed better than the country as a whole and on what account and which phase it performed poorly. The information on this account is presented in Table 3.2.

Comparison of Uttar Pradesh and the country on growth of value of output in agriculture and allied sector suggests that during 1980s and 1990s, Uttar Pradesh was growing at the all-India average growth rates whereas, during the last decade of 2001-2011, agricultural growth in Uttar Pradesh decelerated whereas that of the country as a whole remained the same. Sub-sector-wise comparison suggests that the growth of output of the crop sector in the state remained less than the all-India average growth rate with exception of 1980s, when the state was growing almost at the same level as with the country as a whole. Deceleration in crop sector production seems to be the main reason for poor performance of agriculture and allied sector *vis-à-vis* the country as a whole during the new millennium. The crop sector in Uttar Pradesh grew at almost half of the growth rate attained by the country as a whole.

Comparison of different segments of the crop sector suggests that on the whole, Uttar Pradesh performed better than the all-India average so far as the cereal production is concerned. Here again, is the exception of cereal growth during new millennium that declined not only to one-third of its previous decade growth, but also turned out to be half of the all-India growth rate during this period. However, growth performance of Uttar Pradesh on account of other sub-sectors namely—pulses, oilseeds, sugar, fibres and non-horticulture crops

Table 3.2: Growth Rate of Value of Output from Agriculture in Uttar Pradesh and All India: 1960-61 to 2010-11

	Compound annual growth rates during the period of (per cent per annum)									
	Pre-Green Rev.	*Initial Green Rev.*	*Mature Green Rev.*	*Initial Post-Reform*	*New Mille-nnium*	*Pre-Green Rev.*	*Initial Green Rev.*	*Mature Green Rev.*	*Initial Post-Reform*	*New Mille-nnium*
Period→	*1960-61 to 1965-66*	*1967-68 to 1980-81*	*1981-82 to 1990-91*	*1991-92 to 2000-01*	*2001-02 to 2010-11*	*1951-52 to 1967-68*	*1968-69 to 1980-81*	*1981-82 to 1990-91*	*1991-92 to 2001-02*	*2002-03 to 2011-12*
Value of output↓	*Uttar Pradesh*					*India*				
Cereals	0.5	6.5	5.1	2.8	1.0	4.2	3.4	3.5	2.0	2.0
Pulses	–1.5	–0.02	1.6	–1.5	0.6	3.0	0.7	3.4	0.6	3.0
Oilseeds	4.5	1.7	1.1	1.5	2.2	3.2	1.8	7.4	1.0	6.0
Sugar	3.9	3.8	5.0	1.0	0.7	3.3	4.1	4.2	5.9	2.0
Fibers	3.8	–1.2	–4.8	–6.6	1.8	4.4	2.5	5.3	0.5	12.9
Non-horticulture crops	0.3	3.1	3.1	1.7	1.7	3.2	2.7	3.0	1.9	2.5
Horticulture	2.2	3.9	1.4	9.3	3.6	2.6	4.2	3.1	4.8	3.7
Total Value of Output Agriculture (All crops)	**0.7**	**2.5**	**3.2**	**2.3**	**1.5**	**3.0**	**3.0**	**3.0**	**2.7**	**2.8**
Total Value of Output-Livestock			**3.7**	**2.0**	**4.1**	**1.0**	**3.3**	**4.8**	**3.8**	**4.2**

(*Contd.*)

Period→	Pre-Green Rev. 1960-61 to 1965-66	Initial Green Rev. 1967-68 to 1980-81	Mature Green Rev. 1981-82 to 1990-91	Initial Post-Reform 1991-92 to 2000-01	New Millennium 2001-02 to 2010-11	Pre-Green Rev. 1951-52 to 1967-68	Initial Green Rev. 1968-69 to 1980-81	Mature Green Rev. 1981-82 to 1990-91	Initial Post-Reform 1991-92 to 2001-02	New Millennium 2002-03 to 2011-12
	Compound annual growth rates during the period of (per cent per annum)									
Value of output↓	Uttar Pradesh					India				
Cereals	0.5	6.5	5.1	2.8	1.0	4.2	3.4	3.5	2.0	2.0
Pulses	–1.5	–0.02	1.6	–1.5	0.6	3.0	0.7	3.4	0.6	3.0
Oilseeds	4.5	1.7	1.1	1.5	2.2	3.2	1.8	7.4	1.0	6.0
Sugar	3.9	3.8	5.0	1.0	0.7	3.3	4.1	4.2	5.9	2.0
Fibers	3.8	–1.2	–4.8	–6.6	1.8	4.4	2.5	5.3	0.5	12.9
Non-horticulture crops	0.3	3.1	3.1	1.7	1.7	3.2	2.7	3.0	1.9	2.5
Horticulture	2.2	3.9	1.4	9.3	3.6	2.6	4.2	3.1	4.8	3.7
Total Value of Output Agriculture (All crops)	**0.7**	**2.5**	**3.2**	**2.3**	**1.5**	**3.0**	**3.0**	**3.0**	**2.7**	**2.8**
Total Value of Output-Livestock			**3.7**	**2.0**	**4.1**	**1.0**	**3.3**	**4.8**	**3.5**	**4.2**

Source: (i) Chandhok, H.L. (1990), *India Database*, *The Economy*, Volume 1, New Delhi, The Policy Group.

(ii) GoI (1996), *State-wise and Crop-wise Estimates of Value Output from Agriculture*, Central Statistica Organisation, New Delhi, Department of Statistics, Ministry of Planning and Programme Implementation, Government of India.

(iii) Online data from, GoI, *Ministry of Statistics and Programme Implementation*, (www.mospi.nic.in).

(iv) All India figures are from: GoI (2008), *Twelfth Five Year Plan 2012-2017*, Volume II, New Delhi, Planning Commission of India, Government of India, Sage Publications India Pvt. Ltd.

remained poor compared to the country as a whole. In the case of horticulture crops, though the performance differs across different periods, but on the whole state seems to have performed at par with all-India level.

In the case of livestock production, during 1980s and 1990s performance of Uttar Pradesh was much below the all-India level, whereas it picked up during the new millennium and grew at the all-India level. In case of two allied sectors of forestry and fishery, the performance of Uttar Pradesh again varies considerably during different phases. It seems that comparatively the state performed better than the country as a whole.

On the whole, the performance of Uttar Pradesh agriculture in case of different crop sectors is below the all-India average with exception of only the horticulture crops. For practical purposes, it would be more fruitful to identify the crops so far as the good and poor performance of the state *vis-à-vis* the country as a whole is concerned. This is undertaken in the following sub-section.

3.3 (iii) Performance of Uttar Pradesh Agriculture: Crop-wise Analysis

Information on average growth rate of area, output and yield of all major crops grown in Uttar Pradesh is presented in Table 3.3. Information suggests that both rice and wheat crops that constitute a major share in total crop sector in Uttar Pradesh recorded a decline in growth rate of output after green revolution phase. During initial green revolution phase, the output growth of superior cereals (rice and wheat) was as high as 7.73 per cent per annum. It however decelerated to 5.13 per cent per annum during 1980s—the mature green revolution phase. The main culprit behind this decline seems to be decline in the growth of area under superior cereals from 3.03 per cent during 1967-68 to 1980-81 to only 0.61 per cent during 1980s. Besides area, equally relevant is the decline in output growth of wheat from 8.52 per cent during 1967-68 to 1980-81 to 3.74 per cent per annum during mature green revolution phase. With maturation of the Green Revolution, there seems to be exhaustion of technology that is clearly visible with decline in wheat production. Thereafter, during initial post-reform period though growth in area under superior cereals accelerated to 1.12 per cent per annum, but it was rapid decline in yield growth of superior cereals that led to overall decline in value output growth in the state. The situation worsened thereafter during new millennium. Declining yield growth

Table 3.3: Crop-wise Growth of Area, Value Output and Yield in Uttar Pradesh: 1960-61 to 2010-11

Crops ↓	Area					Value of Output					Yield				
	Pre-Green Rev	Initial Green Rev	Mature Green Rev	Initial Post-Ref	New Mille-nnium	Pre-Green Rev	Initial Green Rev	Mature Green Rev	Initial Pcst-Ref	New Mille-nnium	Pre-Green Rev	Initial Green Rev	Mature Green Rev	Initial Post-Ref	New Mille-nnium
Period →	1960-1965	1967-1980	1981-1990	1991-2000	2001-2010	1960-1965	1967-1980	1981-1990	1991-2000	2001-2010	1960-1965	1967-1980	1981-1990	1991-2000	2001-2010
(1)	(2)	(3)	(4)	(5)	(6)	(7)	(8)	(9)	(10)	(11)	(12)	(13)	(14)	(15)	(16)
Rice	0.15	1.54	0.82	1.05	-0.03	-3.88	6.54	7.40	2.13	0.54	-4.40	5.00	6.35	1.10	0.57
Wheat	0.92	4.28	0.59	1.17	0.42	2.00	8.52	3.74	3.41	1.51	1.04	4.07	3.03	2.25	1.10
Superior cereals	**0.49**	**3.03**	**0.61**	**1.12**	**0.15**	**-1.13**	**7.73**	**5.18**	**2.91**	**1.15**	**-1.62**	**4.70**	**4.52**	**1.79**	**1.00**
Jowar	-0.79	-1.80	-2.15	-3.83	-4.76	5.60	5.41	8.81	-2.31	-3.38	6.09	7.08	10.45	1.48	1.33
Bajra	-1.74	-0.23	-2.16	1.33	0.77	10.11	5.00	3.74	5.54	1.64	11.10	5.12	5.49	4.13	0.87
Maize	2.13	-0.26	-1.11	-1.22	-1.77	13.50	2.33	8.23	3.16	-0.87	11.01	2.50	9.15	4.33	0.90
Barley	-4.26	-4.62	-5.73	-2.96	-4.76	-2.48	-1.94	-2.20	-1.64	-4.88	1.78	2.63	3.66	1.43	-0.13
Ragi (Mandua)	-1.94	0.45	-1.64	0.31	-1.02	9.63	2.85	3.35	1.66	-1.29	11.70	2.23	4.85	1.38	-0.30
Coarse cereals	**-1.67**	**-1.80**	**-2.51**	**-1.10**	**-1.56**	**4.51**	**1.56**	**4.44**	**2.21**	**-0.73**	**6.18**	**3.35**	**6.95**	**3.31**	**0.83**
Small millets and other cereals	-3.05	-2.04	1.30	-8.63	-1.61	1.11	4.44	5.77	-1.27	0.96	4.38	6.18	4.52	7.36	2.56
Total cereals	**-0.44**	**1.46**	**-0.05**	**0.63**	**-0.10**	**0.49**	**6.51**	**5.06**	**2.84**	**1.03**	**0.94**	**5.05**	**5.11**	**2.21**	**1.13**
Gram	0.29	-3.21	-1.42	-4.04	-3.41	-1.31	-1.03	-0.17	-3.57	-0.17	-1.51	2.38	1.55	0.47	3.26
Arhar	-0.17	-1.37	-0.96	-1.27	-1.24	3.50	6.20	-1.73	-0.90	-3.09	3.60	7.46	-0.71	0.37	-1.86
Other pulses	-0.87	-2.63	5.37	0.68	0.80	-3.70	-3.97	7.54	0.06	2.34	-2.36	-1.10	2.12	-0.63	1.54
Total pulses	**-0.18**	**-2.83**	**1.03**	**-1.39**	**-0.78**	**-1.54**	**-0.02**	**1.58**	**-1.48**	**0.60**	**-1.33**	**2.81**	**0.55**	**-0.09**	**1.38**
Total Foodgrains	**-0.38**	**0.63**	**0.09**	**0.35**	**-0.22**	**-0.38**	**4.55**	**4.41**	**2.26**	**0.98**	**-0.01**	**3.90**	**4.32**	**1.91**	**1.20**
Rapeseed and mustard	7.71	7.34	5.76	-1.34	1.12	2.48	3.08	0.24	1.05	2.20	-5.23	-4.18	-5.12	2.79	1.08
Groundnut	9.97	-2.01	-0.09	-2.10	-2.60	7.89	-3.55	5.84	-0.13	0.27	-2.03	-1.54	5.82	1.94	2.85

(Contd.)

(1)	(2)	(3)	(4)	(5)	(6)	(7)	(8)	(9)	(10)	(11)	(12)	(13)	(14)	(15)	(16)
Linseed	-0.43	3.93	1.14	-4.57	-5.04	9.86	1.74	-1.46	-3.35	4.72	10.23	-2.12	-2.58	1.28	9.73
Sesamum	3.80	-0.26	6.78	4.61	14.63	3.15	1.68	6.17	5.89	6.67	-0.65	1.94	-0.61	1.27	-7.59
Soyabean			-3.05	5.86	0.41			-0.85	-3.72	7.88			2.51	-9.03	7.48
Sunflower			2.17	6.62	-3.10			20.28	22.17	-7.19			18.61	15.55	-4.09
Total oilseeds	**7.07**	**2.32**	**1.98**	**-1.32**	**2.45**	**4.51**	**1.67**	**1.11**	**1.54**	**2.25**	**-2.56**	**-0.67**	**-0.87**	**2.86**	**-0.20**
Sugarcane and Gur	**4.07**	**2.08**	**3.49**	**1.15**	**0.91**	**3.90**	**3.57**	**4.99**	**1.01**	**0.68**	**-0.15**	**1.45**	**1.57**	**-0.15**	**-0.23**
Cotton	1.34	-2.88	-7.03	-9.28	0.61	9.69	-0.65	-4.27	-7.03	2.88	8.10	2.52	2.77	2.20	2.73
Jute	-1.43	-2.78	-18.3	-6.92	0.00	-0.97	-2.27	-6.78	-11.2	0.00	0.46	0.51	11.55	-4.30	0.00
Sanhemp	1.13	-2.25	-8.53	-7.09	-11.2			-4.76	-5.67	-2.98			3.67	1.34	8.11
Other fibres	-4.07	-1.26	6.20	-4.75	-3.33	-1.39	-0.12	6.90	-7.39	0.00	2.64	1.13	0.69	-2.64	0.00
Total fibres	**0.24**	**-3.18**	**-9.12**	**-7.89**	**-3.81**	**5.82**	**-1.17**	**-4.78**	**-6.62**	**-1.78**	**5.58**	**2.01**	**4.34**	**1.27**	**5.59**
Tobacco	-5.25	1.17	1.55	3.73	3.46	-9.12	6.82	9.81	8.66	2.23	-3.69	5.52	8.26	4.48	-1.21
Other drugs and narcotics	-12.7	9.86	15.72	16.74	6.01	-15.8	17.52	10.99	8.95	4.42	-3.03	7.39	-4.72	-7.79	-1.60
Total drugs and narcotics (tea, opium)	**-8.98**	**4.36**	**9.26**	**13.55**	**5.65**	**-10.4**	**11.08**	**10.40**	**8.78**	**4.13**	**-1.40**	**6.72**	**1.14**	**-4.77**	**-1.52**
Dry chillies	0.76	3.45	1.94	2.00	-1.72	-3.22	6.91	1.42	2.14	2.66	-3.94	3.44	-0.59	0.14	4.26
Dry ginger			7.06	10.82	12.07			0.96	13.04	9.65			-6.09	2.30	-2.41
Turmeric		-1.14	12.57	10.29	2.26			9.94	4.05	8.05			-2.63	-6.24	5.79
Garlic			5.47	4.98	16.35			9.34	7.80	19.15			3.88	2.82	2.80
Coriander			1.16	-0.06	0.51			-1.74	2.27	7.60			-2.26	2.34	7.10
Other condiments and spices	-2.69	1.34	7.26	1.21	2.65	-2.34	7.41	12.39	2.94	0.37	0.39	6.30	5.13	1.73	-2.27
Total condiments and spices	**-1.90**	**3.36**	**3.90**	**1.56**	**3.41**	**-2.71**	**7.16**	**7.26**	**3.80**	**16.81**	**-0.80**	**3.80**	**3.36**	**2.24**	**13.40**
Potato	5.79	5.30	2.42	2.63	3.20	13.20	11.51	5.98	6.98	5.08	7.60	6.78	3.41	4.33	1.98
Sweet potato			-0.81	-0.81	-3.81			-4.05	-0.46	-2.53			-3.22	0.35	1.31
Onion			3.70	0.18	-1.22			4.63	0.06	1.88			0.92	-0.13	3.07
Total fruits and veg.	**3.82**	**4.13**	**3.08**	**1.24**	**1.74**	**2.24**	**3.99**	**1.40**	**9.34**	**3.63**	**-1.51**	**-0.12**	**-1.60**	**8.10**	**1.81**
Total other crops and by-products	3.49	0.66	-0.66	1.52	4.46	0.13	1.73	0.32	1.05	-0.41	-3.35	1.21	0.98	-0.47	-4.28
Total	**0.32**	**0.69**	**0.37**	**0.41**	**0.11**	**0.76**	**2.47**	**3.16**	**2.32**	**1.47**	**0.44**	**1.77**	**2.72**	**1.91**	**1.38**

Source: (i) Same as in Table 3.2.

(ii) GoI, *Department of Agriculture and Cooperation*, New Delhi, Ministry of Agriculture, Government of India, (agricoop.nic.in) for both rice and wheat crops is a matter of serious concern. There is a need for second green revolution in these crops. All major coarse cereals also display a negative growth in area during 1960-61 to 2010-11. As a result, there is decline in the output growth as well. Contrary to the pattern of growth of superior cereals, the coarse cereals experienced different pattern of growth so far as the growth of value output, area and yield are concerned. First and the foremost is the continuous decline in area under almost all coarse cereal crops in the state during all the phases with exception of marginal increase in area under bajra during the last two decades. It seems that the area from coarse cereals is diversified towards superior cereals—rice and wheat. This diversification may be because of better technological breakthrough in rice and wheat crops as compared to the coarse cereals. However, technological argument is valid only for the initial green revolution phase whereas during the last three decades, the growth of yield of coarse cereals was higher than that of superior cereals. The issue would be examined later on in this chapter. Despite the information on growth of value output along with area changes, suggest that the growth of output of coarse cereals was significantly higher than of superior cereals during the pre-green revolution phase whereas it was other way round during the initial phase of green revolution technology. The technological impact was so strong during 1980s, that the output growth of coarse cereals was three times compared to the earlier periods with only exception of barley. The output growth rate of most of coarse cereals was substantially high and almost comparable to superior cereals. Growth of coarse cereals suffered serious reverses during the new millennium, when with only exception of bajra, all other coarse cereals recorded negative growth. Again, the main culprit was a shift in area away from coarse cereals that led to negative growth in coarse cereals despite a positive growth of crop yield. The story for small millets and other cereals is akin to coarse cereals with exception that due to strong yield effect, small millets recorded positive growth during new millennium despite a rapid shift in area away from small millets and other cereals.

The pattern of area, production and yield growth of pulses in Uttar Pradesh has experienced the same story as in case of coarse cereals and small millets. Area under all pulses taken together and individually, declined very rapidly with only exception of other pulses (moong, urad, moth, masur), for which there was some area growth after 1980s. The negative area growth was so strong that it overcame the yield growth and led to negative output growth of gram and arhar crops. However, the positive area growth for other pulses combined with improvement in yield led to positive and significant growth of other pulses during 1980s and the new millennium. This resulted in overall positive output growth of pulses during 1980s and 2001-2011. Like coarse cereals, the higher yield growth of some pulses during some period failed to check the declining area under pulses. So, the argument put forth in earlier case that it was not only area and yield, it seems that there are some other factors like price, market demand and risk and uncertainty that played key role in diversification of area from pulses to other crops in case of Uttar Pradesh.

In case of total oilseeds, area, output and yield growth rates recorded different pattern of growth during different phases. Growth in area for total oilseeds recorded a continuous decline till 1991-2000, but accelerated thereafter. However growth in value output in total oilseeds declined till 1990s, but with increase in yield growth rates during initial post-reform period, there was acceleration in value output growth rates in total oilseeds. Similarly, it is very difficult to predict any specific pattern of growth in area, output and yield for individual oilseed crops. It may however be noted that there is reversal in growth rates of mainly three oilseed crops during the later period—sesamum, soyabean and sunflower. Considerable improvement in value output growth in sesamum crop is mainly due to very strong area effect. It is however both, growth in area as well as yield in case of soyabean. Though sunflower recorded negative output growth during new millennium, but very high growth in yield as well as output during previous two decades is worth mentioning. The overall pattern of oilseeds crops suggests that soyabean, sesamum as well as rapeseed and mustard crops have recorded an increasing tendency recently. Whereas, groundnut and linseed have faced reverses mainly due to decline in area growth under these crops.

In case of sugarcane crop, there is almost same pattern of growth of area and output during different phases. With acceleration in growth of area and yield during mature green revolution phase, there was overall acceleration in value output growth rates as well. But thereafter with decline in area as well as negative growth in yield, there was sudden decline in value output growth as well, during 1991-2000 and 2001-2011.

In case of fibres, there is negative growth in area as well as value output since initiation of green revolution technology. Pre-green revolution phase however recorded satisfactory growth of 5.82 per cent per annum in value output in total fibres due to very high growth in value output as well as yield in one of the major fibre crop—cotton grown in the state. But thereafter, there is negative growth in area in all fibre crops and even value output also recorded negative growth rates for individual crops as well as total fibre crops. Area effect was so strong that even very high growth in yield (4.34% per annum) during 1980s also could not lead to increase in value output growth of total fibres. The situation however recovered for cotton crop during new millennium and it recorded more than 2 per cent per annum value output growth. Even yield growth in total fibres also accelerated, but value output as well as area growth continued to record negative growth rates for total fibres during this period as well.

Total drugs and narcotics recorded significant acceleration in area growth since 1960s. But growth in value output seems to be more influenced with growth in yield. As acceleration in yield growth led to considerable acceleration in total drugs and narcotics value output growth rates during initial green revolution phase. But thereafter, despite further acceleration in area growth, there was decline in value output growth rates. This was again due to negative yield growth for two decades continuously.

The most important feature of the changing pattern of area, production and yield of Uttar Pradesh is very high growth rate of area, output and yield of almost all condiments and spices in the state. The noteworthy is the exceptional high growth rate of area under dry ginger, turmeric and garlic crops. Though yield of some condiments and spices declined in some periods, but area growth was so strong that almost all crops recorded exceptionally high growth in their production after 1980s. It seems that rising price of these commodities may have induced farmers to allocate increasing area under these high value crops. This seems to be a healthy development especially because of their high labour intensive requirement and even suitable to be grown by small and marginal farmers in the state.

Like condiments and spices, area under potato crop has grown at exceptionally high rate during all sub-periods. The yield of potato also recorded very high growth rate during all the periods except that the new millennium yield growth halved to 2 per cent per annum compared with the earlier decade. Consequently, potato production recorded very high growth exceeding 5 per cent per annum during all sub-periods, though growth of potato output decelerated from 13.2

per cent during pre-green revolution to 5.08 per cent per annum during first decade of new millennium. Unlike potato, onion does not depict any consistent pattern in growth, though the growth of area under onion decelerated during 1980s and 1990s and then turned to be negative during 2001-2010. However, the yield accelerated from negative during 1990s to 3.07 per cent during 2001-2010 resulting in acceleration in onion production growth during the new millennium.

Another interesting pattern of the dynamics of the agriculture in Uttar Pradesh is the high growth rate of fruits and vegetables production in the state. There was considerable acceleration in both area as well as value output growth rates during initial green revolution phase. Though it decelerated thereafter during 1980s, but tremendous growth of 8.10 per cent per annum in yield growth during 1990s changed the whole scenario. This growth in yield was so strong that despite deceleration in growth in area, there was as high as 9.34 per cent per annum growth in value output in total fruits and vegetables. But this momentum of growth could not sustain during the new millennium phase and there was deceleration in growth of yield as well as value output growth rates. Though there was marginal increase in area growth, but it seems that yield growth can play an important role in overall growth of horticulture crops.

The overall crop sector recorded continuous acceleration in growth in yield as well as value output since 1960s till mature green revolution phase. However, growth in area did not follow any uniform pattern during 1960-2011. It declined during 1980s, accelerated during 1990s and decelerated again during new millennium. Yield growth seems to have made significant contribution in overall growth in value output in Uttar Pradesh. Both yield as well as value output growth rates exhibit almost same pattern in growth during 1960-2011.

3.4. PATTERNS OF AGRICULTURAL DEVELOPMENT: LAND AND LABOUR PRODUCTIVITY

3.4 (i) Land Productivity: 1960-63 to 2008-11

As mentioned earlier in this chapter, to examine the patterns of agricultural development, we have measured the same in terms of changing levels of land and labour productivity in Uttar Pradesh. Emerging patterns on these two accounts during different phases are examined as follows.

Table 3.4 presents decade-wise level of land productivity at constant 1993-94 prices. From 1960-63 onwards, level of development improved continuously and almost doubled to Rs. 17,488 per hectare during 1990-93 and further to Rs. 24,224 per hectare during 2008-11. After growing at 1.69 per cent per annum during 1960s, land productivity improved at accelerated rate of 2.24 per cent per annum during 1970s and further to 2.63 per cent per annum during 1980s. However after 1980s, the level of development improved, but at a decelerated pace. The level of land productivity after growing at 2.63 per cent per annum during 1980s grew at decelerated pace of 1.99 per cent per annum during 1990s and further to 1.63 per cent per annum during first decade of the new millennium. The level of land productivity as an improvement in productivity, basically originate from two main sources namely—growth of production and growth of area. Though, growth of area after increasing during 1960s decelerated continuously till 2010-11, but it was growth of output that is mainly responsible for acceleration/deceleration in land productivity, as like land productivity, value of output first accelerated up to 1980s and decelerated thereafter.

Table 3.4: Land Productivity in Uttar Pradesh: 1960-63 to 2008-11

	Land productivity (Rs. per hectare at 1993-94 constant prices)					
Period→	*1960-63*	*1970-73*	*1980-83*	*1990-93*	*2000-03*	*2008-11*
Land productivity	*9135*	*10803*	*13485*	*17488*	*21289*	*24224*

Growth rate (% per annum)

Period→	*1960-63/ 1970-73*	*1970-73/ 1980-83*	*1980-83/ 1990-93*	*1990-93/ 2000-03*	*2000-03/ 2008-11*
Land productivity growth	1.69	2.24	2.63	1.99	1.63
Value output growth	1.71	2.23	2.64	2.14	1.48
Area growth	0.49	0.69	0.32	0.30	0.21
Coefficient of variation	10.48	9.17	8.14	7.71	6.05

Source: Same as in Table 3.3.

The land productivity, though depict inverted 'U' curve behaviour over the period of time, but the yearly variations across different decades show a consistent pattern. Information on variation in land productivity measured in terms of coefficient of variation for different decades is also provided in Table 3.4. There is a consistent pattern of declining coefficient of variation from 10.48 per cent during 1970s to 6.05 per cent during the first decade of new millennium. Comparatively, decline was small in 1980s, but big shift came during 1990s when the coefficient of variation declined from 9.17 per cent to 7.71 per cent. This indicates a significant reduction in year to year instability in the levels of agricultural development in Uttar Pradesh over time. This is a good development as it indicates the reduction of production related risk and uncertainties in the state agriculture. This development is noteworthy in context of optimum use and efficient allocation of inputs and resources by the farmers in their production decisions.

3.4 (ii) Labour Productivity: 1960-63 to 2008-11

Provision of gainful employment and removal of poverty are twin problems that continued to be on the agenda of every Five Year plan in India. Labour Productivity, defined as output per agricultural worker, is considered to be an important indicator of standard of living and well-being of the rural population (Block, 1995). The process of agricultural growth and restructuring of labour market following the liberalization of Indian economy expected to have wide ramification for growth of employment, agriculture labour productivity and earnings (Bhattacharya and Sakthivel, 2005a). It would therefore, be interesting to examine the dynamics in employment and labour productivity of agricultural workers in Uttar Pradesh since 1960s.

Table 3.5 presents information on agricultural workers productivity for triennium ending 1960-63, 1980-83, 1990-93, 2000-03 and 2008-11. We ignored the data for agriculture workers for 1970-73 because during this period the data on the number of female agricultural workers in agriculture was not comparable with other census because of changes in definition of female workers during 1971 and reverting back to 1961 definition in 1981 census of population in India. Information on labour productivity detailed in Table 3.5, suggests that labour productivity increased from Rs. 7223 to Rs. 10,342 during 1960-63 to 2008-11. Growth of labour production suggests that first labour productivity grew at a high rate of 1.05 per cent per annum during 1960s and 1970s. Then the growth rate decelerated to 0.14 per cent per annum during 1980s, but picked up thereafter to 0.64 per cent per annum during 1990s and 0.90 per cent per annum during first decade of twenty first century. The 'U' curve behaviour of growth rate of labour productivity

Table 3.5: Labour Productivity in Uttar Pradesh: 1960-63 to 2008-11

	Labour productivity (Productivity per worker (Rs.) at 1993-94 constant prices)				
Period →	*1960-63*	*1980-83*	*1990-93*	*2000-03*	*2008-11*
Labour productivity	*7223*	*8904*	*9031*	*9630*	*10342*
Growth rate (% Per Annum)					
Period →		*1960-63/ 1980-83*	*1980-83/ 1990-93*	*1990-93/ 2000-03*	*2000-03/ 2008-11*
Labour productivity growth		1.05	0.14	0.64	0.90
Agricultural workers growth		0.95	2.47	1.15	0.92
Value output growth		1.97	2.64	2.14	1.48
Coefficient of variation		8.27	2.64	5.27	3.24

Source: (i) Same as in Table 3.3
(ii) GoI (Various Reports), *Census of India (Uttar Pradesh)*, Primary Census Abstract, Uttar Pradesh, Directorate of Census Operations, Government of India.

is mainly due to behaviour of output growth in the state. The deceleration during 1980s is mainly because the worker growth increased from 0.95 per cent during 1960-80 to 2.47 per cent during 1980s and it declined thereafter. Inverted 'U' curve growth of agriculture workers and agriculture production both superimposed on each other and the differential in growth between the two curves resulted in 'U' curve of labour productivity.

3.5. DIVERSIFICATION IN AGRICULTURE IN UTTAR PRADESH: CROP SHARE

3.5 (i) Crop Share in Area

Table 3.6 presents share of all the crops in gross cropped area in Uttar Pradesh from 1960-63 to 2008-11. The percentage distribution of the total cropped area among crops underwent dramatic changes since 1960s. Total foodgrains registered a considerable variation in the share of area. From 83.64 per cent during 1960-63, the foodgrain share declined to 77.27 per cent during 2008-2011. Among foodgrains, rice and wheat experienced substantial increase in area. The share of area under rice increased from 19.19 per cent to 22.18 per cent till 2008-11. Similarly, the area under wheat doubled from 18.34 per cent in early 1960s to 37.44 per cent during 2008-11. On the other hand, share of area under coarse cereals (jowar, bajra, maize, barley and ragi) in gross cropped area declined continuously from 22.49 per cent during 1960s to 14.75 per cent during 1980s and further to as low as 8.09 per cent during 2008-11. However, total cereals registered increase in share in area from 62.76 per cent in 1960-63 to 68.03 per cent in 2008-11 though it declined during 1990s, but increased thereafter. It is mainly due to increase in area under wheat and rice crops.

Share of pulses in gross cropped area declined by 11.65 per cent since 1960s. This was mainly due to decrease in share of gram from as high as 11.54 per cent in 1960-63 to only 2.18 per cent during 2008-11. However, arhar and other pulses also registered a decline in their shares in total cropped area, but it was only by 1 to 2 per cent respectively. Though share of total foodgrains has declined in total cropped area, still its share is more than 75 per cent in total cropped area.

Total oilseeds recorded an increase in share in area till 1990-93, but thereafter area under all oilseeds declined, with exception of sesamum and sunflower crops. However for the overall period, there is increase in total oilseeds share in gross cropped area by nearly 1.53 per cent. Though some new oilseed crops such as sunflower and soyabean have been introduced in Uttar Pradesh since 1980s, but their shares in total cropped area is less than 1 per cent. Moreover, there is decline in share of soyabean and share of sunflower has remained more or less constant at 0.02 per cent. Groundnut and linseed also registered decline in their shares in total cropped area.

Sugarcane, one of the important cash crops in Uttar Pradesh, registered increase in share in area from 5.70 per cent in 1960-63 to 6.48 per cent in 1980-83 and further to 8.26 per cent in 2000-03, but it declined to about 8 per cent in 2008-11.

Like coarse cereals, total fibres also recorded continuous decline in area share since 1960s. Sudden decline in area under cotton and Sannhemp and almost nil share of jute and other fibres led to overall decline in share of total fibre crops. Total drugs and narcotics crops recorded a considerable increase in share in total gross cropped area. Their share in total cropped area increased from 0.12 per cent to 0.99 per cent during 1960-63 to 2008-11.

The area planted to condiments and spices also registered nearly two times increase from 0.23 per cent during 1960-63 to 0.44 per cent

Table 3.6: Share of Crops in Total Cropped Area in Uttar Pradesh: 1960-63 to 2008-11

Period→	*Share in total cropped area (Percentage)*					
Crops↓	*1960-63*	*1970-73*	*1980-83*	*1990-93*	*2000-03*	*2008-10*
Rice	19.19	19.75	21.26	21.60	22.95	22.18
Wheat	18.34	26.16	32.65	34.16	36.53	37.44
Superior cereals	**37.54**	**45.91**	**53.91**	**55.75**	**59.48**	**59.62**
Jowar	4.00	3.01	2.60	1.91	1.19	0.73
Bajra	4.68	4.56	3.95	3.10	3.26	3.24
Maize	4.88	6.46	4.70	4.22	3.47	2.93
Barley	8.12	5.67	2.83	1.62	1.09	0.73
Ragi (Mandua)	0.79	1.13	0.67	0.55	0.53	0.47
Coarse cereals	**22.49**	**20.84**	**14.75**	**11.40**	**9.55**	**8.09**
Small millets and other cereal	2.74	2.06	1.32	0.82	0.39	0.32
Total cereals	**62.76**	**68.81**	**69.99**	**67.97**	**69.43**	**68.03**
Gram	11.54	8.66	6.17	4.51	3.24	2.18
Arhar	2.90	2.33	2.05	1.99	1.47	1.21
Other pulses	6.45	4.57	3.77	5.54	5.63	5.84
Total pulses	**20.88**	**15.56**	**11.99**	**12.05**	**10.34**	**9.23**
Total foodgrains	**83.64**	**84.36**	**81.98**	**80.02**	**79.77**	**77.27**
Rapeseed and mustard	0.68	1.05	1.76	2.99	2.19	2.35
Groundnut	1.16	1.4[illegible]	1.01	0.52	0.39	0.34
Linseed	0.35	0.3[illegible]	0.32	0.37	0.17	0.13
Sesamum	0.29	0.27	0.19	0.33	0.38	1.08
Soyabean	0.00	0.00	0.58	0.10	0.07	0.06
Sunflower	0.00	0.00	0.02	0.03	0.03	0.02
Total oilseeds	**2.47**	**3.05**	**3.90**	**4.33**	**3.23**	**4.00**
Sugarcane	**5.70**	**5.68**	**6.48**	**7.39**	**8.26**	**8.10**
Cotton	0.32	0.22	0.14	0.05	0.02	0.02
Jute	0.09	0.05	0.04	0.00	0.00	0.00
Sannhemp	0.30	0.23	0.15	0.06	0.03	0.01
Other fibres	0.01	0.01	0.00	0.00	0.01	0.00
Total fibres	**0.72**	**0.51**	**0.33**	**0.12**	**0.05**	**0.03**
Tobacco	0.07	0.05	0.05	0.06	0.07	0.09
Other drugs and narcotics	0.05	0.04	0.05	0.19	0.57	0.90
Total drugs and narcotics	**0.12**	**0.08**	**0.10**	**0.25**	**0.64**	**0.99**
Dry Chillies	0.06	0.09	0.09	0.08	0.08	0.07
Dry Ginger	0.00	0.00	0.00	0.00	0.01	0.01
Turmeric	0.00	0.00	0.00	0.00	0.01	0.01
Garlic	0.00	0.00	0.01	0.02	0.07	0.12
Coriander	0.00	0.02	0.02	0.02	0.02	0.02
Other condiments and spices	0.16	0.09	0.11	0.18	0.20	0.20
Total condiments and spices	**0.23**	**0.21**	**0.24**	**0.32**	**0.38**	**0.44**
Potato	0.51	0.71	1.09	1.36	1.62	2.03
Sweet potato	0.00	0.20	0.17	0.10	0.09	0.07
Onion	0.00	0.00	0.08	0.12	0.09	0.08
Total fruits and vegetables	**1.53**	**1.70**	**2.78**	**3.54**	**3.76**	**4.32**
Total other crops	**5.57**	**4.41**	**4.18**	**4.04**	**3.90**	**4.85**
Total	**100.00**	**100.00**	**100.00**	**100.00**	**100.00**	**100.00**

Source: Same as in Table 3.3.

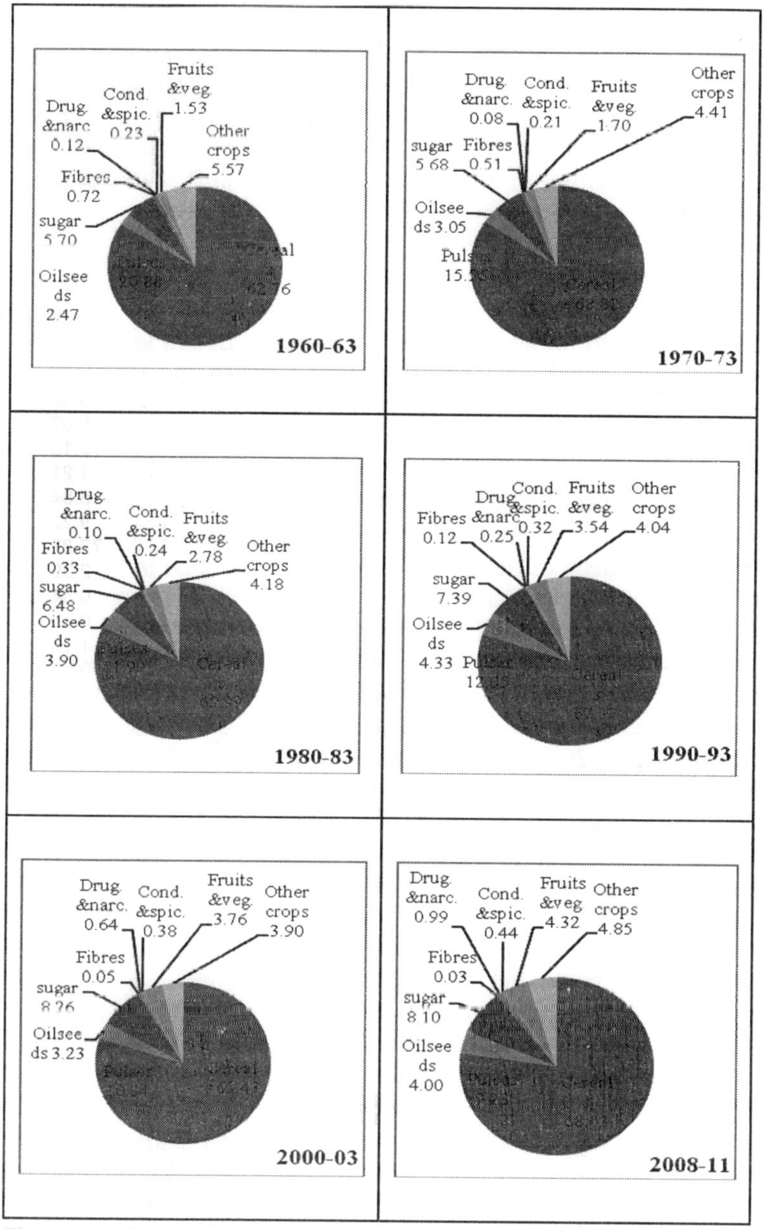

Figure 3.1: Share of Crops in Total Cropped Area in Uttar Pradesh: 1960-63 to 2008-11

Source: Table 3.6.

during 2008-11. There is considerable increase in area under garlic in Uttar Pradesh in recent years. Share of area under total fruits and vegetables also increased from 1.53 per cent during 1960-63 to 2.78 per cent in 1980-83 and nearly doubled to 4.32 per cent during 2008-11. Increase in area under horticulture crops is also a positive sign towards diversification of cropping pattern towards high value and high income elasticity crops.

3.5 (ii) Crop Share in Output

Crop-wise share of all the crops in total value output (all crops) is presented in Table 3.7. The results of share of crop output in total value output depict almost similar pattern as in previous table (share of area). With decrease in share of area under total food-grains, there is also decrease in share of output in total food-grains from 53.94 per cent to 48.07 per cent since 1960-63 to 2008-11. Though it increased during 1980-83 and 1990-93, but thereafter it started declining. However, under food-grains, share of rice and wheat (superior cereals) in total value output has almost doubled from 21.37 per cent to 43.76 per cent during 1960-63 to 2000-03, but declined thereafter for both the crops.

Total coarse cereals, small millets and total pulses recorded considerable decrease in output share. Total pulses recorded five-fold decrease from 23.74 per cent during 1960s to as low as 4.83 per cent during 2008-11. Among coarse cereals, except bajra all other coarse cereals share in total value output is less than 1 per cent during 2008-11. However, the share of bajra remained more or less constant over time. Total coarse cereals also recorded a sudden decline (nearly half) in its share during 1980s and again declined by nearly 50 per cent during 2008-11.

Total oilseeds on one hand registered increase in share in total cropped area, but on the other hand there was continuous decline in share of total oilseeds in total value output since 1980-83. Its share was nearly 10 per cent during 1960s and 1970s, but declined thereafter. However, it is nearly constant at 3 per cent during post-reform period. All oilseeds crops individually also registered decline.

Share of sugarcane in total value output was fluctuating during the study period. It was 20.91 per cent during 1960-63, declined in 1970-73, again increased to 21.47 per cent in 1980s and 22.76 per cent per annum in 1990-93, but declined again thereafter to 17.54 per cent during 2008-11.

Table 3.7: Share of Crops in Total Value Output in Uttar Pradesh: 1960-63 to 2008-11

	Share of crops in total value output (Percentage)					
Crops↓ Period→	*1960-63*	*1970-73*	*1980-83*	*1990-93*	*2000-03*	*2008-10*
Paddy	11.30	10.52	13.42	17.30	16.80	14.17
Wheat	10.07	17.08	24.60	26.13	26.96	26.31
Superior cereals	**21.37**	**27.59**	**38.02**	**43.43**	**43.76**	**40.48**
Jowar	1.06	0.77	0.65	0.49	0.27	0.16
Bajra	1.14	1.41	1.14	1.07	1.06	1.15
Maize	1.72	2.42	1.33	1.54	1.14	0.83
Barley	4.17	3.01	1.53	0.98	0.64	0.36
Ragi (Mandua)	0.25	0.43	0.21	0.18	0.15	0.12
Coarse cereals	**8.34**	**8.05**	**4.86**	**4.27**	**3.25**	**2.62**
Small millets and other cereal	0.49	0.47	0.29	0.22	0.15	0.14
Total cereals	**30.20**	**36.11**	**43.17**	**47.92**	**47.16**	**43.24**
Gram	11.92	9.36	6.07	3.69	2.26	1.54
Arhar	2.94	3.53	3.15	2.04	1.27	0.68
Other pulses	8.88	4.32	2.77	3.52	2.81	2.60
Total pulses	**23.74**	**17.20**	**11.99**	**9.25**	**6.34**	**4.83**
Total food grains	**53.94**	**53.31**	**55.17**	**57.17**	**53.50**	**48.07**
Rapeseed and mustard	6.12	6.84	5.38	3.96	2.62	2.69
Groundnut	2.09	1.77	1.03	0.53	0.28	0.19
Linseed	1.06	1.20	0.47	0.28	0.13	0.12
Sesamum	0.81	0.64	0.50	0.10	0.11	0.14
Soyabean	0.00	0.00	0.28	0.09	0.03	0.03
Sunflower	0.00	0.00	0.01	0.12	0.06	0.03
Total oilseeds	**10.07**	**10.45**	**7.80**	**5.08**	**3.26**	**3.19**
Sugarcane	**20.91**	**19.82**	**21.47**	**22.76**	**20.64**	**17.54**
Kapas	0.20	0.12	0.07	0.03	0.01	0.01
Jute	0.12	0.05	0.03	0.00	0.00	0.00
Sannhemp	0.00	0.00	0.02	0.01	0.00	0.00
Other fibres	0.00	0.00	0.00	0.00	0.00	0.00
Total fibres	**0.32**	**0.18**	**0.13**	**0.05**	**0.01**	**0.01**
Tobacco	0.13	0.08	0.10	0.36	0.49	0.44
Other drugs and narcotics	0.03	0.03	0.03	0.08	0.52	3.68
Total drugs and narcotics	**0.16**	**0.11**	**0.14**	**0.44**	**1.01**	**4.12**
Dry chillies	0.16	0.15	0.33	0.22	0.20	0.17
Dry ginger	0.00	0.00	0.01	0.01	0.01	0.05
Turmeric	0.00	0.00	0.01	0.01	0.02	0.02
Garlic	0.00	0.00	0.05	0.11	0.35	5.14
Coriander	0.00	0.00	0.02	0.02	0.02	0.03
Other condiments and spices	0.24	0.13	0.25	0.45	0.28	0.23
Total condiments and spices	**0.39**	**0.28**	**0.66**	**0.83**	**0.89**	**5.64**
Potato	0.91	1.60	2.79	2.95	3.85	4.42
Sweet potato	0.00	0.00	0.37	0.26	0.20	0.15
Onion	0.00	0.00	0.22	0.38	0.19	0.19
Total fruits and vegetables	**10.99**	**11.89**	**12.25**	**11.73**	**19.12**	**20.13**
Total other crops	**3.21**	**3.96**	**2.39**	**1.95**	**1.54**	**1.30**
Total	**100.0**	**100.0**	**100.0**	**100.0**	**100.0**	**100.0**

Source: Same as in Table 3.3.

The situation of total fibres in Uttar Pradesh is very poor, as in the case of share of fibres in total area, its share in total value output also registered a continuous decline from 0.32 per cent in 1960s to 0.01 per cent during 2000s. Total drugs and narcotics however performed really well. There is significant increase in its share in total value output from 0.16 per cent during 1960-63 to 4.12 per cent during 2008-11 (Fig. 3.2).

Following the same trend as in share in area, share of condiments and spices in total value output registered an increase since 1980s. Though it increased only marginally during 1990s and 2000-03, but thereafter its share in total value output increased to more than 5 per cent. This spurt increase in value output is due to sudden increase in value output of garlic during this period.

Total fruits and vegetables also registered nearly two times increase in its share in 2008-11 as compared in 1960-63. Their share in total value output doubled to 20.13 per cent in 2008-11 from 10.99 per cent during 1960-63.

The overall share of crops in total value output recorded that among foodgrains, only bajra recorded marginal increase in its share in total value output whereas all other food-grains including rice, jowar, maize, barley, ragi as well as pulses that included gram, arhar and other pulses registered decrease in their shares in total value output. The share of wheat is however constant at nearly 26 per cent since 1980s. Total oilseeds as well as oilseeds crops also did not perform well and registered a decline during post-reform period. Total condiments and spices on the other hand improved their share in output significantly. Share of sugarcane in total value output recorded an increase till 1980s, but declined thereafter. There was increase in share of potato, but on the other hand sweet potato and onion registered decline in their shares in total value output. Total fruits and vegetables also recorded nearly two times increase in their share in value output during 2008-11 as compared with 1960s.

3.6. AGRICULTURAL GROWTH IN UTTAR PRADESH: DECOMPOSITION ANALYSIS

3.6 (i) Decomposition of Growth in Total Agricultural Output in Uttar Pradesh: 1960-63 to 2008-11

Following the decomposition methodology illustrated in the

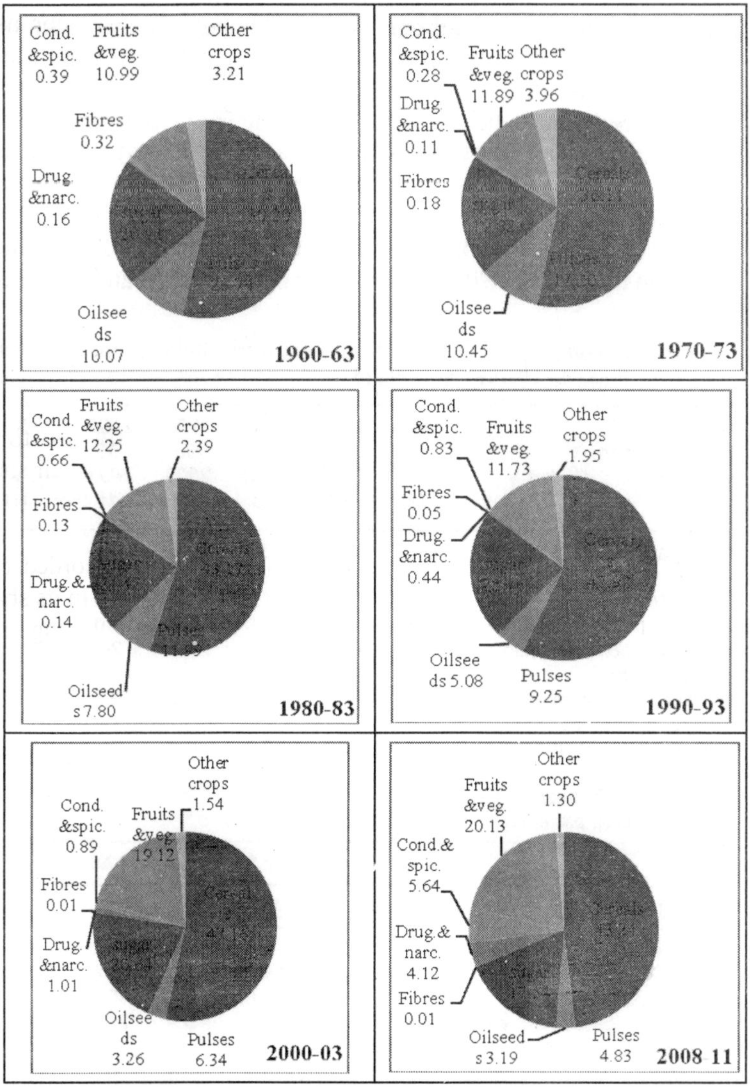

Figure 3.2: Share of Crops in Total Value Output in Uttar Pradesh: 1960-63 to 2008-11.

Source: Table 3.7.

preceding section, the component-wise estimates of decomposition exercise for different periods is detailed in Table 3.8. It may be seen that for the period as a whole from 1960-61 to 2010-11, yield effect turned out to be the most important factor contributing to agricultural growth in Uttar Pradesh. One-third (33.9%) of the total increase in production is contributed by the pure yield effect and about one-fourth (23.4%), has been contributed by the pure cropping pattern effect that has resulted from diversification of cropping pattern in the state. The interaction effect between yield and cropping

Table 3.8: Decomposition of Growth of Total Agricultural Output in Uttar Pradesh: 1960-63 to 2008-11

Decomposition of growth *Period→*	*1960-63 1970-73*	*1970-73 1980-83*	*1980-83 1990-93*	*1990-93 2000-03*	*2000-03 2008-11*	*1960-63/ 2008-11*
Aggregate growth in output	18.6	24.6	32.6	25.6	12.5	166.5
Area effect	5.0	7.1	2.8	4.2	2.4	21.6
Yield effect	10.9	8.1	21.0	13.4	2.2	56.4
Cropping pattern effect	2.0	9.0	9.0	5.7	5.0	38.9
Interaction between yield and crop pattern	0.1	–0.6	–1.0	1.5	2.7	23.9
Interaction between area and cropping pattern	0.1	0.6	0.3	0.2	0.1	8.4
Interaction between area and yield	0.5	0.5	0.6	0.6	0.1	12.2
Interaction between area, yield and crop pattern	0.003	–0.04	–0.03	0.1	0.1	5.2
Total	**18.6**	**24.6**	**32.6**	**25.6**	**12.5**	**166.5**
Share (percentage) of each component in overall output growth						
Area effect	26.9	28.9	8.6	16.4	19.2	13.0
Yield effect	58.6	32.9	64.4	52.3	17.6	33.9
Cropping pattern effect	10.8	36.6	27.6	22.3	40.0	23.4
Interaction between yield and crop pattern effect	0.5	–2.4	–3.1	5.9	21.6	14.4
Interaction between area and crop pattern effect	0.5	2.4	0.9	0.8	0.8	5.0
Interaction between area and yield effect	2.7	2.0	1.8	2.3	0.4	7.3
Interaction between area, yield and crop. pattern	0.0	–0.2	–0.1	0.4	0.8	3.1
Total	100	100	100	100	100	100

Source: Same as in Table 3.3.

pattern contributed about one-seventh (14.4%) of the increase in production. Another 13 per cent of the increase in production over five decades was due to pure area effect which is the combined effect of the expansion of new area under cultivation and intensification of area use in the state.

The overall contribution of various factors notwithstanding, the contribution by different channels to overall production varies across different periods. For example, up to the beginning of the twenty first century, the pure yield effect turned out to be the most important driver of agricultural growth in Uttar Pradesh contributing about half of the increase in production in the state. However during the new millennium, a serious deceleration in the contribution of yield occurred as the contribution of pure yield effect declined to one-third (17.6%) from more than half during the previous decade. The contribution of other two main sources, namely area effect and cropping pattern effect does not depict any consistent pattern across five decades. The area effect first increased marginally from 1960 to 1970 and then experienced big decline during 1980s, but thereafter shows considerable increase in its share. The cropping pattern effect shows a big increase from 10.8 per cent during sixties to 36.6 per cent during seventies. Thereafter, its share declined to 27.6 per cent during 1980s and 22.3 per cent in 1990s. However, the cropping pattern effect emerged as the main contributor to output growth during 2000-2011 as it contributed to 40 per cent of increase in production which is higher than the joint contribution of area and yield effect taken together. Among the interaction terms, interaction between yield and cropping pattern turned out to be the significant contributor to output growth during 1990s and 2000, whereas rest of the factors and during rest of the period, the four interaction terms contributed a negligible proportion to output growth.

To further examine the role of area, yield and their interaction effect for the individual crops, we decomposed the output growth into the pure area and pure yield effect and the impact of the interaction between the two. The results reported in the Appendix 3.3 reveals no consistent pattern about the contribution of these three channels, both across state as well as over time. During 1960s, the contribution of change in area under crop remained the main contributor to agriculture growth in the state. In many crops, button has been passed on from area to yield growth whereas in many other crops, change in area continues to be the major contributor to changes in agriculture

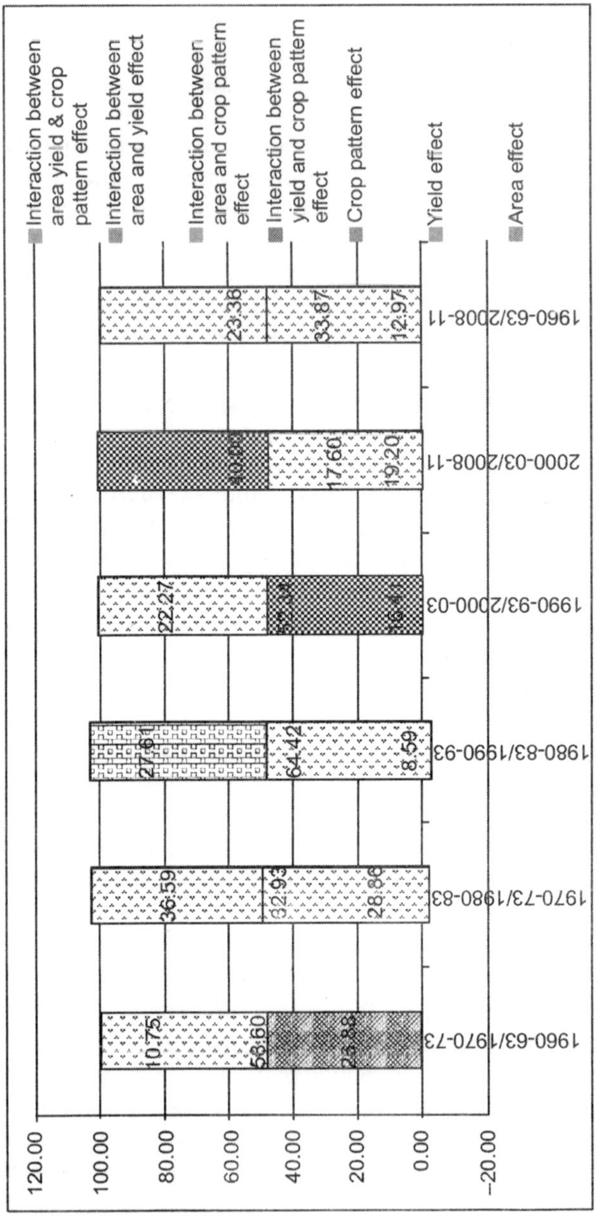

Figure 3.3: Decomposition of Growth of Total Agricultural Output in Uttar Pradesh.

Source: Table 3.8.

production. The wheat and rice crops, which experienced a significant improvement in yield due to green revolution technology follow a different pattern then the remaining food crops. In case of these two crops, improvement in yield turned out to be the major contributor to output growth since 1970s. Whereas, in rest of the food crops namely—coarse cereals and pulses, area continued to play a dominant role in acceleration/deceleration in their production. Same is more or less true about for most of the oilseeds crops with only exception of linseed where yield remained the main contributor during most of the decades.

The impact of area and yield is mixed in sugarcane, where yield remained the same source for three decades whereas the area for the other two decades. For condiments and spices taken together, yield remained the main contributor whereas in fruits and vegetables, it was area which on the whole turned out to be the major source of changes in production over time.

So with this type of evidence, it is difficult to make any definite conclusion regarding the emerging drivers of agriculture growth. Nevertheless with serious deceleration of yield in rice and wheat crops, diversification of area away/towards different crops is expected to play an important role in the near future.

3.7. SUMMARY

The present chapter examined the temporal dynamics of agricultural performance in the state of Uttar Pradesh during the last five decades from 1960-61 to 2010-11. Besides the overall performance, the chapter also analyze the temporal dynamics of changes in area, production and yield of different crops and contribution of area and yield, changes in cropping pattern and their interaction effect with each other and overall changes in agricultural production in the state for the period as a whole as well by sub-dividing it into five periods. The main findings of the chapter are:

1. The state of Uttar Pradesh recorded mediocre performance in agricultural growth during the last half a century. It continues to achieve approximately average growth recorded by the agriculture sector in the country as a whole. The state could not benefit from green revolution technology as much as the benefits harvested by its neighbouring states of Punjab

and Haryana. Nevertheless, the agriculture growth rate accelerated during the green revolution period, decelerated in the first decade of reform period (1990s), but recovered marginally during the first decade of the twenty first century.

2. The recent recovery of agriculture is mainly because of a significant improvement in growth of livestock production. The combined output of the crop sector experienced considerable acceleration in growth from less than 1 per cent per annum during pre-green revolution period to more than 3 per cent during 1980s and decelerated to almost half (1.5%) during the new millennium. However, like crop sector, the fishery production continues to decelerate from a high of 12 per cent per annum growth during 1980s to 5 per cent per annum during 2000s. Forestry production accelerated from negative during 1980s to 20 per cent per annum during 1990s and declining to 4 per cent during 2000s.
3. In crop sector, the temporal pattern of acceleration up to 1980s and serious deceleration thereafter has mainly marked in the cereal sector. The opposite behaviour is shown by oilseeds, its growth decelerated up to 1980s, but recovered thereafter.
4. The growth of land productivity depicts inverted 'U' curve behaviour during the study period. The inverted 'U' curve behaviour of land productivity is mainly because both area and output depict inverted 'U' curve relationship and their superimposition on each other resulted in observed inverted 'U' curve relationship in land productivity. Over time, instability in land productivity has significantly declined.
5. Contrary to land productivity growth, labour productivity experienced 'U' curve behaviour over time. However, like the land productivity, over time temporal variations in growth of workers productivity declined significantly.
6. There is significant diversification of area under foodgrains with corresponding rise in area under non-foodgrains in general and under sugarcane, fruits and vegetables and condiments and spices in particular. Within foodgrains, major shift in area took place from coarse cereals and pulses towards the green revolution superior cereals—rice and wheat.
7. Diversification in value of output is more sharp in case of total non-foodgrains value of output. This is mainly because

of shift in area from low value coarse cereals and pulses towards high value condiments and spices and fruits and vegetable crops.

8. Decomposition of growth brings out that increase in yield was the main contributor to the total agriculture production, but it lost its importance during the last decade whereby its contribution to total production declined from more than 50 per cent to 17.6 per cent during 2001-2011. The changes in cropping pattern from low value to high value crops accounted for almost 40 per cent contribution to growth during 2001-2011. Almost one-fifth of the total production during the last decade was due to interaction between crop yield and changes in cropping pattern effect. Contribution of area effect first declined from one-fourth to a low level of approximately one-tenth during 1980s, but doubled to almost 20 per cent during 2010. The technological deceleration, price and increasing role of markets seems to play a significant role in area, yield and cropping pattern changes as contributor to agricultural performance in the state.

4

Pattern of Agricultural Growth in Uttar Pradesh: Variations Across Districts and Agro-Economic Regions

4.1. INTRODUCTION

The preceding chapter brought out significant dynamic changes in the temporal pattern of agricultural growth and development at the state level in Uttar Pradesh. However, agricultural production being biological in nature is likely to exhibit significant inter-regional variations in a geographically large state like in Uttar Pradesh. This is mainly because agricultural production is intimately affected by variations in physical endowments like quality of the soil, availability of irrigation, accessibility to rural economic infrastructure and agro-climatic conditions like rainfall, temperature, drought and floods. All these factors vary significantly with the size of the state. Therefore, it would be interesting to examine the performance of agriculture sector in the state across various regions and districts. Hence, this chapter is devoted to analyze the temporal and spatial pattern of agricultural growth in Uttar Pradesh. For temporal analysis agricultural performance is measured for the overall period from 1960-61 to 2010-11 as well as during various sub-periods. As mentioned in the previous chapter, these sub-periods are: 1960-61 to 1965-66 representing pre-green revolution phase, 1967-68 to 1980-81 is initial green revolution phase, 1981-82 to 1990-91 is mature green revolution phase and the period from 1991-92 to 2000-01 represents initial post-reform period and the period from 2001-02 to 2010-11 is new millennium. Thereafter, for spatial analysis growth pattern of agriculture is studied at the district-level and also for nine agro-economic regions (including hills) in Uttar Pradesh.

Precisely, the objective of the present chapter is to examine the spatial, i.e. district and region-wise pattern of agricultural growth in Uttar Pradesh from 1960-61 to 2010-11 and various sub-periods, 1960-61 to 1965-66, 1967-68 to 1980-81, 1981-82 to 1990-91, 1991-92 to 2000-01 and 2001-02 to 2010-11.

Wc propose to test the following hypotheses in this chapter:

(i) Given the wide regional disparities in natural and human resources, growth and development of agriculture vary considerably across districts and regions in Uttar Pradesh.

(ii) Given the regional disparities, the temporal pattern during different policy regimes may vary considerably across regions and districts in Uttar Pradesh.

The chapter is organized as follows. After introduction, objective and hypotheses in this section, following section 4.2 details the methodology followed in the chapter. Section 4.3 discusses inter-regional variations in agricultural growth. It compares region-wise growth of value output and instability in Uttar Pradesh from 1960-61 to 2010-11 and also during various sub-periods in sub-section 4.3 (i). We also discussed the trend in value output growth using regression estimates in this section. Sub-section 4.3 (ii) discusses region-wise growth and trend in gross cropped area in Uttar Pradesh for the overall period as well as during various sub-periods. We discussed growth in yield and rate of change in yield growth in sub-section 4.3 (iii). Thereafter, section 4.4 (i) discusses intra-regional and inter-district variations in agricultural value output growth during 1960-61 to 2010-11. Sub-section 4.4 (ii) provides inter-district inequality in agriculture production. Section 4.5 discusses geographical continuity in agricultural growth in Uttar Pradesh during different time periods. Thereafter, the summary of the chapter is presented in last section 4.6.

4.2. METHODOLOGY

To examine the region and district-wise pattern of agricultural growth in Uttar Pradesh, we employed the following methodology:

4.2 (i) Districts covered: For compatibility of information across districts in Uttar Pradesh, we merged the information for 26 newly created districts in the intervening period (1960-61 to 2010-11) with their parental constituent districts in Uttar Pradesh because of non-availability of data for these newly formed districts prior to their formation. Generally, when a new district is formed, no attempt has been made to generate data series for the newly formed districts for the earlier periods. Therefore, the only practical solution is to merge the newly created districts with their parent districts to make the district-level information comparable over time. The information on area and production has been estimated by clubbing total 72 districts into 46 district units and Hills (as 47th district) in Uttar Pradesh. The same problem arose when Uttarakhand as a separate state was formed out of Uttar Pradesh on 9th November, 2000. The districts at present the part of newly formed Uttarakhand, being initially in Uttar Pradesh were also included in the study. However these districts, total 13 in number, were clubbed as hills districts in the study. But Haridwar that at present is a separate district in Uttarakhand, has been clubbed within parental districts—Saharanpur (87%), Muzaffarnagar (6.36 %) and Bijnor (6.64%). The detailed information of formation of districts with their parent districts is presented at the end in Appendix 4.1. To trace out the regional pattern of agricultural performance, these 46 district units in Uttar Pradesh were further divided into eight agro-economic regions and ninth zone with hill districts. Though the region and zone are different regional entities, but they are used as synonyms in the present analysis to avoid any confusion of the present study with the past literature. This is mainly because the words were used interchangeably in the past studies. Based on soil and weather conditions as base of regionalization, the region-wise constituent of districts is provided in Table 4.1.

4.2 (ii) Estimation of Price: Prices used in the analysis are at 2010-11 prices. We estimated implicit prices by using crop-wise value output at current prices used in the 'National Accounts Statistics' compiled by Central Statistical Organization (CSO) and crop-wise production estimated by the Directorate of Economics and Statistics, Ministry of Agriculture.

$$\text{Price of a crop} = \frac{\text{Value output of the crop (Rs.) during 2010-11}}{\text{Physical quantity of the crop output (tons) during 2010-11}}$$

4.2 (iii) Estimation of Value of Output: The crop-wise value of output for major 35 crops was estimated at 2010-11 prices for each district. The estimated value output was aggregated to obtain the value

Table 4.1: Distribution of Districts into Agro-economic Regions

S. No.	*Regions*	*Districts included*
1.	Western Plain Zone	It includes 04 districts namely: Bulandshahr, Meerut, Muzaffarnagar and Saharanpur.
2.	Mid-Western Plain Zone	It includes 07 districts namely: Bareilly, Bijnor, Budaun, Moradabad, Rampur, Piliphit, and Shahjahanpur.
3.	South-Western Semi Arid Zone	It includes 05 districts namely: Agra, Aligarh, Etah, Mainpuri and Mathura.
4.	Central Plain Zone	It includes 11 districts namely: Allahabad, Etawah, Farrukhabad, Fatehpur, Hardoi, Kanpur, Kheri, Lucknow, Rae Bareli, Sitapur and Unnao.
5.	Bundelkhand Zone	It includes 04 districts namely: Banda, Hamirpur, Jalaun and Jhansi.
6.	North-Eastern Plain Zone	It includes 05 districts namely: Bahraich, Basti, Deoria, Gonda, and Gorakhpur.
7.	Eastern Plain Zone	It includes 09 districts namely: Azamgarh, Ballia, Barabanki, Faizabad, Ghazipur, Jaunpur, Sultanpur, Pratapgarh and Varanasi.
8.	Vindhyan Zone	It includes 01 district namely: Mirzapur.
9.	Hills	It includes 12 districts namely: Almora, Bageshwar, Chamoli, Champawat, Dehradun, Nainital, Pauri Garhwal, Pithoragarh, Rudra-Prayag, Tehri Garwhal and Udham Singh Nagar.

Source: GoI (2014), *Uttar Pradesh State Development Report*, Volume II, New Delhi, Planning Commission, Government of India.

of output for 35 crop sectors in each district. However, a pertinent issue related with measurement of value output of all the crops is the availability of the information on the area and production of all the crops grown at district-level in the state. Since authenticated and consistent district-level information on area and output of many fruits and vegetables and various other crops (minor) is not available, we therefore assumed that the yield of gross cropped area over and above covered under 35 crops is same as that of 35 crops:

$$\text{Total value output} = \text{Average yield of 35 crops} \times \text{Total cropped area}$$

where,

$$\text{Average yield} = \frac{\text{Total value output of 35 crops in a year}}{\text{Total area under 35 crops}}$$

4.2 (iv) Estimation of Growth rate: For district and region-wise analysis in the chapter, growth rates of agricultural production, area (gross cropped area), yield and valuc output are estimated by employing the following methodology for compound annual growth rates at different points of time:

$$\text{Annual growth rate } (G_t) = [(V_t/V_{t-1}) - 1]\times 100$$

$$\text{Compound annual growth rate (CAGR)} = \sum_{t=1}^{T} G_t/T$$

where,

V_t – Value of indicator (like area/production/yield) in year t.

V_{t-1} – Value of indicator (like area/production/yield) in year t-1.

T – Number of years for which CAGR is to be estimated.

4.2 (v) Estimation of Instability: To analyze the level of instability across various regions or districts in Uttar Pradesh, we estimated coefficient of variation, which is the ratio of standard deviation to the mean. We used the following formula:

$$\text{Coefficient of variation} = \frac{\text{Standard deviation}}{\text{Mean}}$$

4.2 (vi) Trend analysis: To examine the pattern in trend of agricultural production during different periods, we estimated the following semi-logarithmic trend line with slope differential dummy variables:

$$\log P_t = \alpha + \beta_1(\text{Time}) + \beta_2(\text{D1960-65*Time}) + \beta_3(\text{D1967 – 80*Time}) + \beta_4(\text{D1990s*Time}) + \beta_5(\text{D2000s*Time})$$

where,

P_t = Production in a district/zone during year t

D1960-65 – Dummy = 1 for pre-green revolution (1960-61 to 1965-66) period, otherwise,

D1967-80 – Dummy = 1 for initial green revolution (1967-68 to 1980-81) period.

D1990s – Dummy = 1 for initial post-reform (1991-92 to 2000-01) period.

D2000s – Dummy = 1 for new millennium (2001-02 to 2010-11) period.

1981-82 to 1990-91 is taken as base year.

The dummy variables are introduced to study dynamics of changes in trend growth during different periods.

EMPIRICAL FINDINGS

4.3. AGRICULTURAL GROWTH: INTER-REGIONAL VARIATIONS

4.3 (i) Region-wise Growth of Value Output in Uttar Pradesh: 1960-61 to 2010-11

The information on region-wise growth of value output of agriculture in Uttar Pradesh during the period 1960-61 to 2010-11 as well as during various sub-periods, 1960-61 to 1965-66 representing pre-green revolution phase, 1967-68 to 1980-81—initial green revolution phase, 1981-82 to 1990-91—mature green revolution phase, 1990-91 to 2000-01—initial reform phase and 2001-02 to 2010-11—new millennium phase is provided in Table 4.2 (a).

For the period as a whole from 1960-61 to 2010-11, the three zones namely—Mid-Western Plain Zone, South-Western Semi-Arid Zone and North-Eastern Plain Zone, outperformed all other zones by achieving growth rate exceeding 3 per cent per annum for fifty years. Two zones namely—Hills and Bundelkhand Zone along with Vindhyan Zone performed poorly by recording less than 2.5 per cent per annum growth during the study period. However, the pattern of growth varied significantly over time. At the state level, agriculture growth accelerated five-fold from 0.71 per cent per annum during pre-green revolution period to 3.73 per cent per annum during 1980s, then declined by almost one-third to 2.14 per cent per annum during the new millennium. On the basis of growth recorded by different zones during different periods, different trends emerge. While in the three of the nine zones namely—Western Plain Zone, Mid-Western Plain Zone and Central Plain Zone, agricultural growth follow the overall pattern in the state, i.e. first acceleration up to 1990s and deceleration thereafter. South-Western Semi-Arid Zone, which recorded the highest growth among these zones over the study period follow entirely different pattern of growth. Unlike

Table 4.2(a): Region-wise Growth of Value Output in Uttar Pradesh: 1960-61 to 2010-11

	Compound annual growth rates during the period of (per cent per annum)					
	Pre-Green Revolution	*Initial Green Revolution*	*Mature Green Revolution*	*Initial post-Reform*	*New millennium*	*Overall*
Period → / *Regions ↓*	1960-61 to 1965-66	1967-68 to 1980-81	1981-82 to 1990-91	1991-92 to 2000-01	2001-02 to 2010-11	1960-61 to 2010-11
Western Plain Zone	1.28	2.81	2.97	2.19	0.60	2.10
Mid-Western Plain Zone	1.91	4.78	4.96	2.07	0.88	3.13
South-Western Semi Arid Zone	5.49	1.62	4.88	3.00	2.94	3.24
Central Plain Zone	1.07	3.00	4.08	2.94	1.69	2.74
Bundelkhand Zone	–3.91	1.84	3.67	2.97	4.38	2.34
North-Eastern Plain Zone	3.55	2.79	4.79	3.16	1.87	3.18
Eastern Plain Zone	0.57	3.44	4.56	1.96	2.87	2.93
Vindhyan Zone	2.00	2.25	2.06	4.30	1.47	2.45
Hills	–5.54	3.29	1.05	2.71	0.87	1.28
Uttar Pradesh	0.71	2.55	3.73	2.50	1.41	2.23

Sources: (i) GoI (Various Years), *Agricultural Situation in India (Various Issues)*, New Delhi, Directorate of Economics and Statistics, Government of India.

(ii) GoI, *Department of Agriculture and Cooperation*, Ministry of Agriculture, Government of India, (website: agricoop.nic.in)

(iii) GOUP (Various Years), *Season and Crop Report of Uttar Pradesh (Various Issues)*, Lucknow, Directorate of Economics and Statistics, Government of Uttar Pradesh.

(iv) GOUP (Various Years), *Statistical Abstracts of Uttar Pradesh (Various Issues)*, Lucknow, Economic and Statistics Division, State Planning Institute, Government of Uttar Pradesh.

the overall pattern, agricultural growth declined first during initial phase of green revolution, then accelerated and peaked to almost 5 per cent per annum during 1980s and then stabilized to about 3 per cent annual growth during 1990s and 2000s. Bundelkhand Zone and Eastern Plain Zone follow similar pattern of acceleration in growth rate up to 1991, decelerated during 1990s and again accelerated during 2001-02 to 2010-11. The remaining two zones namely—Vindhyan Zone and Hills depict cyclical pattern of growth by recording acceleration during initial green revolution phase to deceleration during mature green revolution phase, again accelerated during 1990s and again decelerated during 2000s. These two zones are exception in the context that when all regions and states in the country recorded exceptional high growth rate during 1980s, these two zones experienced deceleration and recorded very low crop growth during the period. When agriculture decelerated everywhere during 1990s, agricultural growth accelerated two times in these zones during this period. Besides these two, Bundelkhand Zone is also an exception in its own way, as contrary to very low growth rate recorded by all other zones, Bundelkhand Zone recorded exceptionally high growth rate of 4.3 per cent per annum during 2000s.

These region-wise observations support the general perception of the big role of agro-climatic factors in the dynamics of agriculture growth in a country like India and a big state like Uttar Pradesh. Secondly, observation also seems to suggest that there are some agro-climatic region specific road blocks that constraint the adoption of technological developments that contribute to growth elsewhere. Consequently, some regions emerge the leaders and other laggards in the process of growth and development from new technological and institutional innovations.

Information on coefficient of variation, as an indicator of variation in agriculture growth is detailed in Table 4.2(b). It may be seen that the temporal and spatial pattern of instability also show considerable difference across zones as well as over time variations within each zone. On the whole, the instability shows the opposite behaviour to growth. For example, while growth for the state as a whole accelerated till 1990s and decelerated thereafter, instability of crop production in Uttar Pradesh declined from a high of 30.41 per cent during pre-green revolution period to a low of 0.99 per cent during 1980s and increased thereafter during 1990s with some reduction during 2000s. Like the growth pattern, Hills and Vindhyan Zone, show a cyclical movement of increase in instability up to 1991, declining during 1990s and increasing all time high during 2001-2011. During the new millennium, instability increased almost everywhere with exception of Western Plain Zone and Bundelkhand Zone, where it declined and in Eastern Plain Zone, where it remained same.

On the whole, it seems that the deceleration in agriculture during the reform period in general and during new millennium in particular, the agriculture instability has increased significantly during this period. The instability is generally related with vagaries of nature,

Table 4.2(b): Region-wise Instability in Growth of Crop Production in Uttar Pradesh: 1960-61 to 2010-11

	Coefficient of variation during the period of (per cent)					
	Pre-Green Revolution	*Initial Green Revolution*	*Mature Green Revolution*	*Initial post-Reform*	*New Millennium*	*Overall*
Period→ *Regions↓*	*1960-61 to 1965-66*	*1967-68 to 1980-81*	*1981-82 to 1990-91*	*1991-92 to 2000-01*	*2001-02 to 2010-11*	*1960-61 to 2010-11*
Western Plain Zone	11.67	3.04	1.33	11.72	9.25	5.49
Mid-Western Plain Zone	12.65	1.72	1.46	4.96	5.88	3.04
South-Western Semi Arid Zone	4.46	7.73	1.81	4.60	1.97	3.60
Central Plain Zone	40.79	3.01	1.79	2.63	3.90	4.11
Bundelkhand Zone	–3.34	6.94	1.96	6.19	3.95	6.40
North-Eastern Plain Zone	5.01	3.32	0.99	3.40	4.95	2.95
Eastern Plain Zone	–25.98	2.64	1.19	5.40	5.44	3.87
Vindhyan Zone	3.39	5.41	5.80	2.90	17.61	6.17
Hills	–1.62	2.60	8.10	4.32	11.34	7.45
Uttar Pradesh	30.41	2.52	0.99	4.53	3.68	3.34

Source: Same as in Table 4.2 (a).

disease and pests attack and the instability in agriculture markets. Therefore, it seems that slowdown in growth during the last two decades is partly attributed to the exogenous shocks which not only affect the growth directly, but also affect it indirectly by increasing risk and uncertainty of agriculture production and hence allocation of modern inputs by the farmers in crop production. The other part of deceleration, as noted earlier seems to be due to marked deceleration in production technology leading to slowdown of crop yield in the state. These issues would be examined in the subsequent chapters.

As mentioned earlier, we further tested the zone-wise acceleration/deceleration in agriculture growth by using semi-logarithmic cubic trend equation. From results reported in Table 4.2(c), it may be seen that zones can be clubbed into two parts on the basis of acceleration/deceleration in growth. In case of four zones namely—Western Plain Zone, Mid-Western Plain Zone, South-Western Semi-Arid Zone and Hills Zone, the agriculture growth in the earlier phase does not show any significant change whereas in the middle phase, a significant improvement in growth occurred and in the later phase the growth rate decelerated significantly. In the case of remaining

Table 4.2(c): Trend Growth in Agriculture Output: 1960-61 to 2010-11

Regions↓	*Regression coefficients*					
	Intercept	*Time*	*Time²*	*Time³*	R^2	*N*
Western Plain Zone	13.103 (0.843)	0.004 (0.461)	0.001*** (3.443)	–0.000020*** (4.442)	0.94	49
Mid-Western Plain Zone	11.160 (0.852)	0.004 (0.671)	0.002*** (6.311)	–0.000029*** (7.736)	0.98	49
South-Western Semi-Arid Zone	46.264 (2.769)	–0.013 (1.580)	0.001*** (3.852)	–0.000015*** (3.231)	0.96	49
Central Plain Zone	41.038 (3.386)	–0.010* (1.700)	0.002*** (6.138)	–0.000021*** (6.221)	0.98	49
Bundelkhand Zone	57.317 (2.788)	–0.019* (1.849)	0.002*** (4.022)	–0.000023*** (3.991)	0.91	49
North-Eastern Plain Zone	52.035 (3.892)	–0.016** (2.411)	0.002*** (7.022)	–0.000027*** (7.215)	0.98	49
Eastern Plain Zone	62.629 (4.009)	–0.022*** (2.723)	0.002*** (6.368)	–0.000030*** (6.715)	0.95	49
Vindhyan Zone	84.796 (3.061)	–0.034** (2.419)	0.003*** (4.550)	–0.000040*** (5.046)	0.81	49
Hills	-3.877 (0.199)	0.011 (1.155)	0.001* (1.824)	–0.000015*** (2.727)	0.88	49
Uttar Pradesh	39.708 (3.545)	–0.009 (1.580)	0.002*** (6.898)	–0.000024*** (7.427)	0.98	49

Source: Table 4.2(a).

Notes:
1. Figure in parenthesis is t value of the coefficients.
2. Asterisk *, ** and *** indicate coefficients significant at 10 per cent, 5 per cent and 1 per cent level of significance respectively for two tailed test.

five of the nine zones—Central Plain Zone, Bundelkhand Zone, North-Eastern Plain Zone, Eastern Plain Zone and Vindhyan Zone, it is a reverse 'N' behaviour of the agriculture growth over the study period. It indicates that agriculture growth first experienced a significant declining trend in the mid of the study period, it started growing at accelerated rate thereafter, whereas during the later part of the period of study, the agriculture growth decelerated at a significant rate. All the zones show a significant acceleration in growth during the mid-years of 1960 to 2011 period and a significant deceleration in growth during the latest period. However, regarding the initial years, some zones show no significant acceleration/ deceleration in growth whereas more than half of the zones show a deceleration in growth. Taking our earlier results along with these regression ones, shows that controlling the random variations, there is a significant deceleration in growth in the recent period, specifically during the first decade of the new millennium.

We further tested the acceleration/deceleration in growth through semi-logarithmic trend equation including dummy variable for the four different phases and taking 1981-1990 as the base period to compare it with the others. The results reported in Table 4.2(d) show that there is a significant increasing trend of agriculture growth over time in all the zones. Similarly, the dummy for the initial green revolution (1967-68 to 1980-81) bears the negative sign and significant statistically except in Vindhyan Zone. This supports our earlier finding that during 1980s (1981-82 to 1990-91) all the zones experienced a significant acceleration during the mature phase of green revolution period. The dummy for two post-reform periods however does not show any consistent pattern across zones. For five of nine zones, the coefficient for 2001-02 to 2010-11, dummy bears negative sign and coefficients are significant statistically. This indicates a significant deceleration in growth for most of the zones in Uttar Pradesh during the new millennium. For Bundelkhand Zone, the coefficient for post-reform period is positive and marginally significant indicating slight improvement in agricultural growth during the new millennium. Similarly, for Vindhyan Zone, there seems to be acceleration in growth during the post-reform period. So bearing these two zones, we can safely say that post-reform period bears a significant deceleration in growth compared to the region-wise agriculture growth during the mature phase of green revolution technology when the random factors (captured by the error term in the model) are controlled.

4.3 (ii) Region-wise Growth of Gross Cropped Area in Uttar Pradesh: 1960-61 to 2010-11

Table 4.3(a) details growth in gross cropped area at regional level in Uttar Pradesh for the overall period as well as for various sub-periods from 1960-61 to 2010-11. For the overall period growth in gross cropped area was recorded at 0.41 per cent per annum for the state as a whole. All regions experienced positive growth in gross cropped area with only exception of the Hill Zone. Among the zones, the gross cropped area grew at 0.75 per cent per annum in Bundelkhand Zone followed by Mid-Western Plain Zone (0.68% per annum), South-Western Semi-Arid Zone (0.51% per annum) and Eastern Plain Zone

Table 4.2(d): Trend Growth in Agriculture Output from 1960-61 to 2010-11

Regions↓	Regression coefficients								
	Intercept	*Time*	*Time Dummy for the Period of*				R^2	*N*
			Pre-Green Revolution	*Initial Green Revolution*	*Initial post-Reform*	*New mille-nnium*		
			1960-61 to 1965-66	*1967-68 to 1980-81*	*1991-92 to 2000-01*	*2001-02 to 2010-11*		
Western Plain Zone	–24.147	0.023***	–0.013	–0.007***	–0.002	–0.006***	0.93	49
	(5.155)	(9.587)	(0.893)	(2.769)	(1.316)	(3.915)		
Mid-Western Plain Zone	–52.955	0.037***	–0.006	–0.007***	–0.002	–0.008***	0.98	49
	(12.299)	(17.098)	(0.485)	(2.961)	(1.189)	(5.541)		
South-Western Semi-Arid Zone	–20.083	0.020***	0.012	–0.008***	0.003**	–0.003**	0.96	49
	(4.464)	(8.964)	(0.891)	(3.109)	(1.977)	(2.131)		
Central Plain Zone	–24.108	0.023***	–0.004	–0.006***	0.002**	–0.0000565	0.97	49
	(6.654)	(12.420)	(0.396)	(3.197)	(2.015)	(0.0490)		
Bundelkhand Zone	–6.254	0.013***	–0.048***	–0.014***	0.003*	0.002	0.93	49
	(1.217)	(5.062)	(3.053)	(5.038)	(1.883)	(1.518)		
North-Eastern Plain Zone	–33.351	0.027***	0.006	–0.009***	0.001	–0.002	0.98	49
	(8.998)	(14.485)	(0.534)	(4.706)	(0.756)	(1.645)		
Eastern Plain Zone	–25.357	0.023***	–0.003	–0.009***	0.001	–0.003**	0.95	49
	(5.550)	(10.054)	(0.216)	(3.719)	(0.588)	(2.054)		
Vindhyan Zone	–16.645	0.018***	0.005	–0.004	0.005**	–0.003	0.80	49
	(2.084)	(4.360)	(0.213)	(0.823)	(2.213)	(1.106)		
Hills	–10.016	0.015***	–0.066***	–0.007***	0.002	–0.004***	0.93	49
	(2.417)	(7.031)	(5.240)	(2.997)	(1.435)	(2.611)		
Uttar Pradesh	–25.467	0.024***	–0.007	–0.008***	0.001	–0.002**	0.98	49
	(7.803)	(14.701)	(0.720)	(4.463)	(0.816)	(2.233)		

Source: Table 4.2(a).

Notes: 1. Figure in parenthesis is t value of the coefficients.

2. Asterisk *, ** and *** indicate coefficients significant at 10 per cent, 5 per cent and 1 per cent level of significance respectively for two tailed test.

Table 4.3(a): Region-wise Growth of Gross Cropped Area in Uttar Pradesh: 1960-61 to 2010-11

	Compound annual growth rates during the period of (% per annum)					
	Pre-Green Revolution	*Initial Green Revolution*	*Mature Green Revolution*	*Initial post Reform*	*New Millennium*	*Overall*
Period → *Regions ↓*	*1960-61 to 1965-66*	*1967-68 to 1980-81*	*1981-82 to 1990-91*	*1991-92 to 2000-01*	*2001-02 to 2010-11*	*1960-61 to 2010-11*
Western Plain Zone	0.39	0.97	0.07	–0.25	–0.26	0.21
Mid-Western Plain Zone	–0.12	1.36	0.69	0.63	0.25	0.68
South-Western Semi-Arid Zone	0.26	0.75	0.06	0.85	0.44	0.51
Central Plain Zone	0.51	0.42	0.59	0.75	–0.30	0.39
Bundelkhand Zone	0.01	0.48	0.32	1.16	1.51	0.75
North-Eastern Plain Zone	0.37	0.59	0.20	–0.04	0.06	0.24
Eastern Plain Zone	0.34	0.49	0.65	0.15	0.43	0.42
Vindhyan Zone	0.83	1.21	0.42	0.89	–2.51	0.16
Hills	0.75	0.67	–0.12	–0.69	–0.52	–0.02
Uttar Pradesh	0.32	0.69	0.37	0.41	0.11	0.41

Source: Same as in Table 4.2(a).

(0.42% per annum). The Western Plain Zone, Central Plain Zone, North-Eastern Plain Zone and Vindhyan Zone also recorded positive growth in gross cropped area, but the pace of growth was less than the state average. Different zones, however present different pattern of area growth over time. For example, the Western Plain Zone shows maximum growth during 1967-68 to 1980-81, decelerated thereafter and became negative in the reform period. Mid-Western Plain Zone shows the maximum growth again during 1967-68 to 1980-81 and decelerated thereafter and remained positive and high. The Central Plain Zone shows maximum growth during 1991-92 to 2000-01 period, but negative growth during the following period. Bundelkhand Zone experienced exceptionally high growth rate in the post-reform period, recording 1.16 per cent per annum growth during 1991-92 to 2000-01 and 1.51 per cent per annum during 2001-02 to 2010-11. The Hill Zone shows negative growth for three decades after 1980-81. Since, growth in gross cropped area basically occurs due to three reasons, first is the increase in net area sown under crop sector, second is intensive use of net area sown due to shifting from mono crop to multiple cropping system and third, due to changes in crop composition from perennial to seasonal crops. It is difficult at this stage to find the relative contribution of different factors to acceleration/deceleration in the growth in area in different zones and periods.

We further estimated the semi-logarithmic trend equation by inserting slope dummy variables for the different periods to test the acceleration/deceleration in area growth over the different periods. Results reported in Table 4.3(b) suggest that there was significant growth in gross cropped area in all the zones over the study period.

Table 4.3(b): Trend Growth in Gross Cropped Area from 1960-61 to 2010-11

	Intercept	*Time*	*Time Dummy for the period of*				R^2	*N*
			Pre-Green Revolution	*Initial Green Revolution*	*Initial post-Reform*	*New Millennium*		
Periods→ *Regions↓*			*1960-61 to 1965-66*	*1967-68 to 1980-81*	*1991-92 to 2000-01*	*2001-02 to 2010-11*		
Western Plain Zone	6.329 (1124.94)	0.003*** (12.139)	–0.003* (1.912)	–0.00029 (1.169)	–0.001*** (7.645)	–0.002*** (11.779)	0.90	49
Mid-Western Plain Zone	6.432 (1035.72)	0.004*** (15.304)	–0.004** (2.553)	–0.001* (1.860)	–0.00029* (1.882)	–0.001*** (4.072)	0.97	49
South-Western Semi Arid Zone	6.326 (1189.718)	0.002*** (10.372)	–0.003** (2.470)	0.00026 (1.113)	0.000023 (0.180)	0.000012 (0.085)	0.96	49
Central Plain Zone	6.672 (1082.451)	0.002*** (6.501)	0.00011 (0.072)	–0.001* (1.945)	0.00028* (1.882)	0.000053 (0.331)	0.91	49
Bundelkhand Zone	6.280 (682.089)	0.002*** (4.166)	–0.002 (0.879)	0.000016 (0.039)	0.00044* (1.953)	0.001*** (3.571)	0.90	49
North-Eastern Plain Zone	6.517 (1428.282)	0.002*** (9.615)	0.001 (0.535)	–0.001*** (2.672)	–0.001*** (5.621)	–0.001*** (5.647)	0.88	49
Eastern Plain Zone	6.542 (1506.280)	0.002*** (12.574)	0.001 (0.502)	–0.001*** (5.545)	–0.00026** (2.463)	–0.001*** (4.539)	0.96	49
Vindhyan Zone	5.647 (279.078)	0.003*** (3.274)	0.005 (1.067)	0.001 (0.642)	0.000059 (0.120)	–0.002*** (3.663)	0.48	49
Hills	6.029 (568.45)	0.001*** (2.122)	–0.005* (1.887)	0.001* (1.927)	–0.001*** (2.929)	–0.001*** (4.553)	0.60	49
Uttar Pradesh	7.339 (2000.42)	0.002*** (14.761)	–0.001 (1.255)	–0.00037** (2.297)	–0.00020** (2.256)	– 0.00043*** (4.494)	0.97	49

Source: Table 4.3(a).

Notes:
1. Figure in parenthesis is t value of the coefficients.
2. Asterisk *, ** and *** indicate coefficients significant at 10 per cent, 5 per cent and 1 per cent level of significance respectively for two tailed test.

With the anomalous behaviour of the Central Plain Zone and Bundelkhand Zone, rest of the zones on the whole suggest significant deceleration in growth of gross cropped area during the latest decade of 2001-2011. Similarly, five of the nine zones also show significant less growth in area during 1991-2000 as compared to 1980s. This seems to suggest that a significant higher growth in area during 1980s, was one important contributor to very high growth of agriculture production during this period. Similarly, significant lesser growth during the post-reform period in most of the zones is because of significant less growth in gross cropped area experienced by majority of the zones. A significant positive coefficient of slope dummy for post-reform periods is in line with earlier findings of a high agriculture growth experienced by these zones in the post-reform period. In other words, part of the high growth in Bundelkhand Zone is because of phenomenal expansion of gross cropped area in the zone.

4.3 (iii) Region-wise Growth of Crop Yield in Uttar Pradesh: 1960-61 to 2010-11

The information on growth of crop yield for different regions and periods is detailed in Table 4.4(a). It reveals that almost all zones

Table 4.4(a): Region-wise Growth of Crop Yield in Uttar Pradesh: 1960-61 to 2010-11

	Compound annual growth rates during the period of (% per annum)					
	Pre-Green Revolution	*Initial Green Revolution*	*Mature Green Revolution*	*Initial post-Reform*	*New Millennium*	*Overall*
Period→ / *Regions↓*	*1960-61 to 1965-66*	*1967-68 to 1980-81*	*1981-82 to 1990-91*	*1991-92 to 2000-01*	*2001-02 to 2010-11*	*1960-61 to 2010-11*
Western Plain Zone	0.89	1.84	2.90	2.44	0.86	1.89
Mid-Western Plain Zone	2.03	3.42	4.27	1.44	0.63	2.45
South Western Semi-Arid Zone	5.23	0.87	4.82	2.15	2.50	2.73
Central Plain Zone	0.56	2.58	3.49	2.19	1.99	2.35
Bundelkhand Zone	–3.92	1.36	3.35	1.81	2.87	1.59
North-Eastern Plain Zone	3.18	2.20	4.59	3.20	1.81	2.94
Eastern Plain Zone	0.23	2.95	3.91	1.81	2.44	2.51
Vindhyan Zone	1.17	1.05	1.64	3.42	3.99	2.29
Hills	–6.22	2.67	1.15	3.42	1.41	1.32
Uttar Pradesh	0.39	1.85	3.35	2.09	1.29	1.82

Source: Calculated from Value output and Area data.

experienced a significant acceleration in crop yield during 1980s. However, the picture is slightly mixed across the zones, with Mid-Western Plain Zone, South-Western Semi-Arid Zone and North-Eastern Plain Zone performing exceptionally well recording almost 4.5 per cent per annum increase in crop yield. Whereas Vindhyan and Hill Zones performed poorly. For the state as a whole, crop yield decelerated from 3.35 per cent per annum during 1980s to 2.09 per cent per annum during 1990s to 1.29 per cent per annum during 2000s. Such continuous deceleration on the whole is shown by Western Plain Zone, Mid-Western Plain Zone, North-Eastern Plain Zone and Central Plain Zone. Yield growth also decelerated in the South-Western Semi-Arid Zone during 1990s, but it recorded marginal improvement during 2000s. Bundelkhand Zone, first experienced a decline in growth during 1990s, but then recovered during 2000s. The same is true about Eastern Plain Zone as well. Vindhyan Zone is an exception among all the zones as it experienced almost continuous acceleration in yield from 1.1 per cent per annum up to 1980s to almost 4 per cent per annum during 2001-11 period.

Like output and area growth, we also fitted the semi-logarithmic equation by inserting the slope dummy variable to test statistically the period-wise growth rate of yield in various zones. The results in this context are reported in Table 4.4(b). Again like earlier findings, negative significant coefficient of dummy for 1967-68 to 1980-81 suggests a significant acceleration in yield during 1980s compared with the initial phase of green revolution (1967-68 to 1980-81). However, there is a mixed pattern for differences in growth during 1980s and subsequent post-reform periods. While, in case of the state as a whole, both the post-reform slope dummies are not significant statistically, suggests no acceleration/deceleration in yield during the post-reform period. However, as observed earlier in Table 4.4(a), growth rate during the post-reform period is approximately half of the growth in yield during 1980s. Taken together, it indicates that the random variations were playing a significant role, otherwise there was no significant decline in trend growth rate in the post-reform period for the state as a whole. No trend change in the post-reform period is also evident for Western Plain Zone, Central Plain Zone, Bundelkhand Zone and the Eastern Plain Zone. However, the four zones namely—South-Western Semi-Arid Zone, North-Eastern Plain Zone, Vindhyan Zone and Hill Zone experienced some acceleration in yield growth in the post-reform period compared with 1980s. On

Table 4.4(b): Trend Growth in Crop Yield from 1960-61 to 2010-11

Periods→ *Regions↓*	*Intercept*	*Time*	*Time Dummy for the period of*				R^2	*N*
			Pre-Green Revolution	*Initial Green Revolution*	*Initial post-Reform*	*New Mille-nnium*		
			1960-61 to 1965-66	*1967-68 to 1980-81*	*1991-92 To 2000-01*	*2001-02 To 2010-11*		
Western Plain Zone	2.471	0.007***	–0.003	–0.003***	0.00025	–0.001	0.91	49
	(106.564)	(7.315)	(0.492)	(2.680)	(0.446)	(1.332)		
Mid-Western Plain Zone	2.190	0.012***	0.001	–0.002***	–0.00038	–0.003***	0.97	49
	(108.417)	(14.605)	(0.238)	(2.772)	(0.765)	(5.006)		
South-Western Semi Arid Zone	2.273	0.007***	0.009	–0.004***	0.001**	0.001**	0.94	49
	(96.915)	(6.758)	(1.465)	(3.412)	(1.968)	(2.147)		
Central Plain Zone	2.187	0.008***	–0.002	–0.002***	0.001	–0.000078	0.97	49
	(124.894)	(11.327)	(0.4600)	(2.819)	(1.546)	(0.1705)		
Bundelkhand Zone	2.172	0.004***	–0.019***	–0.006***	0.001	0.00022	0.89	49
	(84.018)	(3.844)	(2.900)	(5.313)	(1.286)	(0.326)		
North-Eastern Plain Zone	2.059	0.010***	0.002	–0.004***	0.001**	–0.00017	0.97	49
	(108.880)	(12.722)	(0.425)	(4.242)	(2.142)	(0.346)		
Eastern Plain Zone	2.175	0.008***	–0.002	–0.003***	0.001	–0.001	0.94	49
	(99.701)	(8.654)	(0.340)	(3.023)	(1.142)	(1.375)		
Vindhyan Zone	2.080	0.005***	–0.003	–0.002	0.002**	0.001	0.83	49
	(62.144)	(3.614)	(0.390)	(1.514)	(2.543)	(0.746)		
Hills	2.138	0.005***	–0.024***	–0.004***	0.001***	–0.00022	0.95	49
	(108.518)	(6.660)	(4.851)	(4.399)	(3.045)	(0.437)		
Uttar Pradesh	2.210	0.008***	–0.002	–0.003***	0.001	–0.00048	0.97	49
	(132.967)	(11.899)	(0.498)	(4.114	(1.500	(1.106)		

Source: Table 4.4(a).

Notes: 1. Figure in parenthesis is t value of the coefficients.

2. Asterisk *, ** and *** indicate coefficients significant at 10 per cent, 5 per cent and 1 per cent level of significance respectively for two tailed test.

the contrary, Mid-Western Plain Zone shows a significant deceleration in yield during the post-reform period. This seems to suggest that at the regional level, the deceleration in growth during the post-reform period cannot be attributed to deceleration in technology, we tried to capture through the yield analysis. However, technological improvement certainly played a significant role in exceptional high performance of production growth during 1980s. Acceleration in growth observed for four zones seems to suggest a further unexploited potential in agriculture in these zones. However, it needs deeper analysis to arrive at definite conclusions about the role of area and yield as contributors to recent deceleration in agriculture growth for majority of the zones in the state. This analysis would be carried out in the subsequent chapters.

4.4. AGRICULTURAL GROWTH: INTRA-REGIONAL AND INTER-DISTRICT VARIATIONS

4.1 (i) Distribution of Districts in Value Output Growth in Uttar Pradesh: 1960-61 to 2010-11

Depending upon growth actually realized districts were classified into three main groups. High growth districts with growth exceeding 3.0 per cent per annum, medium growth with growth falling between 2.0-3.0 per cent and those with growth less than 2.0 per cent as low growth districts. Information on distribution of districts in different zones in this context is presented in Table 4.5 and Table 4.6 presents district-wise growth of value output in Uttar Pradesh during 1960-61 to 2010-11. During the pre-green revolution phase as many as 27 districts that constitute 60 per cent of the districts in the state recorded very low growth rates. These low growth districts were mainly concentrated in Mid-Western Plain Zone, Central Plain and Eastern Plain Zones. 15 of the 46 districts recorded high growth during this period and they were mainly concentrated in South-Western Semi-Arid Zone, Central Plain and North-Eastern Plain Zones. There was remarkable upward shift in distribution of districts among different growth groups during initial phase of the green revolution technology. While the number of low growth districts declined from 27 during previous period to eight during this period, most of these districts graduated to medium growth categories, with some graduating to high growth categories. Almost half of the districts recorded high

Table 4.5: Region-wise Distribution of Districts in Total Value Output in Uttar Pradesh: 1960-61 to 2010-11

	Compound annual growth rates (per cent per annum)	*Number of districts during the period of*					
		Pre-Green Revolution	*Initial Green Revolution*	*Mature Green Revolution*	*Initial Post-Reform*	*New Mille-nnium*	*Overall*
Period→ Regions↓		*1960-61 to 1965-66*	*1967-68 to 1980-81*	*1981-82 to 1990-91*	*1991-92 to 2000-01*	*2001-02 to 2010-11*	*1960-61 to 2010-11*
Western Plain zone	High (>3.0%)	0	3	1	0	0	0
	Medium (2.0%-3.0%)	2	0	3	2	0	3
	Low (<2.0%)	2	1	0	2	4	1
Mid-Western Plain Zone	High (>3.0%)	2	6	7	2	0	5
	Medium (2.0%-3.0%)	0	1	0	1	0	2
	Low (<2.0%)	5	0	0	4	7	0
South-Western Semi-Arid Zone	High (>3.0%)	4	0	5	4	2	3
	Medium (2.0%-3.0%)	0	2	0	0	2	2
	Low (<2.0%)	1	3	0	1	1	0
Central Plain Zone	High (>3.0%)	4	3	8	5	2	3
	Medium (2.0%-3.0%)	0	7	2	2	2	7
	Low (<2.0%)	7	1	1	4	7	1
Bundelkhand Zone	High (>3.0%)	0	0	2	1	3	1
	Medium (2.0%-3.0%)	0	2	2	2	1	1
	Low (<2.0%)	4	2	0	1	0	2

Source: Table 4.6

Table 4.6: District and Region-wise Growth of Total Value Output in Uttar Pradesh: 1960-61 to 2010-11

Districts/Regions↓	*Compound annual growth rates during the period of (% per annum)*					
	Pre-Green Revolution	*Initial Green Revolution*	*Mature Green Revolution*	*Initial Post-Reform*	*New Millennium*	*Overall*
Period→	*1960-61 to 1965-66*	*1967-68 to 1980-81*	*1981-82 to 1990-91*	*1991-92 to 2000-01*	*2001-02 to 2010-11*	*1960-61 to 2010-11*
(1)	(2)	(3)	(4)	(5)	(6)	(7)
Bulandshahr	0.33	1.11	2.19	1.66	0.44	1.23
Meerut	0.20	3.12	2.93	2.67	0.68	2.17
Muzaffarnagar	2.34	3.11	2.70	1.38	0.50	2.04
Saharanpur	2.95	3.39	3.92	2.73	0.74	2.77
Western Plain Zone	**1.28**	**2.81**	**2.97**	**2.19**	**0.60**	**2.10**
Bareilly	–1.87	3.74	5.44	1.54	0.63	2.40
Bijnor	1.98	5.69	5.28	1.06	0.43	3.16
Budaun	8.43	2.99	4.32	3.15	1.87	3.63
Moradabad	3.10	4.29	3.92	1.99	0.29	2.78
Pilibhit	–3.17	7.50	4.64	1.61	1.61	3.34
Rampur	1.73	5.80	5.51	2.48	1.31	3.69
Shahjahanpur	–0.45	4.62	6.28	3.13	0.77	3.33
Mid-Western Plain Zone	**1.91**	**4.78**	**4.96**	**2.07**	**0.88**	**3.13**
Agra	0.37	1.99	5.90	4.38	3.69	3.49
Aligarh	7.25	2.01	3.41	1.21	2.48	2.78
Etah	7.81	1.43	5.75	3.21	1.47	3.37
Mainpuri	3.40	2.53	5.94	3.14	4.79	3.93
Mathura	6.82	0.02	4.24	3.53	2.30	2.81

(Contd.)

(1)	(2)	(3)	(4)	(5)	(6)	(7)
South-Western Semi-Arid Zone	**5.49**	**1.62**	**4.88**	**3.00**	**2.94**	**3.24**
Allahabad	–3.83	4.93	1.51	3.96	0.73	2.23
Etawah	–0.01	2.72	4.43	3.77	1.68	2.79
Farrukhabad	3.18	3.96	6.04	3.91	0.36	3.55
Fatehpur	0.42	2.71	2.24	1.33	2.86	2.12
Hardoi	4.07	0.93	4.33	2.64	2.35	2.62
Kanpur	1.36	3.82	4.32	1.20	0.97	2.53
Kheri	3.43	2.91	5.49	4.21	1.79	3.54
Lucknow	3.92	2.71	2.50	1.40	1.83	2.33
Raebareli	–4.48	2.81	3.76	1.44	–0.83	1.20
Sitapur	1.67	2.13	4.68	3.05	3.08	3.00
Unnao	1.56	2.60	3.18	2.12	3.80	2.76
Central Plain Zone	**1.07**	**3.00**	**4.08**	**2.94**	**1.69**	**2.74**
Banda	–6.81	2.09	2.86	2.22	2.14	1.36
Hamirpur	–2.28	1.41	2.48	1.34	3.26	1.62
Jalaun	–0.25	1.71	4.21	2.27	4.33	2.69
Jhansi	–5.89	2.14	5.21	5.25	6.44	3.49
Bundelkhand Zone	**–3.91**	**1.84**	**3.67**	**2.97**	**4.38**	**2.34**
Bahraich	9.36	2.84	6.02	4.14	2.09	4.30
Basti	0.68	1.91	5.47	3.32	3.23	3.09
Deoria	2.08	3.36	4.23	1.97	0.01	2.42
Gonda	3.49	2.67	4.00	4.36	2.98	3.45
Gorakhpur	4.90	3.18	4.68	2.62	0.86	3.07
North-Eastern Plain Zone	**3.55**	**2.79**	**4.79**	**3.16**	**1.87**	**3.18**
Azamgarh	0.67	3.30	5.61	2.01	2.70	3.11
Ballia	2.71	4.75	3.25	2.66	3.60	3.55
Barabanki	4.58	2.17	4.56	2.24	3.63	3.24

(Contd.)

(1)	(2)	(3)	(4)	(5)	(6)	(7)
Faizabad	–2.76	2.69	4.97	1.81	2.27	2.33
Ghazipur	5.49	3.63	5.55	1.21	2.09	3.40
Jaunpur	–2.36	5.19	3.11	1.98	1.09	2.45
Pratapgarh	0.98	3.75	4.21	1.25	1.53	2.57
Sultanpur	–3.58	2.91	4.31	2.89	5.23	3.01
Varanasi	–0.55	3.14	4.65	1.50	3.08	2.72
Eastern Plain Zone	**0.57**	**3.44**	**4.56**	**1.96**	**2.87**	**2.93**
Mirzapur	2.00	2.25	2.06	4.30	1.47	2.45
Vindhyan Zone	**2.00**	**2.25**	**2.06**	**4.30**	**1.47**	**2.45**
Hills	**–5.54**	**3.29**	**1.05**	**2.71**	**0.87**	**1.28**
Uttar Pradesh	**0.71**	**2.55**	**3.73**	**2.50**	**1.41**	**2.23**

Source: Same as in Table 4.2 (a).

growth rate during this period and they were mainly concentrated in the Western Plain, Mid-Western Plain and Eastern Plain Zones. The initial green revolution technology seems to have made a significant impact in the Western Plain, Mid-Western Plain and Eastern Plain Zones. However, the green revolution technology seems to have bypassed South-Western Semi-Arid Zone, Bundelkhand Zone and Vindhyan Zone.

The most important breakthrough in agricultural growth was witnessed during 1980s when 37 of 46 districts recorded high growth exceeding 3 per cent per annum. Green revolution technology not only consolidated its base in Western Plain, Mid-Western Plain and Eastern Plain Zones, but it extended to South-Western Semi-Arid Zone and North-Eastern Plain Zone with all their districts recording high growth during this period.

The post-reform period experienced many high growth districts slipping to medium and low growth categories. Interestingly, this downward shift has most marked the districts in the regions who were the main gainers during initial phase of the green revolution technology. The technological gain of the leading districts in the adoption of new technology seems to have petered out in the twenty first century. This is evident from the fact as all the 11 districts in Western Plain and Mid-Western Plain Zone recorded low growth rates during 2001-2010. The same is more or less true about Eastern Plain Zone. The only soothing observation during the post-reform period is that three of the four districts in Bundelkhand Zone recorded high growth exceeding 3 per cent per annum during the last about one decade. During the new millennium, more than half of the districts recorded low growth falling short of 2 per cent per annum. Only about one-fourth of the districts were able to attain high growth exceeding 3 per cent per annum. The serious slowdown in specific regions needs to be reversed.

4. 4 (iii) District-wise Instability in Growth of Agriculture Production in Uttar Pradesh: 1960-61 to 2010-11

Table 4.7 provides district-wise instability measured through coefficient of variation in growth of value output in Uttar Pradesh for the overall period from 1960-61 to 2010-11. For the period as a whole, at the district-level in Uttar Pradesh, the highest level of instability was recorded by Banda district with as high as 14.17 per

Table 4.7: District-wise Instability in Growth of Agriculture Production in Uttar Pradesh: 1960-61 to 2010-11

	Coefficient of Variation during the period of (%)					
	Pre-Green Revolution	*Initial Green Revolution*	*Mature Green Revolution*	*Initial post-Reform*	*New Millennium*	*Overall*
Period→ *Districts/Regions↓*	*1960-61 to 1965-66*	*1967-68 to 1980-81*	*1981-82 to 1990-91*	*1991-92 to 2000-01*	*2001-02 to 2010-11*	*1960-61 to 2010-11*
(1)	(2)	(3)	(4)	(5)	(6)	(7)
Bulandshahr	76.23	8.71	3.85	5.86	8.39	8.63
Meerut	48.13	3.39	3.01	8.06	9.98	5.64
Muzaffarnagar	3.83	2.87	1.79	13.41	14.94	5.12
Saharanpur	1.07	3.05	1.47	12.35	7.74	5.83
Western Plain Zone	**11.67**	**3.04**	**1.33**	**11.72**	**9.25**	**5.49**
Bareilly	–9.71	2.11	1.51	6.09	13.81	4.02
Bijnor	7.34	2.20	2.04	15.20	15.20	3.80
Budaun	3.46	4.70	2.15	3.32	4.27	3.65
Moradabad	6.51	1.84	1.71	2.87	11.48	3.01
Pilibhit	–3.96	2.01	1.74	4.71	3.52	3.17
Rampur	11.55	2.61	2.86	4.13	6.28	3.61
Shahjahanpur	–60.46	2.23	1.80	4.85	15.34	4.15
Mid-Western Plain Zone	**12.65**	**1.72**	**1.46**	**4.96**	**5.88**	**3.04**
Agra	101.02	6.01	3.44	4.97	2.08	5.29
Aligarh	1.97	6.72	2.82	9.90	2.29	3.91

(Contd.)

(1)	(2)	(3)	(4)	(5)	(6)	(7)
Etah	4.09	6.14	1.70	2.74	6.26	3.76
Mainpuri	5.53	4.50	1.89	5.10	1.63	3.11
Mathura	2.81	907.37	1.21	3.93	3.47	4.41
South-Western Semi-Arid Zone	**4.46**	**7.73**	**1.81**	**4.60**	**1.97**	**3.60**
Allahabad	–6.75	2.97	9.11	2.85	23.26	6.87
Etawah	–2645.79	3.21	2.89	1.91	5.61	4.17
Farrukhabad	9.44	3.25	1.62	3.64	16.92	3.85
Fatehpur	37.72	3.59	3.20	4.81	4.23	4.52
Hardoi	5.85	17.91	2.76	3.69	2.95	5.06
Kanpur	25.79	3.37	3.01	8.59	9.21	5.83
Kheri	5.00	2.73	1.68	1.76	3.17	2.46
Lucknow	9.05	4.51	4.48	6.89	4.43	6.06
Raebareli	–6.34	3.56	2.56	7.04	–15.96	10.89
Sitapur	17.03	4.68	2.22	2.76	2.41	3.94
Unnao	22.77	5.09	3.55	5.40	2.44	5.36
Central Plain Zone	**40.79**	**3.01**	**1.79**	**2.63**	**3.90**	**4.11**
Banda	–3.32	7.93	7.45	8.36	10.52	14.17
Hamirpur	–5.66	8.43	3.34	12.56	5.95	8.56
Jalaun	–72.18	5.86	2.89	10.28	4.26	5.93
Jhansi	–1.69	5.59	2.22	2.88	2.83	3.96
Bundelkhand Zone	**–3.34**	**6.94**	**1.96**	**6.19**	**3.95**	**6.40**
Bahraich	3.66	5.91	1.84	2.52	2.77	3.51
Basti	21.47	4.51	1.05	5.44	5.82	4.29
Deoria	4.05	3.92	1.10	3.79	1438.08	3.69
Gonda	6.80	2.80	3.59	1.86	2.98	3.30
Gorakhpur	2.61	2.96	1.16	5.02	8.56	3.05
North Eastern Plain Zone	**5.01**	**3.32**	**0.99**	**3.40**	**4.95**	**2.95**

(Contd.)

(1)	(2)	(3)	(4)	(5)	(6)	(7)
Azamgarh	13.23	3.72	1.93	4.77	6.78	3.96
Ballia	3.02	5.00	3.27	4.61	5.60	4.71
Barabanki	9.57	4.86	1.80	6.41	4.14	5.25
Faizabad	–7.07	3.43	1.31	7.32	6.07	5.02
Ghazipur	2.87	4.39	2.02	9.84	8.76	4.21
Jaunpur	–6.26	2.50	2.66	3.65	12.29	4.55
Pratapgarh	31.85	2.93	1.93	6.58	8.04	5.06
Sultanpur	–7.03	2.90	2.37	3.75	3.00	4.31
Varanasi	–31.70	3.16	2.45	11.95	7.03	5.57
Eastern Plain Zone	**–25.98**	**2.64**	**1.19**	**5.40**	**5.44**	**3.87**
Mirzapur	3.39	5.41	5.80	2.90	17.61	6.17
Vindhyan Zone	**3.39**	**5.41**	**5.80**	**2.90**	**17.61**	**6.17**
Hills	–1.62	2.60	8.10	4.32	11.34	7.45
Uttar Pradesh	**30.41**	**2.52**	**0.99**	**4.53**	3.68	**3.34**

Source: Same as in Table 4.2 (a).

cent coefficient of variation followed by 10.89 per cent in Raebareli district from Central Plain Zone. If we look at the value output growth rates of these districts in Table 4.6, it was as low as 1.36 per cent and 1.20 per cent per annum respectively during the overall period. This collaborates our earlier finding that growth rates and level of instability usually have inverse relationship. On the other hand, Kheri district, again from Central Plain Zone recorded the lowest instability level. These extreme values of coefficient of variation from same zone shows the existence of regional variations in the state. Moreover, 17 out of total 47 district units (including hills) recorded low level of variations with coefficient of variation less than 4 per cent for the overall period.

The level of instability was extremely large across districts during pre-green revolution period. On one hand some districts such as Saharanpur and Aligarh recorded comparatively very low levels of instability, while on the other hand there are some others such as Agra, Bulandshahr and Meerut that recorded very high coefficient of variation.

Instability in most of the districts and regions declined with growth of agriculture during initial green revolution phase. All the districts that witnessed very high coefficient of variation during previous period declined considerably during this period. However, Mathura district from South-Western Semi-Arid Zone recorded many fold increase in coefficient of variation, again this is mainly due to sudden decline in output growth rate from 6.82 per cent during previous period to as low as 0.02 per cent during this period.

There was further decline in level of instability during 1980s. Only five districts, Rampur from Mid-Western Plain Zone, Allahabad from Central Plain Zone, Gonda from North-Eastern Plain Zone, Jaunpur from Eastern Plain Zone and Mirzapur from Vindhyan Zone and Hills recorded acceleration in coefficient of variation and hence increase in instability whereas, rest 41 districts recorded a decline. The situation reversed during 1990s. There was increase in variations at the state level as well as at district-level with exception of Allahabad, Etawah, Gonda, Mirzapur and Hill districts. The declining trend of instability was seen again during the new millennium as 19 of the 47 district units (including hills) experienced decline in instability. There seems to be convergence of instability in agricultural growth in the state, regions and for most of the districts in Uttar Pradesh.

4.4 (iv) District-wise Trend Growth in Agriculture Output: 1960-61 to 2010-11

Table 4.8 presents estimates of the trend regression of agricultural growth for all the districts individually for the period as a whole. Three important observations emerging from the table are:

1. All districts experienced a significant improvement in agricultural growth during the last half a century. However, trend growth across districts vary considerably from about 4 per cent per annum growth for Moradabad and Pilibhit districts to about 1 per cent per annum for Bulandshahr and Hamirpur districts. Banda is the only odd man out district that has not recorded any significant change in agriculture production for the last five decades.
2. Agricultural growth accelerated significantly during 1980s in all the districts with exception of Muzaffarnagar, Saharanpur, Bijnor, Mainpuri, Allahabad, Lucknow, Unnao, Ballia, Varanasi and Mirzapur districts. These districts also experienced acceleration in growth, but the same was not significant statistically.
3. Though on contrary of the overall analysis, as well as with region specific analysis, there is mixed picture regarding acceleration/deceleration of growth during the post-reform period. Almost half of the districts experienced significant deceleration during the post-reform period whereas 14 districts experienced the just opposite, i.e. the acceleration in growth during the reform period. The remaining 12 districts do not show any significant change in trend of agriculture growth rate during the post-reform period compared to their trend growth during 1980s. The acceleration/deceleration/ no change however seems to have some region specificity. For example, all districts in the Mid-Western Plain Zone and Eastern Plain Zone experienced significant deceleration in the post-reform period, whereas almost all districts in South-Western Semi-Arid Zone experienced acceleration in growth. The remaining zones present a mixed picture of acceleration/ deceleration in growth.

Table 4.8: Trend Growth in District-wise Agriculture Output from 1960-61 to 2010-11

Periods→ *Districts/Regions↓*	*Intercept*	*Time*	*Time Dummy for the period of*				R^2	*N*
			Pre-Green Revolution	*Initial Green Rev.*	*Initial Post-Reform*	*New Millennium*		
			1960-61 to 1965-66	*1967-68 to 1980-81*	*1991-92 to 2000-01*	*2001-02 to 2010-11*		
(1)	(2)	(3)	(4)	(5)	(6)	(7)	(8)	(9)
Bulandshahr	–2.672	0.011***	–0.012	–0.014***	–0.000066	–0.000228	0.88	49
	(0.572)	(4.654)	(0.838)	(5.492)	(0.048)	(0.154)		
Meerut	–22.880	0.021***	–0.012	–0.006*	0.002	–0.003	0.92	49
	(4.02)	(7.468)	(0.700)	(1.869)	(0.960)	(1.442)		
Muzaffarnagar	–35.202	0.028***	–0.019	–0.004	–0.005***	–0.009***	0.93	49
	(7.095)	(11.008)	(1.267)	(1.565)	(3.196)	(5.707)		
Saharanpur	–39.782	0.030***	–0.006	–0.005	–0.006***	–0.012***	0.87	49
	(6.022)	(8.94)	(0.284)	(1.497)	(2.933)	(5.840)		
Western Plain Zone	**–24.147**	**0.023*****	**–0.013**	**–0.007*****	**–0.002**	**–0.006*****	**0.93**	**49**
	(5.155)	**(9.587)**	**(0.893)**	**(2.769)**	**(1.316)**	**(3.915)**		
Bareilly	–39.298	0.029***	–0.022	–0.008***	0.000114	–0.005***	0.97	49
	(8.557)	(12.621)	(1.534)	(3.280)	(0.084)	(3.319)		
Bijnor	–60.294	0.040***	–0.003	–0.004	–0.003	–0.011***	0.95	49
	(9.669)	(12.714)	(0.164)	(1.210)	(1.394)	(5.335)		
Budaun	–46.218	0.033***	0.031**	–0.004*	–0.001	–0.003**	0.97	49
	(10.534)	(14.779)	(2.336)	(1.730)	(0.445)	(2.426)		
Moradabad	–61.614	0.041***	0.000	–0.008***	–0.003*	–0.010***	0.97	49
	(12.822)	(16.810)	(0.014)	(2.963)	(1.799)	(6.501)		

(*Contd.*)

(1)	(2)	(3)	(4)	(5)	(6)	(7)	(8)	(9)
Pilibhit	–64.791	0.042***	–0.036**	–0.007**	–0.004**	–0.009***	0.97	49
	(11.515)	(14.782)	(2.084)	(2.365)	(2.133)	(4.862)		
Rampur	–52.502	0.036***	–0.015	–0.009***	–0.001	–0.007***	0.96	49
	(8.97)	(12.090)	(0.833)	(2.953)	(0.750)	(4.023)		
Shahjahanpur	–55.954	0.038***	–0.026	–0.009***	0.000226	–0.006***	0.96	49
	(8.995)	(11.989)	(1.372)	(2.779)	(0.122)	(3.164)		
Mid-Western Plain Zone	**–52.955**	**0.037*****	**–0.006**	**–0.007*****	**–0.002**	**–0.008*****	**0.98**	**49**
	(12.299)	**(17.098)**	**(0.485)**	**(2.961)**	**(1.189)**	**(5.541)**		
Agra	–15.088	0.017***	–0.022	–0.009***	0.004**	0.006***	0.92	49
	(2.264)	(5.050)	(1.087)	(2.631)	(2.181)	(2.622)		
Aligarh	–16.640	0.018***	0.013	–0.007**	–0.001	–0.002	0.88	49
	(3.109)	(6.656)	(0.810)	(2.314)	(0.561)	(0.945)		
Etah	–31.378	0.025***	0.024	–0.007**	0.005***	0.004**	0.97	49
	(6.432)	(10.234)	(1.606)	(2.495)	(3.161)	(2.464)		
Mainpuri	–39.787	0.029***	0.015	–0.003	0.002	0.003**	0.97	49
	(7.876)	(11.518)	(1.003)	(1.083)	(1.664)	(2.150)		
Mathura	–12.428	0.016***	0.028	–0.012***	0.003*	0.004**	0.91	49
	(2.081)	(5.189)	(1.538)	(3.593)	(1.906)	(2.229)		
South-Western Semi-Arid Zone	**–20.083**	**0.020*****	**0.012**	**–0.008*****	**0.003****	**0.003****	**0.96**	**49**
	(4.464)	**(8.964)**	**(0.891)**	**(3.109)**	**(1.977)**	**(2.131)**		
Allahabad	–13.253	0.016***	–0.042**	–0.004	0.002	–0.001	0.88	49
	(2.216)	(5.349)	(2.290)	(1.148)	(1.400)	(0.644)		
Etawah	–25.082	0.022***	–0.010	–0.006**	0.003**	0.001	0.97	49
	(5.943)	(10.315)	(0.780)	(2.461)	(2.338)	(1.007)		
Farrukhabad	–56.116	0.038***	0.010	–0.012***	0.000329	–0.006***	0.97	49
	(9.985)	(13.300)	(0.593)	(3.985)	(0.197)	(3.208)		
Fatehpur	–17.498	0.018***	–0.018	–0.007***	0.00016	–0.001	0.94	49
	(4.121)	(8.433)	(1.417)	(2.889)	(0.124)	(1.012)		

(Contd.)

(1)	(2)	(3)	(4)	(5)	(6)	(7)	(8)	(9)
Hardoi	–14.332	0.017***	0.021	–0.005	0.004**	0.004**	0.92	49
	(2.654)	(6.100)	(1.299)	(1.676)	(2.264)	(2.157)		
Kanpur	–29.204	0.024***	–0.004	–0.006*	–0.001	–0.005***	0.90	49
	(4.886)	(8.032)	(0.195)	(1.943)	(0.529)	(2.843)		
Kheri	–46.787	0.033***	0.017	–0.008***	0.003**	–0.001	0.98	49
	(12.192)	(17.109)	(1.458)	(3.859)	(2.500)	(0.630)		
Lucknow	–24.601	0.021***	0.001	–0.005	–0.002	–0.002	0.89	49
	(4.187)	(7.173)	(0.077)	(1.568)	(0.865)	(1.212)		
Raebareli	–13.282	0.016***	–0.054***	–0.007**	0.001	–0.001	0.91	49
	(2.543)	(6.026)	(3.388)	(2.565)	(0.641)	(0.315)		
Sitapur	–19.953	0.019***	0.018	–0.005**	0.006***	0.006***	0.97	49
	(4.502)	(8.681)	(1.319)	(2.230)	(4.923)	(4.598)		
Unnao	–19.082	0.019***	–0.006	–0.00042	0.002	0.003*	0.93	49
	(3.678)	(7.166)	(0.402)	(0.154)	(1.231)	(1.731)		
Central Plain Zone	**–24.108**	**0.023*****	**–0.004**	**–0.006*****	**0.002****	**0.0000056**	**0.97**	**49**
	(6.654)	**(12.420)**	**(0.396)**	**(3.197)**	**(2.015)**	**(0.049)**		
Banda	10.120	0.004***	–0.075***	–0.017***	0.002	0.001	0.68	49
	(1.205)	(0.989)	(2.917)	(3.765)	(0.949)	(0.409)		
Hamirpur	–7.889	0.013***	–0.039**	–0.013***	0.002	–0.001	0.85	49
	(1.229)	(4.095)	(1.965)	(3.853)	(0.992)	(0.600)		
Jalaun	–14.211	0.016***	–0.018	–0.009***	–0.001	0.002	0.90	49
	(2.381)	(5.436)	(0.9690	(2.911)	(0.504)	(0.827)		
Jhansi	–18.444	0.019***	–0.063***	–0.016***	0.007***	0.007***	0.97	49
	(3.429)	(6.844)	(3.829)	(5.386)	(4.326)	(3.826)		
Bundelkhand Zone	**–6.254**	**0.013*****	**–0.048*****	**–0.014*****	**0.003***	**0.002**	**0.93**	**49**
	(1.217)	**(5.062)**	**(3.053)**	**(5.038)**	**(1.883)**	**(1.518)**		
Bahraich	–37.165	0.028***	0.004	–0.010***	0.003	0.001	0.96	49
	(6.157)	(9.190)	(0.241)	(3.209)	(1.639)	(0.744)		

(Contd.)

(1)	(2)	(3)	(4)	(5)	(6)	(7)	(8)	(9)
Basti	–25.054	0.022***	–0.001	–0.010***	0.004**	0.001	0.96	49
	(5.250)	(9.194)	(0.060)	(3.899)	(2.545)	(0.620)		
Deoria	–39.997	0.030***	0.015	–0.010***	–0.002	–0.007***	0.95	49
	(8.508)	(12.533)	(1.073)	(4.080)	(1.286)	(4.892)		
Gonda	–30.964	0.025***	–0.004	–0.009***	0.001	0.003*	0.97	49
	(6.813)	(10.919)	(0.295)	(3.500)	(0.522)	(1.752)		
Gorakhpur	–42.190	0.031***	0.014	–0.008***	–0.00042	–0.006***	0.97	49
	(10.135)	(14.655)	(1.086)	(3.370)	(0.340)	(4.404)		
North-Eastern Plain Zone	**–33.351**	**0.027*****	**0.006**	**–0.009*****	**0.001**	**–0.002**	**0.98**	**49**
	(8.998)	**(14.485)**	**(0.534)**	**(4.706)**	**(0.756)**	**(1.645)**		
Azamgarh	–37.376	0.028***	0.019	–0.010***	0.001	–0.003*	0.94	49
	(6.376)	(9.570)	(1.065)	(3.143)	(0.375)	(1.878)		
Ballia	–22.897	0.021***	0.001	–0.004	0.001	–0.004*	0.87	49
	(3.564)	(6.386)	(0.050)	(1.217)	(0.521)	(1.780)		
Barabanki	–13.912	0.016***	–0.016	–0.013***	0.002	0.002	0.89	49
	(2.005)	(4.671)	(0.766)	(3.365)	(0.945)	(1.078)		
Faizabad	–31.623	0.025***	–0.018	–0.015***	–0.000053	–0.005***	0.94	49
	(5.777)	(9.161)	(1.080)	(4.947)	(0.032)	(2.709)		
Ghazipur	–30.925	0.025***	0.010	–0.007**	0.00022	–0.004**	0.91	49
	(5.062)	(8.045)	(0.547)	(2.125)	(0.122)	(2.293)		
Jaunpur	–36.229	0.028***	–0.014	–0.007**	–0.002	–0.007***	0.93	49
	(6.628)	(9.990)	(0.820)	(2.311)	(1.448)	(3.915)		
Pratapgarh	–25.102	0.022***	–0.018	–0.009***	0.001	–0.005***	0.92	49
	(4.599)	(7.892)	(1.063)	(3.022)	(0.336)	(2.741)		
Sultanpur	–23.817	0.021***	–0.016	–0.010***	0.003	0.001	0.94	49
	(4.136)	(7.309)	(0.934)	(3.052)	(1.552)	(0.380)		
Varanasi	–24.786	0.022***	0.013	–0.006	0.002	–0.004*	0.86	49
	(3.569)	(6.229)	(0.589)	(1.582)	(0.899)	(2.011)		
Eastern Plain Zone	**–25.357**	**0.023*****	**–0.003**	**–0.009*******	**0.001**	**–0.003****	**0.95**	**49**
	(5.550	**(10.054**	**(0.216)**	**(3.719)**	**(0.588)**	**(2.054)**		

(Contd.)

(1)	(2)	(3)	(4)	(5)	(6)	(7)	(8)	(9)
Mirzapur	–16.645	0.018***	0.005	–0.004	0.005**	–0.003	0.80	49
	(2.084)	(4.360)	(0.213)	(0.823)	(2.213)	(1.106)		
Vindhyan Zone	**–16.645**	**0.018*** **	**0.005**	**–0.004**	**0.005** **	**–0.003**	**0.80**	**49**
	(2.084)	**(4.360)**	**(0.213)**	**(0.823)**	**(2.213)**	**(1.106)**		
Hills	–10.016	0.015***	–0.066***	–0.007***	0.002	–0.004***	0.93	49
	(2.417)	(7.031)	(5.240)	(2.997)	(1.435)	(2.611)		
Uttar Pradesh	**–25.467**	**0.024*** **	**–0.007**	**–0.008*** **	**0.001**	**–0.002** **	**0.98**	**49**
	(7.803)	**(14.701)**	**(0.720)**	**(4.463)**	**(0.816)**	**(2.233)**		

Source: Table 4.6.

Notes: 1. Figures in parentheses are t value of the coefficients.

2. Asterisk *, ** and *** indicates coefficient significant at 10 per cent, 5 per cent and 1 per cent level of significance respectively for two tailed t test.

4.5. REGIONAL CONTIGUITY

Growth of agriculture output in high, medium and low growth categories for the pre-green revolution phase, initial green revolution phase, mature green revolution phase, initial post-reform period, new millennium phase as well as overall period from 1960-2011 is presented in Maps 4.1(a) to 4.1(f). Initially, during pre-green revolution phase, there was a long stretch of low developed districts in the lower part of the state neighbouring Madhya Pradesh in South-West, Chhattisgarh in South and Jharkhand in South-East. High growth districts were spread in mostly the upper part of the state and had a narrow strip of contiguity. There are two more small clubs of high growth districts in East. Whereas, middle growth districts had two separate fringes, one in top in North and a small club towards East bordering the state of Bihar. Thereafter, during initial green revolution phase, cluster of high growth districts in the East expanded and formed a continuous stretch from East towards South-West. Another cluster of high growth districts formed in the North. Low growth districts were scattered during this period and middle growth districts formed a big club in the middle of the state with few other small clusters. Thereafter, during mature green revolution, the wave of the high growth spread to most of the areas and a big continuous cluster of districts was formed. During 1990s, some of the districts in South and South-West and few others, adjacent to Haryana and Delhi in North-West recorded medium growth rates. Except for high growth districts forming a long stretch from North-East towards West and South-West, there is no definite pattern of contiguity in low and medium developed districts during this period. However, again during 2000s, some geographical contiguity of low growth districts is seen. Most of the districts in Western region performed poorly and a patch of these districts that formed during 1990s expanded further and formed a long stretch during 2000s. Another cluster of low developed districts emerged in the South. But, except districts in Bundelkhand Zone, there was no definite pattern of high growth districts. The same is true for medium growth districts with no geographical contiguity as such during this period.

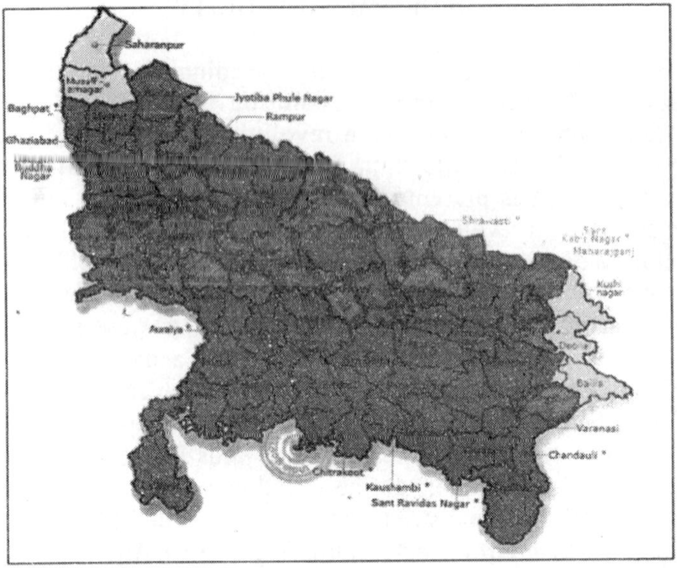

Map 4.1 (a): District-wise growth of value output in Uttar Pradesh: 1960-61 to 1965-66.

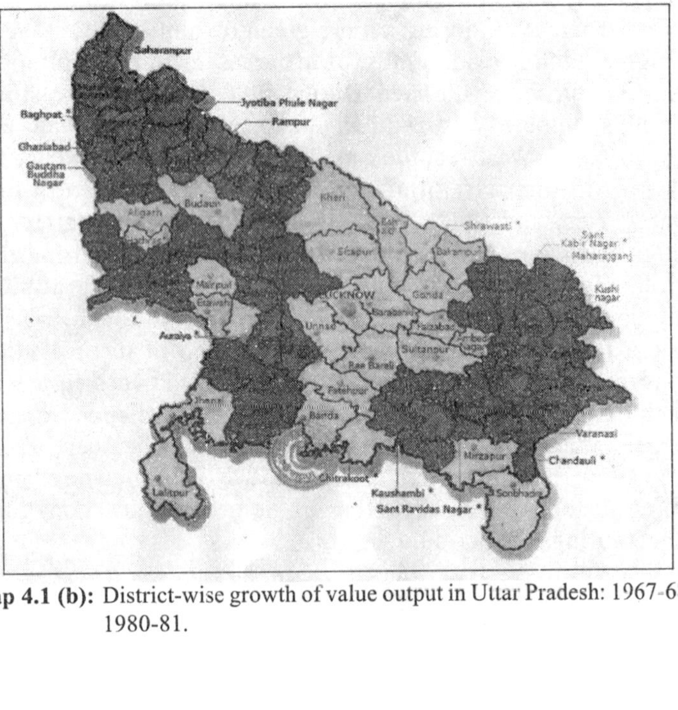

Map 4.1 (b): District-wise growth of value output in Uttar Pradesh: 1967-68 to 1980-81.

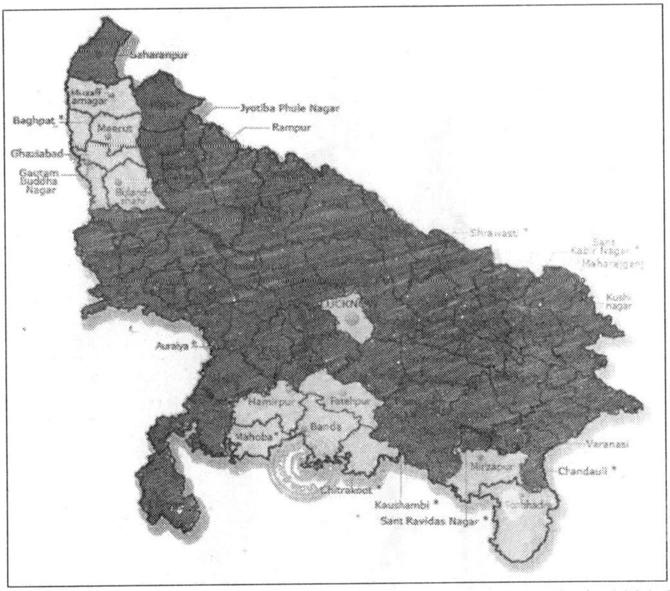

Map 4.1 (c): District-wise growth of value output in Uttar Pradesh: 1981-82 to 1990-91.

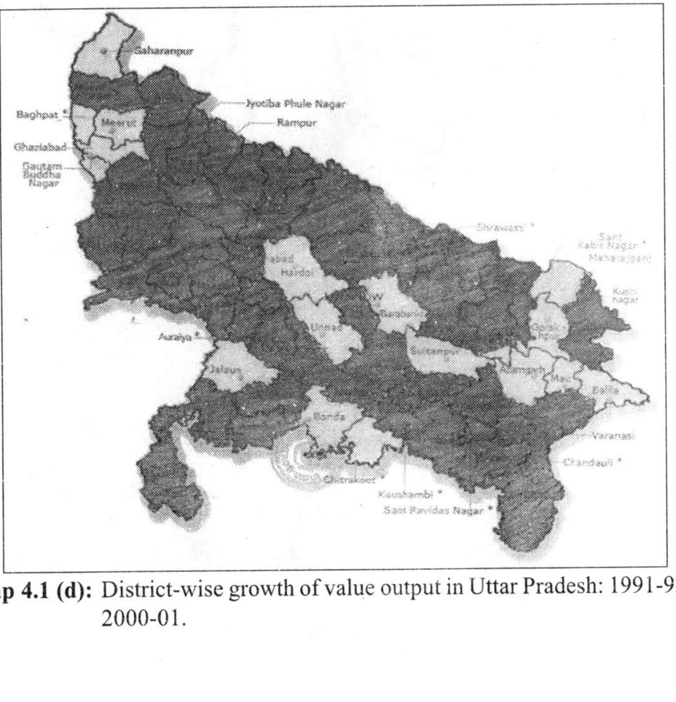

Map 4.1 (d): District-wise growth of value output in Uttar Pradesh: 1991-92 to 2000-01.

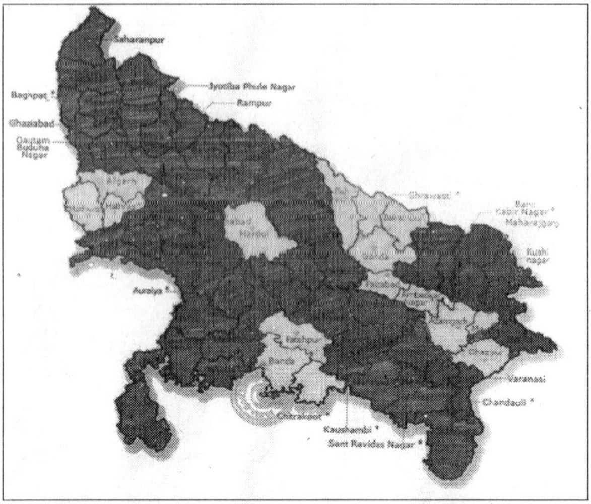

Map 4.1 (e): District-wise growth of value output in Uttar Pradesh: 2001-02 to 2010-11.

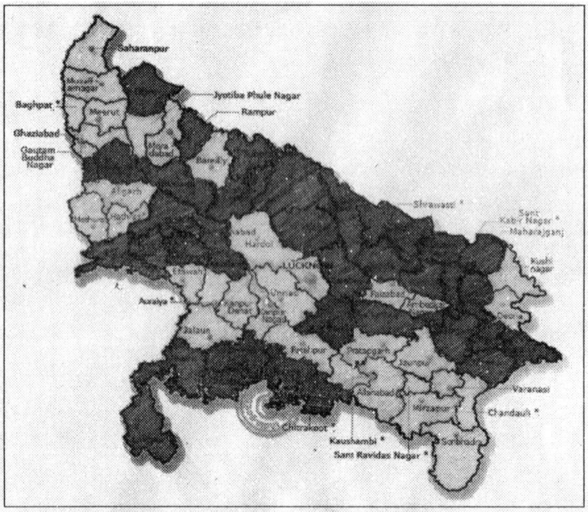

Map 4.1 (f): District-wise growth of value output in Uttar Pradesh: 1960-61 to 2010-11.

High growth rate, Medium growth rate, Low growth rate.

Map 4.1: District-wise growth of value output in Uttar Pradesh: 1960-61 to 2010-11

Source: Table 4.6

Note: These are indicative maps of Uttar Pradesh.

4.6. SUMMARY

The present chapter examined the district and region level performance of Uttar Pradesh agriculture in terms of pattern of growth in area, output and yield of crops over the last five decades and its five sub-periods. Movement of districts across high, medium and low growth categories has been examined to study the changing dynamics of spatial performance of the agriculture in the state. The main findings of this chapter are:

1. For the period as a whole, agricultural performance varies considerably across agro-economic regions in the state. While three of nine zones namely Mid-Western Plain Zone, South-Western Semi-Arid Zone and North-Eastern Plain Zone achieved high growth rates exceeding 3 per cent per annum whereas Hills, Vindhyan and Western Plain Zones recorded low growth during the overall period.
2. The temporal pattern of growth vary considerably across different agro-economic regions, while the agriculture growth in five of the nine agro-economic regions (including Hills) namely-Western Plain Zone, Mid-Western Plain Zone, Central Plain Zone, North-Eastern Plain Zone and Vindhyan Zone follow the overall state pattern of inverted 'U' curve behaviour over time indicating acceleration during the pre-reform period and deceleration in growth during the post-reform period. In rest of the four zones, the agriculture growth accelerated till 1980s, but has not declined thereafter significantly as it accelerated albeit marginally during the post-reform period as well.
3. Like the output growth, the temporal pattern of growth in area under different crops was not uniform over time for the state as a whole as well as for different agro-economic regions. In six of the nine agro-economic regions, namely-Western Plain Zone, Mid-Western Plain Zone, North-Eastern Plain Zone, Eastern Plain Zone, Vindhyan Zone and Hills Zone, there was acceleration in area growth up to 1980s, but it continued to decelerate significantly during the post-reform period. Bundelkhand and Central Plain Zone are the only zones where area continues to accelerate even during the

post-reform period as well. However, there was no significant change in growth of area in South-Western Semi-Arid Zone.

4. Like output and area growth, the growth of crop yield varies considerably across zones and over time. Four agro-economic regions namely-Mid-Western Plain Zone, South-Western Semi-Arid Zone, North-Eastern Plain Zone and Eastern Plain Zone performed extremely well by recording growth exceeding 2.5 per cent per annum. Like the earlier finding, the Hills, Bundelkhand and Western Plain Zones performed poorly on yield growth as well. Therefore, the differential performance of agriculture growth by different agro-economic regions seems to be mainly because of their differential performance in crop yield. Better performing zones achieved high yield growth and poor performing recorded slow yield. There is mix picture regarding acceleration/deceleration of crop yield during the post-reform period. The yield growth accelerated up to mature green revolution phase in all the zones, but the post-reform period does not follow any specific pattern in this context. While, the yield growth decelerated during post-reform period in Mid-Western Plain Zone, it accelerated in South-Western Semi-Arid Zone, North-Eastern Plain Zone, Vindhyan Zone and Hills Zone. In remaining four zones, the crop yield continues to grow at the same pace, it neither accelerated nor decelerated significantly.
5. The number of districts recording different levels of growth vary considerably over time. The number of high growth districts increased from 15 during the pre-green revolution period to 37 during 1980s and declined to 12 during 2000s. The low performing districts depict just opposite behaviour, as the number of districts recording less than 2 per cent per annum growth declined from 27 during the pre-green revolution period to just one during 1980s, but their number increased to 24 during 2000s.
6. Though all districts experienced significant improvement in agriculture growth, but there are large inter-district variations in growth. The growth varies from 4 per cent per annum for Moradabad and Pilibhit districts to about 1 per cent per annum in Bulandshahr and Hamirpur districts. Banda is odd man out district as it has not recorded any significant improvement in growth for the last five decades.

7. Growth accelerated in almost all the districts with exception of Muzaffarnagar, Saharanpur, Bijnor, Mainpuri, Allahabad, Lucknow, Unnao, Ballia, Varanasi and Mirzapur districts. Almost half of the districts recorded significant deceleration during the post-reform period whereas, agriculture growth accelerated in 14 of the 47 districts (including hills) units in the state. 12 districts just continue to grow with the same pattern during the post-reform period at which they were growing during 1980s.
8. During different decades, so far as the geographical contiguity of districts is concerned, they have a definite pattern during pre-green revolution, mature green revolution and during the last period from 2001-02 to 2010-11. During pre-green revolution period, most of the districts were performing poorly and had a continuous stretch with only intrusion of high performing districts in between. During 1980s, except for districts neighbouring Madhya Pradesh and Chhattisgarh in South-West and bordering Haryana and Delhi in North-West that recorded medium growth rates, rest of the districts form a continuous stretch of big landscape recording high growth rates. During 2001-2010, the high growth districts form contiguity in Bundelkhand Zone whereas, they were scattered at all places in the rest of the state. Only low growth districts have a continuous stretch from North to South and South-West. However, for the period as a whole, it indicates that there are forces other than climatic conditions that play a significant role in agriculture growth in a big state like Uttar Pradesh.

5

Dynamics of Agricultural Development in Uttar Pradesh: Variations Across Districts and Agro-Economic Regions

5.1. INTRODUCTION

The preceding chapter was devoted to analyze the pattern of agricultural growth and variations therein across districts and agro-economic regions over the period 1960-61 to 2010-11. This chapter examines the temporal and spatial variations in the level of agricultural development (land productivity) in the state. For temporal analysis, the level of agricultural development is measured for the triennium ending 1960-63, 1970-73, 1980-83, 1990-93, 2000-03 and 2008-11. For spatial analysis, the level of agricultural development is measured for all 46 district units formed after clubbing newly formed districts (among total 72 districts) in the state. Thereafter, like our earlier analysis, these districts are broadly classified into eight agro-economic regions and hill districts are taken as separate heading under Hills and referred as ninth zone. These districts at present are part of newly formed Uttarakhand state bifurcated from Uttar Pradesh. The composition of all these zones is same as explained in the previous chapter.

More specifically, the objective of the present chapter is to examine the spatial (district and region) pattern of agricultural development (land productivity) in the state and study disparities therein across the districts at different points of time in the state.

The chapter is organized into six sections. After a brief introduction and underlying the objective and hypothesis of the chapter in section 5.1, we discussed the methodology used in succeeding section 5.2. Section 5.3 discusses level of agricultural development at the regional level in Uttar Pradesh for triennium ending 1960-63, 1970-73, 1980-83, 1990-93, 2000-03 and 2008-11. Section 5.4 (i) examines distribution of districts into high, medium and low levels of agricultural development in Uttar Pradesh at different points of time since sixties. Thereafter, district-wise level of land productivity is undertaken in sub-section 5.4 (ii). Extent of inter-district inequality in productivity and value output levels across districts in the state have been examined in sub-section 5.4 (iii). Regional contiguity of districts in the level of land productivity is presented with the help of maps in section 5.5. Thereafter, section 5.6 reports the main findings of the chapter.

5.2. METHODOLOGY

We propose to examine the dynamics of agricultural development in Uttar Pradesh in this chapter, we will also compare the dynamics of inter-regional, inter-district disparities in agricultural development. For this empirical analysis following methodology would be used in the present chapter:

5.2 (i) Agricultural development: Level of land productivity has been taken as proxy of agricultural development. The district- and region-wise level of land productivity is measured as:

$$\text{Land productivity} = \frac{\text{Value output of all crops in the district/zone}}{\text{District/zone-wise net sown area}}$$

$$\text{Value Output of all crop} = \frac{\text{Value output of 35 crops}}{\text{Total area under 35 crops}} \times \text{Total cropped area}$$

Land productivity is measured for triennium average to smoothen weather and random shocks.

5.2 (ii) Instability in development: The coefficient of variation (as explained earlier) has been taken as proxy for instability in level of agricultural development over time.

5.2 (iii) Inequality in agricultural development: The inequality in literature has been measured in many different ways. Though the Gini coefficient is the most popular measure of inequality, but being less sensitive to distribution to the low and high level distribution, it needs to be complemented by other more intuitive measures of inequality like share of top to bottom quintiles in production, ratio of top to bottom quintile (quartile or deciles). These measures are as follows:

(a) *Gini coefficient (G):*

$$G = (N+1)/(N-1) - 2/[N(N-1)\mu][\Sigma \downarrow (i=1) \uparrow n\, P_i X_i]$$

Where,

μ is mean of level of land productivity,

P_i is the rank of district i, with level of land productivity X_i, such that the highest district receives a rank of 1 and the lowest a rank of N.

(b) *Share of top quintile districts:* Districts were arranged into ascending order of their productivity levels and then divided into five parts and the share of top and bottom quintile districts were estimated as follows:

$$= \frac{\text{Value output of top (nine) districts}}{\text{Total value output}} \times 100$$

(c) *Share of bottom quintile districts:*

$$= \frac{\text{Value output of bottom (nine) districts}}{\text{Total value output}} \times 100$$

Thereafter, the share of top/bottom quintile districts was estimated as follows:

$$= \frac{\text{\% share of top quintile districts in productivity}}{\text{\% share of bottom quintile districts in productivity}}$$

(d) *Ratio of top to bottom quintile districts*:

$$= \frac{\text{Average productivity level of top quintile districts}}{\text{Average productivity level of bottom quintile districts}}$$

EMPIRICAL FINDINGS

5.3. AGRICULTURAL DEVELOPMENT (LAND PRODUCTIVITY): INTER-REGIONAL VARIATIONS

5.3 (i) Region-wise level of agricultural development in Uttar Pradesh: 1960-63 to 2008-11

Region-wise level of agricultural development measured as total value output of net sown area for triennium ending 1960-63, 1970-73, 1980-83, 1990-93 and 2008-11 is provided in Table 5.1. It is evident that Western Plain Zone was agriculturally most developed zone in Uttar Pradesh during triennium ending 1960-63 recording the highest level of land productivity of Rs. 42,140 per hectare. All other zones were comparatively at very low levels of development. It was only South-Western Semi-Arid Zone that followed the highest developed Western Plain Zone, but the level of productivity in the zone was only Rs. 25,859 per hectare. Bundelkhand Zone with productivity of just Rs. 15,135 per hectare was at the lowest level. Some other zones such as Vindhyan Zone and North-Eastern Plain Zone also recorded very low levels of land productivity. It was less than half of the productivity level as recorded by Western Plain Zone.

Table 5.1: Region-wise Level of Agriculture Productivity in Uttar Pradesh: 1960-63 to 2008-11

Period → *Regions* ↓	*Land Productivity in Triennium (Rs. per hectare at 2010-11 prices)*					
	1960-63	*1970-73*	*1980-83*	*1990-93*	*2000-03*	*2008-11*
Western Plain Zone	42140	50107	66357	86973	84430	89384
Mid-Western Plain Zone	20780	25774	40277	59199	68046	71492
South Western Semi-Arid Zone	25859	30296	35155	49984	60919	76612
Central Plain Zone	20978	23426	29857	42265	51433	58155
Bundelkhand Zone	15135	16576	19409	23249	27463	30495
North-Eastern Plain Zone	17092	18383	25763	38814	47923	53446
Eastern Plain Zone	22055	21393	30292	44233	50059	54923
Vindhyan Zone	15966	17238	20371	24730	33141	29354
Hills	16075	24568	27697	36843	38094	41897
Uttar Pradesh	21988	24861	33130	46440	53283	59085

Source: Same as in Table 4.2(a).

Thereafter, in triennium ending 1970-73, there was an increase in the level of productivity at the state level from Rs. 21,988 per hectare during sixties to Rs. 24,861 per hectare during seventies. All the zones, with exception of Eastern Plain Zone, also recorded an increase in the land productivity. However, it was again the Western Plain Zone and South-Western Semi-Arid Zone that maintained the top two positions by recording productivity of Rs. 50,107 and Rs. 30,296 per hectare respectively. Earlier Mid-Western Plain Zone and Central Plain Zone maintained almost same levels in agricultural development, however during this period, Mid-Western Plain Zone outperformed the Central Plain Zone (*see* Fig. 5.1). The gap between these two zones widened from 0.94 per cent to 9.10 per cent during these periods. There was almost similar pattern of increase in land productivity across zones. Almost all the zones recorded an increase, but most of the zones maintained their relative positions in ranking during this period as well. Bundelkhand Zone was at the lowest level of development among all the zones, though it recorded an increase from Rs. 15,135 to Rs. 16,576 per hectare in land productivity.

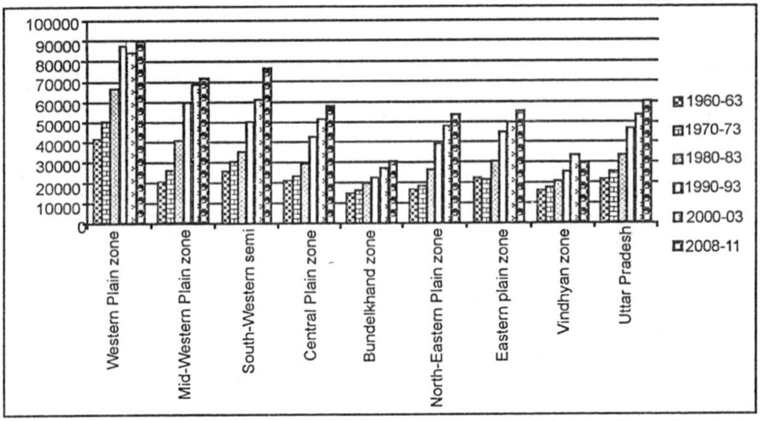

Figure 5.1: Region-wise level of agricultural productivity in Uttar Pradesh: 1960-63 to 2008-11

Source: Table 5.1.

The triennium ending 1980-83, further recorded an increase in land productivity at the state as well as at regional level in Uttar Pradesh. Out of total nine zones (including Hills), Western Plain Zone, Mid-Western Plain Zone and South-Western Semi-Arid Zone recorded productivity levels above the state average. Though Western Plain Zone continued to record the highest level of land productivity during eighties as well, Mid-Western Plain Zone surged ahead of South-Western Semi-Arid Zone and followed Western Plain Zone in highest productivity levels. It recorded significant increase from Rs. 25,774 per hectare during seventies to Rs. 40,277 per hectare during eighties. Bundelkhand Zone continued to be the least developed zone during 1980s also. Vindhyan Zone also performed poorly during this period. There was not much difference in the productivity levels between the lowest developed Bundelkhand Zone and Vindhyan Zone during 1980-83.

On the contrary to deceleration in growth rates in agriculture output and yield levels, as discussed in the previous chapter, the level of agricultural development recorded an increase during the initial phase of reform period in 1990-93. However like the previous periods, the top and bottom positions in agricultural productivity were recorded by same Western Plain Zone and Bundelkhand Zone respectively. The level of productivity in Bundelkhand Zone and Vindhyan Zone was less than three times the level of productivity recorded by Western Plain Zone. Moreover, the state along with almost all the zones recorded considerable improvements in land productivity.

The triennium ending 2000-03 recorded decrease in productivity level by Rs. 2,543 per hectare in Western Plain Zone as compared with 1990s, but even then the zone recorded highest level of land productivity. On the other hand Bundelkhand—the 'Achilles Heel' of Uttar Pradesh agriculture—continued to be the most lagging in terms of agricultural development since 1960s. Among other zones, Mid-Western Plain Zone and South-Western Semi-Arid Zone performed comparatively better than rest of the zones. The North-Eastern Plain Zone, Eastern Plain Zone, Vindhyan Zone and Hills continued to record low productivity. This holds true at all points of time from 1960-63 to 2008-11. During 2008-11 also, Western Plain Zone retained its top position. However, unlike all earlier periods, Bundelkhand Zone seems to have progressed a little and shifted upward from the bottom position. Vindhyan Zone on the other hand recorded a decline in land productivity and was at the lowest level of development among all the zones. There is a wide gap between the most developed and the least developed zones in the state.

To examine relative development across zones, we compared the level of development in each region *vis-à-vis* the level of productivity in the most developed Western Plain Zone. Information in this context is detailed in Table 5.2.

Table 5.2: Regional Gap (Percentage) in Agricultural Development *vis-à-vis* Western Plain Zone in Uttar Pradesh: 1960-63 to 2008-11

Period→ Regions ↓	*Gap (percentage) with respect to Western Plain Zone*					
	1960-63	*1970-73*	*1980-83*	*1990-93*	*2000-03*	*2008-10*
Mid-Western Plain Zone	50.69	48.56	39.30	31.93	19.41	20.02
South-Western Semi-Arid Zone	38.63	39.54	47.02	42.53	27.85	14.29
Central Plain Zone	50.22	53.25	55.00	51.40	39.08	34.94
Bundelkhand Zone	64.08	66.92	70.75	73.27	67.47	65.88
North-Eastern Plain Zone	59.44	63.31	61.17	55.37	43.24	40.21
Eastern Plain Zone	47.66	57.30	54.35	49.14	40.71	38.55
Vindhyan Zone	62.11	65.60	69.30	71.57	60.75	67.16
Hills	61.85	50.97	58.26	57.64	54.88	53.13

Source: Table 5.1.

The three important features emerge regarding the relative performance of different agro-economic zones in the state of Uttar Pradesh over the study period.

1. First is that, the gap between the most developed Western Plain Zone and remaining eight zones (including hills) declined over time with exception of Bundelkhand and Vindhyan Zone. While in Vindhyan Zone the gap increased from 62.11 per cent to 67.16 per cent whereas it increased marginally from 64.08 per cent to 65.88 per cent in Bundelkhand Zone. The gap has declined by more than half in case of Mid-Western Plain and South-Western Semi-Arid Zones, which are in neighbourhood of the Western Plain Zone. Nevertheless, still there is a big difference in Western Plain Zone and these two other developed zones of Uttar Pradesh.

2. Second is that, the overall pattern of declining gap between most developed and other zones notwithstanding, it follow a different pattern over time in different zones. For example the Mid-Western Plain Zone experienced almost continuous decline in gap over the past decades, whereas in rest of the zones, it follows inverted 'U' pattern of widening gap between the Western Plain and the North-Eastern Plain Zone and the other zones and declining thereafter. Even the Bundelkhand Zone which experienced marginal increase in gap also experienced inverted 'U' relationship of first widening the gap up to 1990-93 and declining thereafter. Similarly, Vindhyan Zone continues to experience increasing gap up to 1990-93, it declined

during 2000-03, but increased marginally up to 67.16 per cent in 2008-11. With exception of 1970-73, even Hill Zone also show inverted 'U' curve relationship.

3. Third is, widening and bridging of gap between Western Plain Zone and other zones seems to suggest that the level of agricultural development was first diverging across zones and after 1980s it started converging. However, this observation would be further explored in the subsequent analysis.

5.4. AGRICULTURAL DEVELOPMENT: INTRA-REGIONAL AND INTER-DISTRICT VARIATIONS

5.4 (i) Distribution of Districts by Level of Land Productivity in Uttar Pradesh: 1960-63 to 2008-11

Region-wise distribution of districts in level of land productivity in high, medium and low productivity levels is presented in Table 5.3. The districts having productivity more than Rs. 71,000 per hectare are categorized as high productivity districts, districts with productivity levels between Rs. 52,000 to Rs. 71,000 per hectare are categorized as medium productivity districts and the districts with less than Rs. 52,000 per hectare land productivity comes under low productivity districts.

To begin with, the level of agricultural development in the state was distressing as all the districts from all the zones in the state were having low level of productivity with land productivity less than Rs. 52,000 per hectare during triennium ending 1960-63. This corroborates our earlier findings that during pre-green revolution phase, there was very low level of development with low growth rates. However, during 1970-73, two districts, both from Western Plain Zone, those were in low level of productivity during 1960s graduated to medium productivity levels. Still there was no district in any of the zone to reach high level of development even in this period also.

In triennium ending 1980-83, one district—Muzaffarnagar was able to make its way in high level of development category with productivity exceeding Rs. 71,000 per hectare. Since green revolution technology was mostly concentrated in Western region in Uttar Pradesh, all high and medium developed category districts during this period were from Western Plain Zone only. The level of development in all other zones was still not satisfactory. As many as 42 districts out of total 46 district units were still below Rs. 52,000 per hectare land productivity level.

Table 5.3: Region-wise Distribution of Districts in Level of Land Productivity in Uttar Pradesh: 1960-63 to 2008-11

Period→ Regions ↓	*Level of productivity (Rs. per hectare)*	*Number of districts in triennium*					
		1960-63	*1970-73*	*1980-83*	*1990-93*	*2000-03*	*2008-11*
Western Plain Zone	High (>71000)	0	0	1	3	2	4
	Medium (52000-71000)	0	2	3	1	2	0
	Low (<52000)	4	2	0	0	0	0
Mid-Western Plain Zone	High (>71000)	0	0	0	1	4	4
	Medium (52000-71000)	0	0	0	5	2	3
	Low (<52000)	7	7	7	1	1	0
South-Western Semi-Arid Zone	High (>71000)	0	0	0	0	0	4
	Medium (52000-71000)	0	0	0	2	5	1
	Low (<52000)	5	5	5	3	0	0
Central Plain Zone	High (>71000)	0	0	0	0	1	3
	Medium (52000-71000)	0	0	0	1	2	3
	Low (<52000)	11	11	11	10	8	5
Bundelkhand Zone	High (>71000)	0	0	0	0	0	0
	Medium (52000-71000)	0	0	0	0	0	0
	Low (<52000)	4	4	4	4	4	4
North-Eastern Plain Zone	High (>71000)	0	0	0	0	0	0
	Medium (52000-71000)	0	0	0	1	1	4
	Low (<52000)	5	5	5	4	4	1
Eastern Plain Zone	High (>71000)	0	0	0	0	0	0
	Medium (52000-71000)	0	0	0	0	2	5
	Low (<52000)	9	9	9	9	7	4
Vindhyan Zone	High (>71000)	0	0	0	0	0	0
	Medium (52000-71000)	0	0	0	0	0	0
	Low (<52000)	1	1	1	1	1	1
Uttar Pradesh	High (>71000)	0	0	1	4	7	15
	Medium (52000-71000)	0	2	3	10	14	16
	Low (<52000)	46	44	42	32	25	15

Source: Table 5.4.

The number of districts in the high productivity range increased from one in triennium ending 1980-83 to four districts in 1990-93. Among these, three districts namely—Meerut, Muzaffarnagar and Saharanpur were again from most developed Western Plain Zone and one district—Bijnor was from its neighbouring Mid-Western Plain Zone. In addition, there was nearly three times increase in number of medium productivity districts in the state. Nearly half of the medium productivity districts were concentrated in Mid-Western Plain Zone whereas Western Plain Zone, Central Plain Zone and North-Eastern Plain Zone have one district each in the medium productivity range. South-Western Semi-Arid Zone that recorded no district in this category during previous period could make way for Aligarh and

Etah districts to register themselves in mid-productivity category. Bundelkhand Zone, Eastern Plain Zone and Vindhyan Zone still remained in the low level of development. All the districts from these zones were still trapped in low productivity levels.

By 2000-03, the number of low productivity districts had declined considerably to 25 districts from 32 districts during 1990s. But still, all the districts from Bundelkhand Zone and Vindhyan Zone were in low productivity levels. However, in addition to Western region the development wave made headway to dry sub-humid Central region also. As Farrukhabad district from Central Plain Zone recorded high productivity and two other districts namely—Etawah and Kheri were in medium productivity range. In addition there was a gradual progress in Mid-Western Plain Zone. Four of total five districts in the zone recorded high levels of productivity exceeding Rs. 71,000 per hectare during this period. On the other hand, Western Plain Zone recorded decline in number of high productivity districts from three to two districts. There was a gradual increase from 10 districts during 1990-93 to 14 districts during 2000-03 to record medium levels of productivity.

The scenario in 2008-11 period was favourable for almost all the zones. But there was no change in Bundelkhand and Vindhyan Zones. All the districts in these zones were still under low levels of development. Finally, 15 districts in the state could make headway in high productivity range. It included all the districts from Western Plain Zone, four districts each from Mid-Western Plain Zone and South-Western Semi-Arid Zone and three districts from Central Plain Zone. Another 16 districts registered medium productivity, ranging between Rs. 52,000 to Rs. 71,000 per hectare. These were mainly from North-Eastern Plain Zone and Eastern Plain Zone. The number of low growth districts was all time low at only 15 districts during this period.

To sum up, the agricultural economy of Uttar Pradesh seems to be trapped under low levels of development till 1980s. However in triennium ending 1990-93, there was a gradual shift from low productivity to high and medium productivity levels. Thereafter, the number of low productivity districts declined from 46 in 1960-63 to 25 districts in the period 2000-03 and further to 15 districts during 2008-11. There were 15 districts to join high productivity range and 16 districts recorded medium land productivity range at the end. Except districts in Bundelkhand Zone and Vindhyan Zone districts in other zones made significant comparative improvements in land productivity levels.

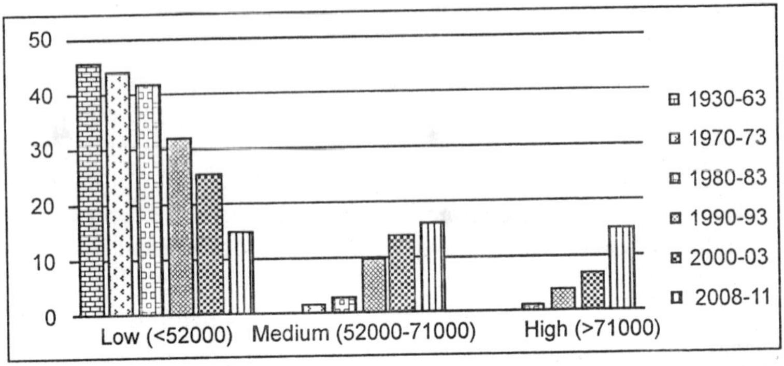

Figure 5.2: Distribution of districts in level of land productivity in Uttar Pradesh: 1960-63 to 2008-11.

The bar diagram presents gradual shifting of districts from low to medium and higher productivity levels. There is continuous decline in low productivity districts during 1960-63 to 2008-11 period. Whereas the distribution of districts across medium and high productivity ranges seems to be improving in each successive period.

5.4 (ii) District-wise Level of Agricultural Development in Uttar Pradesh: 1960-63 to 2008-11

Spatial distribution of districts across zones by their level of development—land productivity detailed in Table 5.4 reveals interesting geographical pattern of agricultural development at the district-level in Uttar Pradesh.

Initially in 1960-63, all the districts recorded low levels in land productivity that was below Rs. 52,000 per hectare. But comparatively Bulandshahr, Meerut and Muzaffarnagar districts from Western Plain Zone recorded more than twice the level of land productivity recorded at the state level in Uttar Pradesh. In addition, the level of development in Saharanpur district from Western Plain Zone, Bareilly, Bijnor and Rampur from Mid-Western Plain Zone, Agra, Aligarh, Etah and Mathura from South-Western Semi-Arid Zone, Etawah, Farrukhabad, Hardoi and Kanpur from Central Plain Zone, Deoria from North-Eastern Plain Zone and Barabanki, Faizabad and Varanasi from

Table 5.4: District-wise Level of Land Productivity in Uttar Pradesh: 1960-63 to 2008-11

Period→ Districts/Regions↓	*Agriculture Productivity in Triennium (Rs. Per Hectare at Rs. 2010-11 prices)*					
	1960-63	*1970-73*	*1980-83*	*1990-93*	*2000-03*	*2008-11*
(1)	(2)	(3)	(4)	(5)	(6)	(7)
Bulandshahr	43393	41282	52358	62558	67367	73753
Meerut	45944	55778	69263	95654	95074	103123
Muzaffarnagar	44364	60759	82654	103412	102168	105275
Saharanpur	34059	43195	60847	83553	70712	71972
Western Plain Zone	**42140**	**50107**	**66357**	**86973**	**84430**	**89384**
Bareilly	22616	24466	36004	53906	62319	63261
Bijnor	26499	34277	50061	78654	83609	79809
Budaun	16473	22616	30881	41937	51986	62016
Moradabad	20365	25582	45653	62582	72475	74776
Pilibhit	21370	25899	43378	65709	75216	78260
Rampur	23785	26797	45091	64265	75333	77707
Shahjahanpur	17586	22197	33468	53136	62013	69833
Mid-Western Plain Zone	**20780**	**25774**	**40277**	**59199**	**68046**	**71492**
Agra	22989	25842	30820	43355	58832	75193
Aligarh	31210	40171	44467	54309	59118	71341
Etah	24183	27714	34805	55445	70275	80273
Mainpuri	20735	25290	31056	48811	58983	88306
Mathura	28617	30154	32276	47455	57927	69645
South-Western Semi-Arid Zone	**25859**	**30296**	**35155**	**49984**	**60919**	**76612**
Allahabad	20488	23917	29171	36442	41035	43718
Etawah	22990	26838	34995	48285	61572	73685
Farrukhabad	22317	25661	38506	64286	80791	85889
Fatehpur	21832	25171	30109	37142	42675	48466
Hardoi	23468	24243	26768	39216	44796	55710
Kanpur	22645	25494	30977	46124	50251	52923
Kheri	19985	23595	31733	49881	67957	71434
Lucknow	20013	19368	29756	35296	42547	49204
Raebareli	19524	22133	26364	35078	39871	48326
Sitapur	18945	19611	26451	37921	50781	58509
Unnao	18068	19775	25263	32211	37444	47790
Central Plain Zone	**20978**	**23426**	**29857**	**42265**	**51433**	**58155**
Banda	17406	17163	20591	20244	23751	22291
Hamirpur	14080	15866	18841	21346	23399	25484
Jalaun	15932	18458	22535	29942	36144	37112
Jhansi	13233	15284	16657	23562	29332	37968
Bundelkhand Zone	**15135**	**16576**	**19409**	**23249**	**27463**	**30495**
Bahraich	12673	12893	17046	28781	39609	44566
Basti	17424	19165	23503	35385	42969	52030
Deoria	22054	22507	35771	53761	58989	58341
Gonda	15402	16806	24072	33260	48432	56658
Gorakhpur	18044	20569	29152	45181	51672	56203
North Eastern Plain Zone	**17092**	**18383**	**25763**	**38814**	**47923**	**53446**

(Contd.)

(1)	(2)	(3)	(4)	(5)	(6)	(7)
North-Eastern Plain Zone	**17092**	**18383**	**25763**	**38814**	**47923**	**53446**
Azamgarh	21411	19535	28092	46750	50728	55458
Ballia	20631	25839	31493	39306	45844	49567
Barabanki	29260	24014	32251	47521	62349	70147
Faizabad	23741	22183	34642	49568	56410	62851
Ghazipur	20710	21315	28701	45446	47501	50934
Jaunpur	20346	21497	32710	44184	48259	53926
Pratapgarh	18174	17783	27036	37829	40807	42806
Sultanpur	19565	19194	26893	41761	49218	53952
Varanasi	23575	22413	31009	42387	47544	51290
Eastern Plain Zone	**22055**	**21393**	**30292**	**44233**	**50059**	**54923**
Mirzapur	15966	17238	20371	24730	33141	29354
Vindhyan Zone	**15966**	**17238**	**20371**	**24730**	**33141**	**29354**
Hills	16075	24568	27697	36843	38094	41897
Uttar Pradesh	**21988**	**24861**	**33130**	**46440**	**53283**	**59085**

Source: Same as in Table 4.2(a).

Eastern Plain Zone was above the state average of Rs. 21,988 per hectare. On the other hand, Bahraich from North-Eastern Plain Zone recorded the lowest level of Rs. 12,673 per hectare followed by Jhansi with Rs. 13,233 per hectare and Hamirpur district with Rs. 14,080 per hectare land productivity, both from Bundelkhand Zone. Concentration of the most developed and chronically underdeveloped districts in specific regions however is a known phenomenon in agriculture sector. As it is evident, the level of development in highest productivity district is more than three times the productivity level recorded by the lowest district in the state.

Thereafter, during triennium ending 1970-73, there was acceleration in land productivity at the state level as well in all zones except Eastern Plain Zone. At the district-level also, almost similar pattern of increase in land productivity is evident, however Bulandshahr from Western Plain Zone, Kheri from Central Plain Zone, Banda from Bundelkhand Zone and as many as six districts of total nine in Eastern Plain Zone recorded reverses in the productivity level. The overall impact of decline in majority of districts in Eastern Plain Zone led to decline in productivity at the regional level as well. However, still Bahraich, Jhansi and Hamirpur remained at the bottom three levels of productivity during this period also. Though majority of the districts, nearly 80 per cent of them recorded an increase in land productivity, among these, Muzaffarnagar district recorded significant increase by Rs. 16,395 per hectare during 1970-73 as compared with triennium ending 1960-63.

The introduction of new technology during 1980s had a profound impact on the levels of agriculture productivity. All the districts in the state recorded considerable increase in land productivity during 1980-83. Muzaffarnagar district carried on the momentum of significant increase during this period as well. Moreover, nearly 15 districts in the state recorded more than Rs. 10,000 per hectare increase in agricultural productivity during this period. Until 1980s, the lowest level of productivity was recorded by Bahraich district in the North-Eastern Plain Zone, but there was a shifting of districts where the least productivity was recorded by Jhansi district from Bundelkhand Zone. Bahraich still remained among the three least productive districts in the state.

During triennium ending 1990-93, there was nearly two times increase in level of productivity at the state level as compared with Rs. 21,988 per hectare in 1960-63. Interestingly as many as 29 districts also recorded more than two fold increase in productivity levels during these two periods. On the contrary, three districts—Banda, Hamirpur and Jhansi from Bundelkhand Zone were at very low levels of development with productivity less than Rs. 25,000 per hectare. There was nearly 80 per cent gap between the lowest—Banda district and the highest developed Muzaffarnagar district in land productivity levels. As compared with the previous period, where all the districts recorded an increase in land productivity, it was only Banda district that experienced a decline by Rs. 345 per hectare during this period, whereas rest all the districts recorded an increase.

Among all the districts in Western Plain Zone that recorded tremendous increase in level of productivity since 1960s, Meerut, Muzaffarnagar and Saharanpur however faced reverses during triennium ending 2000-03. There was decline in productivity levels in these districts. Though, Muzaffarnagar still remained the top district in land productivity levels. But decline in three out of total four districts in one of the highest productivity zone is a matter of serious concern. There is a need to revive technology advancement and shift the composition of crop sector, as the level of development in agriculture depends mainly upon these factors. All other districts in the state, however continued the momentum of increase in land productivity during this period as well. Among these all, Agra and Etah districts from South-Western Semi-Arid Zone, Farrukhabad and Kheri from Central Plain Zone, Gonda from North-Eastern Plain Zone and Barabanki from Eastern Plain Zone recorded a noteworthy improvement in productivity levels during 2000-03 as compared with 1990-93 period.

During 2008-11, the districts in Western Plain Zone made for the reverses in land productivity registered during the previous period. However on the other hand, Bijnor, Deoria and Mirzapur districts that recorded a continuous increase in land productivity till 2000-03, however recorded a decline in 2008-11. In addition, Banda district that did not have any uniform pattern of development also recorded a decline from Rs. 23,751 per hectare during previous period to Rs. 22,291 per hectare during this period.

For the entire period under study, only except during 1960-63, Muzaffarnagar district continued to be the highest productivity district and the districts in Bundelkhand Zone were among the lowest category in level of development. Bahraich district however seems to have made a significant improvement in land productivity over the years. To sum up, agriculture sector in the state seems to have recorded a significant improvement in level of land productivity since the introduction of new technology. Western Plain Zone was the most developed and retained its position till the end. The zone was the earliest to harvest rich dividends on adoption of new technology, moreover, the zone is rich in natural resources as well. On the contrary, Bundelkhand Zone and Vindhyan Zone were the least developed zones with comparatively very low levels of productivity.

5.4 (iii) Agricultural Development and Inter-District Disparities in Uttar Pradesh: 1960-63 to 2008-11

To measure trends in inter-district inequality in the process of agricultural development, as discussed earlier, we estimated the coefficient of variation, Gini coefficient, share of each quintile in total value output for the periods 1960-63, 1970-73, 1980-83, 1990-93, 2000-03 and 2008-11 and cumulative frequency of districts in level of land productivity. The estimates are presented in Table 5.5.

There are two important patterns which emerge:

1. Gini coefficient of inequality, the share of top to bottom quintile in agriculture production as well as the ratio of top to bottom quintile of land productivity shows a marginal increase in inter-district inequality in the level of agricultural development in the state of Uttar Pradesh during 1960-63 to 2008-11.

2. There is no unique pattern of changes in inter-district inequality over the last five decades of study period. The inter-district disparities continuously widened from 1960-63 to 1990-93 and declined thereafter. All the indicators of inequality validate this inverted 'U' shape behaviour of inter-district disparities in agricultural development in the state over the last five decades. These patterns are in line up with earlier observations of inverted 'U' relationship in agriculture productivity at the state level because both area and output also depict inverted 'U' curve relationship.

Table 5.5: Changes in Inter-District Inequality in Average Land Productivity and Output Levels: 1960-63 to 2008-11

Measures	*Inequality in Land Productivity in triennium*					
	1960-63	*1970-73*	*1980-83*	*1990-93*	*2000-03*	*2008-11*
Gini coefficient of inequality	0.162	0.177	0.189	0.198	0.176	0.170
Coefficient of variation	32.66	37.39	37.99	37.06	31.34	30.08
Share (%) of the Bottom quintile	17.37	15.50	14.58	12.67	14.22	14.28
Share (%) of the Middle quintile	53.53	54.69	54.28	57.62	58.62	61.23
Share (%) of the Top quintile	29.10	29.81	31.14	29.71	27.16	24.49
Share of the Top/Bottom quintiles	1.67	1.92	2.14	2.34	1.91	1.71
Level of land productivity of Bottom quintile districts	15249	16740	20986	27684	33421	36133
Level of land productivity of Middle quintile districts	20876	23148	31020	44641	52789	59793
Level of land productivity of Top quintile districts	34170	40019	54864	75630	80628	85982
Ratio of Top to Bottom Quintile districts	2.24	2.39	2.61	2.73	2.41	2.38

Source: Same as in Table 4.2(a).

This may be due to two main reasons: (i) in developed regions technology has almost exhausted and these regions are facing slowdown or stagnation in development levels; and (ii) in low developed regions, technology improved significantly over time and these regions have experienced comparative high growth leading to bridging of inter-district productivity gaps.

The cumulative frequency distribution of districts ranked by land productivity levels in each subsequent period shifted away from the vertical axis towards horizontal axis suggesting a continuous movement of districts towards a more superior distribution (Figure 5.3). The cumulative curves for the period 1960-63 and 1970-73 are very close to each other whereas the movement of districts towards higher productivity levels is more thereafter during 1980s, 1990s and so on. Further downward shifting of cumulative frequency curve during 2008-11 suggests significant improvement in distribution at all levels at district-level in Uttar Pradesh.

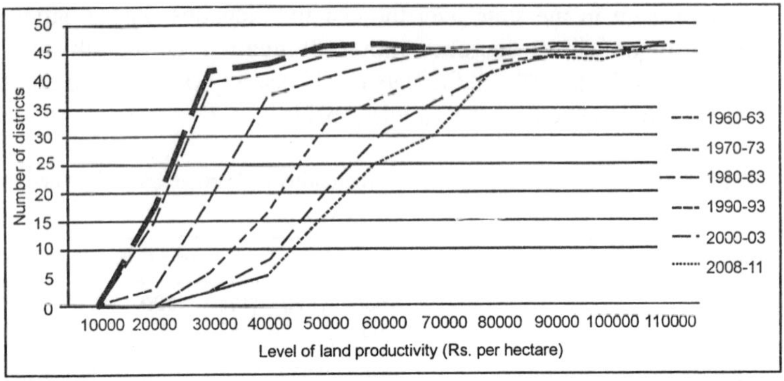

Figure 5.3: Cumulative frequency of districts in level of land productivity in Uttar Pradesh: 1960-63 to 2008-11.

Source: Table 5.3.

5.5. REGIONAL CONTIGUITY

The maps 5.1(a) to 5.1(f) presents the spatial distribution of districts at six points of time namely—1960-63, 1970-73, 1980-83, 1990-93, 2000-03 and 2008-11, by three levels of development i.e. high developed, medium developed and low developed category of districts. As evident from map 5.1(a) to begin with, all districts were in the low level of development. By 1970-73, a cluster of districts emerged in the extreme of the North-Western part adjoining the neighbouring state of Haryana, which graduated to medium level of development, whereas rest of the state continued to be at low levels of development. The observed cluster of developed districts then started expanding on both sides with one district emerged as high developed and rest remained in medium level by 1980-83. Thereafter by 1990-93, cluster further expanded downward with the previous cluster graduating to high levels and the newly joined districts to medium developed levels. This cluster expanded and brought new districts to medium and high level with only exception of Budaun district that remained trapped in low level of development. Interestingly, another cluster developed during 2000-03 near border

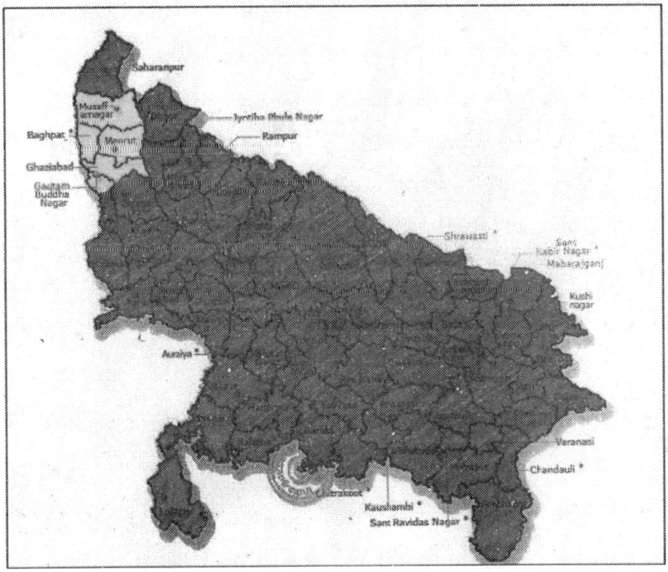

Map 5.1(a): District-wise level of land productivity in Uttar Pradesh: 1960-63.

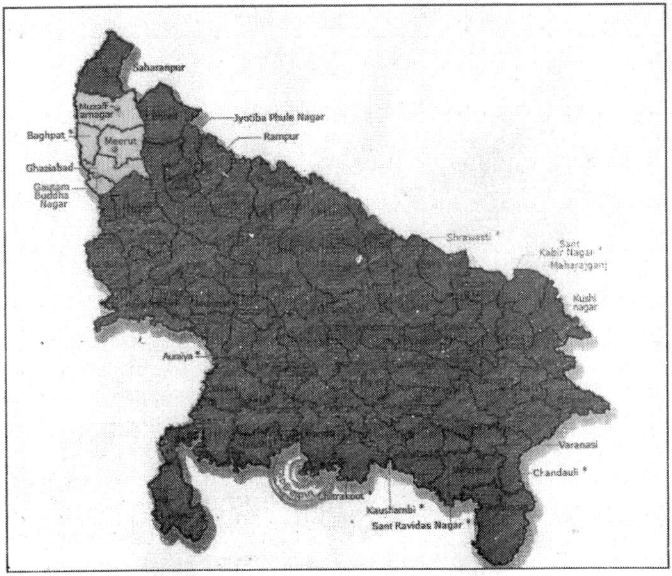

Map 5.1(b): District-wise level of land productivity in Uttar Pradesh: 1970-73.

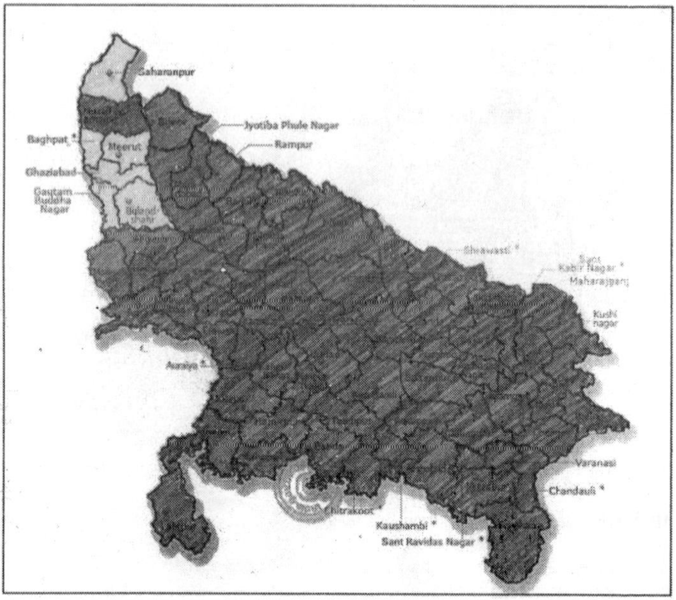

Map 5.1(c): District-wise level of land productivity in Uttar Pradesh:1980-83.

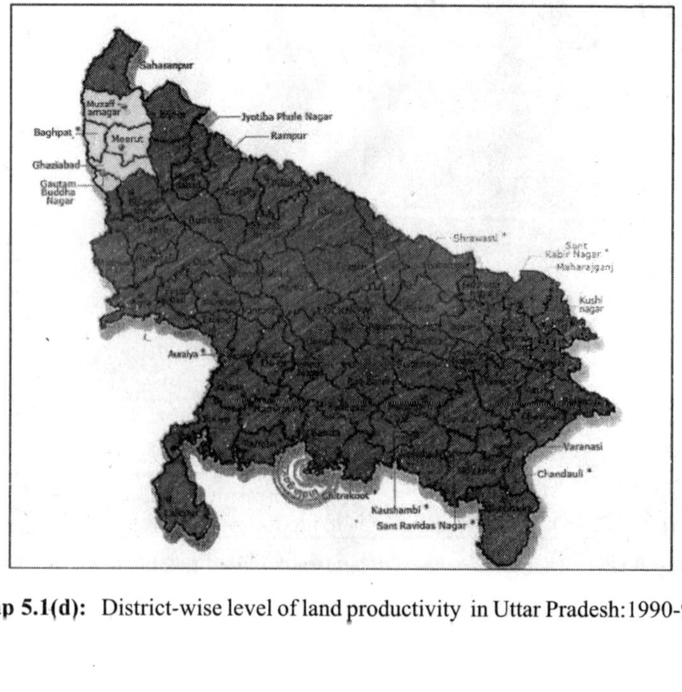

Map 5.1(d): District-wise level of land productivity in Uttar Pradesh:1990-93.

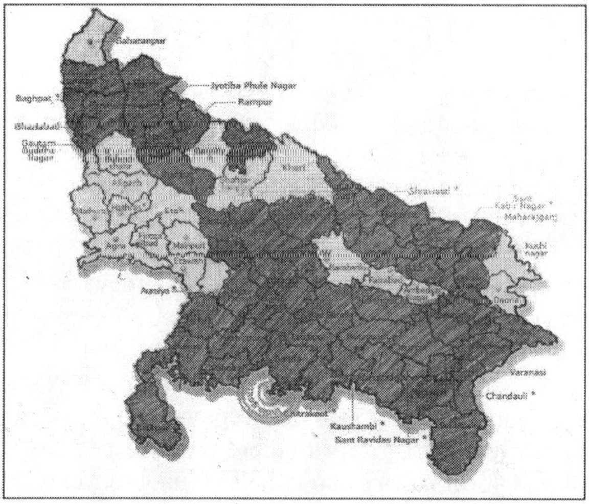

Map 5.1(e): District-wise level of land productivity in Uttar Pradesh:2000-03.

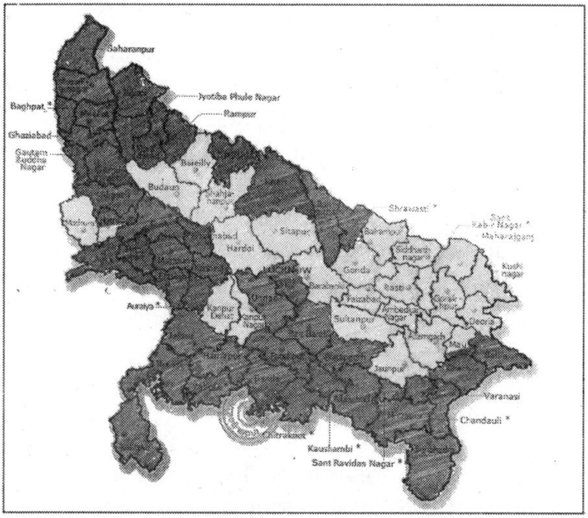

Map 5.1(f): District-wise level of land productivity in Uttar Pradesh:2008-11.
High level of development, Medium level of development,
Low level of development.

Map 5.1: District-wise level of land productivity in Uttar Pradesh:1960-63 to 2008-11.

Source: Table 5.4.

Note: These are indicative maps of Uttar Pradesh.

adjoining the state of Bihar. During this period, another spot emerged in between, where the growth picked up and a few low developed districts graduated to medium level of development. These three spots further expanded and formed a contiguous stretch from North-West to East starting from high development to medium level. Interestingly, with one spot in the upper side, rest of the underdeveloped districts formed a continuous strip adjoining the boarder of the state (Uttar Pradesh) with that of Madhya Pradesh, Chhattisgarh and Jharkhand.

On the whole, the development and underdevelopment in a big state like Uttar Pradesh follow a regional contiguity/proximity. Though in our opinion it needs further exploration, but it seems that first islands of development emerge and then development expands to their neighbourhood areas. The regions which continued to be trapped in low level of development are also trapped in specific situation and form a contiguous belt of underdevelopment. Snow balling of development from islands seems to be due to two main reasons:

1. The earlier developed regions might be having some favourable agro-climatic conditions contrary to the underdeveloped parts being exposed to development constraints and unfavourable climatic conditions.
2. Agriculture being performed openly, the agriculture administrators and farmers in underdeveloped regions may be learning from demonstrations of success stories in their neighbourhood and by adopting better cultured practices, these regions also start replicating the same success story for themselves.

5.6. SUMMARY

The present chapter examines the dynamics of agricultural development in Uttar Pradesh during the last five decades. From the agro-economic regional and district-level analysis of agricultural development measured in terms of land productivity and measurement of inter-regional disparities compared for five different decades, brings out the following main conclusions:

1. To begin with, in beginning of 1960s, Western Plain Zone was much ahead of rest of the zones in terms of agricultural

development. The per hectare productivity in 1960-63 in this zone was as high that even after 50 years, the three zones namely—Bundelkhand Zone, Vindhyan Zone and Hills could not match it even in 2010-11. However, due to very high growth recorded by Mid-Western Plain Zone and South-Western Semi-Arid Zone over time and in comparison low growth recorded by the Western Plain Zone, these three zones emerged as the most developed zones in the State of Uttar Pradesh in 2008-11. However, Bundelkhand Zone, Vindhyan Zone and the Hill zone (which form the present day Uttarakhand), continue to be agriculturally lagging zone of the state. The remaining three zones namely—Central Plain Zone, North-Eastern Plain Zone and Eastern Plain Zone with mediocre growth continues to maintain the middle level of development at par with the state average as a whole.

2. Over time, the gap between the most developed Western Plain Zone and other zones followed inverted 'U' curve path over the last five decades, i.e. the gap first continued to widen till 1980s, but started declining thereafter.
3. Almost all the districts in Uttar Pradesh were trapped in low levels of development till 1980s. There was a gradual shift from low productivity to high and medium productivity levels during 1990s, as the number of low productivity districts declined from 46 during 1960-63 to 32 during 1990-93 and further to 15 during 2008-11. At present while Western Plain Zone, Mid-Western Plain Zone and South-Western Semi-Arid Zone have none of their districts in the low productivity range, Bundelkhand and Vindhyan Zone have all their districts in low productivity category.
4. There are still nine districts in the state namely—Allahabad, Banda, Hamirpur, Jalaun, Jhansi, Bahraich, Pratapgarh, Mirzapur and Hills district unit that are at such low levels of development that they were unable to match the level of development attained by the most developed Meerut district fifty years back, in early 1960s. These districts seem to be the 'Achilles Heel' in Uttar Pradesh agriculture. Apart from this, there are 17 more districts that have not been able to achieve the level of development attained by most developed Muzaffarnagar district forty years from now.

5. For the period as a whole, inter-district disparities in the level of agricultural development increased marginally. Nevertheless, the pattern was not uniform, disparities widened till 1990s, but declined thereafter depicting inverted 'U' curve behaviour over time.
6. There is a definite regional contiguity so far as the district-level development in Uttar Pradesh is concerned. Development started in the extreme North in 1970s then spread to its contiguous districts. By 2000, another spot of prosperity emerged in the East. By 2010, a specific pattern emerged with high developed districts forming a continuous, belt in North-West, medium developed districts forming a continuous strip in the East and underdeveloped districts forming a continuous long strip in South-East and East-West part of the state. Agro-climatic conditions or constraints along with demonstration effect seem to be at play for these regional disparities and spatial pattern of development and underdevelopment in Uttar Pradesh.

6

Convergence of Regional Agricultural Performance in Uttar Pradesh: 1960-61 to 2010-11

6.1. INTRODUCTION

The preceding chapters on growth and level of agricultural development bring out wide regional and inter-district disparities in Uttar Pradesh. The present chapter is devoted to rigorous examination of convergence/divergence of the inter-district disparities in the state. Such information is essential input for planners and policy-makers in the state to device and implement inclusive economic policy and development strategy for the state. In case, the regional differences in agricultural development are converging, there is not much need to deviate from the present policies. However, if the disparities are persisting and/or diverging then planners and policy-makers have to rethink and redesign appropriate plans and programmes for more inclusive balanced regional development of the state. This is highly desirable because persistence/widening of regional disparities have serious economic and political implications. Disillusionment among the underdeveloped regions may lead to social unrest and demand by the people from underdeveloped regions for independent states. Many of the new emerged states like Uttarakhand, Jharkhand, Chhattisgarh, Telangana have their origin in underdevelopment and predominance of rulers from developed parts of the state. Economically also, persistence of regional disparity leads to undesirable capital and labour flight from underdeveloped regions to developed ones and further aggravating problem in the underdeveloped regions.

More specifically the main objective of this chapter is to examine the convergence/divergence of intra-regional and inter-district performance of agriculture in Uttar Pradesh over the last five decades from 1960-61 to 2010-11.

With the spread of new technology and policy initiatives for backward regions, we hypothesize convergence of inter-district disparities in Uttar Pradesh.

The chapter is organized as follows. After a brief introduction, the following section 6.2 discusses briefly the theories of convergence/divergence of development. Section 6.3 explains four main types of convergence used in empirical research to examine the changing pattern of disparities. Section 6.4 deals with methodology followed in this chapter to estimate and examine the regional disparities. Empirical findings regarding convergence/divergence by different types is presented in section 6.5. Section 6.6 concludes the main findings of this chapter.

6.2. THEORIES OF CONVERGENCE/DIVERGENCE

The phenomenon of convergence started with the neo-classical growth model. There are main three theories that predict the convergence pattern of economies (Soukiazis, 2000). The first is 'neo-classical theory' of convergence. It argues that due to diminishing returns to reproductive capital, poor economies or regions with low capital/labour ratios have a higher marginal productivity of capital and therefore, will grow faster than richer ones, given the same level of saving and investment. The theory however assumes that there is free factor mobility, free trade, limited role of government and technical progress is a public good (exogenous) (Soukiazis, 2000; Hossain, 2000; Kane, 2001; Cherodian and Thirlwall, 2013). The conditions of free factor mobility and free trade are essential and contribute to the acceleration of the convergence process through the equalization of prices of goods and factors of production. Therefore, the tendency for disparities to decline over time is due to the fact that factor costs are lower and profit opportunities are higher in poor regions compared to rich regions. Therefore, low income regions will tend to grow faster and will catch-up with the leading ones. In the long run, income differentials will be equalized across regions. This approach to convergence uses and tests sigma (σ) convergence which states that there is convergence if the cross-sectional dispersion of per hectare productivity level decreases over time. Another approach is beta (β) convergence which identifies a negative relationship between the growth of per capita income or productivity over a given period and the initial level of income per head or productivity across regions (Soukiazis, 2000). When all economies are assumed to converge towards the same steady state growth of per capita income or productivity for all regions, beta convergence is said to be absolute or unconditional (Barro and Sala-i-Martin, 1991). This neo-classical approach of convergence is consistent with Ramsey (1928), Domer (1946), Harrod (1939), Solow's (1956), Cass (1965) and Koopmans (1965) growth theory, where growth is determined by the supply of exogenous factor inputs and technology and there is diminishing return to scale. According to them, growth rates tends to be inversely related to initial level of output or income per person. In particular, if economies are similar in respect to preferences and technology, then poor economies grow faster than richer ones. Thus, there is a force that promotes convergence in level of per capita product and income (Barro and Sala-i-Martin, 1992).

The process of convergence due to diminishing returns to scale and exogenity of technical progress was challenged by the 'New Theory' of endogenous growth in the eighties, pioneered by Romer (1986) and Lucas (1988). This theory argues that convergence may come from the externality effects of research and development expenditure (Romer, 1986), and human capital formation (Lucas, 1988). According to this theory, all these factors are endogenous to growth and offset diminishing returns to scale. Regions or countries with more qualified human capital and higher innovation will grow faster. Therefore, according to new theory, convergence process is conditional on all these elements. When productivity depends upon a series of determinants such as factor endowments or institutions, which can vary from one economy to the other in the long run, convergence is said to be conditional [Beta (β) convergence]. At empirical level, when human capital and technical progress are introduced into the neo-classical equation of 'beta' convergence, the significance level of the parameters improves and the speed of convergence (beta coefficient) increases (Barro, 1991). Accordingly, convergence is not the rule as the neo-classical predicts, but is the exception and only takes place when the poor regions are able to absorb technical progress emanating from the advanced regions and improve their human capital efficiency and innovation capacity. Therefore, unconditional convergences occur when the model is tested for regions of same nation or among similar economies (Soukiazis, 2000).

The 'New Theory' of endogenous growth which predicts conditional convergence has some common elements with the early demand oriented approach to growth which explained the phenomenon of divergence in the light of the cumulative causation principle (Myrdal, 1957). According to Myrdal (1957), new theory is static and ignores the dynamic consequences of factor migration and trade. Labour migration from depressed to prosperous regions does not necessarily equalize wage rates and unemployment because movements in labour supply add to labour demand. Labour migration is also a selective process which may denude a depressed region of its human capital, and enhance the productivity capacity of the prosperous regions that it moves to. Equally, capital may not locate where wages are lowest if the future prospective yields of capital are lower in depressed regions than in more depressed regions. Trade may also work to the advantage of more prosperous regions if there are static and dynamic returns to scale, so that fast growing regions become more and more competitive. Moreover leading economies have the ability to exploit, sustain, reinforce, increase and accumulate their initial advantages of economies to state over time and make it difficult for the lagging countries/regions to compete in the same activities. Therefore, the tendency is for regional disparities to increase if the followers become unable to exploit economies of scale in certain activities and to benefit from technological advantages. According to this demand oriented approach, there will be convergence only when poor regions are able to generate a cumulative causation growth process by specializing in products with a high elasticity of demand and improving the supply characteristics of exports related to quality, design, confidence, product differentiation etc. and when regions are not able to promote this cumulative growth process, they will stay backward and divergence will take place (Soukiazis, 2000). Therefore, according to this approach convergence is not the rule, it is conditional depending on certain factors and there can be divergence too.

The majority of empirical studies have examined sigma and beta (unconditional and conditional) convergence processes utilizing econometric or statistical linear models as suggested by neo-classical and other theories. Rather recently, a few empirical studies have asserted the presence of nonlinearities in the growth process implying multiple steady states and convergence clubs (Chatterji, 1992; Quah, 1993b; Durlauf and Johnson, 1995; Hansen, 2000). These studies are based on theoretical models that yield multiple (locally stable) steady state equilibria and classify geographical units into different groups with different convergence characteristics (Azariadis, 1996; David, 1997; Islam, 2003). These models transcend the 'all or nothing' logic behind conventional convergence analysis and maintain that convergence may come about for different groups of economies. Moreover, by testing for a negative relationship between average annual rates of growth and initial levels of income, Boumol (1986) also concluded that industrial countries appear to belong to one convergence club, middle income countries to a separate, only moderately converging club and that low income countries actually diverged over time. He further noted that these groups also exhibit very little convergence with one another.

To summarize these theories, there is neo-classical equilibrium theory predicting unconditional convergence, new growth theory predicting conditional convergence, demand oriented approach of the cumulative causation type associated with Myrdal (1957) and Kaldor (1966, 1972) predicting the possibility of unconditional divergence and a recent concept of club convergence with multiple steady state growths among groups.

6.3. TYPES OF CONVERGENCE

There are four main types of convergence:

(i) Sigma (σ) Convergence

Sigma (σ) convergence concerns with cross-sectional dispersion of per capita income or development. There exists a convergence if the cross-sectional dispersion of per capita income or levels of development decreases over time (Hossain, 2000; Bowman and Felip, 2000; Ralhan and Dayanandan, 2005). It refers to reduction in disparities and captures temporal trend in regional differences across regions over time. Sigma convergence is employed to determine how the distribution of agriculture productivity across regions has behaved in the past or is likely to behave in the future (Monfort, 2008). There are various indices to measure sigma convergence. The most important and frequently used measures are: standard deviation, coefficient of variation and Gini coefficient of productivity levels across districts or regions. Each of these indices has its own advantages and disadvantages. For example, standard deviation is not a standard measure, it is an absolute measure of dispersion. If the scale increases, standard deviation increases automatically even if there is no actual increase in disparity. Therefore, over time comparison with standard deviation measure may not give appropriate results. The Gini coefficient is more sensitive to changes in inequality around the median. It gives more weightege to middle level distribution, giving less importance to values at top and bottom of distribution. The coefficient of variation is more responsive to changes in upper end of the distribution. But it has an advantage over these (standard deviation and Gini coefficient) measures. Coefficient of variation is a standard measure which standardizes changing values of standard deviation to mean of distribution. Moreover, it is often preferred to standard deviation measure which has no interpretable meaning on its own unless the mean value is also reported. For a given standard deviation value, the coefficient of variation indicates a high or low degree of variability only in relation to the mean value (Monfort, 2008). Consequently, these measures may neither rank the distributions the same way, nor will time series patterns necessarily be the same for different measures. It is, therefore, generally required to compute a variety of measures to draw firm conclusions about changes in the extent of disparities (Monfort, 2008). We, therefore, estimated inequalities (sigma convergence) with all these measures and the results were almost same in most of these indices. But in our analysis, we will report the results for coefficient of variation of land productivity to analyze sigma convergence across districts in Uttar Pradesh and the results with standard deviation and Gini coefficient of land productivity and log land productivity are presented in Appendix 6.1. And if there is presence of sigma convergence in the estimates, it suggests a tendency to equalization of productivity levels across regions.

(ii) Beta (β) Unconditional Convergence

Unconditional or absolute beta convergence suggests a tendency towards equalization of per capita income (Kumo, 2011; Hossain, 2000; Soukiazis, 2000). Prevalence of beta convergence indicates an inverse relationship between income growth rate and its initial level. Absolute beta convergence considers the assumption of the high growth rates of the poor entities like countries against the rich ones, regardless of the determinant of growth of the entities. Beta convergence for the present purpose concerns with cross-section regression of the time averaged productivity growth rate on the initial per hectare productivity level. That is, there exists an unconditional beta convergence if the coefficient of initial per hectare productivity level in a cross-sectional regression, for per hectare agriculture productivity growth bears the negative sign (Hossain, 2000). This negative relation is more likely to apply across regions within countries than across countries (Barro and Sala-i-Martin, 1992). This measure suggests that regions with higher initial productivity levels grow slowly than regions with lower initial levels of productivity. When all economies are assumed to converge towards the same steady state, it is absolute or unconditional beta (β) convergence. According to Sala-i-Martin (1994), both concepts, beta and sigma are useful since, they measure convergence or divergence in a different manner and they give different information. However, he suggests that the "beta" convergence is a more interesting concept since it responds to questions, such as, whether poor economies (countries or regions) are predicted to grow faster than rich ones, how fast the convergence process is, whether there is a different convergence process between groups of economies with different structures. He underlined that relation between the two concepts is accurate only to a certain extent which means that "beta" convergence is a necessary, but not a sufficient condition for "sigma" convergence. Therefore, the two concepts seem to be complementary and do not replace each other. Moreover in our analysis also, we will examine the existence of convergence with both these measures as well as with club convergence measures.

(iii) Beta (β) Conditional Convergence

Conditional convergence is the main argument of new theory of growth, which implies that economies converge to a different steady state point of growth since they have different structures (Barro and Sala-i-Martin, 1992). The concept of conditional beta convergence concerns with cross-section regression of the time averaged output/ productivity growth rate on the initial per capita output or per hectare productivity level and a set of additional explanatory variables that define the steady state path for per hectare productivity or per capita output (Barro and Sala-i-Martin, 1992). Under conditional convergence each region converges towards its own unique steady state and per hectare productivity become similar across regions only to the extent that steady states are similar for each region. In addition, when growth depends upon a series of determinants which can vary from one region to the other even in long run, it is said to be conditional beta convergence.

(iv) Club Convergence

The concept of conditional convergence is also related with the notion of club convergence. The term is initially related to Baumol (1986), but its more rigorous formulation owes to Durauf and Johnson (1995) and Galor (1996). In case of unconditional convergence, there is only one steady state to which all economies approach. In case of conditional convergence each economy has its own steady state growth pattern and each one of them approaches its own steady state. In contrast, the idea of club convergence is based on models that yield multiple equilibrium steady states. Which of these different equilibrium an economy will reach, depends on its initial position or some other attributes. More specifically, club convergence implies convergence to a common level only for economies sharing similar characteristics (Galor, 1996). A group of countries may approach a particular state if they share the initial location or attribute corresponding to that steady state or equilibrium (Islam, 2003). This produces club convergence that classifies economies on the basis of indicators like their educational levels, income per capita and other measurable factors. Economies considered poor tend to converge towards one another and create a convergence club at a low level of per capita wealth.

6.4. METHODOLOGY

Methodology followed in empirical testing of inter-district convergence/divergence of disparities is as under:

(i) Sigma (σ) Convergence

Sigma convergence is estimated using the following equation:

$$\text{Inequality}_t = \alpha + \beta_1 \text{time} + \mu_t$$

where,

t is time period from 1960-61 to 2010-11.

μ_t is error term assumed to be independently and identically distributed with zero mean and constant variance.

However, in case the changes over time do not follow a linear pattern, then higher order terms of time needs to be included to capture the real behaviour of inequality over time. Therefore, besides the above linear form, we also estimated the following quadratic form of the inequality function.

$$\text{Inequality}_t = \alpha + \beta_1 \text{time} + \beta_2 \text{time}^2 + \mu_t$$

Any measure of inequality can be used. Following majority of studies, we also measured inequality in terms of standard deviation, coefficient of variation and Gini coefficient.

The negative and significant value of β_1 or β_1 and β_2 indicates the convergence of inequality over time.

(ii) Beta (β) Unconditional Convergence

$$1/T \ln (y_{it} / y_{it-T}) = \alpha + \beta \ln (y_{i,t-T}) + \mu_{it.}$$

where,

y_{it} is per hectare land productivity of the ith state during tth period.

Yi, t-T is productivity of the ith state during its initial/base year (t-T).

$\mu_{it.}$ is white noise or random error term.

Negative and significant value of β indicates the unconditional convergence across states over the study period. It indicates that the poor states tend to grow at higher pace compared with developed states.

(iii) Beta (β) Conditional Convergence

$$\ln (y_{it}/y_{it-T}) = \alpha + \beta \ln (y_{i,t-T}) + \gamma Z_{it} + \mu_{it.}$$

where,

Z_{it} is a set of exogenous determinants of growth of land productivity in the selected states over the period.

y_{it} is per hectare land productivity of the ith state during tth period.

Yi, t-T is productivity of the ith state during its initial/base year (t-T).

γ_{it} is white noise or random error term.

(iv) Club Convergence

To examine whether or not club convergence exists or not, first and the foremost is to group the districts into different clubs classified on the basis of their homogeneity in terms of their indicators which may be related with the contiguity of the clubbed districts that are more or less indicative of common agro-climatic and other conditions for agriculture development. On basis of this classification, we have chosen three clubs of districts namely—Western, Central and Eastern clubs of districts. Composition of each club is given as follows:

Table 6.1: Composition of Geographical Regions of Uttar Pradesh

S.No.	*Regions*	*Districts included*
1.	Western Region	It includes 18 districts namely: Agra, Aligarh, Bareilly, Bijnor, Budaun, Bulandshahr, Etah, Etawah, Farrukhabad, Mainpuri, Mathura, Meerut, Moradabad, Muzaffarnagar, Rampur, Pilibhit, Saharanpur and Shahjahanpur.
2.	Central Region	It includes 09 districts namely: Barabanki, Fatehpur, Hardoi, Kanpur, Kheri, Lucknow, Rae Bareli, Sitapur and Unnao.
3.	Eastern Region	It includes 15 districts namely: Allahabad, Azamgarh, Bahraich, Ballia, Basti, Deoria, Faizabad, Ghazipur, Gonda, Gorakhpur, Jaunpur, Mirzapur, Sultanpur, Pratapgarh and Varanasi.

Source: GoI (2014), *Uttar Pradesh State Development Report*, Volume II, New Delhi: Planning Commission, Government of India.

Note: We did not include Bundelkhand Region because it has just four districts.

The other feasible way is to club the districts on the basis of their level of development. On this basis, we ranked the districts as per their level of development and divided them into three almost equal parts as: with high level of development, medium level of development and low level of development. We tested for both conditional and unconditional beta convergence across these clubs of districts to further explore the issue of convergence/divergence in agricultural development in Uttar Pradesh.

6.5 EMPIRICAL FINDINGS

6.5 (i) Sigma (σ) Convergence

We estimated sigma convergence with three widely used measures of inequality and the results are presented in graphical form in Figure 6.1 with standard deviation of land productivity and standard deviation of log land productivity curves in Figures 6.1(i) and 6.1(ii), coefficient of variation of land productivity and coefficient of variation of log land productivity curves in Figures 6.1(iii) and 6.1(iv) and Gini coefficient of land productivity and Gini coefficient of log land productivity curves in figures 6.1(v) and 6.1(vi). We estimated the regression results in linear form with time as independent variable as well as with quadratic inequality function with time-and-time^2 as independent variables respectively. Most of the studies fit linear pattern, but this approach is not always the appropriate measure. We therefore tested sigma convergence by employing both linear and quadratic regression.

From the visual inspection of all the six graphs of different ways to examine temporal nature of regional inequalities, we observed the following:

1. Both linear as well as log linear measures of standard deviation show an increasing trend of inequalities over time.
2. Both, coefficient of variation as well as Gini coefficient based graphs however does not support the upward movement of inequality during the study period.
3. Though, it seems that the quadratic trend fit better the linear trend to inequalities over time, but it is difficult to say from graph which of these better fit to the data. Nevertheless, it seems that non-log form better fit the data compared to the log forms.
4. Coefficient of variation seems to be a better measure of inequality on our data compared to the Gini coefficient. Standard deviation though seems to better fit the data, but as

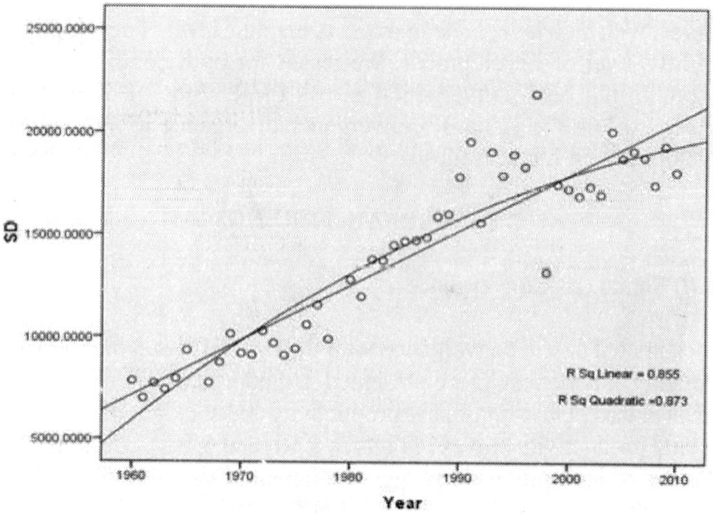

6.1(i): Standard deviation of land productivity.

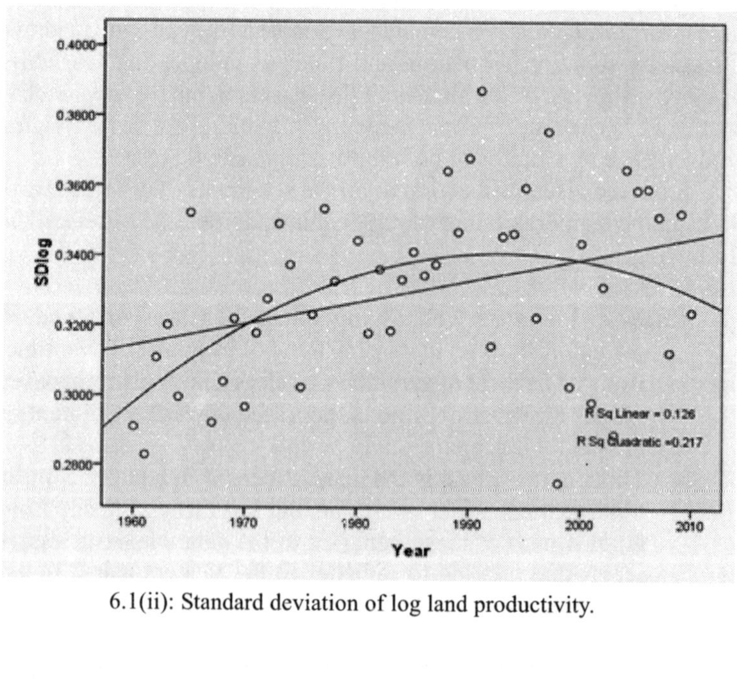

6.1(ii): Standard deviation of log land productivity.

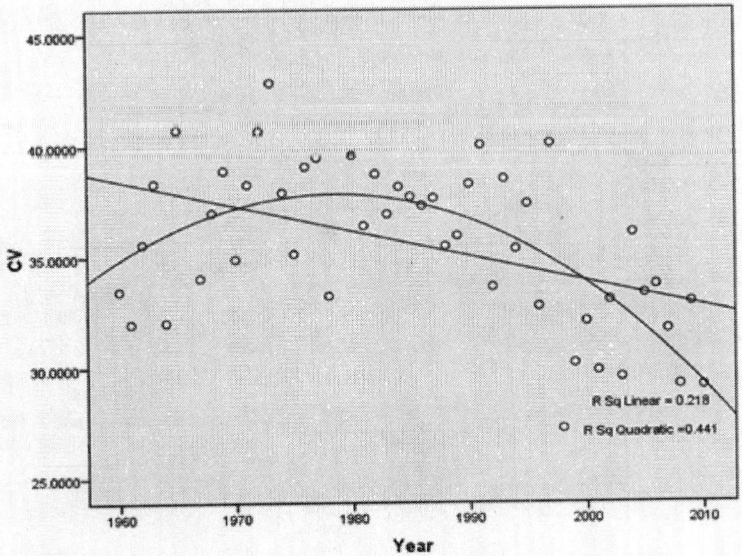

6.1(iii): Coefficient of variation of land productivity.

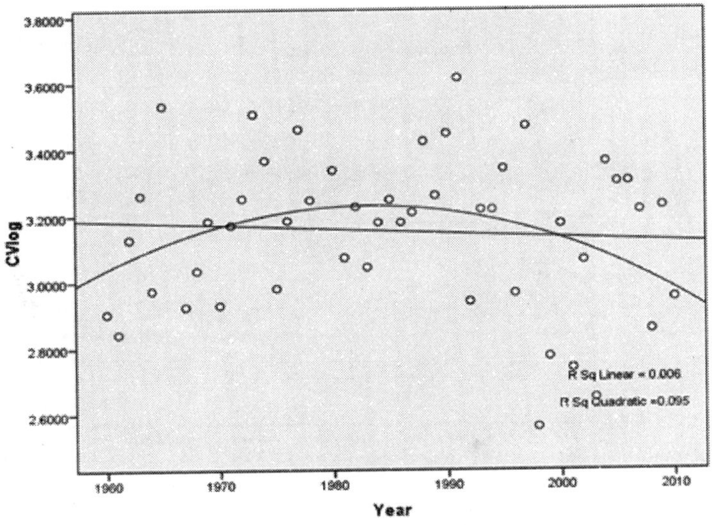

6.1(iv): Coefficient of variation of log land productivity.

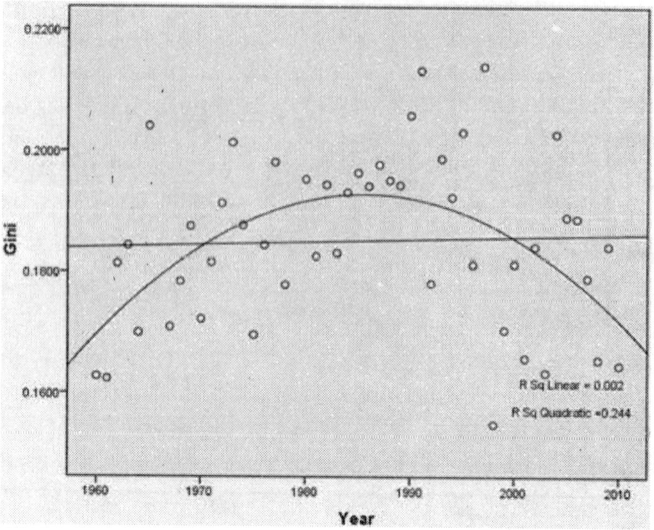

6.1(v): Gini coefficient of land productivity.

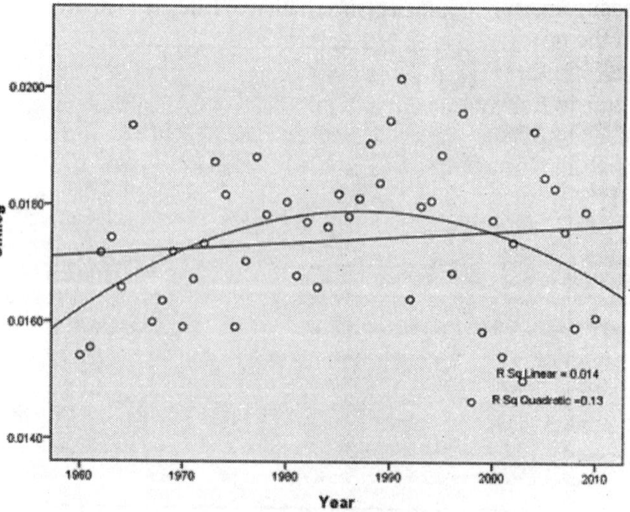

6.1(vi): Gini coefficient of log land productivity.

Figure 6.1: Sigma convergence of inequalities in Uttar Pradesh: 1960-61 to 2010-11.

Sources: (i) Table 6.2(a).
(ii) Appendix 6.1.

pointed out earlier that since the average land productivity almost increased three times over the study period. It tends to overstate rising income inequality because it measures inequality in absolute terms. Therefore, choice lies between coefficient of variation and the Gini coefficient of inequality and their linear and quadratic forms as well as between log and non-log forms. From the graphs, it seems that the coefficient of variation better captures the situation and quadratic form give better fit to data then the linear form. Therefore, on basis of graphical exposition, the coefficient of variation in quadratic form seems to be better choice to test the sigma convergence of inter-district disparity in Uttar Pradesh. In our subsequent analysis, the empirical results are therefore, based on this measure of inequality. Nevertheless, the results by other measures and model forms are presented for reference purposes.

The information in Table 6.2(a) on the linear and quadratic measurement of land productivity validate our earlier observation that the non-log form is better than the log form of the model and the quadratic form of model is better than the linear one. The coefficient of time in linear trend equation is negative and significant statistically. It suggests the prevalence of convergence in land productivity in Uttar

Table 6.2(a): Sigma (σ) convergence in Uttar Pradesh: 1960-61 to 2010-11

Period↓	*Regression coefficients*						
	Dependent variable	*Intercept*	*Time*	*Time²*	*R²*	*(R²)*	*N*
1960-61 to 2010-11	Coefficient of Variation of land productivity	38.512	−0.113***		0.218	0.202	49
			(3.622)				
		34.524	0.337***	−0.009***	0.441	0.416	49
			(3.107)	(4.279)			
	Coefficient of Variation of log land productivity	3.184	−0.001		0.006	−0.014	49
			(0.548)				
		3.021	0.017*	−3.52x10[illegible]**	0.095	0.055	49
			(1.914)	(2.119)			

Source: Table 5.4.

Notes: 1. Figure in parenthesis is t value of the coefficients.

2. Asterisk *, ** and *** indicate coefficients significant at 10 per cent, 5 per cent and 1 per cent level of significance respectively for two tailed test.

Pradesh during the five decades from 1960-61 to 2010-11. In the quadratic equation, the coefficient of time-and-time^2 are significant statistically and bears positive and negative signs respectively. This suggests that there is no consistent pattern of changing inequalities in the state. Though there was sigma convergence for the period as a whole, but there was sigma divergence in the beginning which shifted to convergence over the period of time. Though, the log form equations have low R^2, but they also broadly support the same phenomenon. It seems that there is decline in inter-district disparities whereby the poor districts and the developed ones are coming closer.

To further examine the break in pattern of divergence/ convergence in agriculture over time, we re-estimated the linear equation by switching over the data period. The results reported in this context are presented in Table 6.2(b). On the basis of the size of the slope coefficient as well as the coefficient of determination (R^2), it seems that rising inequalities peaked up to 1980s and show a

Table 6.2(b): Searching Trend Change in Sigma (σ) Convergence in Uttar Pradesh: 1960-61 to 2010-11

Period↓	*Regression coefficients*					
	Intercept	*Coefficient*	*R^2*	*R^2*	*F Significance*	*N*
1960-61 to 1978-79	34.700	0.211 (1.638)	0.143	0.090	0.121	18
1960-61 to 1980-81	34.654	0.218* (1.903)	0.176	0.127	0.074	19
1960-61 to 1981-82	34.968	0.176* (1.681)	0.136	0.080	0.110	20
1960-61 to 1982-83	34.998	0.172* (1.822)	0.149	0.104	0.084	21
1960-61 to 1983-84	35.199	0.148* (1.702)	0.127	0.083	0.104	22
1960-61 to 1984-85	35.264	0.140* (1.765)	0.129	0.088	0.092	23
1960-61 to 1986-87	35.486	0.117* (1.709)	0.113	0.074	0.101	25
1960-61 to 1990-91	35.953	0.069 (1.308)	0.060	0.025	0.202	29

Source: Same as in Table 6.2(a).

Notes:
1. Figure in parenthesis is t value of the coefficients.
2. Asterisk *, ** and *** indicate coefficients significant at 10 per cent, 5 per cent and 1 per cent level of significance respectively for two tailed test.

declining trend thereafter. The coefficient of both, the slope coefficient as well as R^2 continue to decline and cease to be significant statistically in 1991. It seems that whatever inequality increased from 1960-61 to 1980-81 were leveled off by declining trend of inequalities between 1981-82 to 1990-91.

To further test the same, we divided the whole period into two parts—one up to 1980s and other thereafter. We re-estimated the sigma convergence model on these two periods separately. The result in this context, presented in Table 6.2(c), corroborate our earlier observation that there was sigma divergence in agricultural development for the first two decades from 1960-61 to 1980-81 whereas the sigma convergence began from 1981-82 to 2010-11 period. Since, the absolute value for the later period is higher than the former one, the net impact turned out to be negative indicating the sigma convergence of agricultural development in Uttar Pradesh.

Table 6.2(c): Sigma (σ) Convergence in Uttar Pradesh: 1960-61 to 1980-81 and 1981-82 to 2010-11

Period↓	*Regression coefficients*					
	Dependent variable	*Intercept*	*Time*	R^2	R^2	*N*
1960-61 to 1980-81	Coefficient of variation of land productivity	34.654	0.218* (1.903)	0.176	0.127	19
	Coefficient of variation of log land productivity	2.992	0.016* (2.224)	0.225	0.180	19
1981-82 to 2010-11	Coefficient of variation of land productivity	44.779	–0.279*** (4.983)	0.470	0.451	30
	Coefficient of variation of log land productivity	3.394	–0.067 (1.345)	0.061	0.027	30

Source: Same as in Table 6.2(a).

Notes:
1. Figure in parenthesis is t value of the coefficients.
2. Asterisk *, ** and *** indicate coefficients significant at 10 per cent, 5 per cent and 1 per cent level of significance respectively for two tailed test.

The finding of overall convergence and a trend of convergence/divergence over time is also supported by the estimates of sigma convergence model (Appendix 6.1) for the period as a whole as well as for two sub-periods, both for standard deviation and Gini coefficient as a measure of inequality.

6.5 (ii) Beta (β) Unconditional Convergence

To examine the nature of sigma convergence, we estimated the equation of beta convergence by regressing the agriculture growth on initial level of land productivity over the study period. The results are presented in Table 6.3 and presented graphically also in Figure 6.2. For the period as a whole, though the value of R^2 (0.082) is very low, but the slope coefficient is negative and significant statistically. It indicates the prevalence of beta convergence of inequalities in Uttar Pradesh for the period as a whole. When we fit the same regression for beta convergence for two sub-periods, an interesting pattern is observed. For the period during 1960-61 to 1980-81, there was virtual no relation between growth and initial level of productivity indicated both graphically as well as in regression estimates.

Table 6.3: Beta (β) Unconditional Convergence in Uttar Pradesh: 1960-61 to 2010-11

Period↓	*Regression coefficients*			
	Intercept	*β Coefficient*	R^2	*N*
1960-61 to 2010-11	0.086	–0.007** (2.010)	0.082	49
1960-61 to 1980-81	0.020	–5.85x10–4 (0.090)	0.002	19
1981-82 to 2010-11	0.103	–0.008** (2.299)	0.105	30

Source: Same as in Table 6.2(a).

Notes: 1. Figure in parenthesis is t value of the coefficients.

2. Asterisk *, ** and *** indicate coefficients significant at 10 per cent, 5 per cent and 1 per cent level of significance respectively for two tailed test.

Now, combining it with our earlier findings that there was sigma divergence during 1960-80, it seems to suggest that increasing inequality was mainly because of higher growth in more developed districts compared to the less developed districts. In other words, only developed districts benefitted from the initial phase of green revolution technology in Uttar Pradesh. The regression results are however significant for second period from 1981-82 to 2010-11. The negative significant coefficient suggests that there were significant tendencies for underdeveloped districts growing at a faster rate whereas developed districts recording low growth rates. In other

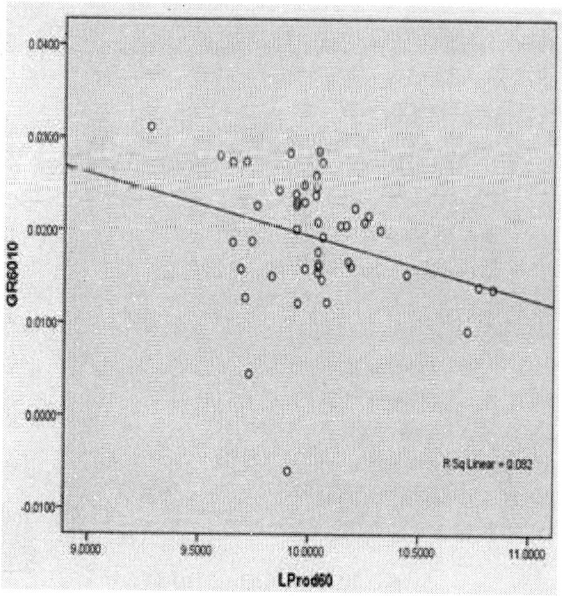

6.2(i) 1960-61 to 2010-11

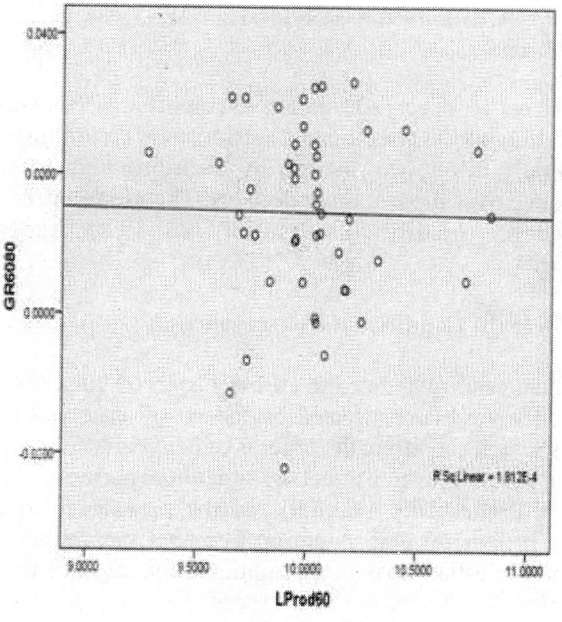

6.2(ii) 1960-61 to 1980-81

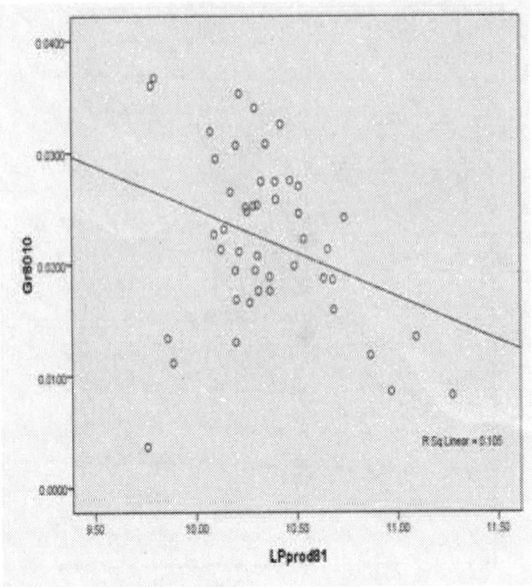

6.2(iii) 1981-82 to 2010-11

Figure 6.2: Beta (β) unconditional convergence of inequalities in Uttar Pradesh: 1960-61 to 2010-11.

Source: Table 6.2.

words, the earlier observed sigma convergence may be mainly due to the fact that underdeveloped districts were catching up with agriculturally developed districts by recording higher agricultural performance over the last three decades. Therefore, the catch-up by the poor developed districts was mainly post-1990s phenomenon in Uttar Pradesh.

6.5 (iii) Beta (β) Conditional Convergence

We further tested whether the earlier observed conditions of beta convergence are being affected by the set of structural exogenous variables which can affect the process of convergence. The two most important variables which affect the agriculture performance in a state like Uttar Pradesh are—rainfall and the prevalence of irrigation facilities in general and irrigation by canal system and rivers in particular. The estimates of beta conditional convergence are presented in Table 6.4.

Table 6.4: Beta (β) Conditional Convergence in Uttar Pradesh: 1960-61 to 2010-11

Period↓	Intercept	β Coefficient	Rainfall	Irrigation	R^2	N
1960-61 to 2010-11	0.099	-0.006 (1.560)	-7.420x10-4 (0.242)	-0.001 (0.817)	0.096	49
1960-61 to 1980-81	0.036	0.001 (0.111)	-0.001 (0.130)	-0.002 (0.645)	0.010	19
1981-82 to 2010-11	0.084	-0.011** (2.556)	1.90x10-4 (0.074)	0.005 (1.352)	0.142	30

Source: Same as in Table 6.2(a).

Notes: 1. Figure in parenthesis is t value of the coefficients.
2. Asterisk *, ** and *** indicate coefficients significant at 10 per cent, 5 per cent and 1 per cent level of significance respectively for two tailed test.

The estimates reveal that even the beta coefficient ceases to be significant statistically for the period as a whole from 1960-61 to 2010-11. Results remained the same during two sub-periods from 1960-61 to 1980-81 and 1981-82 to 2010-11, i.e. the beta coefficient is not significant for the first period and negative significant for the second period. So, it seems that beta unconditional convergence is more relevant than the beta conditional convergence.

6.5 (iv) Club Convergence

(a) Clubs Based on Development

The estimate for unconditional beta convergence for each three clubs of convergence of districts is presented in Table 6.5(a). It may be seen that there is unconditional beta convergence for the period as a whole as well as for the period from 1981-2010 for the club of high developed districts. This implies that there is convergence within high developed districts and that occurred during the last three decades only, whereas for the decades for 1960s and 1970s there was no such convergence/divergence. None of the case, beta coefficient for overall as for two sub-periods turned out to be significant statistically, both for club of medium and club of low developed districts.

The estimates for conditional convergence equations for three clubs of districts are presented in Table 6.5(b). Interestingly, even after controlling for structural factors, the results of unconditional convergence remained the same. In other words, there is conditional

Table 6.5(a): Beta Unconditional Convergence in Uttar Pradesh: 1960-61 to 2010-11

Period↓	*Regression coefficients*			
	Intercept	*β Coefficient*	R^2	*N*
Club of High Developed Districts				
1960-61 to 2010-11	0.117	–0.010** (2.447)	0.300	49
1960-61 to 1980-81	–0.035	0.005 (0.385)	0.010	19
1981-82 to 2010-11	0.277	–0.024*** (6.453)	0.748	30
Club of Medium Developed Districts				
1960-61 to 2010-11	–0.064	0.008 (0.291)	0.006	49
1960-61 to 1980-81	0.339	–0.032 (0.497)	0.017	19
1981-82 to 2010-11	0.205	–0.018 (0.599)	0.025	30
Club of Low developed districts				
1960-61 to 2010-11	0.241	–0.023 (1.431)	0.136	49
1960-61 to 1980-81	0.201	–0.019 (0.727)	0.039	19
1981-82 to 2010-11	–0.013	0.004 (0.227)	0.004	30

Source: Same as in Table 6.2(a).

Notes: 1. Figure in parenthesis is t value of the coefficients.
2. Asterisk *, ** and *** indicate coefficients significant at 10 per cent, 5 per cent and 1 per cent level of significance respectively for two tailed test.

convergence in case of high club districts for 1981-82 to 2010-11 period only. None of the beta coefficient is significant statistically both for the club of medium and club of low developed districts even on controlling the structural factors.

On the whole, the findings from both the unconditional and conditional beta convergence for three different clubs of districts suggest that there is unconditional beta convergence for the club of high developed districts for the period of 1981-82 to 2010-11 only. The clubs of medium and the club of low developed districts do not show any conditional or unconditional beta convergence for the study period as a whole as well as for the two periods separately.

Table 6.5(b): Beta Conditional Convergence in Uttar Pradesh: 1960-61 to 2010-11

Period↓	*Regression Coefficients*					
	Intercept	*β Coefficient*	*Rainfall*	*Irrigation*	R^2	*N*
Club of High Developed Districts						
1960-61 to 2010-11	0.153	–0.006 (1.063)	–0.005 (–0.866)	–0.003* (1.660)	0.454	49
1960-61 to 1980-81	–0.086	0.028 (1.650)	–0.006 (0.359)	–0.012*** (2.587)	0.367	19
1981-82 to 2010-11	0.279	–0.019** (4.729)	0.003 (0.855)	–0.006** (2.205)	0.824	30
Club of Medium Developed Districts						
1960-61 to 2010-11	–0.074	0.007 (0.209)	0.003 (0.245)	3.64x104 (0.074)	0.017	49
1960-61 to 1980-81	0.406	–0.023 (0.325)	–0.015 (0.530)	–0.004 (0.413)	0.041	19
1981-82 to 2010-11	0.221	–0.026 (0.948)	–0.005 (0.609)	0.009** (2.007)	0.283	30
Club of Low Developed Districts						
1960-61 to 2010-11	0.247	–0.023 (1.324)	0.001 (0.118)	–8.50x10–4 (0.186)	0.140	49
1960-61 to 1980-81	0.158	–0.671 (0.019)	0.342 (0.003)	0.239 (0.002)	0.053	19
1981-82 to 2010-11	–0.014	–0.006 (0.312)	–1.42x10–4 (0.031)	0.008 (0.915)	0.081	30

Source: Same as in Table 6.2(a).

Notes: 1. Figure in parenthesis is t value of the coefficients.
2. Asterisk *, ** and *** indicate coefficients significant at 10 per cent, 5 per cent and 1 per cent level of significance respectively for two tailed test.

(b) Clubs Based on Geographical Contiguity

Estimate of the beta unconditional convergence among three different clubs of Western, Central and Eastern regions presented in Table 6.6(a) and Fig. 6.3, suggest that there is strong tendency for unconditional convergence in the club of Western districts both for the overall study period as well as for the two sub-periods separately. Absolute value of beta coefficient during two sub-periods suggests that the beta convergence was more strong during the second period compared with the first one. None of the beta coefficient is significant for Central club of districts indicating no beta unconditional convergence or divergence of development. In the Eastern club, the beta coefficient

Table 6.6(a): Beta Unconditional Convergence within Geographical Regions of Uttar Pradesh: 1960-61 to 2010-11

Period/Regions↓	*Regression coefficients*			
	Intercept	*β Coefficient*	R^2	*N*
Western Region				
1960-61 to 2010-11	0.177	–0.015*** (7.705)	0.790	49
1960-61 to 1980-81	0.154	–0.013* (1.702)	0.153	19
1981-82 to 2010-11	0.283	–0.025*** (8.835)	0.830	30
Central Region				
1960-61 to 2010-11	0.292	–0.027 (1.579)	0.263	49
1960-61 to 1980-81	0.282	–0.027 (0.871)	0.100	19
1981-82 to 2010-11	-0.138	0.016 (0.751)	0.075	30
Eastern Region				
1960-61 to 2010-11	0.170	–0.015*** (2.862)	0.387	49
1960-61 to 1980-81	0.168	–0.015 (1.428)	0.136	19
1981-82 to 2010-11	0.128	–0.010 (1.237)	0.105	30

Source:: Same as in Table 6.1(a).

Notes:
1. Figure in parenthesis is t value of the coefficients.
2. Asterisk *, ** and *** indicate coefficients significant at 10 per cent, 5 per cent and 1 per cent level of significance respectively for two tailed test.

is negative significant for the overall period, but it ceases to be significant for the two sub-periods. It seems to indicate weak tendency of beta convergence in the Eastern club of districts.

We re-estimated the beta convergence by including exogenous structural factors—rainfall and irrigation and the same are reported in Table 6.6(b). All results about beta coefficient remained the same with one exception that beta coefficient for 1960-1980 now ceases to be significant statistically whereas, it was so in case of unconditional convergence for the club of Western districts. Both the results taken together, suggests that there is beta unconditional convergence in the club of Western region districts only. There is no such strong pattern of beta conditional or unconditional convergence evident for the

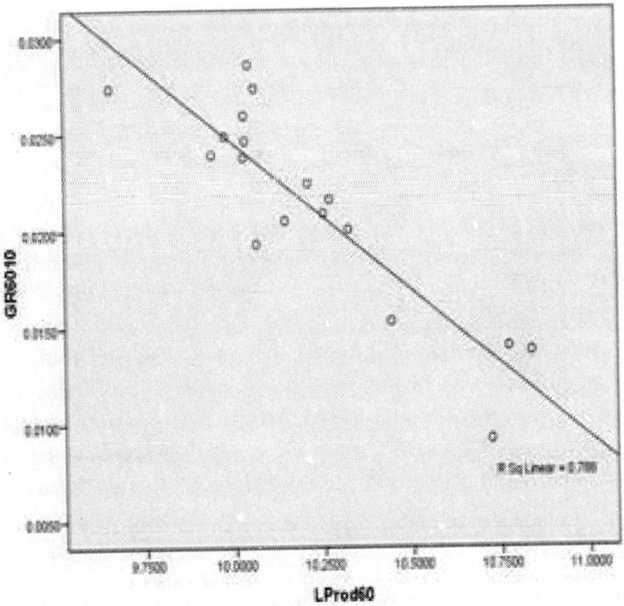

6.3(i) Western Region

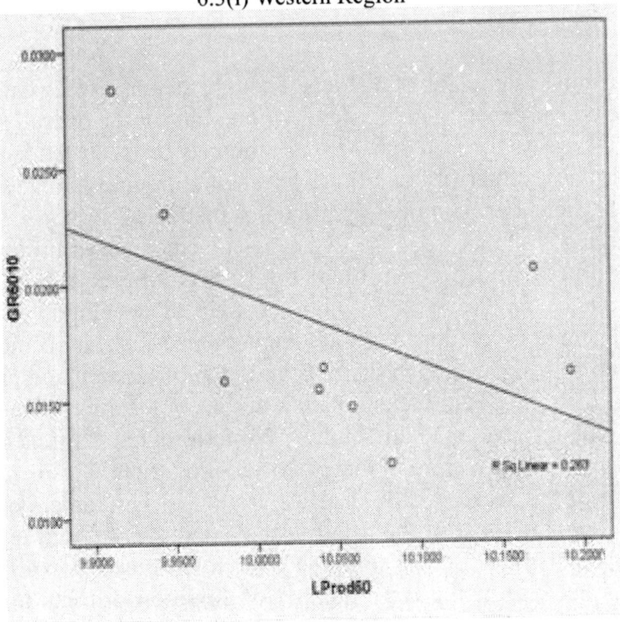

6.3(ii) Central Region

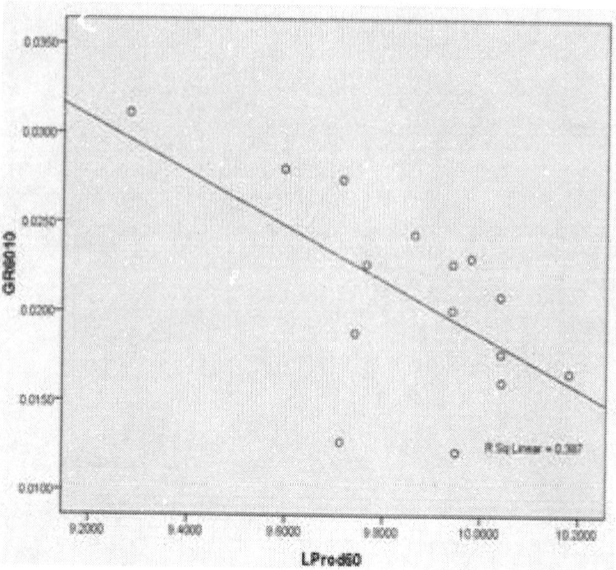

Figure 6.3: Beta (β) unconditional convergence of inequalities within geographical regions of Uttar Pradesh: 1960-61 to 2010-11

Source: Table 6.6(a).

Central and Eastern club of districts. Though, there is a weak tendency of beta convergence in the Eastern region,, but for the overall period only. Whereas, for two sub-periods, there is no such tendency of convergence, either of conditional or unconditional type where the beta coefficient remain non-significant statistically.

Taking findings from the two types of clubs based on level of development and geographical contiguity, there is beta club convergence for the Western club and club of developed districts only. There is no evidence of club convergence for club of medium and club of low developed districts and club of Eastern and club of Central districts. A close examination of the composition of districts in the club of developed and club of Western region districts shows that there is a big overlap in these two set of districts. This is mainly because of the Western club districts are the early adopters of new technology and most of them fall in the categories of high level of developed districts. So, the common behaviour of these two different clubs is because of the large number of common districts in these two categories. Therefore, the club of high developed and club of

Table 6.6(b): Beta Conditional Convergence within Geographical Regions of Uttar Pradesh: 1960-61 to 2010-11

Period/ Regions↓	*Regression coefficients*					
	Intercept	*β Coefficient*	*Rainfall*	*Irrigation*	R^2	*N*
Western Region						
1960-61 to 2010-11	0.214	–0.016*** (5.374)	–0.998 (0.003)	–7.92x10–4 (0.762)	0.805	49
1960-61 to 1980-81	0.231	–0.009 (0.789)	–0.008 (0.669)	–0.005 (1.353)	0.254	19
1981-82 to 2010-11	0.277	–0.024*** (7.892)	0.004 (1.211)	–0.003 (1.036)	0.856	30
Central Region						
1960-61 to 2010-11	0.183	–0.006 (0.242)	–0.004 (0.271)	–0.006 (0.906)	0.401	49
1960-61 to 1980-81	0.121	0.017 (0.359)	–0.017 (0.598)	–0.015 (1.227)	0.327	19
1981-82 to 2010-11	–0.340	0.018 (0.808)	0.015 (0.872)	0.006 (0.661)	0.235	30
Eastern Region						
1960-61 to 2010-11	0.010	–0.013* (1.685)	0.016 (1.210)	0.003 (0.869)	0.501	49
1960-61 to 1980-81	0.388	–0.026 (1.536)	–0.022 (0.776)	0.003 (0.462)	0.190	19
1981-82 to 2010-11	–0.022	–0.008 (0.900)	0.015* (1.962)	0.002 (0.382)	0.369	30

Source: Same as in Table 6.1(a).

Notes:
1. Figure in parenthesis is t value of the coefficients.
2. Asterisk *, ** and *** indicate coefficients significant at 10 per cent, 5 per cent and 1 per cent levei of significance respectively for two tailed test.

Western region districts, broadly are of the same composition. Most of the Central and Eastern region districts fall in the category of medium and low developed districts. Therefore, similar findings of these four clubs seem to be obvious.

On the whole, it seems that there is unconditional club convergence in the club of highly developed Western region districts in the state of Uttar Pradesh. However, there is no club convergence in the club of Central and the club of Eastern districts which virtually are the clubs of medium and club of low developed districts respectively.

6.6. SUMMARY

The present chapter examines the convergence/divergence of regional disparities in agricultural development in Uttar Pradesh for five decades spanning from 1960 to 2010. We tested the phenomenon of convergence/divergence of all the four types, namely—sigma convergence, beta unconditional convergence, beta conditional and club convergence. Contrary to the most of the studies employing a single measure of inequality, we tested the convergence/divergence of sigma type by employing three different concepts of standard deviation, coefficient of variation and Gini coefficient measure of inequality. Rather than relying on single specification of regression to test convergence/divergence, we employed the alternative functional forms of the convergence/divergence regression equations. The main findings in the chapter are:

1. For the period as a whole, there was sigma convergence in regional disparities in agricultural performance in Uttar Pradesh. However, the pattern of inequality was of inverted 'U' type implying sigma divergence from 1960 to 1980 and sigma convergence from 1981 to 2010. The magnitude of convergence was more strong in the later period than the former resulting in overall sigma convergence of declining regional disparities.
2. Besides, sigma convergence, there is evidence of significant beta unconditional convergence mainly during the last three decades, whereas no such convergence occurred during the 1960s and 1970s. In other words, there is evidence of catch-up by the low developed districts with the medium and high developed districts. The results are robust to control for other exogenous structural factors affecting the agricultural development.
3. There is no conclusive evidence on prevalence of club convergence across districts for the last three decades. While, beta convergence occurred in the club of high developed Western region districts during 1981-82 to 2010-11 period, but there is no such evidence from 1960-61 to 1980-81 for the club. However, neither the club of medium developed or low developed districts and nor the clubs of Central region and Eastern region districts provide conclusive evidence

regarding both beta unconditional and beta conditional convergences. Therefore, the overall beta convergence of catch-up by low developed districts seems to be mainly because of very strong catch-up within the club of high developed, Western region districts and partly due to inter-region convergence of development.

7

Dynamics of Labour Productivity in Uttar Pradesh

7.1. INTRODUCTION

The preceding three chapters were mainly devoted to examine the temporal and spatial patterns of agricultural growth and development in the state of Uttar Pradesh over the last five decades. In the present chapter, we propose to examine the dynamics of temporal and spatial patterns of labour productivity of workers employed in agricultural sector for the last five decades. In fact, the growth and level of labour productivity is an important indicator of resource (labour) use efficiency and well-being of the workers and their families employed in the agricultural activities. High labour productivity of the farmers in general and of small and marginal farmers in particular, not only suggests the gainful employment available to them, but is a good indicator of level of living, their capabilities of escaping vulnerability to poverty and their capacities to invest in health and education of their family members in general and their children in particular. The high level productivity is not only an indicator of the availability of more employment opportunities to agricultural workers, but also tends to be significantly associated with high rewards in terms of wages and their capacities to fulfill their basic minimum requirements for food and other basic needs. There is a large empirical evidence establishing inverse relationship between the incidence of rural poverty and the level of labour productivity of workers in the agriculture sector (Ahluwalia 1978; Datt and Ravallion, 1990, 1996, 1998; Mellor 2001; World Bank 2008). Therefore, the information on different dimensions of labour productivity is of crucial importance for planners and policy-makers to provide long-term solution to the problem of vulnerability of poverty and low level of living in the rural areas, where people predominantly rely on agriculture for their livelihood and also have high concentration of poor in the country. The present chapter proposes to generate information on dynamics of labour productivity in Uttar Pradesh in this context.

More specifically, the objective of present chapter is to examine the temporal variations of inter-regional and inter-district variations in growth and level of labour productivity in Uttar Pradesh. The chapter also proposes to examine the dynamics of regional disparities and association between labour productivity and prevalence of rural poverty in the state.

The chapter is outlined as follows. After a brief introduction and objective in section 7.1, section 7.2 presents the methodology used in this chapter. Section 7.3 discusses dynamics of inter-regional variations in agricultural workers, productivity in Uttar Pradesh during 1960-63 to 2008-11. Thereafter, section 7.4 discusses intra-regional and inter-district variations in labour productivity in Uttar Pradesh from 1960-63 to 2008-11. Linkages between labour productivity and poverty are discussed in section 7.5 and section 7.6 presents summary of the main findings.

7.2. METHODOLOGY

In the empirical analysis of dynamics of labour productivity, following methodology is employed in the chapter:

7.2 (i) Labour Productivity: The labour productivity is measured as:

$$\text{Labour productivity} = \frac{\text{Value output of all crops in district/zone}}{\text{Total number of agriculture labourers in the district zone}}$$

The estimate of value of output of total crop sector in the district (value of output of 35 crop sector jacked up/inflated for the total cropped area in the district) has been taken from our earlier estimates at 2010-11 constant prices for all the years from 1960-61 to 2010-11. The information on number of workers employed in agricultural sector is taken from the population census rounds. The agricultural workers include both main and marginal workers in agriculture. We dropped the information in this context for 1971 census because of non-comparable definition of female workers of 1971 census with the preceding (1961) and the succeeding (1981, 1991, 2001 and 2011) census definition. Therefore, we have taken workers from 1961, 1981, 1991, 2001 and 2011 census reports. We interpolated the figures for intervening years between two consecutive census years. For example, between 1991 and 2001, we first estimated the compound growth rate of agricultural workers growth and then assuming the same growth during ten years, interpolated information for all nine intervening years from 1991 to 2001.

To examine the linkages between the workers' productivity in agriculture and the incidence of poverty in Uttar Pradesh, we calculated the district-wise estimate of the incidence of rural poverty in Uttar Pradesh from NSS 61st survey of 2004-05 provided by Chaudhuri and Gupta (2009). It may be mentioned that, probably, these are the only recent district-wise figures generated for the state of Uttar Pradesh. There was no alternative option than to use this 2004-05 information for our present chapter.

The growth rate during different periods has been estimated using compound annual growth rate formula detailed earlier. Similarly, measurement of inequality in labour productivity has been estimated by employing the coefficient of variation, Gini coefficient, ratio of share of top to bottom quintile and the ratio of average productivity of top to bottom quintile. The procedure for estimation for these measures has already been detailed in the previous chapter. The zone-wise dynamics of labour productivity is estimated employing the same agro-economic regionalization of Uttar Pradesh as detailed in previous chapters. Following the earlier procedure, we estimated the dynamics of labour productivity for the period as a whole as well as by sub-dividing period into triennium ending 1960-63, 1980-83, 1990-93, 2000-03 and 2008-11.

EMPIRICAL FINDINGS

7.3. LABOUR PRODUCTIVITY: INTER-REGIONAL VARIATIONS

7.3 (i) Dynamics of Growth of Labour Productivity

Information on the region-wise growth of labour productivity in Uttar

Pradesh is detailed in Table 7.1. For the state as a whole, the growth of labour productivity which has occurred at 1.11 per cent per annum during 1960s and 1970s has declined to 0.95 per cent during 1980s to 0.38 per cent during 1990s and 0.23 per cent during 2000s. Such drastic decline of growth rate is a matter of serious concern for a big state like Uttar Pradesh, housing nearly 16.6 per cent of people in the country. This pattern of consistent decline in growth of labour productivity is contrary to the acceleration of output growth up to 1980s and deceleration thereafter. Furthermore, the growth of agriculture production declined to half, but growth of labour productivity during last decade is one-fifth of growth of labour productivity during 1960s and 1970s. The phenomenon is mainly because of the fact that the growth of workers in agriculture in Uttar Pradesh has grown at a higher pace compared to growth of labour productivity in the state. While labour productivity increased at 0.89 per cent for the period as a whole, the number of agricultural workers in Uttar Pradesh has grown at 1.3 per cent per annum during the last fifty years (Fig. 7.1).

The pattern of labour productivity varies considerably across regions in the state. For the period as a whole, the Mid-Western Plain Zone and North-Eastern Plain Zone, stands apart from rest of the

Table 7.1: Region-wise Growth of Labour Productivity in Uttar Pradesh: 1960-63 to 2008-11

Regions↓	*Growth Rate (% Per Annum) in Triennium*				
Period→	*1960-63/ 1980-83*	*1980-83/ 1990-93*	*1990-93/ 2000-03*	*2000-03/ 2008-11*	*1960-63/ 2008-11*
Western Plain Zone	–0.10	–0.18	0.10	0.03	–0.05
Mid-Western Plain Zone	1.71	1.77	0.50	–0.78	1.05
South-Western Semi-Arid Zone	–0.04	1.32	1.39	1.30	0.76
Central Plain Zone	0.80	1.21	0.73	–0.04	0.73
Bundelkhand Zone	0.09	–1.24	0.93	0.25	0.10
North-Eastern Plain Zone	1.78	1.51	0.42	1.18	1.34
Eastern Plain Zone	1.04	1.20	–0.14	0.54	0.74
Vindhyan Zone	0.22	–1.25	2.56	–5.30	–0.55
Hills	1.55	0.98	0.19	–0.39	0.82
Uttar Pradesh	1.11	0.95	0.38	0.23	0.89

Source: GoI (Various Reports), *Census of India (Uttar Pradesh)*, Primary Census Abstract, Uttar Pradesh, Directorate of Census Operations, Government of India.

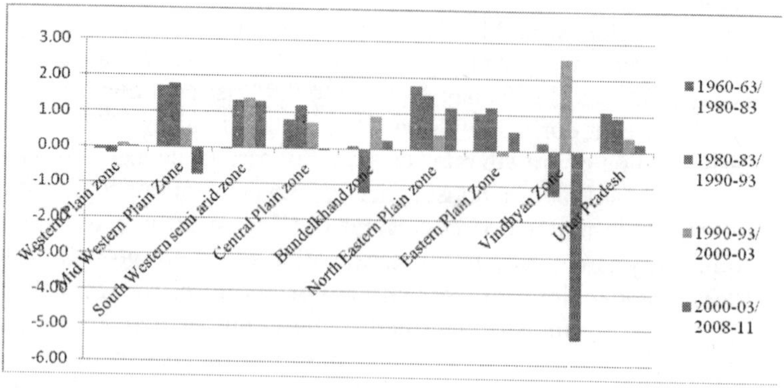

Figure 7.1: Region-wise Growth of Labour Productivity in Uttar Pradesh: 1960-63 to 2008-11.

Source: Table 7.1.

zones as these have recorded growth exceeding 1 per cent per annum. Three other zones, South-Western Semi-Arid Zone, Central Plain Zone and Eastern Plain Zone recorded middle level growth of labour productivity hovering around 0.75 per cent per annum. Three zones performed very badly in terms of growth of labour productivity. While Western Plain Zone and Vindhyan Zone recorded negative growth in labour productivity, Bundelkhand Zone has recorded marginal growth of 0.10 per cent per annum in labour productivity.

The region-wise growth of labour productivity during different sub-periods however does not reveal any consistent pattern over time. With only exception of Hill Zones, that shows consistent decline in labour productivity over time. In rest of the regions, growth rates follow either inverted 'U' curve behaviour, of first increase then decline or cyclical behaviour over time.

7.3 (ii) Dynamics of Level of Labour Productivity

Region-wise level of labour productivity (Rs. per agricultural worker) during 1960-63, 1980-83, 1990-93, 2000-03 and 2008-11 in Uttar Pradesh is presented in Table 7.2.

In 1960-63, the level of labour productivity was Rs. 17,381 per agricultural worker at the state-level in Uttar Pradesh. The level of productivity in most developed Western Plain Zone, Mid-Western Plain Zone, South-Western Semi-Arid Zone was above the state average with per worker productivity above Rs. 22,000. Even,

Table 7.2: Region-wise Level of Labour Productivity in Uttar Pradesh: 1960-63 to 2008-11

Regions↓	*Labour productivity in triennium (Rs. per agricultural worker at 2010-11 constant prices)*				
Period→	*1960-63*	*1980-83*	*1990-93*	*2000-03*	*2008-11*
Western Plain Zone	49336	48367	47525	47984	48093
Mid-Western Plain Zone	22291	31278	37287	39203	36808
South-Western Semi-Arid Zone	28780	28535	32546	37364	41430
Central Plain Zone	16413	19255	21708	23352	23286
Bundelkhand Zone	22664	23054	20358	22324	22774
North-Eastern Plain Zone	9459	13453	15634	16305	17903
Eastern Plain Zone	12606	15517	17482	17240	18000
Vindhyan Zone	13251	13842	12203	15710	10159
Hills	9655	13136	14483	14757	14307
Uttar Pradesh	17381	21686	23833	24766	25227

Source: Same as in Table 7.1.

Bundelkhand Zone recorded significant productivity of Rs. 22,664 per agricultural worker during this period. Whereas, North-Eastern Plain Zone recorded the lowest level of Rs. 9,459 per agricultural worker during this period. There is nearly 80 per cent gap in labour productivity between the highest developed Western Plain Zone and the least developed North-Eastern Plain Zone. Even South-Western Semi-Arid Zone, being second after Western Plain Zone in the level of workers productivity recorded considerable gap of nearly 42 per cent in the productivity levels during this period. This high difference in the levels of agricultural workers productivity signifies existence of wide inter-regional disparities in labour productivity in the state.

The period from 1980-83, marked a significant improvement in levels of labour productivity at the state level as well as in most of the zones in Uttar Pradesh. There was increase by Rs. 4,305 per agricultural worker at the state-level in Uttar Pradesh. All the zones, only except Western Plain Zone and South-Western Semi-Arid Zone, also followed the state-level pattern of increase in labour productivity. The highest increase in the level of labour productivity was recorded by Mid-Western Plain Zone from Rs. 22,291 per agricultural worker in triennium ending 1960-63 to Rs. 31,278 per agricultural worker in 1980-83. In addition, North-Eastern Plain Zone, being the lowest zone in labour productivity during previous period also recorded substantial increase in labour productivity during this period. Though the level of agricultural workers' productivity increased in most of the zones, but still there was considerable gap of nearly 73 per cent between the highest and lowest productivity level Western Plain Zone and Hill Zone.

The triennium ending 1990-93 further recorded increase from Rs. 21,686 to Rs. 23,833 per agricultural worker in the state as compared with eighties. On the other hand, Western Plain Zone continued to record decline in labour productivity during this period as well. Even Bundelkhand Zone and Vindhyan Zone also recorded decline in agricultural workers' productivity during this period. Vindhyan Zone was the most hard hit, as the zone not only recorded decline in productivity levels, but it was at the lowest level of agricultural workers' productivity among all the zones in the state. The gap between the highest and lowest productivity zones further increased to 74 per cent during this period. Though, Western Plain Zone, being at the highest level of development recorded a decline, but on the other hand lowest developed Vindhyan Zone also registered a decline in workers' productivity and hence widening the gap further across zones.

During 1990s, there was significant improvement in the level of labour productivity in the state as well as at the regional level in Uttar Pradesh. Among all the zones, only Eastern Plain Zone recorded a marginal decline in level of agricultural workers productivity. Even Western Plain Zone, that recorded continuous decline till 1990-93, also recorded an increase during this period. The gap between highest and lowest developed zones also declined to nearly 69 per cent during this period. Not only the gap declined among the zones, even Vindhyan Zone made a significant improvement. It was at the lowest level of development during the previous period, whereas, it recorded a significant increase of Rs. 3,507 per agricultural worker during this period.

Thereafter during 2000s, four of total nine zones (including hills) recorded decline in labour productivity. Vindhyan Zone again recorded retrogression in levels of productivity during this period. It was mainly due to deceleration in growth in value output on one hand and due to considerable increase in workers in the zone on the other. Excessive population pressure along with decline in agriculture output led to serious reverses in agricultural workers' productivity in the zone, as most of the growth in output is eaten up by rapid growth in number of agricultural workers. Whereas, at the state level, there was increase in agricultural workers' productivity from Rs. 24,766 per agricultural worker during 2000-03 to Rs. 25,227 per agricultural worker during 2008-11. Moreover, Western Plain Zone, South-Western Semi-Arid Zone, Bundelkhand Zone, North-Eastern Plain Zone and Eastern Plain Zone also recorded an increase in labour productivity during this period. An increase in agricultural workers' productivity is a positive indication of agricultural development in the state. As discussed before, improvement in workers productivity increases wages of labour and hence their living standards.

7. 4. LABOUR PRODUCTIVITY: INTRA-REGIONAL AND INTER-DISTRICT VARIATIONS

7.4 (i) Distribution of Districts by Levels of Labour Productivity in Uttar Pradesh: 1960-63 to 2008-11

Table 7.3 presents region-wise distribution of districts according to their level of labour productivity in Uttar Pradesh during 1960-63, 1980-83, 1990-93, 2000-03 and 2008-11. For analysis all the districts are divided into three broad categories of high, medium and low developed categories according to their levels of labour productivity. High developed districts are those having agricultural workers' productivity above Rs. 34,000 per agricultural worker, medium level districts are, the districts with agricultural workers productivity lying between Rs. 19,000 to Rs. 34,000 per agricultural worker and low developed districts are less than Rs. 19,000 per agricultural worker.

To begin with, during 1960-63 there were only seven high productivity districts out of total 46 district units (excluding hills) that recorded high labour productivity exceeding Rs. 34,000 per agricultural worker. This included all four districts from Western Plain Zone, two districts from South-Western Semi-Arid Zone and one district from Mid-Western Plain Zone. None of the district from any other zone recorded productivity above Rs. 34,000 per agricultural worker in the state. Further, there were as many as 15 mid-productivity districts in the state. Among these, five districts were from Central Plain Zone, four from Mid-Western Plain Zone and three districts each from South-Western Semi-Arid Zone and Bundelkhand Zone respectively. Finally more than half of the districts, 24 districts in the state belonged to low productivity levels with less than Rs. 19,000 per agricultural worker. These low developed districts included all the districts from North-Eastern Plain Zone, Eastern Plain Zone and

Table 7.3: Region-wise Distribution of Districts in Level of Labour Productivity in Uttar Pradesh: 1960-63 to 2008-11

Regions↓ *Period→*	*Level of labour productivity*	*Number of Districts in Triennium*				
		1960-63	*1980-83*	*1990-93*	*2000-03*	*2008-11*
Western Plain Zone	High (>34000)	4	4	4	4	4
	Medium (19000-34000)	0	0	0	0	0
	Low (<19000)	0	0	0	0	0
Mid-Western Plain Zone	High (>34000)	1	2	5	5	5
	Medium (19000-34000)	4	5	2	2	2
	Low (<19000)	2	0	0	0	0
South-Western Semi-Arid Zone	High (>34000)	2	1	1	5	5
	Medium (19000-34000)	3	4	4	0	0
	Low (<19000)	0	0	0	0	0
Central Plain Zone	High (>34000)	0	0	0	2	2
	Medium (19000-34000)	5	5	6	4	4
	Low (<19000)	6	6	5	5	5
Bundelkhand Zone	High (>34000)	0	0	0	0	0
	Medium (19000-34000)	3	4	3	3	3
	Low (<19000)	1	0	1	1	1
North-Eastern Plain Zone	High (>34000)	0	0	0	0	0
	Medium (19000-34000)	0	0	1	0	1
	Low (<19000)	5	5	4	5	4
Eastern Plain Zone	High (>34000)	0	0	0	0	0
	Medium (19000-34000)	0	0	1	1	4
	Low (<19000)	9	9	8	8	5
Vindhyan Zone	High (>34000)	0	0	0	0	0
	Medium (19000-34000)	0	0	0	0	0
	Low (<19000)	1	1	1	1	1
Uttar Pradesh	High (>34000)	7	7	10	16	16
	Medium (19000-34000)	15	18	17	10	14
	Low (<19000)	24	21	19	20	16

Source: Table 7.4.

sole district of Vindhyan Zone and six districts from Central Plain Zone, two from Mid-Western Plain Zone and one district from Bundelkhand Zone. It is interesting to note that there was no district from Western Plain Zone and South-Western Semi-Arid Zone that recorded agricultural workers' productivity below Rs. 19,000 per agricultural worker.

By 1980-83, there was no significant change in distribution of districts across productivity levels. Only three low worker productivity districts graduated to mid-productivity level. Two of them were from the Mid-Western Plain Zone and one from Bundelkhand Zone. By

1990-93, there occurred again marginal change in distribution of districts across productivity levels. While three low productivity districts, one each from Central Plain Zone, North-Eastern Plain Zone and Eastern Plain Zone joined the mid-productivity range, whereas one mid-productivity district of Bundelkhand slipped to low productivity level. The notable change, however is in case of three mid-productivity districts in Mid-Western Plain Zone, joining the high productivity group of districts. Rest distribution of the districts remained same, as was during 1980-83.

The situation underwent a notable change during 2000-03. The number of high productivity districts increased substantially from seven during eighties to 16 during this period. All the districts from South-Western Semi-Arid Zone and Western Plain Zone along with five districts from Mid-Western Plain Zone and two from Central Plain Zone recorded productivity exceeding Rs. 34,000 per agricultural worker. On the other hand, number of mid-productivity districts declined from 17 to 10. This was due to upward shift of four districts from South-Western Semi-Arid Zone and two districts from Central Plain Zone, whereas one district from North-Eastern Plain Zone recorded a decline and moved down in low productivity range. This led to increase in number of low workers' productivity districts from 19 to 20 districts during 2000-03.

The decade of 2000s witnessed marginal change in inter-productivity range distribution of districts. Only change occurred during the period was one district from North-Eastern Plain Zone and three from Eastern Plain Zone joining the mid-productivity level range. At the end, two of types of regions emerged clearly. On the one side are the Western, Mid-Western and South-Western regions having none of the districts falling in the low productivity range, whereas on the other side are rest of the four zones, having none of their districts in the high productivity range. The regional divide in terms of labour productivity seems to be more sharp compared with land productivity in Uttar Pradesh.

7.4 (ii) District-wise Level of Labour Productivity in Uttar Pradesh: 1960-63 to 2008-11

District-wise level of labour productivity during triennium ending 1960-63, 1980-83, 1990-93, 2000-03 and 2008-11 is presented in Table 7.4. During 1960-63, Muzaffarnagar and Meerut districts

Table 7.4: District-wise Level of Labour Productivity in Uttar Pradesh: 1960-63 to 2008-11

Districts/ Regions↓	*Labour Productivity in Triennium (Rs. Per Agricultural Worker at 2010-11 Constant Prices)*				
Period→	*1960-63*	*1980-83*	*1990-93*	*2000-03*	*2008-11*
(1)	(2)	(3)	(4)	(5)	(6)
Bulandshahr	44513	40107	36741	35956	38651
Meerut	51598	49741	49161	58519	56417
Muzaffarnagar	52604	57397	49870	49009	52166
Saharanpur	49273	45289	52907	45669	42048
Western Plain Zone	**49336**	**48367**	**47525**	**47984**	**48093**
Bareilly	21300	25410	31073	31700	30117
Bijnor	37982	46124	56925	56069	49728
Budaun	16329	22659	25389	29759	31705
Moradabad	20988	33896	36674	36654	34843
Pilibhit	27084	38109	46016	50979	43143
Rampur	24903	31975	35676	39765	34438
Shahjahanpur	18500	27395	37967	41498	40201
Mid-Western Plain Zone	**22291**	**31278**	**37287**	**39203**	**36808**
Agra	28629	27001	32076	41102	42210
Aligarh	36477	36381	32534	36896	39844
Etah	22925	23675	30335	38103	38129
Mainpuri	19457	22676	31046	35218	44557
Mathura	37649	32805	38331	35745	43516
South-Western Semi-Arid Zone	**28780**	**28535**	**32546**	**37364**	**41430**
Allahabad	12001	16533	14384	14487	13538
Etawah	21767	27285	30891	32796	33736
Farrukhabad	19049	23809	32763	37950	34068
Fatehpur	16143	19743	18401	18501	18734
Hardoi	19597	17625	20768	21605	24358
Kanpur	23837	23983	30331	26656	24122
Kheri	21539	25922	33899	40478	37188
Lucknow	12451	15686	15455	17044	17930
Raebareli	10607	12918	13982	13828	13876
Sitapur	16569	17407	20330	24648	24740
Unnao	12582	14276	14844	15746	18906
Central Plain Zone	**16413**	**19255**	**21708**	**23352**	**23286**
Banda	21740	19384	14325	16199	14015
Hamirpur	23870	26900	21982	23033	23894
Jalaun	28631	31454	30884	31798	29473
Jhansi	18827	19331	20287	23041	27106
Bundelkhand Zone	**22664**	**23054**	**20358**	**22324**	**22774**
Bahraich	9491	11329	13493	15871	16746
Basti	8518	12055	14793	14763	17714
Deoria	11054	14808	19061	18054	18390
Gonda	9635	14043	13542	16879	19432
Gorakhpur	8966	14530	16978	16216	17127

(Contd.)

(1)	(2)	(3)	(4)	(5)	(6)
North-Eastern Plain Zone	**9459**	**13453**	**15634**	**16305**	**17903**
Azamgarh	12065	12640	17974	17417	19000
Ballia	13599	16931	16681	17674	18494
Barabanki	16796	15896	18559	20222	20938
Faizabad	12653	17671	18826	16765	20109
Ghazipur	13081	17050	20722	17754	16393
Jaunpur	10378	16755	17726	15709	15554
Pratapgarh	8704	13621	13936	12781	13410
Sultanpur	11678	14297	16858	18132	20764
Varanasi	15250	16893	15873	18644	16325
Eastern Plain Zone	**12606**	**15517**	**17482**	**17240**	**18000**
Mirzapur	13251	13842	12203	15710	10159
Vindhyan Zone	**13251**	**13842**	**12203**	**15710**	**10159**
Hills	9655	13136	14483	14757	14307
Uttar Pradesh	**17381**	**21686**	**23833**	**24766**	**25227**

Source: Same as in Table 7.1.

outperformed in labour productivity levels with Rs. 52,604 and Rs. 51,598 per agricultural worker respectively. These districts were highest developed districts in land productivity levels as well. It is evident from the table that only four districts and that too from Western Plain Zone recorded these high levels of productivity whereas when we move towards other zones and districts, there is considerable decline in the level. There was no district in any other zone to record agricultural workers' productivity above Rs. 38,000 per agricultural worker. However, even this level of productivity is confined to districts in Mid-Western Plain Zone and South-Western Semi-Arid Zone only. But even in these zones, there is wide variability in productivity levels. Such as Budaun, Shahjahanpur and Mainpuri districts recorded very low levels of productivity which was below Rs. 19,500 per agricultural worker, whereas some of the districts like Bijnor, Aligarh and Mathura recorded comparatively high productivity above Rs. 36,000 per agricultural worker. It is worth mentioning that even districts in Bundelkhand Zone recorded considerable labour productivity, unlike very low level of development in land productivity. On the other hand, performance of Basti and Gorakhpur districts from North-Eastern Plain Zone and Pratapgarh district from Eastern Plain Zone was below average. Among these districts, Basti recorded the lowest productivity of Rs. 8,518 per agricultural worker in the state. Most of the districts in the state during this period were gripped in low levels of productivity.

Thereafter during triennium ending 1980-83, three of total four districts in Western Plain Zone recorded decline in labour productivity. However, Muzaffarnagar being the highest developed district further recorded increase in labour productivity during this period as well. In addition, only six districts—Agra, Aligarh and Mathura from South-Western Semi-Arid Zone, Hardoi from Central Plain Zone, Banda from Bundelkhand Zone and Barabanki from Eastern Plain Zone also recorded decline in agricultural workers' productivity during this period. Whereas, rest 37 district units recorded an increase in per worker productivity. Among these, Pilibhit district from Mid-Western Plain Zone recorded an impressive increase by Rs. 11,025 per agricultural worker productivity. However during this period also, though Basti district from North-Eastern Plain Zone recorded an increase, but it remained at the lowest level of labour productivity among all the districts in the state.

By 1990-93, Muzaffarnagar district from Western Plain Zone suffered a setback and recorded decline along with Bulandshahr and Meerut districts from the zone. On the other hand, Saharanpur district from this zone only, recorded an increase from Rs. 45,289 to Rs. 52,907 per agricultural worker and recorded highest level of workers' productivity among all the districts in the state. All seven districts from Mid-Western Plain Zone further recorded an increase in productivity levels during this period as well. On the other hand, Aligarh and Banda along with nine more districts from other zones recorded a decline in labour productivity during this period. Basti district from North-Eastern Plain Zone, being at the lowest level during earlier periods, however marked a significant improvement and shifted upward in the productivity levels. Whereas, Mirzapur district from Vindhyan Zone slipped downward and was at the lowest level of productivity of Rs. 12,203 per agricultural worker. Though, there is increase in levels of development in majority of the districts, but still there exists wide extent of disparity in workers' productivity at the district-level. Districts in Western regions still recorded substantial levels of labour productivity whereas populated districts in Eastern regions and its neighbouring parts lagged behind with comparatively low levels of per workers productivity.

There was tremendous improvement in Meerut, Aligarh and Banda districts during triennium ending 2000-03. All these districts recorded continuous decline in agricultural workers' productivity till 1990s. However during this period, among these districts, Meerut from Western Plain Zone not only recorded an increase in per worker productivity, but it was at the highest level of productivity of Rs. 58,519 per agricultural worker. In addition, all the districts in Bundelkhand Zone also made up for previous reverses and recorded an increase in workers' productivity during this period. On the other hand, nearly 16 districts in the state recorded a decline and more than half of the districts in the state recorded productivity below the state average of Rs. 24,766 per agricultural worker. As mentioned before, all these districts were from Central and Eastern regions only, whereas high developed districts were mostly concentrated in Western parts of the state only.

During 2008-11, nearly 19 districts (including hills) recorded a decline in agricultural workers' productivity. The maximum number of districts to receive a setback was from Mid-Western Plain Zone. Only Budaun district from the zone recorded an increase, whereas rest six districts recorded a downward trend in agricultural workers' productivity. Whereas all districts from South-Western Semi-Arid Zone and North-Eastern Plain Zone recorded an increase in productivity levels though Meerut from Western Plain Zone recorded a decline in per worker productivity, but even then it was at the highest level, with productivity of Rs. 56,417 per agricultural worker followed by Muzaffarnagar with productivity of Rs. 52,166 per agricultural worker. At the lowest level, it was again Mirzapur district from Vindhyan Zone with productivity of only Rs. 10,159 per agricultural worker. Nevertheless, there is increase in levels of productivity at the state-level as well as in most of the districts, but still majority of them are at very low levels of workers' productivity that is even below the state average. This is mainly due to ever increasing population pressure moreover, the state as well as districts have also received a serious blow in value output as well since 1990s.

7.4 (iii) Mobility of Districts Across Labour Productivity Quintiles in Uttar Pradesh during 1980-83 to 2008-11

We further provided movement of districts in levels of labour productivity during 1980-83 to 2008-11 in Table 7.5. For comparison we took the period from 1980-83 to 2008-11 because the period during eighties was the green revolution phase and agricultural growth was highest during this period, but after that it declined with initiation of economic reforms during nineties. Moreover, 2008-11 is the end period of our study, therefore our objective was to analyze the movement of districts from the period of maximum agricultural growth till the end. For analysis, we divided the districts into five categories (quintiles) according to their ranks in labour productivity levels. The districts with rank from one to nine are categorized as Q_5, districts from rank 10 to 19 in agricultural workers productivity are categorized as Q_4, districts from rank 20 to 28 are categorized as Q_3, districts from rank 29 to 38 are Q_2 and very low level districts, above 38th rank in productivity levels and categorized as Q_1.

Table 7.5: Mobility of Districts Across Labour Productivity Quintiles in Uttar Pradesh during 1980-83 to 2008-11

Rank		*2008-11*				
		Q_1 *(Rank 39-47)*	Q_2 *(Rank 29-38)*	Q_3 *(Rank 20-28)*	Q_4 *(Rank 10-19)*	Q_5 *(Rank 01-09)*
1980-83	Q_1 (Rank 39-47)	Mirzapur Pratapgarh Hills Raebareli	Unnao Gonda Azamgarh Basti Bahraich			
	Q_2 (Rank 29-38)	Ghazipur Varanasi Jaunpur Allahabad	Ballia Lucknow Deoria Gorakhpur	Barabanki Sultanpur		
	Q_3 (Rank 20-28)	Banda	Fatehpur	Jhansi Faizabad Hardoi Sitapur	Etah Budaun	Mainpuri
	Q_4 (Rank 10-19)			Jalaun Hamirpur Kanpur	Rampur Etawah Kheri Bareilly Farrukhabad	Shahjahanpur Agra
	Q_5 (Rank 01-09)				Bulandshahr Aligarh Moradabad	Muzaffarnagar Meerut Bijnor Saharanpur Pilibhit Mathura

Source: Table 7.4.

It may be seen from Table 7.5 that the dynamism of quintile-wise mobility of districts is more dynamic at the low level while compared with the districts among the top two quintile of the distribution. As indicated by the number of districts along the diagonal that maintained their *status quo* in relative position in productivity levels. It may be seen that six districts in the top quintile maintained their top slot during almost two decades from 1980-83 to 2008-11. However, three districts namely—Bulandshahr, Aligarh and Moradabad slipped to the fourth quintile while two districts from the fourth quintile namely—Agra and Shahjahanpur and one district—Mainpuri from mid-quintile joined the top quintile. Similarly, five districts in the second top quintile (Q_4) maintained their *status quo* whereas three of its districts namely-Jalaun, Hamirpur and Kanpur lost their position and slipped to Q_3, whereas two districts as stated earlier (Agra and Shahjahanpur) joined the league of top quintile in productivity distribution. In middle quintile (Q_3), two districts namely—Banda and Fatehpur slipped to low productivity quintile, whereas three of its districts namely—Etah, Budaun and Mainpuri joined the top two quintiles. The most remarkable shift is in case of bottom second quintile districts where only four districts could maintain their earlier positions whereas four slipped to the bottom quintile of the districts in 2008-11. Only two of its districts—Barabanki and Sultanpur were able to improve their position in joining Q_3 in 2008-11. At bottom of the distribution, five districts—Unnao, Gonda, Azamgarh, Basti and Bahraich graduated to next quintile (Q_2), whereas four districts namely—Mirzapur, Pratapgarh, Raebareli and hills continued to be trapped at the bottom level. The serious problem with these districts in agriculture development needs to be tackled on priority level as it is not only the distribution of districts, but the agricultural workforce in these districts that remained trapped in very low level of earnings for the last three decades.

7.4 (iv) Regional Contiguity

The map 7.1(a) to 7.1(e) presents the spatial distribution of districts in high, medium and low levels of labour productivity at five points of time, namely--1960-63, 1980-83, 1990-93, 2000-03 and 2008-11 based on the worker productivity. Initially, during 1960-63, a cluster of high developed districts was formed in North and North-West, adjoining the neighbouring states of Delhi and Haryana. On the other side, towards East, neighbouring the States of Bihar, Jharkhand and Chhattisgarh, a huge club of low developed districts was formed. In addition, two small fringes of low developed districts existed in the state. The middle part of the state was under medium developed districts, forming a contiguous stretch from North to West

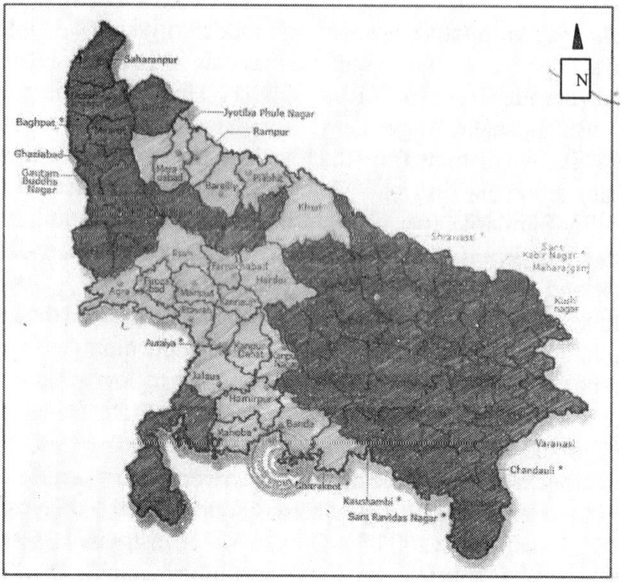

Map 7.1(a): District-wise level of labour productivity in Uttar Pradesh:1960-63.

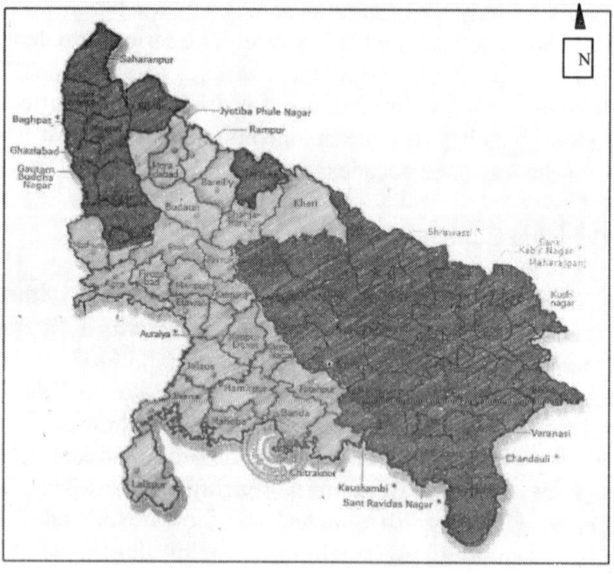

Map 7.1(b): District-wise level of labour productivity in Uttar Pradesh:1980-83.

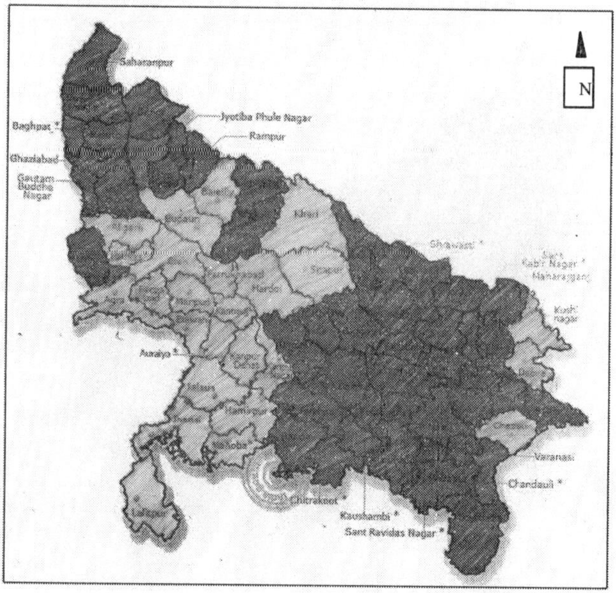

Map 7.1(c): District-wise level of labour productivity in Uttar Pradesh:1990-93.

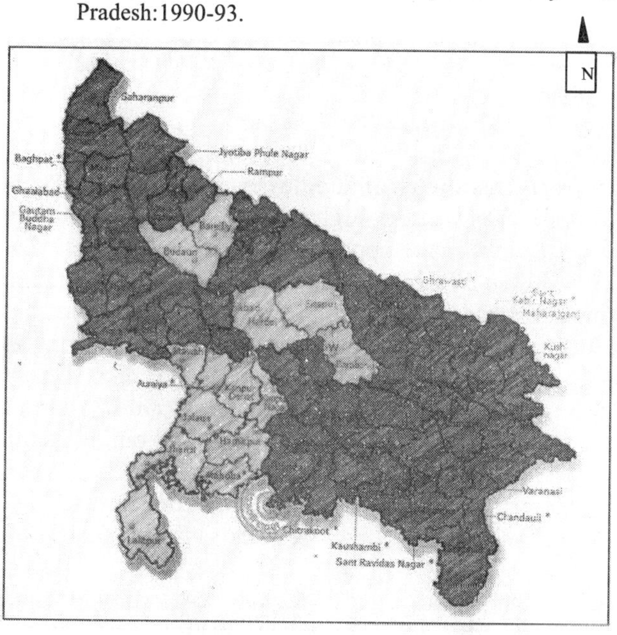

Map 7.1(d): District-wise level of labour productivity in Uttar Pradesh:2000-03.

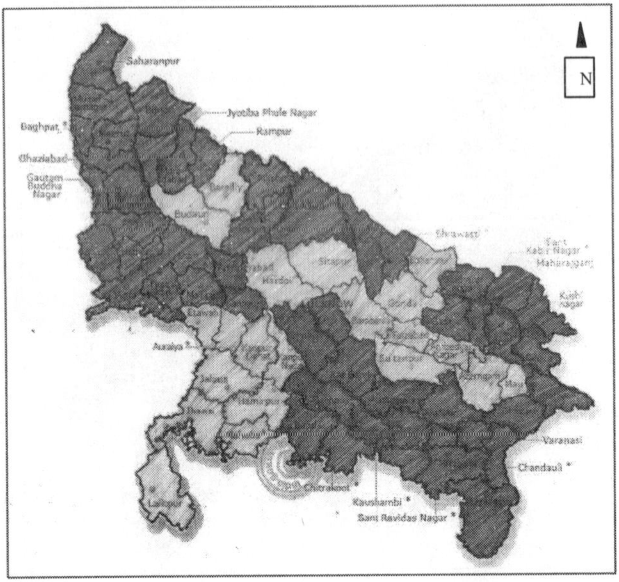

Map 7.1(e): District-wise level of labour productivity in Uttar Pradesh:2008-11.

Map 7.1: District-wise labour productivity in Uttar Pradesh:1960-63 to 2008-11.

Source: Table 7.4.

Note: These are indicative maps of Uttar Pradesh.

and South-West. This stretch of middle developed districts expanded further during 1980s, whereas high and low developed districts had their own huge clubs in the opposite directions in the state. During 1990s, a small club of medium developed districts emerged in the East, adjoining Bihar. Small island of high developed district, that emerged during 1980s, in the North expanded further during 1990s and a small club of high developed districts was also seen in the West. These clubs expanded further during 2000-03, forming a contiguous stretch of high developed districts adjoining Delhi and Haryana in the North-West, Rajasthan in West and Uttarakhand in North. The pattern more or less remained the same during 2008-11, only the group of medium developed districts expanded towards East.

During all the periods there is regional contiguity among high and low developed districts, forming huge clusters on the opposite sides in the state. High and medium growth districts expanded to its contiguous districts over time.

7.4 (v) Labour Productivity: Inter-district Disparities

The information on inter-district disparities in labour productivity at five different points of time is detailed in Table 7.6. Interestingly, there is no unanimity in the temporal pattern of inter-district inequalities measured through different inequality measures. For example, in terms of coefficient of variation, the inequalities consistently declined from 0.561 per cent during 1960-63 to 0.439 per cent in 2008-11. However, in terms of Gini coefficient, there was a big decline in inequality from 0.295 in 1960-63 to 0.250 in 1980-83, increased marginally to 0.253 in 1990-93 and 0.255 in 2000-03 and again marginally declined to 0.248 in 2008-11.

Table 7.6: Changes in Inter-District Inequality in Labour Productivity and Output Levels in Uttar Pradesh: 1960-63 to 2008-11

Measures↓	*Inequality in Labour Productivity in Triennium*				
Periods→	*1960-63*	*1980-83*	*1990-93*	*2000-03*	*2008-11*
Gini Coefficient of Inequality	0.295	0.250	0.253	0.255	0.248
Coefficient of Variation	0.561	0.467	0.460	0.459	0.439
Share (%) of the Bottom quintile	18.77	16.20	16.14	15.60	12.79
Share (%) of the Middle quintile	52.75	52.42	53.80	57.98	61.93
Share (%) of the Top quintile	28.48	31.38	30.05	26.41	25.28
Share of the Top/Bottom quintiles	1.52	1.94	1.86	1.69	1.98
Level of Workers' Productivity of Bottom quintile districts	9668	13096	13905	14850	14175
Level of Workers' Productivity of Middle quintile districts	17925	21058	23732	25209	25886
Level of Workers' Productivity of Top quintile districts	40817	42205	44955	47010	45998
Ratio of Top to Bottom Quintile districts	4.22	3.22	3.23	3.17	3.24

Source: Estimated from District-Level Data on Inflated Value Output and Labour Productivity.

In terms of the share of top to bottom quintile inequality, the gap between top/bottom districts increased from 1.52 per cent to 1.94 per cent, then declined to 1.69 per cent in 2000-03, but again increased to 1.98 per cent in 2008-11. Similar evidence is seen on the basis of the ratio of labour productivity between top to bottom quintile districts. Taken all the measures together, it seems that disparities declined for the first two decades, but almost stagnated thereafter. This is contrary to the trend of agricultural development and growth and rigorous testing of the same through convergence and divergence models, where we found that the regional disparity in agricultural performance first deteriorated during 1960s and 1970s, but inequality declined during subsequent three decades. This seems to indicate that the observed pattern of persistence of inter-district disparity during the last three decades is due to the labour dynamic differentials across districts.

Persistence of regional disparity in labour productivity during last three decades notwithstanding, the pattern of gains across districts at bottom, middle and top-level are not same over the period. It is highly disturbing that the share of bottom quintile districts in total agricultural production consistently and substantially declined from 18.77 per cent to 12.79 per cent. On the other end of the distribution at the top, while the share of top 20 districts in agricultural production first increased from 28.48 per cent in 1960-63 to 31.38 per cent in 1980-83. However, the share of these top districts on labour productivity declined from 31.38 per cent in 1980-83 to 25.28 per cent in 2008-11. The middle 60 per cent of the districts gained at the cost of the districts at the bottom and top of the labour productivity ladder. While the top quintile districts still have high proportionate share in production, but a big decline at the bottom is worrisome. The declining share tends to have a significant bearing on returns to the vulnerable segment of the rural population like small and marginal farmers and agricultural labourers who have very high probability of falling in poverty. It is serious issue for attention of the policy-makers in the state, to check the deteriorating position of the low labour productivity districts in income distribution.

7.5. LINKAGE BETWEEN WORKERS' PRODUCTIVITY AND POVERTY IN UTTAR PRADESH

Table 7.7 presents the region-wise level of workers' productivity and proportion of rural and total population in each zone below poverty line at beginning of the twenty first century. There seems to be inverse relationship between the level of productivity and agricultural development across the districts as the coefficient of correlation comes

Table 7.7: Correlation between Labour Productivity and Poverty in Uttar Pradesh

Regions	*Total poor (percentage)*	*Rural poor (percentage)*	*Labour productivity (Rs. per agricultural worker)*	*Correlation (Total)*	*Correlation (Rural)*
Western Plain Zone	25.5	20.2	47984	0.36	0.95
Mid-Western Plain Zone	26.8	26.9	39203	–0.23	–0.22
South-Western Semi-Arid Zone	31.6	34.7	37364	–0.32	–0.36
Central Plain Zone	30.2	28.5	23352	–0.23	0.12
Bundelkhand Zone	40.9	42.9	22324	–0.55	0.11
North-Eastern Plain Zone	48.1	51.1	16305	–0.04	0.38
Eastern Plain Zone	34.5	29.9	17240	–0.56	0.22
Vindhyan Zone	34.4	43.2	15710		
Hills	41.4	42.3	14717		
Uttar Pradesh	35.1	33.3	24766	–0.47	–0.25

Sources: (i) Same as in table 7.2.

(ii) Poverty figures are calculated from NSS 61st round Survey given in, Chaudhuri, Siladitya and Nivedita Gupta (2009), "Levels of Living and Poverty Patterns: A District-wise Analysis for India", *Economic and Political Weekly*, Vol. 44, No. 9, pp. 94-110.

out to be –0.47 for the overall poverty and --0.25 for the rural poverty. This indicates that the agricultural development not only plays an important role in alleviation of rural poverty, but it plays equally important role in mitigation of poverty in urban centres in Uttar Pradesh. This relationship is evident across districts as poverty is least (20.2%) in the most developed Western Plain Zone to more than double in the low productivity zones namely—Hills, Vindhyan Zone and North-Eastern Plain Zone. North-Eastern Plain Zone is odd man out so far as the poverty is concerned, as it is not only having half of its population living in poverty, but is also having almost one-third of the labour productivity in agriculturally most developed Western Plain Zone. Besides the North-Eastern Plain Zone, Bundelkhand Zone has more than 40 per cent population below poverty and very low level of agricultural development and workers' productivity.

The poverty-labour productivity relationship has been tested econometrically by regressing poverty on labour productivity, both in linear and log linear form. The results are as follows:

(i) Poverty (%) = 46.315-0.426 (labour productivity, Rs. 000), $R^2 = 0.22$, N = 48 (3.581)

(ii) log (Poverty %) = 7.056-0.352 log (labour productivity), $R^2 = 0.21$, N = 48 (3.467)

The econometric results confirm the statistical significance of inverse relationship between labour productivity and incidence of poverty across districts. The first equation suggests that within one thousand rupee increase in per worker productivity in a district, on an average reduces 0.426 per cent poverty in Uttar Pradesh. More specifically as suggested by equation (ii) a 10 per cent increase in labour productivity in a district on an average enables 3.52 per cent people to come out of poverty in Uttar Pradesh. Poverty is a very complex phenomenon determined by a number of economic, political, social and cultural factors. Nevertheless, the estimates suggest that about 22 per cent inter-district differentials in the incidence of poverty are due to inter-district differentials in the level of labour productivity. This seems to suggest the strong poverty alleviation impact of agricultural development through labour productivity in Uttar Pradesh. Since, the poor are highly concentrated in low productivity regions, therefore special focus on agriculturally backward regions and districts may provide a substantial long-term solution to the serious problem of poverty in Uttar Pradesh (see Fig. 7.2).

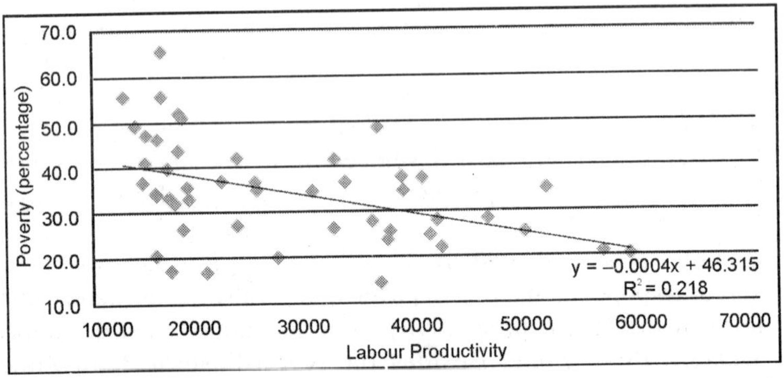

Figure 7.2: Correlation between labour productivity and poverty in Uttar Pradesh.
Source: Table 7.7.

7.6. SUMMARY

This chapter analyses the temporal and spatial dynamics of workers' productivity in the Uttar Pradesh agriculture over the last five decades. Besides labour productivity performance, also examined in the chapter are issues of the regional disparities in labour productivity and linkages between incidence of poverty and the level of productivity across districts in Uttar Pradesh. The main findings are as follows:

1. Contrary to acceleration/deceleration in temporal pattern of agricultural performance, labour productivity growth continuously decelerated over the last five decades.
2. During the last five decades, labour productivity recorded negative growth in Western Plain Zone and Vindhyan Zone whereas the North-Eastern Plain Zone and Mid-Western Plain Zone recorded very high growth of labour productivity exceeding 1 per cent per annum. There is no unique pattern of temporal variations in growth of labour productivity in each of the agro-economic regions.
3. There is continuous increase in labour productivity at the state level in Uttar Pradesh. Whereas, no such consistent pattern of continuous increase is recorded at the regional level except in North-Eastern Plain Zone. Though like the level of land productivity, Western Plain Zone recorded the highest level of labour productivity as well, but there was decline in the productivity in the zone till 1990s that increased only marginally thereafter. Bundelkhand Zone remained almost at the same level of productivity between Rs. 20,000-23,000 per worker productivity. Moreover, four out of nine zones recorded a decline in labour productivity during the later period.
4. All the districts in Western Plain Zone remained at the highest productivity levels since 1960s. Thereafter, except Budaun and Bareilly from Mid-Western Plain Zone, rest all districts joined the high productivity levels during 1990s and districts from South-Western Semi-Arid Zone during 2000s. With exception of Deoria, Ghazipur, Barabanki, Gonda, Azamgarh, Faizabad and Sultanpur, all other districts from North-Eastern Plain Zone, Eastern Plain Zone, Vindhyan

Zone and Hills remained trapped in low levels of labour productivity for last five decades, during 1960-63 to 2008-11.

5. Contrary to inverted 'U' relationship of regional/zone disparities in agriculture growth, the labour productivity depicts 'L' type relationship over time. Disparities in labour productivity declined during 1960-1980 period, but stagnated thereafter during 1981-2010 period. However, this pattern is mainly due to the fact that the main gain of agriculture growth went to the middle 60 per cent of the districts. These middle group districts gained immensely in their share of agriculture production at the cost of bottom and top quintile districts. The most worrisome is substantial decline in share of bottom low productivity districts whose share in agriculture production declined from 18.8 per cent to 12.8 per cent.
6. There is inverse relationship in the incidence of poverty and level of labour productivity across districts in Uttar Pradesh. Persistence of very high incidence of poverty in low productive districts and zones suggests that the policies to overcome agriculture backwardness in these districts may go a long way in overcoming the serious problem of very high incidence of poverty and low level of living of overall population in general and that of small and marginal farmers and agricultural workers in particular.
7. There is a definite regional contiguity in the level of labour productivity in Uttar Pradesh. Districts in the North recorded high levels of development during 1960s and it spread to its contiguous districts thereafter. On the other end, towards East, low developed districts had their own huge cluster. By 2000, some of these low developed districts shifted to medium levels of development. On the whole, a specific pattern emerged with high developed districts forming a contiguous stretch in the North-West and West, and low developed districts forming a contiguous belt in low developed Eastern parts.

8

Sources of Agricultural Performance in Uttar Pradesh

8.1. INTRODUCTION

Having analyzed the level and growth of agriculture production at state, regional and district-level along with level of disparities in Uttar Pradesh in the previous chapters, the present chapter aims at identification of sources of agricultural growth and productivity differences across regions and districts in Uttar Pradesh. Agriculture being biological in nature, the level of output is influenced by both natural and man-made factors. The natural factors include type and texture of soil and topography of land, agro-climatic conditions like rainfall, temperature and sunshine and geographical locations. The man-made factors include: (i) modern inputs and machines like quantity and consumption of fertilizers, cropping pattern, quality of seed, machinery and investment in land; (ii) some traditional factors like manpower, animal power; (iii) infrastructural facilities like roads, electrification, credit facilities; and (iv) institutions like agricultural markets, land-man relations, agriculture research and development and extension services, agriculture price policy, education and priority given to agriculture by planners and policy-makers in the state. Though all these man-made and natural factors are intimately related with growth and development of agriculture sector, but information on these all aspects is rarely available at the district-level. Consequently, in an analysis of the inter-district differences in agriculture productivity, it is not feasible to undertake a comprehensive exercise of the role of all these factors. Therefore, the analysis in this chapter is focussed on the impact of only those factors for which consistent and authenticated information is available for all the districts over the study period. These factors include: fertilizer consumption, number of tractors, number of pumpsets, irrigation facilities and cropping intensity categorized under modern inputs and machinery and road length, manpower, level of literacy rate, average rainfall, structure (small and marginal) of landholdings as resource endowments. Therefore, the present chapter aims at identifying the role of these factors as determinants of agricultural development at the district-level in Uttar Pradesh.

Further, we propose to test the following hypotheses in this chapter:

(i) Differences in physical and human resource endowments (land and human resources), use of modern technology (chemical and mechanical) and physical facilities (road, irrigation) are hypothesised to be responsible for inter-regional disparities in agricultural performance.
(ii) Agro-climatic conditions, such as rainfall, soil quality and other idiosyncratic factors play an important role in inter-district differentials in agricultural development.

The rest of the chapter is organized as follows. Section 8.2 discusses the conceptual framework of the inputs used and the methodology used in this exercise. Thereafter, empirical findings are presented in succeeding sections 8.3, 8.4 and 8.5. Section 8.3 is devoted to regional level analysis of agriculture productivity and inputs used. Section 8.4 correlates the district-wise level of inputs used with level of agricultural development in Uttar Pradesh. Section 8.5 presents results from econometric exercise of sources of agricultural performance. Main findings of the chapter are summarized in concluding section 8.6.

8.2. METHODOLOGY

To examine the role of various sources of agriculture growth and to examine the inter-regional disparities in agricultural performance in the state of Uttar Pradesh, we have examined the input-output relationship at three levels. First, we compared the level of agriculture development with use of various inputs across nine agro-economic regions (including hills) as well as for the state of Uttar Pradesh as a whole at six different points of time, 1960-63, 1970-73, 1980-83, 1990-93, 2000-03 and 2008-11. The idea is to examine the role of different inputs enabling some zones to surge ahead of others and some to be left behind in agriculture development in the state of Uttar Pradesh. We further propose to re-examine the role of various inputs by dividing the all districts into three broad groups of agriculturally high developed, medium developed and low developed districts categorized on the basis of land productivity. Both of these regional and development level analysis would be based on the tabular analysis. This would be followed by graphical analysis of relationship between land productivity and use of various inputs individually. For more rigorous analysis of role of various inputs and other factors in explaining inter-district differences, the district-wise data on agriculture production would be regressed on various inputs and factors using the following form of Cob Douglas production function:

$$\text{Log (Value Output)} = \beta_0 + \beta_1 \log(\text{Land}) + \beta_2 \log(\text{Labour}) + \beta_3 \log(\text{Land structure}) + \beta_4 \log(\text{Literacy}) + \beta_5 \log(\text{Fertilizer}) + \beta_6 \log(\text{Tractors}) + B_7 \log(\text{Pumpsets}) + \beta_8 \log(\text{Cropping Intensity}) + \beta_9 \log(\text{Roads}) + \beta_{10} \log(\text{Irrigation}) + \beta_{11} \log(\text{Rainfall}) + \beta_{12}\,\text{Dummy 1990-93} + \beta_{13}\,\text{Dummy 2000-03} + \beta_{14}\,\text{Dummy 2008-11} + \Sigma^{6}_{i=1}\,{}_{\gamma i} DZ_i + \mu$$

where,

Value Output = Value output of crops in lakhs at 2010-11 prices.

Land = Net Sown Area in hectares.

Labour = Number of agricultural workers both male and female and main and marginal.

Landholdings = Percentage of small and marginal holdings in total holdings in the district.

Literacy = Literacy Rate.

Fertilizer = Chemical fertilizers (NPK in tonnes) consumed in the district.

Tractors = Number of tractors in the district.

Pumpsets = Number of pumpsets in the district.

Cropping Intensity = Ratio of Gross Cropped Area to Net Sown Area in district.

Roads = Road length in km.
Irrigation = Percentage of the Gross Cropped Area under irrigation in the district.
Rainfall = Average rainfall in mm.
DZ_i = 6 agro-climatic dummies one each for Western Plain zone, Mid-Western Plain zone, South-Western Semi-Arid Zone, Central Plain Zone, Bundelkhand Zone and North-Eastern Plain Zone.
B's γs = are regression coefficients.
μ = Stochastic error term.

The Cob Douglas form of production function would be based for the pooled data from 1980-83, 1990-93, 2000-03, 2008-11 trienniums. The sixties and seventies data will not be included because of non-availability of consistent information of some variables for this period. The pooled data OLS model would be used because the cross-section and/or times series production function models suffer from serious implicit problem of heteroscedasticity and multicollinearity. The pooled data model especially in log-log form mitigates these problems substantially (Gujrati, 2007).

In a panel of data, there are some region/district specific idiosyncratic fixed or quasi fixed factors that play important role as a determinant of dependent event like level of agriculture development. Similarly, there may be some factors and developments which are related with time and play a significant role as a determinant of the dependent variable. Panel Data Models facilitate to incorporate the role of such factors as determinants of the dependent event. Fixed Effect Panel Data Model and the Random Effect Panel Data Model, are two Panel Data Models which are used to capture the impact of such idiosyncratic factors. Though, the model generally leads to similar conclusions, the only difference between the two is about the underlying assumptions of the idiosyncratic effects. While, the Fixed Effect Model assumes that these individual observation (district) specific factors are correlated with other independent variable included in the model, the Random Effect Model assumes that such independent factors are random and independent of the other individual specific variables included in the model (Johnston and Dinardo, 2001).

The basic question for the researcher is, regarding the choice between these two models. So for that, Hausman specification test help researchers to choose among these two competing models. These two models would be estimated implying the feasible generalized least square (FGLS) and the maximum likelihood methods (MLE).

EMPIRICAL FINDINGS

8.3. SOURCES OF AGRICULTURAL DEVELOPMENT: TEMPORAL AND SPATIAL ANALYSIS-I

8.3 (i) Agricultural Development and Modern Inputs

Region-wise information on level of agriculture productivity and use of fertilizer consumption, number of tractors, number of pumpsets, cropping intensity and irrigation per unit of area for triennium ending 1960-63, 1970-73, 1980-83, 1990-93, 2000-03 and 2008-11 are presented in Table 8.1(a). Like wide regional disparities in the level of growth and development of agricultural productivity in Uttar Pradesh, almost similar level of variations can be observed in the use of modern inputs and machines across the zones and over time. During all the sub-periods, maximum fertilizer consumption was recorded by the highest developed Western Plain Zone, on the other hand Bundelkhand Zone, being at the lowest level of development recorded the least use of fertilizers. The fertilizer consumption in Western Plain Zone is more than three times as compared with the Bundelkhand Zone. This clearly indicates a direct relationship in use of fertilizers and level of productivity across zones in the state. However, with the increase in level of development, there is more than 50 times increase in the use of fertilizers at the state level during 1960-63 to 2008-11. But there are wide inter-regional differences in fertilizer use.

Almost same relationship is observed in number of tractors used and level of agricultural development. The highest developed Western Plain Zone recorded the maximum number of tractors per thousand hectares. Moreover, wide differentials can be seen in the tractor use across zones. The number of tractors used in Western Plain Zone is nearly double the number of tractors in almost all other zones.

Unlike fertilizers and tractors, there is no direct relationship in agriculture productivity and use of pumpsets. For example, during 2007, the number of pumpsets used is higher in Mid-Western Plain Zone, North-Eastern Plain Zone, Eastern Plain Zone whereas these

Table 8.1(a): Region-wise Level of Modern Inputs Used in Uttar Pradesh: 1960-63 to 2008-11

	Agriculture Productivity (Rs. per hectare)						*Fertilizer Consumption (kg/hectare)*					
Period→ / *Regions↓*	*1960-63*	*1970-73*	*1980-83*	*1990-93*	*2000-03*	*2008-11*	*1960-63*	*1970-73*	*1980-83*	*1990-93*	*2000-03*	*2008-11*
Western Plain Zone	42140	50107	66357	86973	84430	89384	6	39	85	119	188	201
Mid-Western Plain Zone	20780	25774	40277	59199	68046	71492	4	23	65	119	159	180
South-Western Semi-Arid Zone	25859	30296	35155	49984	60919	76612	3	19	42	75	116	176
Central Plain Zone	20978	23426	29857	42265	51433	58155	3	15	50	84	125	183
Bundelkhand Zone	15135	16576	19409	23249	27463	30495	1	4	15	27	40	60
North-Eastern Plain Zone	17092	18383	25763	38814	47923	53446	3	23	46	79	127	167
Eastern Plain Zone	22055	21393	30292	44233	50059	54923	4	23	64	100	135	170
Vindhyan Zone	15966	17238	20371	24730	33141	29354	2	9	31	42	58	121
Hills	16075	24568	27697	36843	38094	41897	1	12	37	72	84	143
Uttar Pradesh	21988	24861	33130	46440	53283	59085	3	20	52	87	126	164

Regions↓	*Tractors (No. per 000 hectare of NSA)*						*Pumpsets (No. per 000 hectare of NSA)*					
Period→	*1961*	*1972*	*1982*	*1992*	*2003*	*2007*	*1961*	*1972*	*1982*	*1992*	*2003*	*2007*
Western Plain Zone	1	6	24	47	79	88	3	40	115	179	273	263
Mid-Western Plain Zone	1	2	11	28	50	54	1	21	90	194	311	330
South-Western Semi-Arid Zone	0.3	2	8	21	41	45	1	26	76	152	200	261
Central Plain Zone	0.3	1	5	12	30	34	0.4	16	53	116	147	224
Bundelkhand Zone	0.3	1	5	15	30	31	0.2	4	16	53	90	79
North-Eastern Plain Zone	0.3	1	6	16	34	38	1	16	68	143	214	317
Eastern Plain Zone	0.2	0	6	18	38	40	0.3	18	67	139	195	305
Vindhyan Zone	0.3	1	7	15	35	41	0.1	8	18	65	108	117
Hills	1	4	10	16	17	18	0.1	6	19	35	51	45
Uttar Pradesh	0.4	2	8	20	40	44	1	18	64	132	191	245

(*Contd.*)

Regions↓ Period→	Cropping Intensity (Percentage)						Irrigation (Percentage of GCA)					
	1960-63	1970-73	1980-83	1990-93	2000-03	2008-11	1960-63	1970-73	1980-83	1990-93	2000-03	2008-11
Western Plain Zone	138	152	161	162	151	156	50.1	67.1	79.1	89.7	96.3	97.7
Mid-Western Plain Zone	122	131	144	154	159	165	13.3	36.8	53.9	75.9	86.0	87.9
South-Western Semi-Arid Zone	127	140	149	150	156	162	36.9	54.2	63.5	76.4	78.2	83.2
Central Plain Zone	127	129	137	142	147	149	19.3	29.9	44.0	60.1	73.6	79.2
Bundelkhand Zone	110	111	113	113	118	132	14.9	20.5	22.2	31.7	40.3	43.2
North-Eastern Plain Zone	136	138	151	153	155	154	23.1	27.8	35.0	39.6	47.7	58.0
Eastern Plain Zone	132	130	147	157	159	163	33.8	38.0	48.5	63.1	80.0	87.4
Vindhyan Zone	131	128	135	139	141	126	18.3	22.3	33.7	39.7	46.0	43.5
Hills	120	170	163	164	163	166	11.5	15.5	28.1	34.3	37.6	40.9
Uttar Pradesh	127	133	143	148	150	154	25.4	36.1	47.4	60.4	70.3	75.3

Sources: (i) Same as in Table 4.2(a).

(ii) FAI (Various Issues), *Fertilizer Statistics*, New Delhi, Fertilizer Association in India.

(iii) GoI (Various Reports), *Livestock Census,* Uttar Pradesh, (Agriculture Machinery and Implements), New Delhi, Ministry of Agriculture, Department of Animal Husbandry and Dairying, Government of India.

zones recorded lower productivity levels in comparison to the highest developed Western Plain Zone and second highest South-Western Semi-Arid Zone. However, there is considerable increase in number of pumpsets used in the state.

There are lesser differences in cropping intensity across zones as compared to productivity levels. This seems to suggest that cropping intensity does not have any direct relationship in explaining inter-regional differences in the state. For example, Hills Zone mostly recorded higher percentage of cropping intensity, but recorded very low levels of agriculture productivity. Similarly, during 2008-11, Mid-Western Plain Zone, South-Western Semi-Arid Zone, Eastern Plain Zone and Hills recorded almost same percentage of cropping intensity, but had wide differences in productivity levels.

There is low level of irrigation mostly in underdeveloped zones. Initially wide inter-regional differences can be seen in the highest developed Western Plain Zone and low developed Hill, Vindhyan and Bundelkhand Zones. It seems that very low irrigation during 1960-63 was one of the reasons among others, for low level of productivity in Mid-Western Plain Zone and a high proportion on the other hand. 50 per cent of area under irrigation in Western Plain Zone during this period led it to early adoption of green revolution technology. However during the later period, excluding four low developed zones namely—Bundelkhand Zone, North-Eastern Plain Zone, Vindhyan Zone and Hills, rest other zones have almost same level of irrigation intensity whereas there are differences in their productivity levels.

8.3 (ii) Agricultural Development and Resource Endowments

There is substantial increase in the road density standardized to the net sown area in the zones. Over the period of time, road density has gone up to seven times from 159 to 1121 km of road length per ten thousand hectare of the net sown area in Uttar Pradesh. There seems to be positive correlation between road density and agricultural productivity. This positive relationship between road density and agricultural development can be observed uniformly for all the agro-economic zones. However, no such direct association between road density and agricultural development can be inferred from inter-zone comparison of the two variables. For example, the level of agricultural development during 2008-11 triennium, is same in the Bundelkhand and Vindhyan Zones, however, the road density in Vindhyan Zone is

Table 8.1(b): Region-wise Level of Resource Endowments Used in Uttar Pradesh: 1960-63 to 2008-11

	Agriculture Productivity (Rs. per hectare)						Road Length (Km. per 00000 hectare of NSA)				
Regions↓ Period→	*1960-63*	*1970-73*	*1980-83*	*1990-93*	*2000-03*	*2008-11*	*1970-73*	*1980-83*	*1990-93*	*2000-03*	*2008-11*
Western Plain Zone	42140	50107	66357	86973	84430	89384	174	263	462	640	959
Mid-Western Plain Zone	20780	25774	40277	59199	68046	71492	129	215	306	533	795
South-Western Semi-Arid Zone	25859	30296	35155	49984	60919	76612	147	272	478	694	1017
Central Plain Zone	20978	23426	29857	42265	51433	58155	138	256	381	624	1081
Bundelkhand Zone	15135	16576	19409	23249	27463	30495	114	218	271	442	585
North-Eastern Plain Zone	17092	18383	25763	38814	47923	53446	142	205	281	553	1025
Eastern Plain Zone	22055	21393	30292	44233	50059	54923	158	297	456	896	1440
Vindhyan Zone	15966	17238	20371	24730	33141	29354	178	306	460	663	1778
Hills	16075	24568	27697	36843	38094	41897	523	1276	1478	2486	3734
Uttar Pradesh	21988	24861	33130	46440	53283	59085	159	290	418	699	1121

	Agricultural Workers (No. per 000 hectare)					Literacy Rate (Percentage)					
Regions↓ Period→	*1960-63*	*1980-83*	*1990-93*	*2000-03*	*2008-11*	*1961*	*1971*	*1981*	*1991*	*2001*	*2011*
Western Plain zone	619	1135	1118	1182	1195	22.6	28.3	31.0	46.8	62.9	72.5
Mid-Western Plain Zone	766	1107	1140	1223	1209	16.0	19.3	20.4	29.2	44.5	57.2
South-Western Semi Arid Zone	707	1040	1122	1191	1181	24.0	29.3	31.2	45.4	62.3	71.8
Central Plain Zone	1008	1429	1573	1671	1721	22.5	27.3	28.6	41.6	59.3	71.0
Bundelkhand Zone	609	1047	1141	1146	1034	22.0	27.1	28.7	42.0	60.3	70.4
North-Eastern Plain Zone	1330	1624	1918	1929	1945	15.1	18.5	19.9	31.3	46.5	62.6
Eastern Plain Zone	1330	1700	1842	1918	1899	19.3	23.2	25.5	40.9	58.3	72.2
Vindhyan Zone	917	1499	1632	1745	2377	20.1	23.4	23.6	39.7	53.0	68.3
Hills	1386	1504	1504	1692	1791	18.1	34.6	37.8	57.8	71.6	78.8
Uttar Pradesh	994	1362	1479	1545	1548	20.7	25.4	27.2	41.6	57.4	67.7

(Contd.)

Regions↓ Period→	Land Structure (small+marginal) (% share in Total holdings)					Average Rainfall (mm)					
	1970-71	1980-81	1990-91	2000-01	2010-11	1960-63	1970-73	1980-83	1990-93	2000-03	2008-11
Western Plain Zone	72.9	78.0	82.1	85.1	88.4	75	60	64	65	63	46
Mid-Western Plain Zone	81.3	83.1	86.3	89.2	91.0	90	71	83	73	68	51
South Western Semi-Arid Zone	76.7	80.0	82.6	87.1	88.1	69	50	67	49	39	41
Central Plain Zone	85.2	88.2	90.5	92.3	93.2	96	74	96	59	51	47
Bundelkhand Zone	60.5	67.7	74.8	77.4	79.2	80	56	96	73	61	43
North-Eastern Plain Zone	88.4	91.6	93.3	94.8	95.8	101	85	132	91	75	64
Eastern Plain Zone	91.2	93.3	95.2	95.5	96.4	84	84	97	72	71	45
Vindhyan Zone	76.2	80.4	86.1	86.9	88.5	88	74	84	81	87	34
Hills	88.1	87.0	88.0	88.7	91.1	142	83	118	101	117	120
Uttar Pradesh	84.0	86.8	89.4	91.0	92.4	95	73	95	74	63	55

Sources: (i) Same as in Table 4.2(a).

(ii) GoI (Various Reports), *Census of India (Uttar Pradesh)*, Primary Census Abstract, Uttar Pradesh, Directorate of Census Operations, Government of India.

(iii) GoI, *Agricultural Census*, New Delhi, Department of Agriculture and Cooperation, Agricultural Census Division, Ministry of Agriculture, Government of India.

three times of the road density in Bundelkhand Zone. Among the non-hill zones, Vindhyan Zone has the highest road density and least land productivity during 2008-11 period. Similarly, during the earlier periods, there are considerable inter-regional disparities in agricultural development, but these are not so in case of the road density in these zones. On the whole, it seems that the role of road density in agricultural development is not very clear at this level of analysis, even though there is an indication of the positive relationship between the two over time and within each zone of the state.

Like road length, the relationship between the number of workers and agricultural development is complex and no definite conclusions can be drawn regarding the same. For example, the number of workers per thousand hectare of net sown area remained same in Western Plain Zone for the past four decades from 1980-83 to 2008-11 in spite of the fact that agriculture productivity has gone up to 150 per cent in the zone during the same period. Workers' concentration is generally low in more developed zones, but Bundelkhand is an exception, which is second from below in terms of agricultural development, but having the least workers concentration among all the zones. Bundelkhand and Vindhyan Zones have almost same level of land productivity, but the labour concentration in agriculture in Vindhyan Zone is more than twice than in Bundelkhand Zone. In some zones, there is no increase in concentration of workers though the agriculture productivity has increased many folds. Therefore, it is very difficult to conclude about the role of agricultural workers in affecting the level of development in a district or zone. This is mainly because many of the agricultural machines and implements as well as chemicals like weedicides are substitutes of human labour to considerable existence. However, across zone comparison brings out that though agricultural workers tends to be concentrated more in agriculturally low developed zones, but again this lacks generalization for all zones and all times.

There is consistent improvement in level of literacy for the state as a whole as well as for all the zones. It indicates contribution of literacy in agricultural development. Nevertheless, there is a problem in explaining the role of literacy in inter-zone differences in agriculture productivity. For example, during 2008-11, Western Plain Zone, South-Western Semi-Arid Zone, Central Plain Zone and Bundelkhand Zone have almost same level of literacy, but are not so in terms of land productivity. Though the literacy rate is almost same, but Western

Plain Zone is the top ranking among the zones, whereas Bundelkhand Zone is the second lowest ranked in agricultural development. Similarly, the Mid-Western Plain Zone has the lowest level of literacy, but ranked second highest in terms of agricultural productivity.

Like the other infrastructural variables, information on land structure in terms of proportion of small and marginal farm holdings shows that this proportion is increasing over time. This is true for the state as a whole as well as for all the individual agro-economic regions. From this behaviour of land structure and land productivity, it seems to indicate the validity of inverse farm size productivity relationship in Uttar Pradesh agriculture and within each agro-economic region. However, generalization of this inverse relationship is problematic in cross-sectional comparison of the level of land productivity and the proportion of small farmers. The picture is obscure across zones. For example, Eastern Plain Zone continues to have the highest proportion of small and marginal farmers for all the periods, but it recorded average level of land productivity. The relationship needs further exploration to arrive at definite conclusions.

No definite conclusion regarding the average rainfall and level of land productivity can be drawn, either by comparison of agricultural development and rainfall over time as well as for cross-sectional comparison of productivity differentials and rainfall differential for almost all the years. This is mainly because the artificial irrigation substantially compensate for low rainfall in some zones where the availability of irrigation is low whereas it is not relevant for other zones where irrigation is not that developed.

8.4. SOURCES OF AGRICULTURAL DEVELOPMENT: TEMPORAL AND SPATIAL ANALYSIS-II

8.4 (i) Distribution of Districts in Agricultural Development and Resource Use

As discussed earlier, the temporal and spatial analysis of agricultural development and use of modern inputs and resource endowments is re-examined by re-clubbing the district-level information into three main set of districts on basis of their land productivity. Information in this context for all the inputs and resource endowment variables is detailed in Table 8.2 by three group of districts namely—high developed, medium developed and low developed districts.

Table 8.2: Distribution of Districts and Input Use by Level of Agriculture Productivity in Uttar Pradesh: 1980-83 to 2008-11

Agriculture Productivity (Rs. per hectare)	*No. of Districts*				*Fertilizer Consumption (kg/hectare)*			
	1980-83	*1990-93*	*2000-03*	*2008-11*	*1980-83*	*1990-93*	*2000-03*	*2008-11*
High (>71000)	1	4	7	15	82	127	184	188
Medium (52000-71000)	3	10	14	16	86	112	145	172
Low (<52000)	42	32	25	15	49	75	103	130

Agriculture Productivity (Rs. per hectare)	*Tractors (No. per 000 hectare of NSA)*				*Pumpsets (No per 000 hectare of NSA)*			
	1980-83	*1990-93*	*2000-03*	*2008-11*	*1980-83*	*1990-93*	*2000-03*	*2008-11*
High (>71000)	35	49	70	60	123	176	308	285
Medium (52000-71000)	20	24	45	41	112	188	216	298
Low (<52000)	6	15	31	33	61	115	159	166

Agriculture Productivity (Rs. per hectare)	*Cropping Intensity (Percentage GCA/NSA*100)*				*Irrigation (Percentage of GCA)*			
	1980-83	*1990-93*	*2000-03*	*2008-11*	*1980-83*	*1990-93*	*2000-03*	*2008-11*
High (>71000)	155	154	154	159	79.7	84.5	90.0	89.0
Medium (52000-71000)	162	158	157	159	79.0	78.2	81.2	77.7
Low (<52000)	140	143	145	142	44.7	53.1	61.5	61.4

Agriculture Productivity (Rs. per hectare)	*Road Length (km per 000 hectare of NSA)*				*Average Rainfall (mm)*			
	1980-83	*1990-93*	*2000-03*	*2008-11*	*1980-83*	*1990-93*	*2000-03*	*2008-11*
High (>71000)	258	473	617	956	57	75	67	46
Medium (52000-71000)	264	346	637	1066	66	64	55	54
Low (<52000)	247	369	632	1050	95	69	63	42

Agriculture Productivity (Rs. per hectare)	*Agricultural Workers (No. per 000 hectare GCA)*				*Structure of Small+ Marginal Landholdings (Percentage of total holdings)*			
	1980-83	*1990-93*	*2000-03*	*2008-11*	*1980-83*	*1990-93*	*2000-03*	*2008-11*
High (>71000)	927	1144	1179	1231	77.4	81.9	88.2	90.0
Medium (52000-71000)	833	1157	1274	1652	78.2	88.0	90.4	94.8
Low (<52000)	1080	1381	1582	1631	87.5	90.4	92.0	91.0

Agriculture Productivity (Rs. per hectare)	*Literacy Rate (Percentage)*			
	1980-83	*1990-93*	*2000-03*	*2008-11*
High (>71000)	30.1	42.2	52.5	67.8
Medium (52000-71000)	31.3	36.8	58.0	67.3
Low (<52000)	25.7	39.7	55.9	70.0

Sources: (i) Table 5.3.
(ii) Same as in Table 8.1(a) and 8.1(b).

The direct and positive relationship between use of modern inputs and the level of agricultural development as observed in the previous agro-economic region-wise analysis is confirmed by information provided in Table 8.2. This relationship is very strong and clear for fertilizer consumption, tractors and irrigation. However, for pumpsets and cropping intensity, though the low developed districts have low availability of pumpsets for irrigation as well as low cropping intensity, but there is not much difference on these two accounts between high and medium developed districts. This indicated that both pumpsets and cropping intensity lead to agricultural development, but relationship is not that strong as in case of other three inputs.

Like the earlier observation of weak association of resource endowments with agricultural development, the same thing is evident regarding this relationship from Table 8.2 as well. This is true about association of agricultural development with road density, average rainfall and level of literacy. However, there seems to be inverse relationship between per hectare productivity and number of workers employed in agriculture. This inverse relationship is true only for cross-sectional comparison, but when we analyze this relationship temporally then it seems to be the other way round, i.e. both the number of workers employed in agriculture as well as land productivity is increasing over time. Therefore, it is very difficult to conclude about the exact role of workers in agricultural development. Same is true about the structure of landholdings which are increasing over time in the zones, indicating a positive relationship, but relationship seems to be negative when we compare it across zones.

8.4 (ii) Agricultural Development and Resource use: Inter-District Graphical Examination

The foregoing analysis of agricultural development and use of various resources presents contradictory conclusions in the case of many resources, so far as their temporal and spatial relations are concerned. Furthermore, the analysis was for clubbed group of districts on the basis of the level of development and agro-economic conditions as base of clubbing the districts into spatial entities. To re-examine resource-wise association with agricultural development afresh, we pooled the district-level data at all six points of time, plotted the same on graph and fitted the trend equation to the scatter points. The graphs in this context are presented in Figures 8.1 (i) to 8.1 (x). The graphical presentation bring out a positive relationship between agricultural development and fertilizer consumption, use of tractors, availability of pumpsets, cropping intensity, percentage of area under irrigation, road density, number of workers per thousand hectares and level of literacy. Not only the fitted lines bear positive slope, but the slope coefficient in all cases turned out to be significant statistically. The relationship is particularly very strong between agricultural development and use of fertilizers, tractors, irrigation intensity and literacy rate as indicated by the coefficient of determination (R^2).

The graph between agriculture productivity and landholdings however does not present any relationship between the two as the fitted linear line to the scatter points is almost flat and the slope coefficient is not significant statistically.

The relationship between agriculture productivity and rainfall in the districts is however contradictory to the general expectation that rainfall is the decisive factor in agriculture production in semi-arid tropic region like Uttar Pradesh. The negative relationship is contrary to our expectation. There can be many reasons for that. For example, it may be possible that high rainfall may be leading to floods and waterlogging that not only destroy the standing crops, but repeated exposure of such area to floods, leads to low use of modern inputs

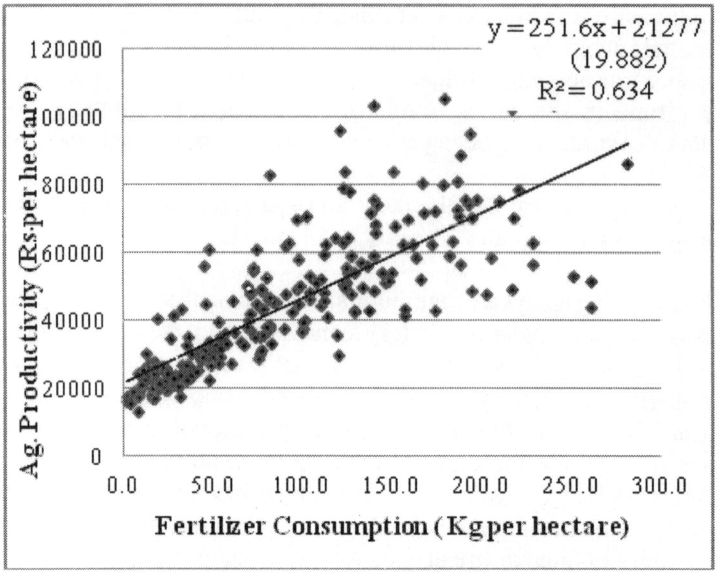

Fig. 8.1(i): Agriculture productivity and Fertilizer consumption.

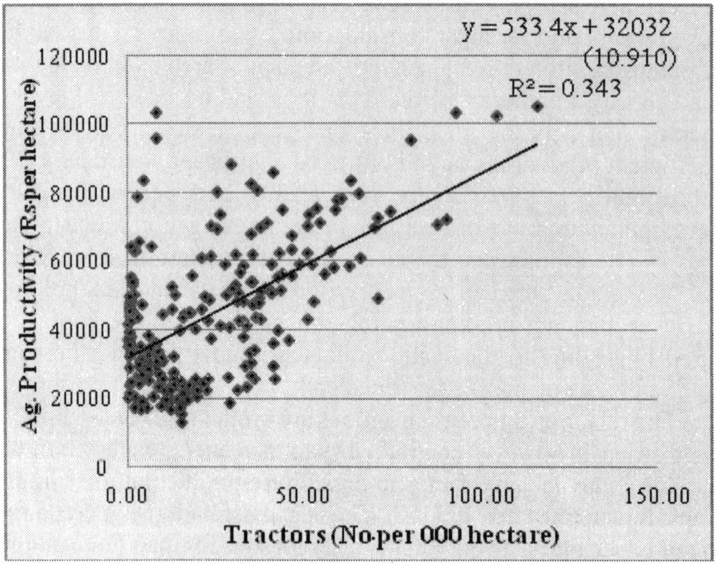

Fig. 8.1(ii): Agriculture productivity and Tractors.

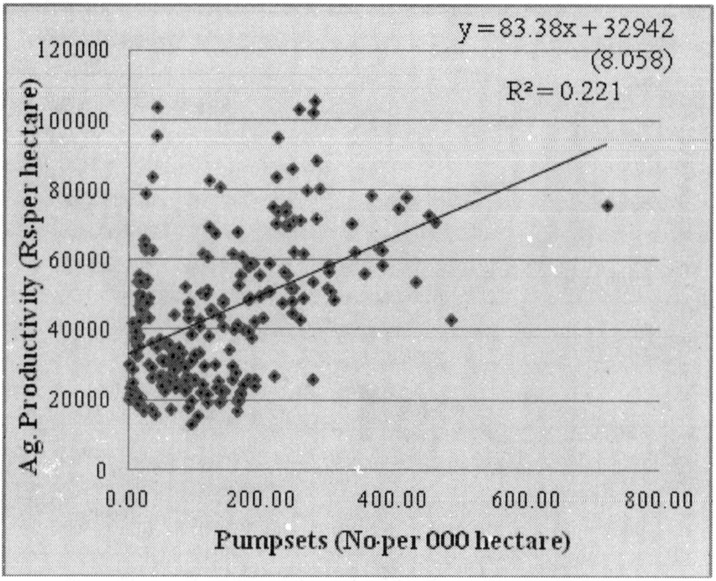

Fig. 8.1(iii): Agriculture productivity and Pumpsets.

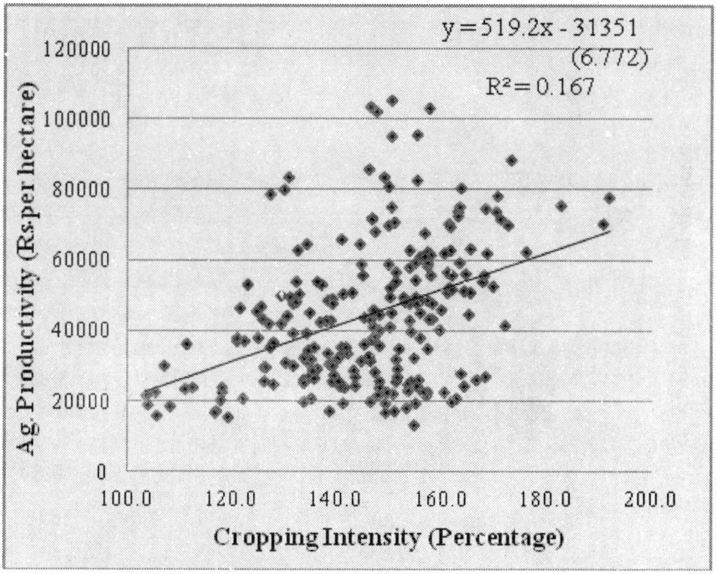

Fig. 8.1(iv): Agriculture productivity and Cropping Intensity.

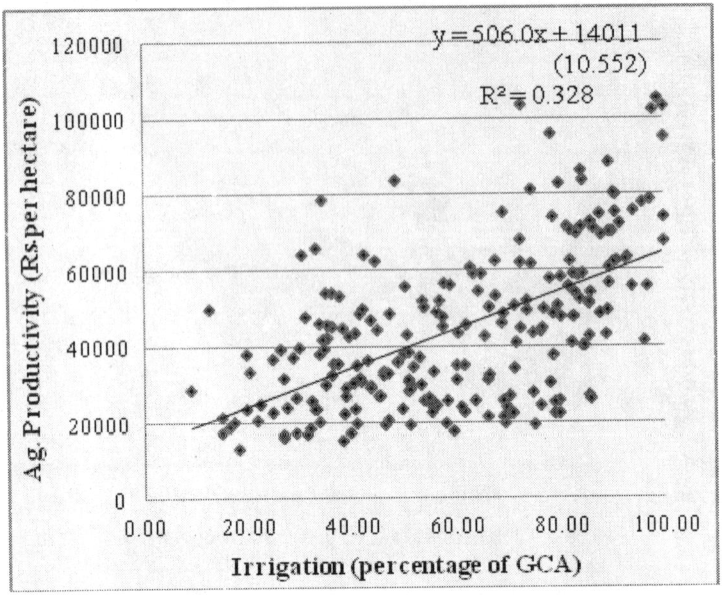

Fig. 8.1(v): Agriculture productivity and Irrigation.

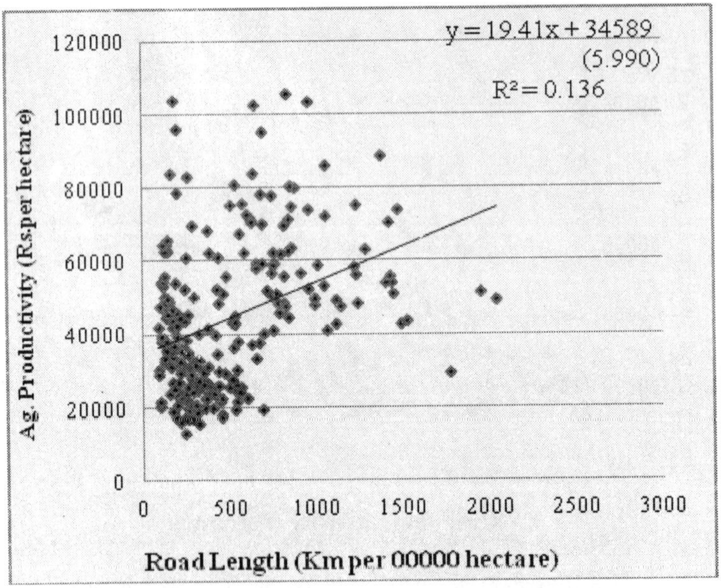

Fig. 8.1(vi): Agriculture productivity and Road length.

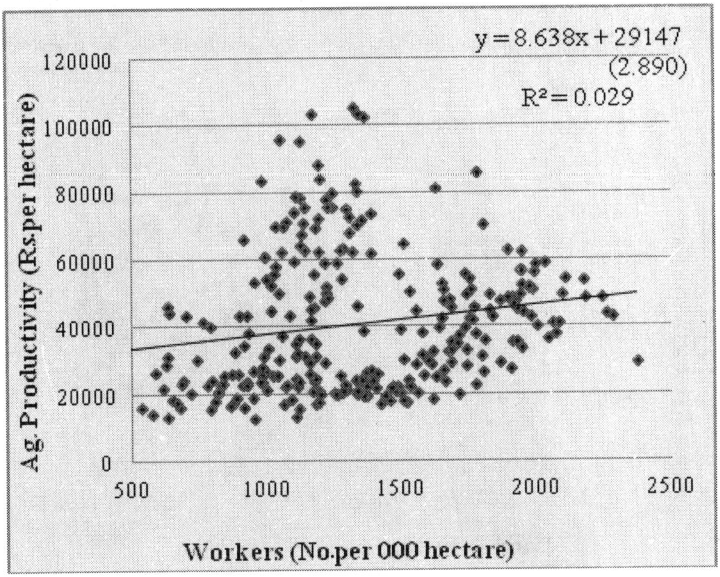

Fig. 8.1(vii): Agriculture productivity and Workers.

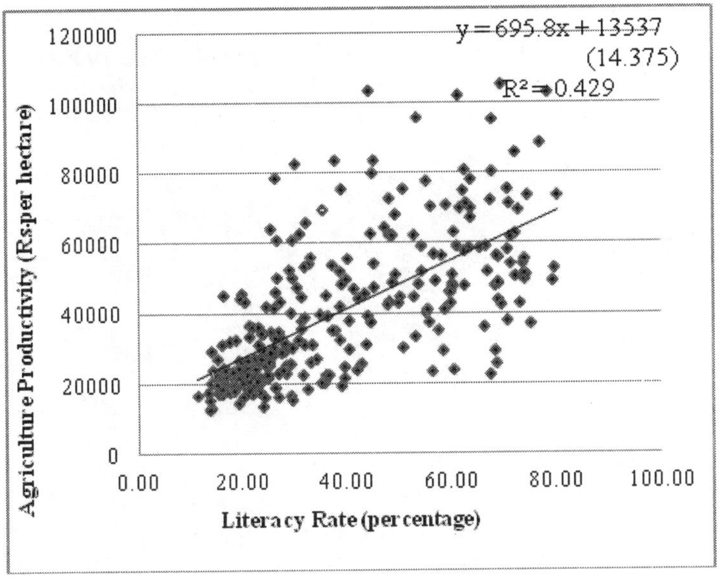

Fig. 8.1(viii): Agriculture productivity and Literacy Rate.

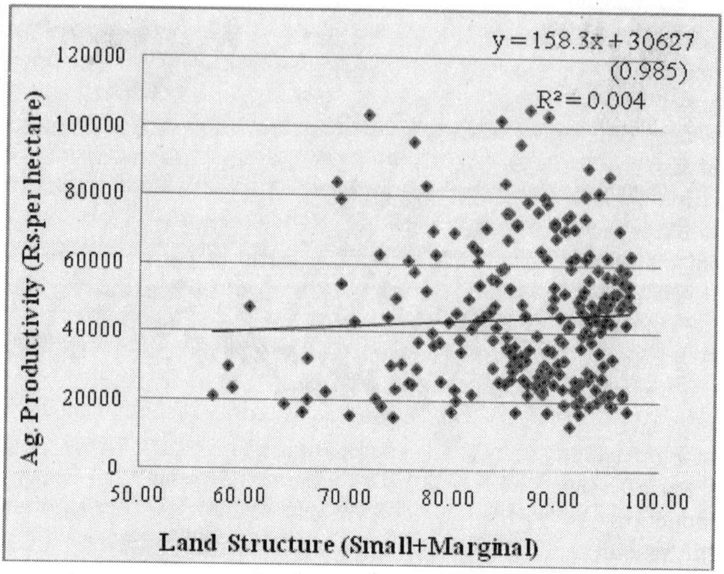

Fig. 8.1(ix): Agriculture productivity and Land Structure.

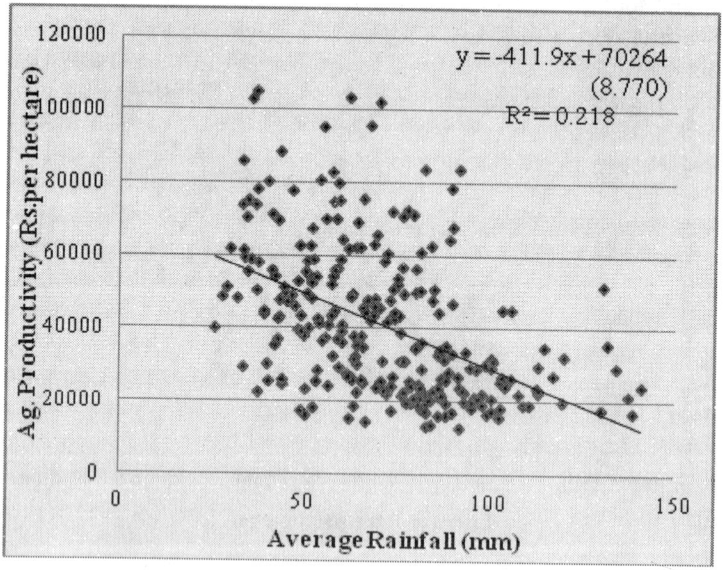

Fig. 8.1(x): Agriculture productivity and Rainfall.

Figure 8.1: District-wise input use and level of agriculture productivity in Uttar Pradesh: 1960-63 to 2008-11.

Source: Appendix 8.1.

and on farm investments by the farmers due to high risk and uncertainty. Alternatively, the relationship may be due to reason that comparatively low rainfall areas may be having higher irrigation intensity that not only overcomes the normal deficiency of rainfall, but also fulfils the need of water during off monsoon season and by facilitating more use of modern inputs. Which of such situation is more relevant is very difficult to conclude with this type of bivariate analysis. A multivariate analysis may probably provide better answer to such questions, which is to be undertaken in the following section.

8.5. SOURCES OF AGRICULTURAL DEVELOPMENT: AN ECONOMETRIC ANALYSIS

In the preceding section, we examined the association between level of agricultural development and resource use in agricultural production through the tabular analysis as well as through graphical analysis on the pooled data. Though, the graphical analysis resolved many of the paradoxes and controversies of the tabular analysis, but it is still too early to draw any definite conclusion of the contribution of various resources in development of agriculture in Uttar Pradesh. This is mainly because the observed graphical bivariate relationship may be due to some other confounding factors leading to spurious conclusions. Therefore, to test the findings from the graphical analysis and bivariate regression line fitted to scatter points on graphs, the present section examines the same afresh through multivariate regression analysis. As stated earlier, we fitted the Cob-Douglas regression to pooled data at four points of time from 1980-83 to 2008-11 by employing the OLS regressions, Random Effect Model and the Fixed Effect Model. The information in this context is presented in Table 8.3. We applied the Hausman specification test to choose between Random Effect and Fixed Effect Panel data Models, but it has not helped us in choosing between Fixed and Random Effect Models. Therefore, we presented the results for all three models.

Interestingly, the results of Random Effect and Fixed Effect Panel Data Models are very close to each other, but differ with the pooled data regression on some accounts. The coefficient of land area, fertilizer, tractor, cropping intensity, turned out to be positive and significant for all the three models and high t-value in all cases, show strong contribution of these inputs to agriculture production. The coefficient of labour variable is positive and significant for Fixed

Table 8.3: Sources of Agricultural Development: Econometric Analysis

Variables	Pooled Regression	Random Effect Model		Fixed Effect Model
	OLS	FGLS	MLE	
	Coefficient (t value)	Coefficient (t value)	Coefficient (t value)	Coefficient (t value)
(1)	(2)	(3)	(4)	(5)
A. Resources				
(i) Land	0.97***	0.73***	0.73***	1.26***
	(8.17)	(6.10)	(6.44)	(4.98)
(ii) Labour	–0.25**	0.10	0.10	0.39***
	(2.31)	(0.97)	(0.92)	(3.17)
(iii) Land structure (% of	–0.07	–0.61*	–0.60**	–0.96***
Small & marg. holdings)	(0.18)	(1.94)	(2.01)	(2.68)
(iv) Literacy	0.01	0.11	0.11	0.06
	(0.15)	(1.56)	(1.64)	(0.74)
B. Technology Variables				
(i) Fertilizers	0.25***	0.19***	0.20***	0.15***
	(4.61)	(4.31)	(4.49)	(3.12)
(ii) Tractors	0.10***	0.10***	0.10***	0.08***
	(2.60)	(3.58)	(3.76)	(2.64)
(iii) Pumpsets	0.04	0.01	0.01	0.01
	(0.94)	(0.32)	(0.35)	(0.24)
(iv) Cropping Intensity	0.46**	0.71***	0.71***	0.75***
	(2.28)	(3.95)	(4.12)	(3.89)
C. Infrastructure				
(i) Roads	–0.07	–0.03	–0.03	0.01
	(1.18)	(0.83)	(0.88)	(0.35)
(ii) Irrigation	0.16*	0.09	0.09	0.02
	(1.91)	(1.18)	(1.24)	(0.31)
D. Fixed/Quasi fixed factors				
(i) Rainfall	0.05	0.04	0.04	0.03
	(1.02)	(1.05)	(1.10)	(0.71)
(ii) Dummy-1990-93	0.05**			
	(1.97)			
(iii) Dummy-2000-03	0.05			
	(1.28)			
(iv) Dummy-2008-11	0.08			
	(1.44)			
(v) Dummy-Western Plain	0.12***	0.16***	0.16***	
Zone	(3.86)	(3.62)	(3.81)	
(vi) Dummy-Mid-Western	0.02	0.10***	0.10***	
Plain Zone	(0.81)	(2.77)	(2.86)	
(vii) Dummy-South-Western	0.05	0.09***	0.09***	
Semi-Arid Zone	(1.55)	(2.24)	(2.34)	

(Contd.)

(1)	(2)	(3)	(4)	(5)
(viii) Dummy-Central Plain Zone	0.02 (1.33)	0.05* (1.94)	0.05** (2.05)	
(ix) Dummy-Bundelkhand Zone	–0.06 (1.46)	–0.03 (0.56)	–0.03 (0.60)	
(x) Dummy-North Eastern Plain Zone	0.005 (0.20)	–0.01 (0.28)	–0.01 (0.28)	
Constant term	1.49 (1.71)	1.50 (1.80)	1.52 (1.90)	–2.09 (1.43)
R^2 Within		0.90		0.91
Between		0.91		0.56
Overall	0.92	0.90		0.62
Log Likelihood			290.45	
Chi^2			427.19	
No. of observations	184	184	184	184

Source: Appendix 8.1.

Notes:

1. Figure in parenthesis is t value of the coefficients.
2. Asterisk *, ** and *** indicate coefficients significant at 10 per cent, 5 per cent and 1 per cent level of significance respectively for two tailed test.

Effect Model, but it is not significant statistically, both for FGLS and MLE Random Effect Model. Literacy, though have positive coefficient, but it is not significant statistically even at 90 per cent confidence level. However, in case of bivariate regression and graphical presentation, literacy shows very strong positive association with level of agricultural development. Same is true about two infrastructural variables namely—roads and irrigation, which are not significant in both Random and Fixed Effect Models, but depict very strong relationship in bivariate and graphical analysis. This validate our earlier conjecture that one has to be little careful in drawing definite conclusion from graphical and bivariate regressions. Same is true about rainfall variable which was highly significant in bivariate regression, but turned out to be not significant statistically when other factors are controlled in multivariate regression. The impact of agro-climatic conditions which we tried to capture by introducing zone dummies, turned out to be significant in case of Western Plain Zone, Mid-Western Plain Zone, South-Western Semi-Arid Zone and Central Plain Zone suggesting strong favourable climatic conditions for agricultural development in these zones *vis-à-vis* the rest of the zones. In other words, low level of development in Bundelkhand Zone, North-Eastern Plain Zone, Eastern Plain Zone and Vindhyan Zone, to a significant extent are due to unfavourable agro-climatic conditions prevailing therein *vis-à-vis* the rest of the Uttar Pradesh.

The most interesting result is relating to coefficient of land structure variable which turned out to be negative and significant, both for Random Effect and Fixed Effect Models. This indicates that even after controlling the availability of land, labour, modern inputs—fertilizers, tractors, pumpsets as well as cropping intensity, increasing proportion of small and marginal farmers in a district tend to reduce agricultural production. The evidence is contrary to no such relation observed from graphical and bivariate regression in the preceding section as well as to the widely held perceptions and empirical evidence of inverse farm size productivity in Indian agriculture (Sen, 1962, 1964; Rao, 1966; Bardhan 1973; Chand, Prasana and Singh, 2011). Productivity seems to decline with increasing proportion of small and marginal farmers in a district. Though the issue require further deep exploration, nevertheless, the present evidence suggests that the large farmers are more efficient agricultural producers as compared to small farmers. The model is giving very high fit to the data as R^2 turns out to be 0.9 not only for Random and Fixed Effect Models, but also for OLS regression.

8.6. SUMMARY

The chapter aimed at identification of the sources of agricultural growth and inter-regional and inter-district differential of agricultural productivity in Uttar Pradesh for the last five decades spanning from 1960-2010. We compared the input used with agricultural development across various agro-economic regions and group of districts formed on the basis of agricultural development. We also examined the relationship of agricultural development with various inputs by pooling the district-level data and fitting the scatter point to straight line and bivariate regression. The relationship was ultimately tested by fitting the data to Random Effect and Fixed Effect Panel Data econometric models. Taking an overall view from this empirical analysis, the following conclusions emerge:

1. Inter-district disparities in agricultural development are significantly related with differential use of modern inputs which include use of chemical fertilizers and tractors and intensification of land use differentials across districts.

2. Favourable agro-climatic conditions in Western and Central Uttar Pradesh and unfavourable agro-climatic conditions in Bundelkhand, Eastern and Vindhyan Zones are significantly related to higher and low level of agricultural development in these two set of zones in the state.
3. Contrary to general perception, inter-district differentials in two most important infrastructure facilities namely—road density and extent of irrigation are not significantly related with inter-district disparities in agricultural development in Uttar Pradesh. Same is true about the role of literacy and rainfall variables.
4. Contrary to widely accepted inverse farm size productivity relationship in Indian agriculture, higher proportion of small farmers turned out to be a constraint on agricultural development suggesting that there is positive farm size productivity relationship in Uttar Pradesh agriculture. However, in our opinion this needs further deep exploration to arrive at a more definite conclusion.

9

Summary and Conclusions

In the state of Uttar Pradesh, agriculture is still the mainstay of livelihood to majority of the population. About two-third of the population still rely on agriculture for their livelihood. The farming community in general and small and marginal farmers in particular have low level of living and almost one-third of them are trapped in poverty. Human resources are underdeveloped and well-being of the majority of the population is directly or indirectly related with agriculture development. But, the agriculture is grossly underdeveloped in the state as compared with its neighbouring states of Punjab and Haryana. Furthermore, there is serious tendency of deceleration in agriculture during the post-reform period in the state. The state not only failed to match the feet of Punjab and Haryana during the green revolution period, but it also could not benefit from the recent developments that led to spectacular performance of Gujarat and Bihar agriculture. Almost whole of the theoretical and empirical literature unanimously bring out the importance of agriculture not only in assuring food security and well-being of the rural population, but also suggests a significant role of agriculture in development of the non-agriculture sector through forward and backward linkages. First and the foremost requirement for development of any sector or region is the information on ground realities, emerging dynamics, constraints and available opportunities. Though, empirical studies are available on some of these accounts, but most of these are either undertaken at the state level or for a specific region or segment of the farmers or cover few crops or are for a limited period. There is no comprehensive analysis on Uttar Pradesh agriculture dealing with different dimensions of its agriculture at the district-level over a longer period. The present study was a humble attempt to fill the gap in this context.

The main objectives of the present study were:

1. To analyze the temporal pattern of agricultural performance in Uttar Pradesh during different policy regimes (Pre-green revolution, initial phase of green revolution, mature phase of green revolution, initial post-reform period and new millennium phase) over the last half a century (1960-61 to 2010-11).
2. To examine the spatial (district and region) pattern of agricultural performance (level of development, output growth and disparities) in Uttar Pradesh over 1960-61 to 2010-11 period.
3. To identify the sources and constraints of agricultural development at the district-level in Uttar Pradesh.

The present study is based on secondary data mainly collected and compiled by the Ministry of Agriculture, New Delhi, Government of India; Central Statistical Organization (CSO) of the Ministry of Statistics and Programme Implementation, Government of India and Directorate of Economics and Statistics (DES), Government of Uttar Pradesh. The temporal trend in agriculture production for the state as a whole is mainly based on the value of output of agriculture and allied sector publication brought out by the CSO. Information on land use pattern has been taken from the statistics compiled by the Directorate of Economics and Statistics (DES), Government of India.

The district-level information on area and production of major agriculture crops grown in the state has been taken from the publication of DES, the online information available on its website, from Season and Crop Reports for various years published by the Directorate of Land Records, Uttar Pradesh and Statistical Abstracts of Uttar Pradesh. Information on workers employed in agriculture sector and level of literacy has been taken from various publications of Census of India (Uttar Pradesh), Primary Census Abstract, Directorate of Census Operations, Government of India. District-wise data on fertilizers and rainfall has been obtained from the publication of Fertilizer Association of India and Indian Metrological Department, Pune, respectively.

The district-wise information on area, production and yield has been compiled from 1960-61 to 2010-11. To estimate the total production in a district, individual crop production has been converted into value terms using 2010-11 constant prices. These prices were derived indirectly from the National Accounts Statistics for the relevant years.

The overall period from 1960-61 to 2010-11 was divided into five sub-periods namely—pre-green revolution phase during 1960-61 to 1965-66, initial green revolution phase from 1967-68 to 1980-81, mature green revolution phase during 1981-82 to 1990-91, initial post-reform period from 1991-92 to 2000-01 and new millennium period from 2001-02 to 2010-11 to study the temporal dynamics of growth at the state and zone level in Uttar Pradesh.

The number of districts increased from 46 to 72 during the study period (till 2010) in Uttar Pradesh. The current information on newly formed districts was available, but the past information (before creation) was not available. Therefore, we converted 72 districts into 46 district units for spatial comparison. Besides the state and district-level study of temporal and spatial pattern, we also clubbed these districts into eight agro-economic regions to get better insight into the spatial and temporal pattern of agricultural performance as well as dynamics of labour productivity in the state. The districts of current state of Uttarakhand, bifurcated from Uttar Pradesh during 2000 have been clubbed under Hill districts.

Besides measuring the growth and development, the inter-district disparities were examined using standard inequality measures of Gini coefficient, coefficient of variation, ratio of top to bottom quintile productivity, top to bottom quintile shares. Dynamics of disparity has been studied by analysing the sigma convergence, beta unconditional convergence, beta conditional convergence and club convergence approaches.

To find the correlates of agricultural performance, district-wise growth and development has been compared with use of modern inputs—fertilizers, tractors, pumpsets, cropping intensity, irrigation, infrastructure facilities like roads and resource endowments, that include—agricultural workers, level of literacy, land structure and rainfall. Findings from the tabular and graphical analysis were tested using Random Effect Panel Data and Fixed Effect Panel Data Models.

Hence, a brief summary from findings of our empirical analysis is as follows:

FIVE DECADES OF AGRICULTURAL PERFORMANCE IN UTTAR PRADESH

Uttar Pradesh recorded mediocre performance in agriculture growth during the last half a century. It continues to achieve approximately average growth recorded by the agriculture sector in the country as a whole. The state could not benefit from green revolution technology as much as the gains harvested by its neighbouring states of Punjab and Haryana. Similarly, the state also could not match the big catch-up recorded by many other states like West Bengal, Gujarat and Bihar. Nevertheless, the agriculture growth rate in Uttar Pradesh accelerated significantly during the green revolution period, decelerated in the first decade of reform period (1990s), but recovered marginally during the first decade of the twenty first century. The recent recovery of agriculture is mainly because of a significant improvement in growth of livestock production. The combined output of the crop sector experienced considerable acceleration in growth from less than 1 per cent per annum during pre-green revolution period to more than 3 per cent during 1980s and decelerated to almost half (1.5%) during the new millennium. However, like crop sector, the fishery production continues to decelerate from a high of 12 per cent per annum growth during 1980s to 5 per cent per annum growth during 2000s. Forestry production accelerated from negative during 1980s to 20 per cent per annum during 1990s and declining to 4 per cent during 2000s. In crop sector, the temporal pattern of acceleration up to 1980s and serious deceleration thereafter has mainly marked the cereal crops. The opposite behaviour is shown by oilseeds. Their combined growth decelerated up to 1980s, but recovered thereafter. There is significant diversification of area under foodgrains with corresponding rise in area under non-foodgrains in general and under sugarcane, fruits and vegetables and condiments and spices in particular. Within foodgrains, major shift in area took place from coarse cereals and pulses towards the green revolution superior cereals—rice and wheat. Diversification in value of output is more sharp in the case of total non-foodgrains. This is mainly because of shift in area from low value coarse cereals and pulses towards high value condiments and spices and fruits and vegetable crops.

Decomposition of growth brings out that increase in yield was the main contributor to total agriculture production, but it lost its importance during the last decade whereby, its contribution to total production declined from more than 50 per cent to 17.6 per cent during 2001-2011. The changes in cropping pattern from low value to high value crops accounted for considerable contribution to growth during 2001-2011. Almost one-fifth of the total production during the last decade was due to interaction between crop yield and changes in cropping pattern effects. Contribution of area effect first declined from one-fourth to a low level of approximately one-tenth during 1980s, but doubled to almost 20 per cent during 2000s. In wake of technological deceleration, price and increasing role of markets seems to have played a significant role in changing relative contribution of area, yield and cropping pattern to agricultural performance in the state.

AGRICULTURAL GROWTH IN UTTAR PRADESH: SPATIAL AND TEMPORAL PATTERN

A regional and district-level analysis of agricultural performance during 1960-61 to 2010-11 brings out different characteristics of temporal and spatial pattern of agricultural growth in Uttar Pradesh. For the period as a whole, agricultural performance varies considerably across agro-economic regions in the state. While three of the nine zones, namely Mid-Western Plain Zone, South-Western Semi-Arid Zone and North-Eastern Plain Zone achieved high growth rates exceeding 3 per cent per annum, whereas Hills, Vindhyan and Western Plain Zones recorded low growth during the overall period. The temporal pattern of growth also varies considerably across agro-economic regions. The agricultural growth in five of the nine agro-economic regions namely—Western Plain Zone, Mid-Western Plain Zone, Central Plain Zone, North-Eastern Plain Zone and Vindhyan Zone follow the overall state pattern of inverted 'U' curve behaviour over time, indicating acceleration during the pre-reform period and deceleration in growth during the post-reform period. In rest of the four zones, the agriculture growth accelerated till 1980s, but has not declined thereafter significantly as it accelerated albeit marginally, during the post-reform period as well.

Like the output growth, the temporal pattern of growth in area under different crops is not uniform over time for the state as a whole as well as for different agro-economic regions. In six of the nine agro-economic regions namely—Western Plain Zone, Mid-Western Plain Zone, North-Eastern Plain Zone, Eastern Plain Zone, Vindhyan

Zone and Hills, there was acceleration in area growth up to 1980s, but it continued to decelerate significantly during the post-reform period. Bundelkhand and Central Plain Zones were the only zones, where area continues to accelerate even during the post-reform period as well. However, there was no significant change in growth of area in South-Western Semi-Arid Zone. The growth of crop yield also varies considerably across zones and over time. Four agro-economic zones namely—Mid-Western Plain Zone, South-Western Semi-Arid Zone, North-Eastern Plain Zone and Eastern Plain Zone performed extremely well by recording growth exceeding 2.5 per cent per annum. Like the earlier finding, the Hills, Bundelkhand and Western Plain Zones performed poorly on yield growth as well. Therefore, the differential performance of agriculture growth by different agro-economic regions seems to be mainly because of their differential performance in crop yield. There is mix picture regarding acceleration/deceleration of crop yield during the post-reform period. The yield growth accelerated up to mature green revolution phase in all the zones, but the post-reform period does not follow any specific pattern in this context. While, the yield growth decelerated in post-reform period in Mid-Western Plain Zone, it accelerated in South-Western Semi-Arid Zone, North-Eastern Plain Zone, Vindhyan Zone and Hills zone. In remaining four zones, the crop yield continues to grow at the same pace, it neither accelerated nor decelerated significantly.

The number of districts, recording different levels of growth, differs considerably over time. The number of high growth districts increased from 15 during the pre-green revolution period to 37 during 1980s and declined to 12 during 2000s. The low performing districts depict just opposite behaviour, as the number of districts recording less than 2 per cent per annum growth declined from 27 during the pre-green revolution period to just one during 1980s, but their number increased to 24 during 2000s. Though all districts experienced significant improvement in agriculture growth, but there are large inter-district variations in growth. The growth varies from 4 per cent per annum for Moradabad and Pilibhit districts to about 1 per cent per annum in Bulandshahr and Hamirpur districts. Banda is odd man out district as it has not recorded any significant improvement in growth for the last five decades. Growth accelerated in almost all the districts with exception of Muzaffarnagar, Saharanpur, Bijnor, Mainpuri, Allahabad, Lucknow, Unnao, Ballia, Varanasi and Mirzapur districts. Almost half of the districts recorded significant deceleration in the post-reform period, whereas agriculture growth accelerated in 14 of the 47 districts (including hills) units in the state. Twelve districts just continued to grow with the same pattern during the post-reform period at which they were growing during 1980s.

AGRICULTURAL DEVELOPMENT IN UTTAR PRADESH: TEMPORAL AND SPATIAL DYNAMICS

There are large spatial disparities in the level of agricultural development in Uttar Pradesh. The Western Plain Zone even though recorded mediocre agriculture growth during last five decades, yet continued to be much ahead of rest of the zones in terms of agricultural development. The per hectare productivity in 1960-63 in this zone was so high that even after 50 years, the three other zones namely—Bundelkhand, Vindhyan and Hill Zones could not match it even in 2010-11. However, due to very high growth recorded by Mid-Western Plain and South-Western Semi-Arid Zones over time and in comparison low growth recorded by the Western Plain Zone, these three zones emerged as the most developed zones in the State of Uttar Pradesh in 2008-11. However, Bundelkhand Zone, Vindhyan Zone and the Hill Zone (which form the present day Uttarakhand) continue to be agriculturally lagging zones of the state. The remaining three zones namely—Central Plain Zone, North-Eastern Plain Zone and Eastern Plain Zone with mediocre growth, continues to maintain the middle level of development. Over time, gap between the most developed Western Plain Zone and other zones followed inverted 'U' curve path over the last five decades, i.e. the gap first continued to widen till 1980s, but started declining thereafter.

Almost all the districts in Uttar Pradesh were trapped in low levels of development till 1980s. There was a gradual shift from low productivity to high and medium productivity levels during 1990s, as the number of low productivity districts declined from 46 during 1960-63 to 32 during 1990-93 and further to 15 during 2008-11. At present, while Western Plain Zone, Mid-Western Plain Zone and South-Western Semi-Arid Zone have none of their districts in the low productivity range, Bundelkhand and Vindhyan Zones have all their districts in low productivity category. There are still nine districts in the state namely—Allahabad, Banda, Hamirpur, Jalaun, Jhansi, Bahraich, Pratapgarh, Mirzapur and Hills district unit that are at such low levels of development that they were unable to match the level of development attained by the most developed Meerut district fifty years back in early 1960s. These districts seem to be the 'Achilles Heel' of the Uttar Pradesh agriculture. Apart from this, there are 17 more districts that have not been able to achieve the level of development attained by most developed Muzaffarnagar district forty years back from now. For the period as a whole, inter-district disparities in the level of agriculture development increased marginally. Nevertheless, the pattern was not uniform, disparities widened till 1990s, but declined thereafter depicting inverted 'U' curve behaviour over time.

There is a definite regional contiguity so far as the district-level development in Uttar Pradesh is concerned. Development started in the extreme North in 1970s then started spreading to its contiguous districts. By 2000, another spot of prosperity emerged in the East. By 2010, a specific pattern emerged with high developed districts forming a continuous belt in North-West, medium developed districts forming a continuous strip in the East, and underdeveloped districts forming a continuous long strip in South-East and East-West part of the state. Agro-climatic conditions along with demonstration effect seem to be at play for these regional disparities and spatial pattern of development and underdevelopment in Uttar Pradesh.

CONVERGENCE/DIVERGENCE OF REGIONAL DISPARITIES IN AGRICULTURAL DEVELOPMENT

For the period as a whole, there was sigma convergence in regional disparities in agricultural development in Uttar Pradesh. However, the pattern of inequality was of inverted 'U' type implying sigma divergence from 1960 to 1980 and sigma convergence from 1981 to 2010. The magnitude of convergence was more strong in the later period than the former, resulting in overall sigma convergence of declining regional disparities.

Besides sigma convergence, there is also significant evidence of beta unconditional convergence. It occurred mainly during the last three decades, whereas no such convergence occurred during the 1960s and 1970s. In other words, there is evidence of catch-up by the low developed districts with the medium and high developed districts from 1980s onward. The results are robust to control for other exogenous structural factors affecting the agricultural development.

There is no conclusive evidence on prevalence of club

convergence across districts for the last three decades. While beta convergence occurred in the club of high developed Western region districts during 1981-82 to 2010-11 period, but there is no such evidence from 1960-61 to 1980-81 for the club. However, neither the club of medium developed or the low developed districts and nor the clubs of Central region and Eastern region districts provide conclusive evidence regarding beta unconditional and beta conditional convergence. Therefore, the overall beta convergence of catch-up by low developed districts seems to be mainly because of very strong catch-up within the club of high developed, Western region districts and partly due to inter-region convergence of development.

DYNAMICS OF LABOUR PRODUCTIVITY

Contrary to acceleration-deceleration in temporal pattern of agricultural performance, labour productivity growth continuously decelerated over the last five decades. During the last five decades, labour productivity recorded negative growth in Western Plain Zone and Vindhyan Zone whereas, the North-Eastern Plain Zone and Mid-Western Plain Zone recorded very high growth of labour productivity exceeding 1 per cent per annum. There is no unique pattern of temporal variations in growth of labour productivity in each of the agro-economic regions.

There is continuous increase in labour productivity at the state level in Uttar Pradesh. Whereas no such consistent pattern of continuous increase is recorded at the regional level except in North-Eastern Plain Zone. Though, like the level of land productivity, Western Plain Zone recorded the highest level of labour productivity as well, but there was decline in the productivity in the zone till 1990s and increased only marginally thereafter. Bundelkhand Zone remained almost at the same level of productivity between Rs. 20,000-23,000 per worker productivity. Moreover, four out of nine zones recorded a decline in labour productivity during the later period. All the districts in Western Plain Zone remained at the highest productivity levels since 1960s. Thereafter, except Budaun and Bareilly from Mid-Western Plain Zone, rest all districts joined the high productivity levels during 1990s and districts from South-Western Semi-Arid Zone during 2000s. With exception of Deoria, Ghazipur, Barabanki, Gonda, Azamgarh, Faizabad and Sultanpur districts all other districts from the North-Eastern Plain Zone, Eastern Plain Zone, Vindhyan and Hills

Zones remained trapped in low levels of labour productivity for the last five decades. Stagnation of labour productivity in these zones along with Bundelkhand Zone districts is worrisome situation.

Contrary to inverted 'U' relationship of regional disparities in agriculture growth, the labour productivity depicts 'L' type relationship over time. Disparities in labour productivity declined during 1960-1980 period, but stagnated thereafter for the last three decades (1981-2010). However, this pattern is mainly due to the fact that the main gain of agriculture growth went to the middle 60 per cent of the districts. These middle group districts gained immensely in their share of agriculture production at the cost of the districts in the bottom and top quintiles. The most worrisome is substantial decline in share of bottom low productivity districts whose share in agriculture production declined from 18.8 per cent to 12.8 per cent.

Revival of growth in low and stagnate labour productivity districts is urgently required as the level of labour productivity and the incidence of poverty are inversely related in the state. Persistence of very high incidence of poverty in low productive districts and zones suggests that the policies to overcome agricultural backwardness in these districts may go a long way in overcoming the serious problem of very high incidence of poverty and low level of living of overall population in general, and that of small and marginal farmers and agricultural workers in particular.

SOURCES OF AGRICULTURAL PERFORMANCE IN UTTAR PRADESH

The inter-district differentials in agricultural performance in the state of Uttar Pradesh arises both due to differentials in resource endowments in zones as well as due to differentials in use of modern inputs in agriculture. Among the modern inputs, the use of chemical fertilizers, tractors and pumpsets contribute to agricultural development, but the impact on inter-district differentials is significant in case of the former two. Among the resource endowments, increasing area under cultivation contributes to higher growth, whereas the labour force employed in agriculture is not significantly related to production differentials in the state. Not only the expanding area leads to higher growth,, but the structure of land distribution plays an equally important role in this context.

Contrary to widely accepted inverse farm size productivity relationship in Indian agriculture, higher proportion of small farmers turned out to be a constraint on agricultural development suggesting that there is positive farm size productivity relationship in Uttar Pradesh agriculture.

Infrastructure facilities do not contribute significantly to agriculture growth and development. But inter-district differentials in the state of Uttar Pradesh are not significant due to differentials in road density and the extent of irrigation facilities in the district when other factors are controlled in the Panel Data Models. Besides the man-made resources, the natural endowments of zones in the form of agro-climatic conditions play a very significant role in inter-district disparities in the performance of agriculture in the state. The favourable agro-climatic conditions in Western and Central regions and unfavourable agro-climatic conditions in Bundelkhand, Eastern and Vindhyan zones are significantly related with high and low level of development achieved by the districts falling in these climatic zones.

SOME POLICY IMPLICATIONS

The low level of development and a serious deceleration in Uttar Pradesh agriculture since initiation of economic reforms along with existence of inter-district disparities is a major concern for planners and policy-makers in the state. To achieve the objective of inclusive, sustained and balanced regional development of national planning and attaining 5.1 per cent growth in agriculture sector during twelfth plan period and transforming the state into a 'Granary of the Nation', the agriculture sector needs to be rejuvenated in the state. The need for rejuvenation is not only an important issue in itself for revival of the momentum of growth,, but is equally important to address many other crucial socio-economic concerns like alleviation of poverty, generation of more remunerative rural farm and non-farm employment opportunities, diversification of rural economy by generating surplus processable raw material for industrial use. The findings from this study as well as drawing from the experience of other developed states like Punjab and Haryana along with recent spectacular growth recorded by Gujarat and Bihar agriculture, to us, it seems that the state agriculture is operating under serious constraints. Five of these important constraints are: the natural constraints, technological constraints, market constraints, information constraints and the financial constraints. Therefore, policy initiatives are required in these areas to reverse the deceleration tendencies as well as to put the state agriculture on path of high sustainable and equitable growth. Some of the initiatives in this context are as follows:

1. Significant low level of development in Bundelkhand Zone, Vindhyan Zone and some districts in Eastern and Central Plain Zones indicate adverse agro-climatic conditions and low level of irrigation facilities. Therefore, besides low level of irrigation, some districts in the Eastern region are prone to flooding during monsoon season. Therefore, risk and uncertainty related with low and untimely rainfall as well as excess rainfall leading to floods, needs to be tackled on priority basis. Development of ground water irrigation facilities therefore, needs to be taken at the priority basis along with bunding of rivers to check the devastation caused by floods. Hence, along with provision of credit, some incentive (subsidy) for plantation of tubewells and provision of electricity for running the tubewells may be provided on priority basis, especially in the low irrigation intensity districts.
2. The state of Uttar Pradesh could not benefit from the earlier green revolution technology and the recent gains from breakthrough in biotechnological developments to the extent as other agriculturally leading states have benefitted. A big gap in yield of major crops in Uttar Pradesh and other leading states (Appendix 9.1), suggest the need to develop the suitable technology of different crops for different agro-economic regions in the state.
3. Besides improvement of technology of existing major crops, policy initiative needs to be taken to benefit from the emerging market opportunities for high value commercial crops like condiments and spices, fruits and vegetables. There is already a shift towards some of these crops which further needs to be accelerated for other crops as well.
4. The biggest problem encountered in the farming sector is the imperfections in the agriculture market and high market demand and price risk, for both inputs and outputs. With indication of government's phased withdrawal from agriculture markets and poor capacity of the small and

marginal farmers to participate and benefit from the commodity markets, we feel the need of some protection mechanism for farmers against the vagaries of agriculture markets. There is a need to promote the cooperative agriculture markets, development of agro-processing industries for surplus agriculture products in general and for processing of fruits and vegetables in particular. Contract farming with the agro-processing firms and big retail market chains are rapidly emerging in the country. Since small and marginal farmers are too weak to deal with such strong and big firms, there is an urgent need to evolve the strong institutional mechanism that facilitate and regulate such contracts to protect the interest of farming community in case of moral hazards by contracting parties.

5. Recent situation assessment survey of the farmers, suggest a big information gap in the state of Uttar Pradesh so far as the scientific knowledge about modern agriculture practices and policies, programmes and extension services provided to the farmers are concerned (Appendix 9.2). The existing large gap in potential and actual yield to a greater extent is because of such information gap among the farmers in the state. Dissemination of information on these accounts and strengthening of the extension network of agricultural departments, Universities, research stations, Krishi Vigyan Kendra's and involvement of NGOs is the need of the hour.
6. Evidence suggests low level of both public and private capital formation in state agriculture compared with the other agriculturally leading states in the Northern and Southern parts of the country (Pandeya, 2015). Evidence also suggests that the public sector play a complimentary role in this context. Therefore, besides more efforts for public investment in rural areas, there is an urgent need to promote private investment in agriculture. Investment in groundwater irrigation, tractor and other implements, improvement in land and other allied agriculture activities require investment that has long gestation period. Small and marginal farmers in the state who have very low level of living may not be having enough savings to undertake these investments. The rural credit institutions can play a significant role in this context. Compared with other leading states, the per hectare credit

supply to Uttar Pradesh farmers is grossly low and inadequate (Appendix 9.3). There is an urgent need for augmenting the institutional credit supply to agriculture in the state.

7. Besides improvement in production and productivity, equally important are the initiatives to reduce the cost of production in the agriculture sector. Such measures are urgently required not only to augment returns to the farmers and to improve their socio-economic well-being, but initiative is equally important to make farming a more remunerative activity. Thus, the state may emulate many successful initiatives undertaken in Punjab agriculture in this context. Some of these initiatives are: promotion of farmer's machinery cooperatives with most modern implements which include tractors, laser leveller, rotavator, tractor driven insecticide spray facilities, sowing machines and thresher services. Similarly, provision of cattle and buffalo breed improvement, through imported artificial insemination services provided to the farmers, are likely to go a long way to facilitate the development of dairy farming in the state. Special incentive scheme for small and marginal farmers for economy net/poly farming can prove to be a boom to small-marginal farmers, located adjoining to big cities for vegetable farming. The state must take initiative to implement these and other similar initiatives in Uttar Pradesh as well.
8. Last, but not the least, we feel the need of more intensive efforts for development of agricultural backward districts in the state. In our opinion, there is a need to undertake micro-level studies for the lagging districts in the state to find out the local constraint and to design the most appropriate policy initiatives for development of such districts.

Appendix 3.1

Price of Crops at (2010-11 Constant Prices)

Crop	*Price (Rs./ton)*
Bajra	10608.93
Barley	9578.54
Coriander	37166.67
Cotton	40298.00
Dry Chillies	69680.00
Dry Ginger	30748.03
Garlic	67546.67
Gram	26038.30
Groundnut	36363.10
Guarseed	9900.00
Jowar	11401.93
Jute	1250.00
Linseed	49383.60
Maize	9657.54
Masur	32633.41
Moong	60610.00
Moth	34625.29
Onion	12078.95
Potato	4669.11
Ragi (Mandua)	4500.00
Rapeseed and mustard	39213.81
Rice	15174.84
Sanhemp	54687.50
Sesamum	55477.27
Small Millets	8183.33
Soyabean	20464.29
Sugarcane	1466.32
Sunflower	23700.00
Sweet Potato	7057.77
Tobacco	76152.76
Total Pulses	32813.35
Tur	37409.06
Turmeric	49650.00
Urad	45623.37
Wheat	11558.37

Sources: (i) GoI, *National Accounts Statistics*, New Delhi, Ministry of Statistics and Programme Implementation, (www.mospi.nic.in).

(ii) GoI, *Department of Agriculture and Cooperation*, New Delhi, Ministry of Agriculture, Government of India, (agricoop.nic.in).

Appendix 3.2
Crops Covered in the Study

Sl. No.	Crops covered	S. No.	Crops covered
1.	Rice	19.	Castor seed
2.	Wheat	20.	Sunflower
3.	Jowar	21.	Soyabean
4.	Bajra	22.	Sugarcane
5.	Maize	23.	Turmeric
6.	Barley	24.	Coriander
7.	Ragi (Mandua)	25.	Dry Chillies
8.	Small Millets	26.	Sesamum
9.	Gram	27.	Garlic
10.	Tur (Arhar)	28.	Dry Ginger
11.	Urad	29.	Potato
12.	Moong	30.	Onion
13.	Moth	31.	Guarseed
14.	Masur	32.	Sweet Potato
15.	Tobacco	33.	Sanhemp
16.	Rapeseed and mustard	34.	Cotton
17.	Groundnut	35.	Jute
18.	Linseed		

Source: Same as in Table 4.2(a).

Appendix 3.3

Crop-wise Decomposition of Growth in Agriculture Output in Uttar Pradesh: 1960-63 to 2008-11

Periods → *Crops↓*	*Decomposition of growth*	*1960-63/ 1970-73*	*1970-73/ 1980-83*	*1980-83/ 1990-93*	*1990-93/ 2000-03*	*2000-03/ 2008-11*	*1960-63/ 2008-11*
Rice	Area effect	76.1	25.1	6.7	43.7	45.2	15.7
	Yield effect	22.1	65.0	89.0	51.4	55.8	60.1
	Interaction between area and yield effect	1.8	9.9	4.3	4.9	–1.0	24.2
	Total	**100.0**	**100.0**	**100.0**	**100.0**	**100.0**	**100.0**
Wheat	Area effect	49.2	41.1	19.1	34.6	37.7	22.9
	Yield effect	33.9	44.1	74.9	59.4	59.7	31.0
	Interaction between area and yield effect	16.9	14.8	6.0	6.0	2.5	46.0
	Total	**100.0**	**100.0**	**100.0**	**100.0**	**100.0**	**100.0**
Jowar	Area effect	174.8	–164.0	–12751.0	116.0	126.0	141.0
	Yield effect	–94.5	285.3	16986.6	–24.8	–41.7	–185.5
	Interaction between area and yield effect	19.8	–21.4	–4135.6	8.8	15.7	144.5
	Total	**100.0**	**100.0**	**100.0**	**100.0**	**100.0**	**100.0**
Bajra	Area effect	4.9	–709.2	–75.1	33.4	4.8	–8.4
	Yield effect	92.9	873.4	216.1	61.5	94.2	128.8
	Interaction between area and yield effect	2.2	–64.2	–41.0	5.0	1.1	–20.5
	Total	**100.0**	**100.0**	**100.0**	**100.0**	**100.0**	**100.0**
Maize	Area effect	55.8	70.0	–13.4	203.9	81.9	–71.5
	Yield effect	31.8	38.5	122.5	–122.4	21.1	235.0
	Interaction between area and yield effect	12.4	–8.5	–9.1	18.5	–3.0	–63.5
	Total	**100.0**	**100.0**	**100.0**	**100.0**	**100.0**	**100.0**
Barley	Area effect	185.5	129.1	297.0	159.0	91.4	118.2
	Yield effect	–116.5	–54.6	–332.0	–85.0	12.7	–167.1
	Interaction between area and yield effect	31.0	25.5	135.1	25.9	–4.2	148.9
	Total	**100.0**	**100.0**	**100.0**	**100.0**	**100.0**	**100.0**

(Contd.)

Periods → *Crops↓*	*Decomposition of growth*	*1960-63/ 1970-73*	*1970-73/ 1980-83*	*1980-83/ 1990-93*	*1990-93/ 2000-03*	*2000-03/ 2008-11*	*1960-63/ 2008-11*
Ragi	Area effect	46.0	98.0	–114.0	5.7	141.1	–71.5
	Yield effect	36.1	3.1	252.5	94.1	–46.1	239.2
	Interaction between area and yield effect	17.9	–1.1	–38.5	0.1	5.1	–67.7
	Total	**100.0**	**100.0**	**100.0**	**100.0**	**100.0**	**100.0**
Gram	Area effect	320.1	130.5	129.9	112.4	139.9	122.0
	Yield effect	–279.3	–39.9	–39.7	–16.7	–58.3	–96.0
	Interaction between area and yield effect	59.2	9.4	9.8	4.4	18.4	74.0
	Total	**100.0**	**100.0**	**100.0**	**100.0**	**100.0**	**100.0**
Arhar	Area effect	–35.6	–49.5	–2.9	107.8	42.1	147.8
	Yield effect	160.4	159.0	102.5	–10.3	69.1	–94.6
	Interaction between area and yield effect	–24.8	–9.5	0.4	2.5	–11.2	46.8
	Total	**100.0**	**100.0**	**100.0**	**100.0**	**100.0**	**100.0**
Rapeseed and mustard	Area effect	183.5	–4377.2	–6190.9	143.0	55.9	1257.9
	Yield effect	–51.6	2480.4	3593.5	–57.1	40.3	–274.6
	Interaction between area and yield effect	–31.9	1996.7	2697.4	14.1	3.9	–883.3
	Total	**100.0**	**100.0**	**100.0**	**100.0**	**100.0**	**100.0**
Groundnut	Area effect	2021.9	139.3	119.1	67.5	49.8	87.0
	Yield effect	–1488.3	–51.7	–36.0	41.8	56.5	33.8
	Interaction between area and yield effect	–433.6	12.4	16.9	–9.3	–6.3	–20.8
	Total	**100.0**	**100.0**	**100.0**	**100.0**	**100.0**	**100.0**
Linseed	Area effect	–19.2	–49.5	–22.2	126.3	–558.7	82.4
	Yield effect	128.0	119.2	116.9	–54.1	878.1	39.5
	Interaction between area and yield effect	–8.8	30.3	5.2	27.8	–219.4	–21.9
	Total	**100.0**	**100.0**	**100.0**	**100.0**	**100.0**	**100.0**
Sesamum	Area effect	35.4	1101.4	–104.6	55.4	440.5	–697.4
	Yield effect	65.9	–1298.9	116.2	37.4	–117.4	173.4
	Interaction between area and yield effect	–1.3	297.5	88.4	7.1	–223.2	624.0
	Total	**100.0**	**100.0**	**100.0**	**100.0**	**100.0**	**100.0**

(*Contd.*)

Periods → *Crops↓*	*Decomposition of growth*	*1960-63/ 1970-73*	*1970-73/ 1980-83*	*1980-83/ 1990-93*	*1990-93/ 2000-03*	*2000-03/ 2008-11*	*1960-63/ 2008-11*
Total oilseeds	Area effect	122.1	–582.6	–104.7	118.2	222.2	–1049.6
	Yield effect	–17.1	493.1	180.5	–23.6	–97.2	584.7
	Interaction between area and yield effect	–5.0	189.5	24.2	5.4	–25.0	564.9
	Total	**100.0**	**100.0**	**100.0**	**100.0**	**100.0**	**100.0**
Sugarcane	Area effect	36.3	60.4	42.7	110.6	4.6	52.2
	Yield effect	60.9	32.4	48.7	–9.2	95.6	27.7
	Interaction between area and yield effect	2.8	7.2	8.6	–1.4	–0.1	20.2
	Total	**100.0**	**100.0**	**100.0**	**100.0**	**100.0**	**100.0**
Cotton	Area effect	107.5	118.3	131.1	95.7	–107.6	104.4
	Yield effect	–10.2	–26.8	–79.7	11.9	226.0	–74.0
	Interaction between area and yield effect	2.7	8.5	48.6	–7.6	–18.3	69.5
	Total	**100.0**	**100.0**	**100.0**	**100.0**	**100.0**	**100.0**
Total Fibres	Area effect	77.1	380.6	116.7	83.9	200.2	102.6
	Yield effect	30.9	–402.2	–44.5	37.3	–176.4	–52.9
	Interaction between area and yield effect	–7.9	121.6	27.8	–21.2	76.2	50.2
	Total	**100.0**	**100.0**	**100.0**	**100.0**	**100.0**	**100.0**
Tobacco	Area effect	126.1	23.6	3.9	46.1	1291.4	6.1
	Yield effect	–38.0	66.3	84.3	40.6	–925.7	60.9
	Interaction between area and yield effect	11.9	10.1	11.8	13.3	–265.6	33.0
	Total	**100.0**	**100.0**	**100.0**	**100.0**	**100.0**	**100.0**
Total drugs and Narcotics	Area effect	135.7	49.6	46.0	87.8	15.8	12.3
	Yield effect	–50.7	38.5	21.3	4.6	53.6	9.0
	Interaction between area and yield effect	15.0	11.8	32.8	7.6	30.6	78.7
	Total	**100.0**	**100.0**	**100.0**	**100.0**	**100.0**	**100.0**
Dry chillies	Area effect	304.3	6.8	65.3	8.8	297.2	16.2
	Yield effect	–140.6	83.6	36.9	90.1	–227.8	62.7
	Interaction between area and yield effect	–63.6	9.6	–2.2	1.1	30.6	21.1
	Total	**100.0**	**100.0**	**100.0**	**100.0**	**100.0**	**100.0**

(*Contd.*)

Periods → *Crops↓*	*Decomposition of growth*	*1960-63/ 1970-73*	*1970-73/ 1980-83*	*1980-83/ 1990-93*	*1990-93/ 2000-03*	*2000-03/ 2008-11*	*1960-63/ 2008-11*
Total Condi-ments and Spices	Area effect	43.4	13.7	50.1	68.4	2.7	3.2
	Yield effect	60.8	67.7	37.4	25.6	83.5	42.4
	Interaction between area and yield effect	–4.2	18.6	12.5	6.1	13.8	54.4
	Total	**100.0**	**100.0**	**100.0**	**100.0**	**100.0**	**100.0**
Potato	Area effect	42.5	52.3	69.7	36.5	88.4	29.5
	Yield effect	39.3	29.3	23.5	51.6	9.1	14.6
	Interaction between area and yield effect	18.2	18.5	6.8	11.9	2.5	55.8
	Total	**100.0**	**100.0**	**100.0**	**100.0**	**100.0**	**100.0**
Total fruits and Vegetables	Area effect	56.7	252.1	111.8	8.9	84.7	57.1
	Yield effect	37.3	–86.7	–9.0	83.3	13.1	12.7
	Interaction between area and yield effect	6.1	–65.3	–2.8	7.7	2.2	30.2
	Total	**100.0**	**100.0**	**100.0**	**100.0**	**100.0**	**100.0**

Source: Same as in Table 3.3.

Appendix 4.1
Formation of District Units in Uttar Pradesh

Sl. No.	*District Unit in 1960-61*	*Comparable Unit in 2010-11*
1.	Agra	Agra + 32.94% of Firozabad
2.	Aligarh	Aligarh + 64.3% of Hatharas
3.	Allahabad	Allahabad + Kaushambi
4.	Azamgarh	Azamgarh + 25% of Ambedkar Nagar + 88.36% of Mau
5.	Badaun	Badaun
6.	Bahraich	Bahraich + Shivasti
7.	Ballia	Ballia + 11.64% of Mau
8.	Banda	Banda + Chitrakut
9.	Barabanki	Barabanki
10.	Bareilly	Bareilly
11.	Basti	Basti + Sant Kabir Nagar + Siddharth Nagar
12.	Bijnor	Bijnor + 6.64% of Haridwar
13.	Bulandshahr	Bullandshahr + 54% of Gautam Budha Nagar
14.	Deoria	Deoria + Kushi Nagar
15.	Etah	Etah
16.	Etawah	Etawah + Auraiya
17.	Faizabad	Faizabad + 75% of Ambedkar Nagar
18.	Farrukhabad	Farrukhabad + Kannauj
19.	Fatehpur	Fatehpur
20.	Ghazipur	Ghazipur
21.	Gonda	Gonda + Balrampur
22.	Gorakhpur	Gorakhpur + Maharahganj
23.	Hamirpur	Hamirpur + Mahoba
24.	Hardoi	Hardoi
25.	Jalaun	Jalaun
26.	Jaunpur	Jaunpur
27.	Jhansi	Jhansi + Lalitpur
28.	Kanpur	Kanpur Dehat + Kanpur City
29.	Kheri	Kheri
30.	Lucknow	Lucknow
31.	Mainpuri	Mainpuri + 67.06% of Firozabad
32.	Mathura	Mathura + 35.7% of Hatharas
33.	Meerut	Meerut + Ghaziabad + Bagpat
34.	Mirzapur	Mirzapur + Sonbhadra

(*Contd.*)

Sl. No.	*District Unit in 1960-61*	*Comparable Unit in 2010-11*
35.	Moradabad	Moradabad + Jyotir Bai Phule Nagar
36.	Muzaffarnagar	Muzaffarnagar + 6.36% of Haridwar
37.	Pilibhit	Pilibhit
38.	Pratapgarh	Pratapgarh
39.	Raebareli	Raebareli
40.	Rampur	Rampur
41.	Saharanpur	Saharanpur + 87 % of Haridwar
42.	Shahjahanpur	Shahjahanpur
43.	Sitapur	Sitapur
44.	Sultanpur	Sultanpur
45.	Unnao	Unnao
46.	Varanasi	Varanasi + Chandauli + Sant Ravi Das Nagar

Source: Bhalla, G.S. and Gurmail Singh (2010), *Growth of Indian Agriculture: A District Level Study,* New Delhi, Centre for Study of Regional Development, Planning Commission Report.

Appendix 6.1
Sigma (σ) Convergence in Uttar Pradesh: 1960-61 to 2010-11

Dependent Variable: Standard Deviation of Land Productivity

Period	*Intercept*	*Regression Coefficients*				
		Time	*Time*^{2}	R^2	R^2	*N*
1960-61 to 2010-11	5499.579	423.860***	−2.977***	0.873	0.867	49
		(6.831)	(2.581)			
1960-61 to 1980-81	7001.854	208.275***		0.742	0.727	19
		(6.991)				
1980-81 to 2010-11	10705.89	172.777***		0.431	0.411	30
		(4.606)				

Dependent Variable: Standard Deviation of Log Land Productivity

Period	*Intercept*	*Regression Coefficients*				
		Time	*Time*^{2}	R^2	R^2	*N*
1960-61 to 2010-11	0.295	0.003***	−3.98*10−5**	0.217	0.183	49
		(2.909)	(2.310)			
1960-61 to 1980-81	0.295	0.002***		0.358	0.321	19
		(3.081)				
1980-81 to 2010-11	0.343	−0.002		0.003	−0.033	30
		(0.263)				

Dependent Variable: Gini Coefficient of Land Productivity

Period	*Intercept*	*Regression Coefficients*				
		Time	*Time*^{2}	R^2	R^2	*N*
1960-61 to 2010-11	0.168	0.002***	−3.52*10-5***	0.244	0.211	49
		(3.805)	(3.837)			
1960-61 to 1980-81	0.172	0.009**		0.021	0.160	19
		(2.101)				
1980-81 to 2010-11	0.214	−0.0007**		0.186	0.157	30
		(2.533)				

Dependent Variable: Gini Coefficient of Log Land Productivity						
Period	*Intercept*	*Regression Coefficients*				
		Time	*Time*^{2}	R^2	$\bar{R}^2$	*N*
1960-61 to 2010-11	0.016	1.28x10*** (2.610)	–2.25*10-6** (2.478)	0.130	0.092	49
1960-61 to 1980-81	0.016	8.15x10** (1.989)		0.189	0.141	19
1980-81 to 2010-11	0.018	–3.47x10□5 (1.201)		0.049	0.015	30

Source: Same as in Table 6.1(a).

Notes:
1. Figure in parenthesis is t value of the coefficients.
2. Asterisk *, ** and *** indicate coefficients significant at 10 per cent, 5 per cent and 1 per cent level of significance respectively for two tailed test.

Appendix 8.1
District-wise level of agricultural productivity and Input use in Uttar Pradesh: 1960-63 to 2008-11

Periods→	*Ag Productivity (Rs. per hectare) at 2010-11 Constant Prices*						*Fertilizer Consumption (kg/hectare)*					
Districts/ Region ↓	*1960-63*	*1970-73*	*1980-83*	*1990-93*	*2000-03*	*2008-10*	*1960-63*	*1970-73*	*1980-83*	*1990-93*	*2000-03*	*2008-11*
Bulandshahr	43393	41282	52358	62558	67367	73753	5	29	81	93	152	194
Meerut	45944	55778	69263	95654	95074	103123	7	46	97	122	195	241
Muzaffarnagar	44364	60759	82654	103412	102168	105275	7	48	82	140	218	180
Saharanpur	34059	43195	60847	83553	70712	71972	4	33	75	124	188	175
Western Plain Zone	**42140**	**50107**	**66357**	**86973**	**84430**	**89384**	**6**	**39**	**85**	**119**	**188**	**201**
Bareilly	22616	24466	36004	53906	62319	63261	3	23	57	130	162	184
Bijnor	26499	34277	50061	78654	83609	79809	4	27	70	123	152	179
Budaun	16473	22616	30881	41937	51986	62016	3	18	50	95	111	114
Moradabad	20365	25582	45653	62582	72475	74776	5	24	62	123	187	210
Pilibhit	21370	25899	43378	65709	75216	78260	3	23	78	142	192	221
Rampur	23785	26797	45091	64265	75333	77707	4	37	85	126	140	127
Shahjahanpur	17586	22197	33468	53136	62013	69833	2	16	66	105	173	219
Mid-Western Plain Zone	**20780**	**25774**	**40277**	**59199**	**68046**	**71492**	**4**	**23**	**65**	**119**	**159**	**180**
Agra	22989	25842	30820	43355	58832	75193	2	22	46	79	128	198
Aligarh	31210	40171	44467	54309	59118	71341	4	20	46	73	113	168
Etah	24183	27714	34805	55445	70275	80273	3	18	37	73	103	168

(*Contd.*)

Periods→ Districts/ Region ↓	Ag Productivity (Rs. per hectare) at 2010-11 Constant Prices						Fertilizer Consumption (kg/hectare)					
	1960-63	1970-73	1980-83	1990-93	2000-03	2008-10	1960-63	1970-73	1980-83	1990-93	2000-03	2008-11
Mainpuri	20735	25290	31056	48811	58983	88306	3	20	45	78	140	189
Mathura	28617	30154	32276	47455	57927	69645	2	13	36	71	99	160
South-Western Semi-Arid Zone	**25859**	**30296**	**35155**	**49984**	**60919**	**76612**	**3**	**19**	**42**	**75**	**116**	**176**
Allahabad	20488	23917	29171	36442	41035	43718	4	18	51	100	158	261
Etawah	22990	26838	34995	48285	61572	73685	2	15	55	72	91	142
Farrukhabad	22317	25661	38506	64286	80791	85889	10	35	82	119	187	282
Fatehpur	21832	25171	30109	37142	42675	48466	1	11	41	83	130	140
Hardoi	23468	24243	26768	39216	44796	55710	2	9	36	54	75	137
Kanpur	22645	25494	30977	46124	50251	52923	3	15	52	81	124	251
Kheri	19985	23595	31733	49881	67957	71434	2	14	53	99	141	139
Lucknow	20013	19368	29756	35296	42547	49204	5	25	77	120	138	218
Raebareli	19524	22133	26364	35078	39871	48326	2	12	49	74	102	196
Sitapur	18945	19611	26451	37921	50781	58509	2	11	33	70	126	163
Unnao	18068	19775	25263	32211	37444	47790	1	10	42	68	101	112
Central Plain Zone	**20978**	**23426**	**29857**	**42265**	**51433**	**58155**	**3**	**15**	**50**	**84**	**125**	**183**
Banda	17406	17163	20591	20244	23751	22291	1	3	11	22	26	48
Hamirpur	14080	15866	18841	21346	23399	25484	1	2	6	21	30	37
Jalaun	15932	18458	22535	29942	36144	37112	1	9	28	38	63	91
Jhansi	13233	15284	16657	23562	29332	37968	1	5	18	32	47	70
Bundelkhand Zone	**15135**	**16576**	**19409**	**23249**	**27463**	**30495**	**1**	**4**	**15**	**27**	**40**	**60**
Bahraich	12673	12893	17046	28781	39609	44566	1	9	32	44	70	99
Basti	17424	19165	23503	35385	42969	52030	3	24	39	79	157	167
Deoria	22054	22507	35771	53761	58989	58341	5	37	73	151	182	206

(*Contd.*)

Periods→ Districts/ Region ↓	Ag Productivity (Rs. per hectare) at 2010-11 Constant Prices						Fertilizer Consumption (kg/hectare)					
	1960-63	1970-73	1980-83	1990-93	2000-03	2008-10	1960-63	1970-73	1980-83	1990-93	2000-03	2008-11
Gonda	15402	16806	24072	33260	48432	56658	1	17	34	48	78	134
Gorakhpur	18044	20569	29152	45181	51672	56203	4	29	54	84	149	230
North-Eastern Plain Zone	**17092**	**18383**	**25763**	**38814**	**47923**	**53446**	**3**	**23**	**46**	**79**	**127**	**167**
Azamgarh	21411	19535	28092	46750	50728	55458	3	17	44	83	108	125
Ballia	20631	25839	31493	39306	45844	49567	2	18	55	101	105	135
Barabanki	29260	24014	32251	47521	62349	70147	6	25	52	91	157	195
Faizabad	23741	22183	34642	49568	56410	62851	6	35	77	124	188	230
Ghazipur	20710	21315	28701	45446	47501	50934	4	19	76	112	128	147
Jaunpur	20346	21497	32710	44184	48259	53926	7	24	84	111	104	127
Pratapgarh	18174	17783	27036	37829	40807	42806	2	16	61	80	115	174
Sultanpur	19565	19194	26893	41761	49218	53952	2	20	53	71	97	145
Varanasi	23575	22413	31009	42387	47544	51290	6	30	78	130	204	261
Eastern Plain Zone	**22055**	**21393**	**30292**	**44233**	**50059**	**54923**	**4**	**23**	**64**	**100**	**135**	**170**
Mirzapur	15966	17238	20371	24730	33141	29354	2	9	31	42	58	121
Vindhyan Zone	**15966**	**17238**	**20371**	**24730**	**33141**	**29354**	**2**	**9**	**31**	**42**	**58**	**121**
Hills	16075	24568	27697	36843	38094	41897	1	12	37	72	84	143
Uttar Pradesh	**21988**	**24861**	**33130**	**46440**	**53283**	**59085**	**3**	**20**	**52**	**87**	**126**	**164**

Source: Same as in Tables 8.1 and 8.2.

Appendix 8.1 (*Contd.*)

Periods →	*Tractors (No. per 1000 Hectare of NSA)*						*Pumpsets (No. per 1000 Hectare of NSA)*					
Districts/Region ↓	*1961-62*	*1972-73*	*1982-83*	*1992-93*	*2003-04*	*2007-08*	*1961-62*	*1972-73*	*1982-83*	*1992-93*	*2003-04*	*2007-08*
Bulandshahr	0.7	2	13	26	47	51	2	36	86	167	132	227
Meerut	1	8	25	46	80	93	3	43	122	172	227	258
Muzaffarnagar	2	8	35	66	104	116	4	44	123	174	281	282
Saharanpur	0.9	5	21	51	88	90	1	36	122	204	464	284
Western Plain Zone	**1**	**6**	**24**	**47**	**79**	**88**	**3**	**40**	**115**	**179**	**273**	**263**
Bareilly	0.4	1	8	20	43	47	0.4	15	57	177	252	380
Bijnor	0.9	2	13	36	63	66	1	26	118	154	223	270
Budaun	0.1	0	4	12	30	35	1	11	54	147	252	266
Moradabad	0.8	2	13	42	71	74	2	26	125	279	454	407
Pilibhit	0.9	3	15	28	59	61	0.4	24	93	184	220	366
Rampur	2	7	17	35	54	60	0.5	25	91	223	722	421
Shahjahanpur	0.3	1	9	22	31	37	0.5	26	83	172	160	238
Mid-Western Plain Zone	**0.6**	**2**	**11**	**28**	**50**	**54**	**1**	**21**	**90**	**194**	**311**	**330**
Agra	0.3	3	10	23	41	44	0.4	31	96	159	190	238
Aligarh	0.3	2	10	19	52	55	1	29	71	161	214	250
Etah	0.3	1	4	13	23	25	0.5	17	62	164	226	290
Mainpuri	0.1	1	4	15	27	29	1	30	80	138	183	285
Mathura	0.2	4	13	35	59	70	0.4	20	69	133	184	245
South-Western Semi-Arid Zone	**0.3**	**2**	**8**	**21**	**41**	**45**	**1**	**26**	**76**	**152**	**200**	**261**
Allahabad	0.1	1	5	13	34	36	0.1	11	35	82	109	140
Etawah	0.2	1	4	9	24	26	0.5	19	43	88	114	240
Farrukhabad	0.3	1	6	19	37	41	1	26	97	194	141	248

(*Contd.*)

Periods → Districts/Region ↓	Tractors (No. per 1000 Hectare of NSA)						Pumpsets (No. per 1000 Hectare of NSA)					
	1961-62	*1972-73*	*1982-83*	*1992-93*	*2003-04*	*2007-08*	*1961-62*	*1972-73*	*1982-83*	*1992-93*	*2003-04*	*2007-08*
Fatehpur	0.1	0	3	6	23	23	0.3	14	32	87	109	146
Hardoi	0.2	0	3	9	18	18	0.2	12	53	114	128	201
Kanpur	0.2	0	6	13	28	31	0.4	19	54	102	111	169
Kheri	1	2	9	17	35	39	1	16	74	135	167	260
Lucknow	0.4	1	5	14	32	71	1	15	67	142	194	265
Raebareli	0.1	0	4	10	43	53	0.2	15	47	111	176	311
Sitapur	0.2	1	3	12	32	33	0.3	18	36	95	213	303
Unnao	0.1	0	4	11	24	37	0.5	15	63	166	188	234
Central Plain Zone	**0.3**	**1**	**5**	12	**30**	**34**	**0.4**	**16**	**53**	**116**	**147**	**224**
Banda	0.1	0	2	5	15	15	0.1	3	14	34	50	55
Hamirpur	0.2	1	4	15	34	36	0.2	4	13	40	89	73
Jalaun	0.6	3	12	29	41	46	0.1	2	9	19	35	49
Jhansi	0.3	1	3	15	33	33	0.3	4	25	106	160	122
Bundelkhand Zone	**0.3**	**1**	**5**	**15**	30	31	0.2	**4**	**16**	**53**	**90**	**79**
Bahraich	0.2	0	2	15	14	16	0.2	8	35	97	183	248
Basti	0.2	1	9	15	38	39	0.3	17	73	139	261	301
Deoria	0.4	1	8	19	49	63	0.5	19	63	143	186	384
Gonda	0.3	1	3	12	31	32	1	13	78	166	182	305
Gorakhpur	0.5	1	8	20	40	44	1	21	87	168	247	358
North-Eastern Plain Zone	**0.3**	**1**	**6**	**16**	**34**	**38**	**1**	**16**	**68**	**143**	**214**	**317**
Azamgarh	0.3	0	6	17	41	43	0.3	18	70	169	215	242
Ballia	0.1	0	3	10	21	22	0.3	12	51	101	128	201
Barabanki	0.2	1	7	21	51	51	1	29	68	193	343	339
Faizabad	0.1	1	6	31	56	57	0.2	21	77	172	237	384

(Contd.)

Periods → Districts/Region ↓	Tractors (No. per 1000 Hectare of NSA)						Pumpsets (No. per 1000 Hectare of NSA)					
	1961-62	1972-73	1982-83	1992-93	2003-04	2007-08	1961-62	1972-73	1982-83	1992-93	2003-04	2007-08
Ghazipur	0.1	1	6	15	36	37	0.2	20	70	120	144	307
Jaunpur	0.0	1	6	16	33	35	0.2	22	102	171	249	281
Pratapgarh	0.0	0	4	9	29	33	0.1	13	64	92	144	487
Sultanpur	0.1	0	3	16	37	35	0.2	8	47	121	185	435
Varanasi	0.3	1	8	19	37	43	0.2	16	52	86	93	121
Eastern Plain Zone	**0.2**	**0**	**6**	**18**	**38**	**40**	**0.3**	**18**	**67**	**139**	**195**	**305**
Mirzapur	0.3	1	7	15	35	41	0.1	8	18	65	108	117
Vindhyan Zone	**0.3**	**1**	**7**	**15**	**35**	**41**	**0.1**	**8**	**18**	**65**	**108**	**117**
Hills	1	4	10	16	17	18	0.1	6	19	35	51	45
Uttar Pradesh	**0.4**	**2**	**8**	**20**	**40**	**44**	**1**	**18**	**64**	**132**	**191**	**245**

Source: Same as in Tables 8.1 and 8.2.

Appendix 8.1 (*Contd.*)

Periods→ Districts/Region↓	Cropping Intensity						Irrigation (Percentage of GCA)					
	1960-63	1970-73	1980-83	1990-93	2000-03	2008-11	1960-63	1970-73	1980-83	1990-93	2000-03	2008-11
Bulandshahr	139	154	170	172	157	170	55.1	67.6	83.6	96.2	99.9	100.0
Meerut	141	155	162	162	151	158	62.7	78.3	87.7	96.8	99.9	100.0
Muzaffarnagar	132	146	155	156	148	151	54.0	72.5	79.7	89.1	98.1	98.9
Saharanpur	139	149	157	158	151	147	25.4	48.3	62.8	74.5	86.4	91.3
Western Plain Zone	**138**	**152**	**161**	**162**	**151**	**156**	**50.1**	**67.1**	**79.1**	**89.7**	**96.3**	**97.7**
Bareilly	127	132	145	154	157	165	13.0	35.9	48.5	76.2	90.8	92.7

(*Contd.*)

Periods→	*Cropping Intensity*						*Irrigation (Percentage of GCA)*					
Districts/Region↓	*1960-63*	*1970-73*	*1980-83*	*1990-93*	*2000-03*	*2008-11*	*1960-63*	*1970-73*	*1980-83*	*1990-93*	*2000-03*	*2008-11*
Bijnor	119	127	133	135	131	130	11.4	34.4	53.5	71.1	84.2	90.4
Budaun	117	127	139	154	161	169	16.3	35.0	41.7	61.4	73.4	72.2
Moradabad	118	133	147	154	163	168	20.1	44.5	61.6	79.7	85.6	87.4
Pilibhit	128	141	158	167	164	171	8.2	32.9	60.4	85.6	90.6	97.3
Rampur	138	144	156	168	183	192	6.3	30.2	57.3	85.5	94.0	95.8
Shahjahanpur	118	123	142	157	161	173	10.1	37.4	55.4	78.7	90.3	89.8
Mid-Western Plain Zone	**122**	**131**	**144**	**154**	**159**	**165**	**13.3**	**36.8**	**53.9**	**75.9**	**86.0**	**87.9**
Agra	118	126	135	134	145	150	25.1	40.4	50.6	63.5	63.3	68.8
Aligarh	135	155	165	160	164	171	46.7	64.3	72.1	84.5	82.5	83.9
Etah	132	145	157	164	161	164	36.2	50.0	59.9	74.5	81.9	90.0
Mainpuri	130	139	146	151	157	173	36.0	56.2	66.0	78.7	84.2	89.2
Mathura	121	132	140	139	154	150	38.1	57.1	66.3	78.0	78.0	83.0
South-Western Semi-Arid Zone	**127**	**140**	**149**	**150**	**156**	**162**	**36.9**	**54.2**	**63.5**	**76.4**	**78.2**	**83.2**
Allahabad	128	128	136	141	147	145	18.4	24.6	38.7	60.8	71.3	76.0
Etawah	126	132	141	152	158	163	35.1	47.2	61.3	70.0	74.4	78.6
Farrukhabad	126	134	147	148	150	146	27.4	42.2	50.8	69.0	74.3	83.7
Fatehpur	121	123	132	134	138	138	23.2	28.6	40.2	55.5	65.5	68.8
Hardoi	122	134	135	144	151	158	11.2	26.1	44.9	56.0	76.5	81.6
Kanpur	122	122	130	139	141	137	25.0	33.8	50.8	58.0	66.2	67.4
Kheri	129	130	135	141	147	147	4.2	12.4	26.7	49.4	72.2	81.3
Lucknow	128	127	139	141	154	153	22.9	36.2	53.1	74.8	85.3	89.1
Raebareli	137	136	136	151	148	156	30.9	40.8	54.6	79.6	84.2	87.4
Sitapur	129	125	136	134	143	150	8.9	19.4	29.0	41.0	71.2	83.3
Unnao	131	134	140	146	147	154	20.5	36.0	54.7	69.2	78.6	80.1

(*Contd.*)

Periods→ Districts/Region↓	Cropping Intensity						Irrigation (Percentage of GCA)					
	1960-63	1970-73	1980-83	1990-93	2000-03	2008-11	1960-63	1970-73	1980-83	1990-93	2000-03	2008-11
Central Plain Zone	**127**	**129**	**137**	**142**	**147**	**149**	**19.3**	**29.9**	**44.0**	**60.1**	**73.6**	**79.2**
Banda	120	118	122	117	118	118	15.8	17.2	21.5	29.1	33.1	38.3
Hamirpur	103	104	104	106	111	126	10.8	14.7	16.1	26.9	32.6	32.0
Jalaun	104	107	105	108	111	121	21.0	34.9	24.8	32.0	42.8	52.8
Jhansi	111	113	117	119	127	156	13.5	19.6	26.8	38.0	51.2	49.8
Bundelkhand Zone	**110**	**111**	**113**	**113**	**118**	**132**	**14.9**	**20.5**	**22.2**	**31.7**	**40.3**	**43.2**
Bahraich	139	135	151	155	154	148	5.6	8.9	14.9	18.1	29.7	38.1
Basti	134	142	148	149	146	150	33.7	37.2	40.4	46.3	50.4	56.8
Deoria	130	136	148	150	155	157	28.1	34.8	48.7	55.3	64.7	80.0
Gonda	142	138	155	149	157	151	18.2	20.1	27.5	31.4	41.5	57.5
Gorakhpur	133	135	152	163	162	165	28.6	35.9	43.6	46.8	53.5	58.8
North-Eastern Plain zone	**136**	**138**	**151**	**153**	**155**	**154**	**23.1**	**27.8**	**35.0**	**39.6**	**47.7**	**58.0**
Azamgarh	126	126	147	162	165	168	41.0	43.5	50.8	57.8	79.4	93.8
Ballia	129	132	151	155	160	155	28.9	34.6	41.4	53.6	68.7	76.8
Barabanki	143	139	155	164	176	191	21.8	31.0	46.0	69.5	81.8	89.3
Faizabad	138	131	152	161	161	162	38.9	41.9	51.7	70.3	89.4	92.5
Ghazipur	123	125	143	148	158	161	31.3	35.1	51.0	68.9	82.4	85.5
Jaunpur	125	131	146	157	153	168	43.0	44.6	46.9	65.9	78.4	82.7
Pratapgarh	129	121	139	153	150	139	31.3	33.8	45.4	59.4	82.1	88.6
Sultanpur	133	129	144	155	150	151	28.9	34.2	38.8	50.9	73.5	85.5
Varanasi	137	137	145	156	155	164	35.7	39.4	59.9	70.6	82.4	85.3
Eastern Plain Zone	**132**	**130**	**147**	**157**	**159**	**163**	**33.8**	**38.0**	**48.5**	**63.1**	**80.0**	**87.4**
Mirzapur	131	128	135	139	141	126	18.3	22.3	33.7	39.7	46.0	43.5
Vindhyan Zone	**131**	**128**	**135**	**139**	**141**	**126**	**18.3**	**22.3**	**33.7**	**39.7**	**46.0**	**43.5**

(Contd.)

Periods→ Districts/Region↓	Cropping Intensity						Irrigation (Percentage of GCA)					
	1960-63	1970-73	1980-83	1990-93	2000-03	2008-11	1960-63	1970-73	1980-83	1990-93	2000-03	2008-11
Hills	120	170	163	164	163	166	11.5	15.5	28.1	34.3	37.6	40.9
Uttar Pradesh	**127**	**133**	**143**	**148**	**150**	**154**	**25.4**	**36.1**	**47.4**	**60.4**	**70.3**	**75.3**

Source: Same as in Tables 8.1 and 8.2.

Appendix 8.1 (Contd.)

Periods → Districts/Region ↓	Road Length (per 00000 hectare)					Workers (No. per 000 Hectare)				
	1970-73	1980-83	1990-93	2000-03	2008-11	1960-63	1980-83	1990-93	2000-03	2008-11
Bulandshahr	146	242	377	562	965	701	1020	1144	1132	1106
Meerut	199	285	485	699	957	631	1186	1052	1130	1173
Muzaffarnagar	183	258	434	648	840	641	1335	1345	1370	1330
Saharanpur	165	256	532	629	1061	498	1001	984	1138	1196
Western Plain Zone	**174**	**263**	**462**	**640**	**959**	**619**	**1135**	**1118**	**1182**	**1195**
Bareilly	108	219	314	585	865	836	1171	1285	1325	1289
Bijnor	201	294	428	642	878	588	1050	1112	1205	1251
Budaun	91	162	214	428	759	865	1186	1170	1225	1197
Moradabad	125	202	306	606	862	822	1180	1280	1310	1300
Pilibhit	143	240	314	509	687	618	902	921	1146	1128
Rampur	140	259	371	582	749	691	1170	1130	1230	1227
Shahjahanpur	117	172	243	386	696	808	1008	958	1063	1040
Mid-Western Plain Zone	**129**	**215**	**306**	**533**	**795**	**766**	**1107**	**1140**	**1223**	**1209**
Agra	176	320	541	758	1231	682	993	1089	1220	1248
Aligarh	123	217	319	657	846	636	1022	1004	1107	1078
Etah	132	263	522	633	856	798	1184	1179	1342	1338
Mainpuri	153	274	501	769	1377	822	1112	1166	1266	1196

(Contd.)

Periods → Districts/Region ↓	Road Length (per 00000 hectare)					Workers (No. per 000 Hectare)				
	1970-73	*1980-83*	*1990-93*	*2000-03*	*2008-11*	*1960-63*	*1980-83*	*1990-93*	*2000-03*	*2008-11*
Mathura	153	297	545	661	819	628	887	1219	1040	1066
South-Western Semi-Arid Zone	**147**	**272**	**478**	**694**	**1017**	**707**	**1040**	**1122**	**1191**	**1181**
Allahabad	181	351	544	761	1531	1338	1871	2050	2067	2263
Etawah	124	247	370	805	1473	837	1113	1231	1392	1394
Farrukhabad	123	248	389	538	1056	930	1361	1511	1632	1787
Fatehpur	125	230	348	538	819	1118	1509	1714	1842	1914
Hardoi	112	208	291	533	816	982	1389	1499	1560	1492
Kanpur	133	233	421	746	1045	779	1149	1338	1535	1656
Kheri	127	202	253	379	628	719	1117	1225	1313	1357
Lucknow	230	440	697	1120	2045	1257	1604	1691	1756	1831
Raebareli	170	347	437	702	1241	1341	1808	1916	2006	2246
Sitapur	106	175	257	464	1013	889	1374	1579	1660	1635
Unnao	128	261	400	677	999	1096	1584	1676	1783	1682
Central Plain Zone	**138**	**256**	**381**	**624**	**1081**	**1008**	**1429**	**1573**	**1671**	**1721**
Banda	104	198	246	384	609	665	1195	1284	1350	1374
Hamirpur	103	169	213	412	567	575	951	1003	927	847
Jalaun	92	217	311	524	637	536	912	1052	1124	1063
Jhansi	152	289	327	473	549	635	1069	1178	1164	933
Bundelkhand Zone	**114**	**218**	**271**	**442**	**585**	**609**	**1047**	**1141**	**1146**	**1034**
Bahraich	96	187	241	416	843	960	1428	1616	1740	1828
Basti	137	187	273	517	956	1521	1664	1936	1984	1953
Deoria	190	240	355	699	1223	1537	1817	2180	2039	2001
Gonda	132	204	261	442	916	1126	1530	1950	1901	1945
Gorakhpur	156	213	282	718	1238	1509	1690	1931	1978	1995
North-Eastern Plain Zone	**142**	**205**	**281**	**553**	**1025**	**1330**	**1624**	**1918**	**1929**	**1945**
Azamgarh	177	283	358	776	1433	1409	1744	1921	1763	1737
Ballia	201	310	434	794	997	1176	1580	1640	1689	1745
Barabanki	98	215	560	847	1420	1219	1619	1662	1951	1806
Faizabad	145	260	368	751	1288	1357	1712	2100	1950	1899

(*Contd.*)

Periods → Districts/Region ↓	Road Length (per 00000 hectare)					Workers (No. per 000 Hectare)				
	1970-73	1980-83	1990-93	2000-03	2008-11	1960-63	1980-83	1990-93	2000-03	2008-11
Ghazipur	144	281	451	830	1448	1287	1557	1776	1926	1992
Jaunpur	141	325	545	786	1406	1563	1687	1959	2187	2112
Pratapgarh	138	325	453	1065	1493	1620	1913	2075	2088	2286
Sultanpur	172	299	532	1117	1442	1260	1661	1771	1944	1759
Varanasi	197	380	454	1147	1956	1126	1804	1652	1873	1977
Eastern Plain Zone	**158**	**297**	**456**	**896**	**1440**	**1330**	**1700**	**1842**	**1918**	**1899**
Mirzapur	178	306	460	663	1778	917	1499	1632	1745	2377
Vindhyan Zone	**178**	**306**	**460**	**663**	**1778**	**917**	**1499**	**1632**	**1745**	**2377**
Hills	523	1276	1478	2486	3734	1386	1504	1504	1692	1791
Uttar Pradesh	**159**	**290**	**418**	**699**	**1121**	**994**	**1362**	**1479**	**1545**	**1548**

Source: Same as in Tables 8.1 and 8.2.

Appendix 8.1 (*Contd.*)

Periods → Districts/Region ↓	Literacy Rate (Percentage)						Small + Marginal Share in Total Holdings				
	1961	1971	1981	1991	2001	2011	1970-71	1980-81	1990-91	2000-01	2010-11
Bulandshahr	20.5	26.0	29.0	44.7	63.6	74.4	73.0	77.5	81.8	85.2	90.9
Meerut	26.5	33.2	35.5	53.3	67.8	78.4	76.2	80.1	83.8	86.4	89.0
Muzaffarnagar	19.7	26.8	30.1	44.3	61.3	69.6	71.8	77.4	82.4	84.5	87.2
Saharanpur	23.6	27.3	29.6	45.0	59.1	67.5	68.7	75.8	79.7	83.2	86.1
Western Plain Zone	**22.6**	**28.3**	**31.0**	**46.8**	**62.9**	**72.5**	**72.9**	**78.0**	**82.1**	**85.1**	**88.4**
Bareilly	17.9	21.1	22.0	32.8	48.0	60.5	82.7	85.3	88.7	91.8	93.1
Bijnor	21.1	24.0	26.7	26.3	37.9	44.8	69.2	74.7	80.9	85.0	88.7
Budaun	11.3	14.9	16.1	24.6	38.8	52.9	84.2	85.7	88.8	90.8	92.8
Moradabad	16.3	20.3	19.8	31.0	48.0	62.2	78.4	80.4	85.2	89.8	91.2
Pilibhit	15.8	19.7	20.4	32.1	50.9	63.6	81.9	82.5	84.5	85.1	87.1
Rampur	14.4	15.3	16.3	25.4	39.0	55.1	82.4	83.0	85.6	88.2	89.1
Shahjahanpur	15.4	19.9	21.4	32.1	48.8	61.6	85.5	86.7	87.3	89.0	90.8

Periods → Districts/Region ↓	Literacy Rate (Percentage)						Small + Marginal Share in Total Holdings				
	1961	1971	1981	1991	2001	2011	1970-71	1980-81	1990-91	2000-01	2010-11
Mid-Western Plain Zone	**16.0**	**19.3**	**20.4**	**29.2**	**44.5**	**57.2**	**81.3**	**83.1**	**86.3**	**89.2**	**91.0**
Agra	28.5	33.1	33.5	48.0	65.4	70.7	70.6	75.1	79.0	84.7	85.3
Aligarh	23.3	29.4	31.4	45.2	61.1	71.0	69.3	73.9	78.2	84.9	86.2
Etah	19.4	25.7	27.1	40.2	56.2	67.8	84.2	85.5	88.3	91.7	92.7
Mainpuri	23.2	28.5	33.3	48.6	66.5	76.8	86.8	89.0	88.2	91.3	93.0
Mathura	25.5	29.6	30.6	45.0	62.5	72.8	60.6	66.1	74.2	76.4	78.2
South-Western Semi-Arid Zone	**24.0**	**29.3**	**31.2**	**45.4**	**62.3**	**71.8**	**76.7**	**80.0**	**82.6**	**87.1**	**88.1**
Allahabad	23.0	27.9	28.0	21.3	55.5	69.1	85.9	89.5	91.8	92.9	93.3
Etawah	27.1	34.4	37.3	53.7	71.1	80.1	84.0	85.5	88.9	91.4	92.7
Farrukhabad	25.0	29.3	32.0	47.1	62.4	72.3	88.5	90.3	92.4	94.0	95.0
Fatehpur	19.6	24.5	26.0	44.7	59.7	68.8	78.8	83.9	88.5	91.3	92.3
Hardoi	18.1	22.5	22.2	36.3	52.6	68.9	85.3	86.8	88.2	93.0	93.1
Kanpur	36.8	42.8	43.7	59.7	72.1	79.4	83.6	86.5	87.3	89.8	92.7
Kheri	14.0	17.0	17.7	29.7	49.4	62.7	81.7	86.1	88.7	89.9	89.7
Lucknow	35.0	39.0	40.3	57.5	69.4	79.3	87.5	89.3	92.2	94.6	95.1
Raebareli	15.4	21.3	23.1	37.8	55.1	69.0	89.6	91.8	94.7	93.3	94.5
Sitapur	15.5	19.2	19.4	31.4	49.1	63.4	84.0	89.0	90.9	92.3	94.0
Unnao	17.7	22.9	25.3	38.7	55.7	68.3	87.2	89.8	92.0	93.4	94.9
Central Plain Zone	**22.5**	**27.3**	**28.6**	**41.6**	**59.3**	**71.0**	**85.2**	**88.2**	**90.5**	**92.3**	**93.2**
Banda	17.6	21.9	23.3	35.7	60.5	67.3	66.1	72.8	80.0	80.2	81.8
Hamirpur	19.3	24.2	26.3	39.6	56.2	68.6	57.0	63.9	70.2	74.6	75.8
Jalaun	27.0	32.6	36.0	50.7	66.1	75.2	58.6	67.9	73.2	78.2	76.8
Jhansi	23.9	29.6	29.2	41.9	58.3	70.7	58.9	65.7	74.4	76.7	80.8
Bundelkhand Zone	**22.0**	**27.1**	**28.7**	**42.0**	**60.3**	**70.4**	**60.5**	**67.7**	**74.8**	**77.4**	**79.2**
Bahraich	13.7	14.0	15.6	24.4	35.0	50.1	85.9	89.3	91.4	92.5	94.8
Basti	13.5	18.2	20.2	31.3	50.0	66.8	89.2	91.8	93.3	95.3	95.9
Deoria	16.6	21.0	23.2	37.3	54.1	70.6	89.8	92.4	95.4	96.3	96.8
Gonda	13.7	16.3	16.3	27.3	38.9	56.5	86.0	90.7	92.2	93.5	94.9
Gorakhpur	18.3	23.1	23.9	36.1	54.3	68.8	90.4	93.0	93.9	95.7	96.3
North-Eastern Plain Zone	**15.1**	**18.5**	**19.9**	**31.3**	**46.5**	**62.6**	**88.4**	**91.6**	**93.3**	**94.8**	**95.8**
Azamgarh	19.3	22.3	25.1	41.4	60.1	73.9	92.4	93.4	95.3	95.5	96.4
Ballia	22.7	25.1	28.2	43.9	59.5	74.0	88.1	90.2	92.1	93.7	94.6

(Contd.)

Periods →	Literacy Rate (Percentage)						Small + Marginal Share in Total Holdings				
Districts/Region ↓	1961	1971	1981	1991	2001	2011	1970-71	1980-81	1990-91	2000-01	2010-11
Barabanki	14.0	16.5	18.9	30.4	48.7	63.8	89.6	90.8	93.8	94.8	96.1
Faizabad	16.7	22.5	25.6	39.9	58.2	72.2	92.1	94.1	95.2	95.6	97.2
Ghazipur	21.3	23.3	27.6	43.3	60.1	74.3	87.0	90.4	92.3	94.2	94.7
Jaunpur	20.3	24.9	26.3	42.2	60.0	73.7	93.9	95.5	96.5	97.2	97.1
Pratapgarh	16.1	21.5	23.8	40.4	58.7	73.1	90.7	94.5	96.9	94.2	96.8
Sultanpur	15.1	20.6	22.4	38.7	56.9	71.1	91.1	93.1	95.4	96.6	96.8
Varanasi	27.9	31.8	31.9	47.7	62.4	74.0	91.3	94.5	96.5	96.2	97.0
Eastern Plain Zone	**19.3**	**23.2**	**25.5**	**40.9**	**58.3**	**72.2**	**91.2**	**93.3**	**95.2**	**95.5**	**96.4**
Mirzapur	20.1	23.4	23.6	39.7	53.0	68.3	76.2	80.4	86.1	86.9	88.5
Vindhyan Zone	**20.1**	**23.4**	**23.6**	**39.7**	**53.0**	**68.3**	**76.2**	**80.4**	**86.1**	**86.9**	**88.5**
Hills	18.1	34.6	37.8	57.8	71.6	78.8	88.1	87.0	88.0	88.7	91.1
Uttar Pradesh	**20.7**	**25.4**	**27.2**	**41.6**	**57.4**	**67.7**	**84.0**	**86.8**	**89.4**	**91.0**	**92.4**

Source: Same as in Tables 8.1 and 8.2.

Appendix 8.1 (*Contd.*)

Periods → Districts/Region ↓	Average Rainfall (mm)					
	1960-63	*1970-73*	*1980-83*	*1990-93*	*2000-03*	*2008-11*
Bulandshahr	69	54	52	49	52	37
Meerut	69	58	64	68	55	36
Muzaffarnagar	75	72	57	62	70	37
Saharanpur	87	57	81	82	76	74
Western Plain Zone	**75**	**60**	**64**	**65**	**63**	**46**
Bareilly	113	44	82	58	64	69
Bijnor	74	80	81	90	91	59
Budaun	99	64	77	68	57	30
Moradabad	79	78	70	84	78	58
Pilibhit	137	88	76	69	59	37
Rampur		62	103	89	66	47
Shahjahanpur	130	83	94	52	62	55
Mid-Western Plain Zone	**90**	**71**	**83**	**73**	**68**	**51**
Agra	72	44	76	49	36	35
Aligarh	63	51	67	53	34	41
Etah	73	62	66	50	34	40
Mainpuri	81	53	71	47	53	44
Mathura	54	40	58	45	38	43
South-Western Semi-Arid Zone	**69**	**50**	**67**	**49**	**39**	**41**
Allahabad	81	79	95	55	56	39
Etawah	93	62	80	52	33	33
Farrukhabad	87	63	76	60	54	33
Fatehpur	98	66	99	59	54	28
Hardoi	113	56	91	60	39	41
Kanpur	85	71	101	47	37	48
Kheri	119	92	100	80	90	79
Lucknow	95	77	113	64	43	63
Raebareli	83	81	106	42	26	32
Sitapur	110	79	87	63	74	71
Unnao	95	93	103	64	56	44
Central Plain Zone	**96**	**74**	**96**	**59**	**51**	**47**
Banda	82	49	101	82	73	38
Hamirpur	66	50	109	76	50	41
Jalaun	86	63	86	64	60	43
Jhansi	84	62	90	69	59	50
Bundelkhand Zone	**80**	**56**	**96**	**73**	**61**	**43**
Bahraich	92	83	139	96	48	58
Basti	100	81	113	88	74	75
Deoria	108	93	132	75	60	51
Gonda	102	83	141	90	63	76

(*Contd.*)

Periods → *Districts/Region ↓*	*Average Rainfall (mm)*					
	1960-63	*1970-73*	*1980-83*	*1990-93*	*2000-03*	*2008-11*
Gorakhpur	103	87	134	106	130	59
North-Eastern Plain Zone	**101**	**85**	**132**	**91**	**75**	**64**
Azamgarh	87	82	89	90	85	35
Ballia	80	65	88	49	69	45
Barabanki	100	104	120	67	65	58
Faizabad	86	72	115	77	80	51
Ghazipur	97	96	82	66	73	45
Jaunpur	84	84	86	86	69	42
Pratapgarh	52	82	117	65	60	44
Sultanpur	88	98	103	72	51	52
Varanasi	81	77	77	74	85	29
Eastern Plain Zone	**84**	**84**	**97**	**72**	**71**	**45**
Mirzapur	88	74	84	81	87	34
Vindhyan Zone	**88**	**74**	**84**	**81**	**87**	**34**
Hills	142	83	118	101	117	120
Uttar Pradesh	**95**	**73**	**95**	**74**	**63**	**55**

Source: Same as in Tables 8.1 and 8.2.

Appendix 9.1

Yield (kg/hectare) Gap in Crops in Uttar Pradesh and other Leading States

Crops↓	*Uttar Pradesh*	*Leading States*	
Rice	2243	3919 (Punjab)	3133 (Andhra Pradesh)
Wheat	3038	4617 (Punjab)	4544 (Haryana)
Barley	2312	3582 (Punjab)	3473 (Haryana)
Foodgrains	2407	4273 (Punjab)	3572 (Haryana)
Pulses	889	1319 (Mizoram)	1087 (Arunachal Pradesh)
Sugarcane	57574	105044 (Tamil Nadu)	88591 (Karnataka)
Rapeseed and Mustard	1162	1674 (Haryana)	1484 (Gujarat)
Oilseeds	837	2047 (Tamil Nadu)	1664 (Haryana)
Potato	24502	26635 (West Bengal)	19074 (Bihar)

Source: GoI, *Department of Agriculture and Cooperation*, Ministry of Agriculture, Government of India, (website: agricoop.nic.in)

Appendix 9.2

Farmer Households (Per thousand) Accessing Information on Modern Agricultural Technology in Uttar Pradesh and Other Leading States

Sl. No.	*State →* *Sources ↓*	*Uttar Pradesh*	*Gujarat*	*Tamil Nadu*	*All India*
1.	Extension worker	11	219	133	57
2.	TV	65	104	196	93
3.	Radio	150	62	163	130
4.	Newspaper	40	68	143	70
5.	Input dealer	83	243	94	131
6.	Other progressive farmers	189	300	210	167
7	Any source	336	552	500	404

Source: GoI (2005), *Situation Assessment Survey of Farmers, Acess of Modern Technology for Farming,* 2003, NSS 59th Round, National Sample Survey Organization, Ministry of Statistics and Programme Implementation, Government of India.

Appendix 9.3

Per Hectare Agricultural credit outstanding in Uttar Pradesh and other leading States

Periods→ *States↓*	*Credit Rs. Per Hectare of NSA (at 2004-05 prices) in Triennium*		
	1990-93	*2000-03*	*2008-11*
Uttar Pradesh	3798.6	12266.8	27276.2
Andhra Pradesh	7067.1	24020.1	53029.7
Haryana	9161.5	23972.8	62106.3
Karnataka	3739.7	21339.3	33711.3
Kerala	24767.1	42252.1	102179.7
Punjab	10296.2	40064.3	65930.8
Tamil Nadu	10518.9	60420.8	93055.6

Sources: (i) NABARD (Various Years), *Statistical Statements Relating to Cooperative Movement in India (Various Issues)*, Institutional Development Department-Cooperative Statistics Division, Mumbai, National Bank for Agriculture and Rural Development.

(ii) NAFSCOB (Various Years), *Basic Data on Performance of District Central Cooperative Bank, Statewise,* (Various Years), Mumbai, National Federation of State Cooperative Banks Ltd.

(iii) RBI (Various Years), *Report on Currency and Finance*, Volume 2 (Various Issues), Statistical Tables Relating to Banks in India, Mumbai, Reserve Bank of India.

Appendix 9.4

Districts with High and Low Growth and Development in Uttar Pradesh

	Development (Low, < 59,000 Rs. per hectare)	Development (High, >59,000 Rs. per hectare)
Growth (High, > 2.0%)	**High Growth/Low Development** Azamgarh Bahraich Ballia Banda Basti Fatehpur Ghazipur Gonda Hamirpur Hardoi Jalaun Jhansi Sitapur Sultanpur Unnao Varanasi	**High Growth/High Development** Agra Aligarh Barabanki Faizabad Mainpuri Mathura
Growth (Low, < 2.0 %)	**Low Growth/Low Development** Allahabad Deoria Gorakhpur Hills Jaunpur Kanpur Lucknow Mirzapur Pratapgarh Raebareli	**Low Growth/High Development** Bareilly Bijnor Budaun Bulandshahr Etah Etawah Farrukhabad Kheri Meerut Moradabad Muzaffarnagar Pilibhit Rampur Saharanpur Shahjahanpur

Sources: (i) Table 4.6.
(ii) Table 5.4.

Note: Growth: From 2001-02 to 2010-11.
Development: In 2008-11.

References

Abraham, T.P. and S.K. Raheja (1967), "An Analysis of Growth of Production of Rice and Wheat in India", *Indian Journal of Agricultural Economics*, Vol. 22, No. 3, pp. 1-15.

Afzal, Naila and Shahid Ahmad (2009), "Agricultural Input Use Efficiency in Pakistan: Key Issues and Reform Areas", *Managing Natural Resources for Sustaining Future Agriculture Research Briefings,* Vol. 1, No. 3, pp. 1-12.

Ahluwalia, Montek Singh (1978), "Rural Poverty and Agricultural Performance in India", *Journal of Development Studies,* Vol. 14, No. 3, pp. 298-323.

Ahluwalia, Montek Singh (2000), "Economic Performance of States in the Post-Reform Period", *Economic and Political Weekly*, Vol. 35, No. 19, pp. 1637-1648.

Alagh, Y.K., G.S. Bhalla and A. Bhaduri (1978), *Agricultural Growth and Manpower Absorption in India—Some Explanation Investigation*, Bangkok: Asian Regional Programme for Employment Promotion, International Labour Organisation.

Alagh, Y.K. and P.S. Sharma (1980), "Growth of Crop Production: 1960-61 to 1978-79: Is it Decelerating", *Indian Journal of Agricultural Economics*, Vol. 35, No. 2, pp. 104-118.

Alamian, M., F. Eshraghi, and R. Joolaie, (2013), "Decomposition of Growth of Agricultural Products Value in Golestan Province", *International Journal of Agriculture and Crop Sciences*, Vol. 6, No. 3, pp. 139-143.

Alshi, M.R. and C.K. Joshi (1997), "Inter-State Disparities in Performance of Cereals, Pulses and Foodgrains in India", *Indian Journal of Agricultural Economics,* Vol. 52, No. 3, pp. 462-463.

Arora, V.P.S., S.K. Srivastava and T.S. Bhogal (1997), "Changing Agricultural Performance in Uttar Pradesh: A Regional Analysis", *Indian Journal of Agricultural Economics,* Vol. 52, No. 3, pp. 463-464.

Azariadis, C. (1996), "The Economics of Poverty Traps, Part One: Complete Markets", *Journal of Economic Growth*, Vol. 1, No. 4, pp. 449-486.

Bairoch, Paul (1973), "Agriculture and the Industrial Revolution, 1700-1914", in Carlo M. Cipolla (eds.), *The Fontana Economic History of Europe: The Industrial Revolution,* Vol. 3. London: Collinis/Fontana.

Bajpai, Nirupam and Nicole Volavka (2005), *Agricultural Performance in Uttar Pradesh: A Historical Account*, Working Paper No. 23, Centre on Globalization and Sustainable Development, The Earth Institute at Columbia University.

Balakrishnan, Pulapre (2000), "Agriculture and Economic Reforms: Growth and Welfare", *Economic and Political Weekly*, Vol. 35, No. 12, pp. 999-1004.

Balakrishnan, Pulapre, Ramesh Golait and Pankaj Kumar (2008), *Agricultural Growth in India Since 1991*, Mumbai: Reserve Bank of India.

Bardhan, P.K. (1973), "Size, Productivity and Returns to Scale: An Analysis of Farm-Level Data in India Agriculture", *Journal of Political Economy,* Vol. 81, No. 6, pp. 1370-1386.

Barrios, Erniel B. (2007), *Convergence in Agriculture of Some Asian Countries*, Asian Discussion Paper No. 71, Tokyo: Asian Development Bank Institute.

Barro, R.J. (1991), "Economic Growth in a Cross-Section of Countries", *Quarterly Journal of Economics*, Vol. 106, No. 2, pp. 407-443.

Barro, R.J. and Xavier Sala-i-Martin (1991), "Convergence Across States and Regions", *Brooking Papers on Economic Activity*, Vol. 1, No. 4, pp. 107-182.

Barro, R., and Xavier Sala-i-Martin (1992), "Convergence", *Journal of Political Economy*, Vol. 100, No. 2, pp. 223–251.

Baumol, W. (1986), "Productivity Growth, Convergence and Welfare: What the Long-Run Data Show", *American Economic Review*, Vol. 76, No. 5, pp. 1072-1085.

Bhalla, G.S. and Y.K. Alagh (1979), *Performance of Indian Agriculture: A District Wise Study*, New Delhi: Sterling Publishers.

Bhalla, G.S. and D.S. Tyagi (1989) *Patterns in Indian Agricultural Development: A District Level Study,* New Delhi: Institute for Studies in Industrial Development.

Bhalla, G.S. (1995), "Globalization and Agricultural Policy in India", *Indian Journal of Agricultural Economics*, Vol. 50, No. 1, pp. 7-26.

Bhalla, G.S. and Gurmail Singh (1997), "Recent Developments in Indian Agriculture: A State Level Analysis", *Economic and Political Weekly,* Vol. 32, No. 13, pp. A3-A18.

Bhalla, G.S. and Gurmail Singh (2001), *Indian Agriculture: Four Decades of Development*, New Delhi: Sage Publications.

Bhalla, G.S. and Gurmail Singh (2009), "Economic Liberalization and Indian Agriculture: A State Wise Analysis", *Economic and Political Weekly,* Vol. 64, No. 52, pp. 34-44.

Bhalla, G.S. and Gurmail Singh (2010), *Growth of Indian Agriculture: A District Level Study,* New Delhi: Centre for Study of Regional Development, Planning Commission Report.

Bhalla, G.S. and Gurmail Singh (2012), *Economic Liberalization and Indian Agriculture: A District Level Study*, New Delhi: Sage Publications.

Bhattacharjee, Jyoti P. (1955), "Resource Use and Productivity in World Agriculture", *Journal of Farm Economics*, Vol. 37, No. 1, pp. 57-58.

Bhattacharya, B.B. and S. Sakthivel (2005a), "Economic Reforms and Jobless Growth in India in the 1990s", in A.K. Sinha (eds.), *India Towards Economic Superpower: A Journey of Economic Reforms*, New Delhi: Deep & Deep Publications.

Bhide, Shashanka, K.P. Kalirajan and R.T. Shand (1998), "India's Agricultural Dynamics: Weak Link in Development", *Economic and Political Weekly*, Vol. 33, No. 39, pp. A118-A127.

Birthal, Pratap S., Harvinder Singh and Shiv Kumar (2011), "Agriculture, Economic Growth and Regional Disparities in India", *Journal of International Development*, Vol. 23, No. 1, pp. 119-131.

Birthal, Pratap S., Pramod K. Joshi, Digvijay S. Negi and Shaily Agarwal (2014), *Changing Sources of Growth in Indian Agriculture: Implications for Regional Priorities for Accelerating Agricultural Growth*, Discussion Paper No. 01325, New Delhi: International Food Policy Research Institute.

Block, S.A. (1995), "The Recovery of Agricultural Productivity in Sub-Saharan Africa", *Food Policy*, Vol. 20, No. 5, pp. 385-405.

Bowman, Kirk and Jesus Felipe (2000), *Convergence, Catch up, and the Future of Latin America*, Working Paper No. 00/01-011, Atlanta: Georgia Institute of Technology.

Breisinger, Clemens, Xinshen Diao, James Thurlow and Ramatu M.Al Hassan (2008), *Agriculture for Development in Ghana: New Opportunities and Challenges*, Working Paper No. 00784, Washington, DC, USA: International Food Policy Research Institute.

Brown, D. Dorris (1971), *Agricultural Development in India's Districts*, Cambridge, Massachusetts: Harvard University Press.

Cass, David (1965), "Optimum Growth in an Aggregative Model of Capital Accumulation." *The Review of Economic Studies*, Vol. 32, No. 3, pp. 233-240.

Chandlok, H.L. (1990), *India Database, The Economy, Annual Time Series Data*, Vol. 1, L.M. Books, The Policy Group.

Chand, Ramesh (2001), "Emerging Trends and Issues in Public and Private Investments in Indian Agriculture: A State Wise Analysis", *Indian Journal of Agricultural Economics*, Vol. 56, No. 2, pp. 161-184.

Chand, Ramesh and Dayanatha Jha (2001), "Trade Liberalization, Agricultural Prices and Social Welfare", in S.S. Acharya and D.P. Chaudhri (eds.), *Indian Agricultural Policy at the Crossroads*, Jaipur: Rawat Publications.

Chand, Ramesh (2003), *Government Intervention in Foodgrain Markets in the Changing Context*, Policy Paper No. 19, New Delhi: National Centre for Agricultural Economics and Policy Research.

Chand, Ramesh, S.S. Raju, and L.M. Pandey (2007), "Growth Crises in Agriculture—Severity and Options at National and State Levels", *Economic and Political Weekly*, Vol. 42, No. 26, pp. 2528-2533.

Chand, Ramesh, P.A. Lakshmi Prasanna and Aruna Singh (2011), "Farm Size and Productivity: Understanding the Strengths of Small holders and Improving their Livelihoods", *Economic and Political Weekly*, Vol. 46, No. 26-27, pp. 5-11.

Chand, Ramesh and Shinoj Parappurathu (2012), "Temporal and Spatial Variations in Agricultural Growth and Its Determinants", *Economic and Political Weekly*, Vol. 47, No. 26-27, pp. 55-64.

Chaudhuri, S. and N. Gupta (2009), "Levels of Living and Poverty Patterns: A District-wise Analysis from India", *Economic and Political Weekly*, Vol. 44, No. 9, pp. 94-110.

Chatterji, Monojit (1992), "Convergence Clubs and Endogenous Growth", *Oxford Review of Economic Policy*, Vol. 8, No. 4, pp. 57-69.

Chatterjee, Tirtha (2014), *Spatial Convergence and Growth in Indian Agriculture: 1967-2010*, Working Paper No. 035, Mumbai: Indira Gandhi Institute of Development Research.

Cherodian, Rowan and A.P. Thirlwall (2013), *Regional Disparities in Per Capita Income in India: Convergence or Divergence?*, School of Economics Discussion Papers, KPDE 1313, UK: University of Kent.

Chopra (1986), *Green Revolution in India*, New Delhi: Intellectual Publishing House.

Datt, Gaurav and Martin Ravallion (1990), *Regional Disparities, Targeting, and Poverty in India*, Policy Research Working Paper No. 375, Washington, DC.: The World Bank.

Datt, Gaurav and Martin Ravallion (1996), "How Important to India's Poor is the Sectoral Composition of Economic Growth?", *The World Bank Economic Review*, Vol. 10, No. 1, pp. 1-25.

Datt, Gaurav and Martin Ravallion (1998), "Why Have Some Indian States Done Better Than Others at Reducing Rural Poverty?", *Economica*, Vol. 65, No. 257, pp. 17-38.

Datt, Gaurav and Martin Ravallion (1998), "Farm Productivity and Rural Poverty in India", *Journal of Development Studies,* Vol. 34, No. 4, pp. 62-85.

David, Dan Ben (1997), *Convergence Clubs and Diverging Economies*, Israel: Tel Aviv University.

Dayal, R. (1966), "Agricultural Growth Rates and Their Components", *Indian Journal of Agricultural Economics*, Vol. 21, No. 4, pp. 227-237.

Dayal, Edison (1984), "Agricultural Productivity in India: A Spatial Analysis", *Annals of the Association of American Geographers,* Vol. 74, No. 1, pp. 98-123.

Debela, Adane Tuffa, Almas Heshmati and Ragnar Oygard (2004), *An Evaluation of the Impacts of Economic Reform on Performance of Agriculture in Ethiopia*, Discussion Paper No. 2, Finland: MTT Economic Research, Agrifood Research.

Dev, Mahendra S. (1985), "Direction of Change in Performance of all Crops in Indian Agriculture in late 1970s—A Look at the Level of District and Agro-climatic Regions", *Economic and Political Weekly*, Vol. 20, No. 51-52, pp. A130-A136.

Dev, Mahendra S. (2000), "Economic Reforms, Poverty, Income Distribution and Employment", *Economic and Political Weekly*, Vol. 35, No. 10, pp. 823-835.

Diao, Xinshen, Peter Hazell, Danielle Resnick, and James Thurlow (2005), *The Role of Agriculture in Pro-Poor Growth in Sub-Saharan Africa,* Washington, DC.: International Food Policy Research Institute.

Domar, E.D. (1946), "Capital Expansion, Rate of Growth, and Employment", *Econometrica,* Vol. 14, No. 2, pp. 137-147.

Durlauf, S. and P. Johnson (1995), "Multiple Regimes and Cross-Country Growth Behaviour", *Journal of Applied Econometrics*, Vol. 10, No. 4, pp. 365-384.

Easter, W.K., E.A. Martin and N. George (1977), "Regional Differences in Agricultural Productivity in Selected Areas of India", *American Journal of Agricultural Economics,* Vol. 59, No. 2, pp. 257-260.

Etienne, Gilbert (1968), *Studies in Indian Agriculture*, Bombay: Oxford University Press.

FAI (Various Years), *Fertilizer Statistics* (Various Issues), New Delhi: Fertilizer Association in India.

Galor, Oded (1996), "Convergence? Inferences From Theoretical Models", *Economic Journal,* Vol. 106, No. 437, pp. 1056–1069.

GoI (1994), *Economic Survey, 1994*, New Delhi: Ministry of Finance, Government of India.

GoI (1996*), Statewise and Cropwise Estimates of Value Output from Agriculture*, Central Statistical Organisation, New Delhi: Department of Statistics, Ministry of Planning and Programme Implementation, Government of India.

GoI (2005), *Situation Assessment Survey of Farmers, Access of Modern Technology for Farming,* 2003, NSS 59th Round, New Delhi: National Sample Survey Organization, Ministry of Statistics and Programme Implementation, Government of India.

GoI (2007), *Census of Minor Irrigation, 2006-07,* New Delhi: Ministry of Water Resources, Government of India.

GoI (2008), *Twelfth Five Year Plan, 2012-2017*, Volume II, New Delhi: Planning Commission of India, Government of India, Sage Publications India Pvt. Ltd.

GoI (2014), *State of Indian Agriculture 2013-2014*, New Delhi: Department of Agriculture, Ministry of Agriculture.

GoI (2014), *Economic Survey, 2014,* New Delhi: Ministry of Finance, Government of India.

GoI (2014), *Uttar Pradesh State Development Report*, Volume II, New Delhi: State Plan Division, Planning Commission, Government of India.

GoI, *Agricultural Census*, New Delhi: Department of Agriculture and Cooperation, Agricultural Census Division, Ministry of Agriculture, Government of India.

GoI (Various Years), *Agricultural Situation in India*, (Various Issues), New Delhi: Directorate of Economics and Statistics, Government of India.

GoI (Various Years), *Agricultural Statistics at a Glance* (Various Issues), New Delhi: Directorate of Economics and Statistics, Department of Agriculture and Cooperation, Ministry of Agriculture, Government of India.

GoI (Various Years), *Census of India (Uttar Pradesh) for 1961, 1971, 1981, 1991, 2001, 2011,* Primary Census Abstract, Uttar Pradesh: Directorate of Census Operations, Government of India.

GoI (Various Years), *Livestock Census for 1961, 1972, 1982, 1992, 2003,* Uttar Pradesh, (Agriculture Machinery and Implements), New Delhi: Ministry of Agriculture, Department of Animal Husbandry and Dairying, Government of India.

Gordan, McClelland Donald (1974), *Agricultural Productivity in India's Districts: An Empirical Analysis*, USA: Graduate School of Arts and Sciences, University of Pennsylvania.

GoUP (Various Years), *Statistical Abstracts of Uttar Pradesh* (Various Issues), Lucknow: Economic and Statistics Division, State Planning Institute, Government of Uttar Pradesh.

GoUP (Various Years), *Season and Crop Report of Uttar Pradesh* (Various Issues), Lucknow: Directorate of Economics and Statistics, Government of Uttar Pradesh.

GoUP, *Zila Sankyikiya Patrika*, Lucknow: Economics and Statistics Division, Department of Planning, Government of Uttar Pradesh.

Goyal, Aloka Kumar and Sandeep Kumar (2013), "Agricultural Production Trends and Cropping Pattern in Uttar Pradesh: An Overview", *International Journal of Agriculture Innovations and Research,* Vol. 2, No. 2, pp. 229-235.

Gujarati, Damodar (2007), *Basic Econometrics*, New York: McGraw Hill.

Hansen, B. (2000), "Sample Splitting and Threshold Estimation", *Econometrica,* Vol. 68, No. 3, pp. 575-603.

Harrod, R.F. (1939), "An Essay in Dynamic Theory", *The Economic Journal*, Vol. 49, No. 193, pp. 14-33.

Hayami, Yujiro and Vernon W. Ruttan (1985), *Agricultural Development—An International Perspective*, Baltimore: Johns Hopkins University Press.

Hayami, Yujiro and Vernon W. Ruttan (1970), "Agricultural Productivity Differences Among Countries", *American Economic Review*, Vol. 60, No. 5, pp. 895-911.

Hossian, Akhtar (2000), *Convergence of Per Capita Output Levels Across Regions of Bangladesh, 1982-97,* Working Paper No. 00/121, Washington, DC.: International Monetary Fund.

Hsiao, Cheng (2003), *Analysis of Panel Data*, Cambridge: Cambridge University Press.

Islam, N. (2003), "What Have We Learnt From the Convergence Debate?", *Journal of Economic Surveys*, Vol. 17, No. 3, pp. 309–362.

Jain, Reena (1990), "High Yielding Varieties and Correlated Response of Yields of Wheat and Rice in Uttar Pradesh", *Indian Journal of Agricultural Economics,* Vol. 45, No. 1, pp. 61-68.

Jamal, H. and A. Zaman (1992), "Decomposition of Growth Trend in Agriculture: Another Approach", *Indian Journal of Agricultural Economics,* Vo. 47, No. 4, pp. 644-651.

Joshi, P.K, Pratap Singh Birthal and Nicholas Minot (2006), *Sources of Agricultural Growth in India: Role of Diversification Towards High-Value Crops,* Discussion Paper No. 98, Washington, DC, USA: International Food Policy Research Institute Publication.

Johnston, J. and J. DiNardo (2001), *Econometric Methods,* Irvine: University of California, McGraw Hill.

Kaldor, N. (1966), *Cases of the Slow Rate of Economic Growth of the United Kingdom,* UK: Cambridge University Press.

Kaldor, N. (1972), "The Irrelevance of Equilibrium Economics", *Economic Journal,* Vol. 82, No. 328, pp. 1237-1255.

Kannan, Elumalai and Sujata Sundaram (2011), *Analysis of Trends in India's Agricultural Growth,* Working Paper No. 276, Bangalore, The Institute for Social and Economic Change.

Kane, Richard (2001), "Investigating Convergence of the US Regions: A Time-Series Analysis", *The Journal of Regional Analysis and Policy,* Vol. 31, No. 1, pp. 1-22.

Karshenas, Massoud (1999), *Agriculture and Economic Development in Sub-Saharan Africa and Asia,* London: Department of Economics, University of London.

Kawagoe, Toshihko and Yujrao Hayami (1983), "The Production Structure of World Agriculture: An Inter-Country Cross-Section Analysis", *Developing Economics,* Vol. 21, No. 3, pp. 189-206.

Koopmans, T. (1965), *On the Concept of Optimal Economic Growth,* Amsterdam, North Holland: The Economic Approach to Development Planning.

Kumar, Arun (2000), *Agricultural Development in Uttar Pradesh,* New Delhi: Anmol Publications Pvt. Ltd.

Kumar, Anjani and Rajni Jain (2013), "Growth and Instability in Agricultural Productivity: A District Level Analysis", *Agricultural Economics Research Review,* Vol. 26 (Conference Number) 2013, pp. 31-42.

Kumar, Shiv, Kamble Ankush Lala and Khyali Ram Chaudhary (2014), "Agricultural Growth and Economic Convergence in Indian Agriculture", *Indian Journal of Agricultural Economics,* Vol. 69, No. 2, pp. 211-227.

Kumo, W.L. (2011), *Growth and Macroeconomic Convergence in Southern Africa,* Series No. 130, Tunis, Tunisia: African Development Bank.

Kurosaki, Takashi (2001), *Agriculture in India and Pakistan, 1900-95: A Further Note,* Tokyo: Hitotsubashi University.

Lewis, W.A. (1954), "Economic Development with Unlimited Supplies of Labour", *Manchester School of Economic and Social Studies,* Vol. 22, No. 2, pp. 139-191.

Lucas, Robert E. (1988), "On Mechanics of Economic Development", *Journal of Monetary Economics,* Vol. 22, No. 1, pp. 3-42.

Mathur, Archana S., Surajit Das and Subhalakshmi Sircar (2006), "Status of

Agriculture in India—Trends and Prospects", *Economic and Political Weekly,* Vol. 41, No. 52, pp. 5327-5336.

Mellor, John W. (1966), *The Economics of Agricultural Development,* Ithaca, New York: Cornell University Press.

Mellor, John W. (2000), *Agricultural Growth, Rural Employment, and Poverty Reduction: Non-Tradables, Public Expenditure, and Balanced Growth,* Prepared for the World Bank Rural Week 2000.

Mellor, John W. (2001), *Faster, More Equitable Growth: The Relation Between Growth in Agriculture and Poverty Reduction,* CARE II Discussion Paper No. 70, Harvard: The Harvard Institute of International Development.

Minhas, B.S. and A. Vidhyanathan (1965), "Growth of Crop Output in India, 1951-54 to 1958-61: Analysis by Component Elements", *Journal of Indian Society of Agricultural Statistics,* Vol. 28, No. 2, pp. 230-252.

Minhas, B.S. (1966), "Rapporteur's Report on Measurement of Agricultural Growth", *Indian Journal of Agricultural Economics,* Vol. 21, No. 4, pp. 165-182.

Mishra, S.N. and Ramesh Chand (1995), "Private and Public Capital Formation in Indian Agriculture: Comments on Complementarity Hypothesis and Others", *Economic and Political Weekly,* Vol. 30, No. 25, pp. A64-A79.

Mishra, S.K. (2007), *Trends in Growth of Agriculture Sector of the Indian Economy,* Working Paper No. 882, e-Social Sciences.

Montfort, P. (2008), *Convergence of EU Region, Measures and Evolution,* Working Paper No. 01/2008, Luxembourg: European Union Regional Policy.

Myrdal, G. (1957), *Economic Theory and Underdeveloped Regions,* London: Duckworth.

NABARD (Various Years), *Statistical Statements Relating to Cooperative Movement in India (Various Issues),* Institutional Development Department—Cooperative Statistics Division, Mumbai: National Bank for Agriculture and Rural Development.

NAFSCOB (Various Years), *Basic Data on Performance of District Central Cooperative Bank, Statewise,* (Various Years), Mumbai: National Federation of State Cooperative Banks Ltd.

Naher, Firdousi (1997), "Green Revolution in Bangladesh—Production Stability and Food Self-Sufficiency", *Economic and Political Weekly,* Vol. 32, No. 26, pp. A84-A89.

Nair, K.S. (1980), *Technological Change in Agriculture*, New Delhi: Birla Institute of Scientific Research.

Narain, Dharm (1977), "Growth of Productivity in Indian Agriculture", *Indian Journal of Agricultural Economics,* Vol. 32, No. 1, pp. 1-44.

Pandey, Lalmani and A. Amrender Reddy (2012), "Farm Productivity and Rural Poverty in Uttar Pradesh: A Regional Perspective", *Agricultural Economics Research Review*, Vol. 25, No. 1, pp. 25-35.

Pandeya, Niti (2015), *Capital Formation in Indian Agriculture: Patterns and Determinants*, (Forthcoming), Ph.D. Thesis, Chandigarh: Department of Economics, Panjab University.

Parikh, A. (1966), "Analysis of Growth Components and Methods of Constructing the Index Number of Agricultural Production Under Constant Cropping Pattern", *Indian Journal of Agricultural Economics,* Vol. 21, No. 3, pp. 41-47.

Piya, Sujan, Akira Kiminami and Hironori Yagi (2011), "Sources of Agricultural Productivity Growth in South and South-east Asia", *Trends in Agricultural Economics*, Vol. 4, No. 1, pp. 18-29.

Prabha, Chandar (1971), "District wise Measurement of Decomposition of the Growth of Agricultural Output in the Punjab During Post-Independence Period", *Indian Economic Review,* Vol. 6, No. 1, pp. 49-63.

Prabha, Kishore Goswami and Bani Chatterjee (2010), "Linkage Between Rural Poverty and Agricultural Productivity Across the Districts of Uttar Pradesh in India", *Journal of Development and Agricultural Economics*, Vol. 2, No. 2, pp. 26-40.

Quah, D. (1993b), "Empirical Cross-Section Dynamics in Economic Growth", *European Economic Review*, Vol. 37, No. 2-3, pp. 426–434.

Quah, D. (1996), "Convergence Empirics Across Economies With (some) Capital Mobility", *Journal of Economic Growth,* Vol. 1, No. 1, pp. 95-124.

Ralhan, Mukesh and Ajit Dayanandan (2005), *Convergence of Income Among Provinces in Canada—An Application of GMM Estimation,* Econometrics Working Paper No. 0502, Victoria, B.C., Canada: University of Victoria.

Raman, Rakesh and Reena Kumari (2012), "Regional Disparity in Agricultural Development: A District Level Analysis for Uttar Pradesh", *Journal of Regional Development and Planning,* Vol. 1, No. 2, pp. 71-90.

Ramsey, Frank P. (1928), "A Mathematical Theory of Saving." *The Economic Journal*, Vol. 38, No. 152, pp. 543-559.

Rana, R.K. (1990), "Land Productivity Differentials in India: An Empirical Study", *Indian Journal of Agricultural Economics,* Vol. 45, No. 1, pp. 51-55.

Ranade, C.G. (1986), "Growth of Productivity in Indian Agriculture: Some Unfinished Components of Dharm Narain's Work", *Economic and Political Weekly,* Vol. 21, No. 25-26, pp. A75-A80.

Rao, C.H. Hanumantha (1966), "Alternative Explanations of the Inverse Relationship Between Farm Size and Output Per Acre in India", *Indian Economic Review*, Vol. 1, No. 2, pp. 1-12.

Rao, S.K. (1971), "Inter-regional Variations in Agricultural Growth, 1952-53 to 1964-65: A Tentative Analysis in Relation to Irrigation", *Economic and Political Weekly,* Vol. 6, No. 27, pp. 1333-1346.

Rao, V.M. (1994), "Agriculture and Liberalization: Some Implications for Development Policies", *Economic and Political Weekly*, Vol. 29, No. 16-17, pp. 999-1004.

Rao, C.H. Hanumantha (2001), "WTO and Viability of Indian Agriculture", *Economic and Political Weekly*, Vol. 36, No. 36, pp. 3453-3457.

Rao, C.H. Hanumantha (2003), "Reform Agenda for Agriculture", *Economic and Political Weekly*, Vol. 33, No. 29, pp. 615-20.

RBI (Various Years), *Report on Currency and Finance*, Volume 2 (Various Issues), Statistical Tables Relating to Banks in India, Mumbai: Reserve Bank of India.

Reddy, D. Narasimha and Srijit Mishra (2009), "Agriculture in the Reforms Regime", in D Narasimha Reddy and Srijit Mishra (eds.), *Agrarian Crisis in India*, New Delhi: Oxford University Press.

Rehman, Hifzur, Abdul Wahab and Asif (2008), "Agricultural Productivity and Productivity Regions in Ganga-Yamuna Doab", *The Geographer*, Vol. 55, No. 1, pp. 10-21.

Rehman, F.U., Ikram Saeed and Abdul Salam (2011), "Estimating Growth Rates and Decomposition Analysis of Agriculture Production in Pakistan: Pre and Post SAP Analysis", *Sarhad Journal of Agriculture*, Vol. 27, No. 1, pp. 125-131.

Romer, P. (1986), "Increasing Returns and Long-Run Growth", *Journal of Political Economy*, Vol. 98, No. 5, pp. 71-102.

Ruttan, Vernon W. (1984), "Models of Agricultural Development", in Carl K. Eicher and John M. Staatz (eds.), *Agricultural Development in the Third World,* Baltimore: Johns Hopkins University Press.

Ruttan, Vernon W. and Yujiro Hayami (1984), "Induced Innovation Model of Agricultural Development", in Carl K. Eicher and John M. Staatz (eds.), *Agricultural Development in the Third World,* Baltimore: Johns Hopkins University Press.

Ruttan, Vernon W. (1987), *Lectures on Technical and Institutional Change in Agricultural Development*, Islamabad: Pakistan Institute of Development Economics.

Sagar, Vidya (1977), "A Component Analysis of Growth of Agricultural Productivity in Rajasthan: 1956-61 to 1969-74", *Indian Journal of Agricultural Economics,* Vol. 3, No. 1, pp. 108-119.

Sagar, Vidya (1980), "Decomposition of Growth Trends and Certain Related Issues", *Indian Journal of Agricultural Economics,* Vol. 35, No. 2, pp. 42-59.

Sahoo, Bimal Kishore and Simantini Mohapatra (2008), "Agricultural Disparity Across Indian States: Determinants and Policy Implication", *IUP Journal of Agricultural Economics,* Vol. 5, No. 2, pp. 64-82.

Sala-i-Martin, Xavier (1994), "Cross-Sectional Regressions and the Empirics of Economic Growth", *European Economic Review*, Vol. 38, No. 3-4, pp. 739-747.

Sala-i-Martin, Xavier (1996), "The Classical Approach to Convergence Analysis," *The Economic Journal*, Vol. 106, No. 437, pp. 1019-1036.

Sala-i-Martin, Xavier (1996), "Regional Cohesion: Evidence and Theories of Regional Growth and Convergence", *European Economic Review*, Vol. 40, No. 6, pp. 1325-1352.

Schultz, T.W. (1964), *Transforming Traditional Agriculture,* New York, CT: Yale University Press.

Sen, A.K. (1962), "An Aspect of Indian Agriculture", *The Economic Weekly*, Vol. 14, No. 4-6, pp. 243-446.

Sen, A.K. (1964), "Size of Holdings and Productivity", *The Economic Weekly*, Vol. 16, No. 5-7, pp. 323-326.

Shaffi, M. (1984), *Agricultural Productivity and Regional Imbalances: A Case Study of Uttar Pradesh,* New Delhi: Concept Publishing Company (P) Ltd.

Shafiqullah (2013), "Impact of Regional Disparities on Agricultural Development in Uttar Pradesh—A Geographical Analysis", *Global Journal of Human Social Science, Geography, Geo-sciences, Environment and Disaster Management*, Vol. 13, No. 5, pp. 36-46.

Shetty, S.A. (1970), "Agricultural Production Trends and Components", *Indian Journal of Agricultural Economics,* Vol. 25, No. 2, pp. 28-48.

Shukla, O.P. (2002), "Agricultural Development in Uttar Pradesh: Some Institutional Issues". *Journal of Agricultural Economics,* Vol. 57, No. 3, pp. 564-565.

Singh, R.V., A.S. Sirohi and K.R. Singh (1973), *Allocation Efficiency in Transitional Agriculture,* Research Bulletin No. 2, New Delhi: Division of Agricultural Economics, Indian Agriculture Research Institute.

Singh, J.P. (1975), "Resource Use, Farm Size and Returns to Scale in a Backward Agriculture", *Indian Journal of Agricultural Economics*, Vol. 30, No. 2, pp. 32-46.

Singh, A.L. and A.P. Saxena (1985), "Agricultural Development in Uttar Pradesh", *The* Geographer, Vol. 32, No. 1, pp. 20-28.

Singh, Chhotan and Puran Chand (1990), "Inter-Regional Disparities in Technological Change and Agricultural Growth in India", *Indian Journal of Agricultural Economics,* Vol. 45, No. 1, pp. 314-315.

Singh, I.J., K.N. Rai and J.C. Karwasra (1997), "Regional Variations in Agricultural Performance in India", *Indian Journal of Agricultural Economics,* Vol. 52, No. 3, pp. 374-385.

Singh, Gurmail (2007), *Growth of Indian Agriculture: A District Level Study,* Chandigarh: Department of Economics, Panjab University.

Singh, Richa and A.K. Singh (2009), Agricultural Growth in the Reform Period—A Inter-State Study, *Changing Contours of Asian Agriculture—Policies, Performance and Challenges*, New Delhi: Academic Foundations.

Solow, R.M. (1956), "A Contribution to The Theory of Economic Growth," *Quarterly Journal of Economics*, Vol. 70, No. 1, pp. 65-94.

Solow, R.M. (1957), "Technical Change and the Aggregate Production Function", *Review of Economics and Statistics*, Vol. 39, No. 3, pp. 312-320.

Soukiazis, E. (2000), *What We Have Learnt About Convergence in Europe? Some Theoretical and Empirical Considerations*, Discussion Paper No. 2, Coimbra (Portugal): University of Coimbra.

Srivastava, S.K. (2003), "A Temporal View of Cropping Pattern in Western Uttar Pradesh: Pre and Post Liberalisation Analysis", *Indian Journal of Agricultural Economics,* Vol. 58, No. 3, pp. 401-402.

Taffesse, Alemayehu Seyoum, Paul Dorosh and Sinafikeh Asrat (2011), *Crop Production in Ethiopia: Regional Patterns and Trends,* Ethiopia Strategy Support Programme II, Working Paper No. 0016, Washington, DC: International Food Policy Research Institute.

Thamarajakshi, R. (1999), "Agriculture and Economic Reforms", *Economic and Political Weekly,* Vol. 34, No. 33, pp. 2393-2395.

Thunen, J.H. Von (1826), *Die Isolierte Staat in Beziehung auf Landwirtshaft und Nationalökonomie*, New York: Pergamon Press.

Timmer, C.P. (1988), "The Agricultural Transformation", in H. Chenery and T.N. Srinivasan (eds.), *Handbook of Development Economics*, Vol. 1, Amsterdam, North-Holland.

Tripathi, Amarnath and A.R. Prasad (2009), "Agricultural Development in India Since Independence: A Study on Progress, Performance and Determinants", *Journal of Emerging Knowledge on Emerging Markets,* Vol. 1, No. 1, pp. 63-92.

Udensi, A.I., J.S. Orebiyi, D.O. Ohajianya, and C.C. Eze (2012), "Determinants of Macro-economic Variables that Affect Agricultural Production in Nigeria", *International Journal of Agriculture and Rural Development,* Vol. 15, No. 3, pp. 1169-1173.

Vaidyanathan, A. (2010), *Agricultural Growth in India, Role of Technology, Incentives, and Institutions,* New Delhi, Oxford University Press.

Venkateswarlu, A. (2008), *Agricultural Development in India: Policies and Performance,* Reforming Indian Agriculture: Towards Employment Generation and Poverty Reduction, New Delhi, Sage Publications.

Vyas, V.S. (2001), "Agriculture: Second Round of Economic Reforms", *Economic and Political Weekly*, Vol. 36, No. 14, pp. 829-836.

World Bank (2008), *World Development Report 2007: Agriculture for Development*, Washington DC.

Wu, Harry X. (1997), *Reform in China's Agriculture—Trade Implications*, Briefing Paper Series, No. 9, Canberra, Department of Foreign Affairs and Trade, Government of Australia.

Xin, Xiangfei and Fu Qin (2009), *Decomposition of Agricultural Labour Productivity Growth and its Regional Disparity in China,* Beijing, China, Paper presented at The International Association of Agricultural Economists Conference 2009.

Index